Friends Exposed

1500 Fun Facts About the Show

Dennis Bjorklund

PRAETORIAN PUBLISHING

Library of Congress Cataloging-in-Publication Data
Bjorklund, Dennis
Friends Exposed: 1500 Fun Facts About the Show / Dennis Bjorklund.
p. cm
"A Maizeland Books book"

1. Friends (Television program)–Miscellaneous. I. Title.

First published in the United States of America in 2004
ISBN: 9798223981770

TABLE OF CONTENTS

Author..iii

Casting, Characters & Crew...1
    Casting...1
    Character Development..8
    Recurring Regulars..10
    Guest Stars...14
    Stand-Ins..15
    Body Doubles...15
    Extras..16

Series..17
    Concept..17
    Pilot...17
    Character Names...17
    Pilot Changes..18
    Show Titles...18
    Pilot Filming..19
    Script Ideas...21
    Unused Script Ideas...22
    Recycled Jokes..22
    Phoebe's Songs...23
    Real-Life Inspirations...23
    NBC Censors..23
    Directors...24
    Title Sequence..24
    Theme Song..25
    Music Video..26

Pilot Debut..26
Cast Camaraderie..26
Friend Pairings..26
Love Interests..28
Pregnancy Issues...28
Sets..29
Taping Episodes...30
Location Shooting...32
Series Facts..32

Episodes..35
Season 1: 1994-95..35
Season 2: 1995-96..50
Season 3: 1996-97..64
Season 4: 1997-98..79
Season 5: 1998-99..93
Season 6: 1999-2000..106
Season 7: 2000-01..122
Season 8: 2001-02..137
Season 9: 2002-03..153
Season 10: 2003-04..167

Episode Index...179

General Index..181

Author

Author Dennis Bjorklund is an accomplished and well-respected television authority who published many small-screen books covering some of the best sitcoms in network history. In addition to writing books, the author has provided literary contributions to numerous entertainment magazines and authoritative interviews for A&E network, E! Entertainment, The Biography Channel, Bio channel, and FYI.

Bjorklund is considered one of the foremost authorities on television sitcoms, and the only individual to write multiple in-depth and thoroughly comprehensive books in this genre. He has written a multitude of books on other television shows:

Seinfeld Reference: The Complete Encyclopedia

Seinfeld Secrets: 1500 Fun Facts About the Show

Seinfeld Ultimate Episode Guide

Seinfeld Trivia: Everything About Nothing

Seinfeld Trivia: Everything About Nothing, Challenging

Seinfeld Trivia: Everything About Nothing, Multiple Choice

Cheers TV Show: A Comprehensive Reference

Cheers Trivia: It's a Little Known Fact...

Friends Trivia Quiz & Fun Facts: Channel Your Inner Unagi

Friends Secrets: 236 Episodes, Thousands of Facts

Friends Exposed: 1500 Fun Facts About the Show

Friends Behind the Scenes: Backstage Pass to the Series, A Comprehensive History

Modern Family Trivia Quiz & Fun Facts: Early Years

The Big Bang Theory Trivia Quiz & Fun Facts: Challenging

The Big Bang Theory Trivia Quiz & Fun Facts: Casual Fan

The author continues to reside in California to remain close to the heart of network television programming.

Casting, Characters & Crew

Casting

Lead actor auditions were held in New York City and Los Angeles. Casting director Ellie Kanner received more than 1,000 glossy black-and-white photographs for each role. She pared the list to 75 actors for each part and scheduled callbacks. After an audition with her, promising prospects received another audition callback to read for cocreator Marta Kauffman and executive producer Kevin Bright. Cocreator David Crane abstained from the early screening process because he wanted to hire every actor and felt guilty when he had to reject them.

All six lead roles were cast simultaneously. David Crane claims the six *Friends* costars were the only actors who "nailed" their parts.

The order of casting decisions: Schwimmer, Kudrow, LeBlanc, Cox, Aniston and Perry. Although cast in April 1994, Aniston was the last to officially sign, in mid-September, because she was under contract with another series.

Ross

Having worked with David Schwimmer as a guest performer in Dream On and during casting for the Couples pilot, the Friends creators had him in mind when writing the character Ross (his "hang dog expression" stuck in their minds). He was their one and only choice for the role. When they offered him the part without an audition, however, he turned them down.

After a bad experience on Henry Winkler's short-lived sitcom series *Monty*, which aired from January 11, 1994 to February 15, 1994, David Schwimmer moved to Chicago and vowed never to work in television again. NBC was thrilled because it wanted a big-name star to anchor "Friends Like Us" (aka *Friends*), namely Jonathan Silverman.

This was not the first time NBC chose Silverman over Schwimmer. One year prior, both actors were finalists for the male lead in *Couples*. Although Marta Kauffman and David Crane lobbied for Schwimmer, the network execs had final veto authority and insisted on casting Silverman. Kevin Bright opined that NBC saw Silverman as a handsome Jew, worthy of leading man stature, whereas Schwimmer was not.

Eric McCormack (*Will & Grace*) was invited to read for the part. He progressed through three auditions and read for the studio, but didn't make it any further.

After lengthy casting sessions, the creators settled on Noah Wyle to test (final audition) for the network. Alas, he also auditioned for ER and was offered a starring role, which he accepted. Wyle was signed in second position, meaning he would be available for the sitcom but only if ER was not picked up. He subsequently guest starred on Friends, along with George Clooney, in Season 1.

With Wyle in second position, Mitchell Whitfield became the top prospect. He received a call from a staffer who claimed he was going to get the role. The next day the producers said, "We're bringing in one more guy to read." That guy was actor David Schwimmer. Whitfield was later cast as Dr. Barry Farber, Rachel's ex-fiancé.

The cast in high school (senior year) and Season 9 (2002)

David Schwimmer's agent repeatedly urged her client to read the script, emphasizing an ensemble cast, which he preferred, and it being written by Kauffman and Crane, whose work he highly regarded. But he held firm. The creators then begged, sent gift baskets, and promised that their show would not be like *Monty*. Schwimmer remained steadfast. Then two phone calls from distinguished directors, Robby Benson and James Burrows, tipped the scales. The thespian then thought to himself, "Well, it's quite disrespectful [to decline] with all this talent asking to meet and just consider it. I'd be an idiot not to go."

Although there was no formal audition, David Schwimmer read for the showrunners and casting director Ellie Kanner. No studio or network executives were involved. After finishing the reading, everyone knew he was perfect for the part.

Phoebe
According to the creators' original pilot pitch, Phoebe was "sweet, flaky, a waif, a hippie" and goth. When the casting call went out for a "New Age waif," many actresses arrived for the audition sporting "bell bottoms and clunky shoes and nose rings."

The audition involved a monologue from the pilot script where Phoebe discusses her sad life: "I remember when I first came to this city. I was 14. My mom had just killed herself and my stepdad was back in prison, and I got here, and I didn't know anybody. And I ended up living with this albino guy who was, like, cleaning windshields outside port authority, and then he killed himself, and then I found aromatherapy. So believe me, I know exactly how you feel."

Numerous sources falsely reported that Jane Lynch auditioned for the role of Phoebe. The actress confirmed it was a "Hollywood myth." She later appeared in Season 10 as a real estate agent.

Kathy Griffin previously appeared in an episode of *Dream On*, so the creators were very familiar with her talents but felt she was not right, partly because of her age (33). She could play a flake but lacked experience. She received only one audition callback.

Megan Mullally advanced quite far in the audition process but never became a finalist mostly due to her age (35). FYI: She tested for the role of Elaine on *Seinfeld*, which went to Julia Louis-Dreyfus.

Lar Park Lincoln attracted attention from the casting director because of her successful recurring role in *Knots Landing* as Linda Fairgate, but she was too old (34) for the part.

Although initially considered to play the part of Monica, Janeane Garofalo was asked to audition for the role of Phoebe as a goth girl. Instead, she opted to join *Saturday Night Live* for its infamous 1994-95 season. She received the job after Jennifer Aniston turned down the role.

Countless reports indicate that Ellen DeGeneres auditioned for the role of Phoebe. She did not. Her name was at the top of their list of potential leads when casting started but she had already committed to starring in the sitcom *These Friends of Mine* (aka *Ellen*), which debuted on March 29, 1994. Sources misreported her involvement in "Friends Like Us" (aka *Friends*) because of the similar sitcom titles.

In 1985, long before costarring in *Friends*, Lisa Kudrow was a Vassar College graduate with a degree in biology (with an emphasis in neurobiology) and co-authored a scientific research paper on "Handedness and Headache" with three others, including her father, Dr. Lee Kudrow, who founded the California Medical Clinic for Headache, which is now headed by her brother, Dr. David Kudrow. It was her intention to follow her father as a headache researcher. The paper was published in 1994.

A few months after graduation, Lisa Kudrow realized if she wanted to try acting, now was the time. Her father supported the decision. She stopped researching and became a receptionist at the clinic. Kudrow worked on her father's staff for eight years while breaking into acting.

Kudrow's first big break was being cast on *Frasier* as radio producer Roz Doyle. After three days of rehearsals she was fired for giving a weak performance. The role was then offered to Peri Gilpin.

A few months after that, Kudrow was offered a recurring role on *Mad About You* but her agent encouraged her to turn it down—it required Kudrow to be on set in one hour and accept the part without first reading the script. The actress was desperately low on cash so she jumped at the opportunity. She did so well on the first show that creator Danny Jacobson immediately offered her a recurring role.

Kudrow also impressed *Mad About You* staff writer Jeffrey Klarik, who gushed to his life partner, David Crane, about her skills, claiming she would be perfect as Phoebe. Crane invited her to audition. Kudrow thought an audition would give her leverage, prompting Jacobson to offer her a permanent part on *Mad About You*. The ploy didn't work. He actually encouraged her to audition.

After reading the script, Kudrow was drawn to the Rachel character—she could identify with the Long Island JAP persona—but the producers insisted she audition for Phoebe.

Kudrow auditioned multiple times. Each one was perfect. Although excited about earning a costarring role, she was more concerned whether a failed pilot would impact her recurring role on *Mad About You*. Even after the series was picked up, she kept pulling the producers aside during rehearsal breaks to ask, "Are the ratings good enough?" She needed to know her level of job security and whether she should prepare for yet another round of auditions during pilot season.

Joey

The Joey character was written as a womanizer, city slicker, and arrogant self-centered jerk. He acts in children's theater, which he finds unfulfilling, and accepts a variety of gigs to pay the rent, including bouncer, bike messenger, and "the guy in the department store saying 'Aramis? Aramis? Aramis?'"

For the casting call, Joey was described as a "handsome, smug, macho guy in his 20s." According to casting director Ellie Kanner, there was a slew of actors displaying ample chest hair.

All the actors read the "grab a spoon" monologue from the pilot: "What are you talking about? One woman? That's like saying there's only one flavor of ice cream for you. Let me tell you something, Ross. There's lots of flavors out there. There's Rocky Road, and Cookie Dough, and Bing Cherry Vanilla. You could get 'em with jimmies, or nuts, or whipped cream! This is the best thing that ever happened to you! You got married, you were, like, what, eight? Welcome back to the world! Grab a spoon!"

Hank Azaria thought he was perfect for the role and had his heart set on playing the part. In fact, after receiving a rejection, he begged for a second audition. "It was a very fast no," he honestly admitted. Azaria ended up having a five-episode arc as Phoebe's scientist-boyfriend David.

Vince Vaughn was youthful (23) and inexperienced at the time of his audition. He had seven TV roles and a couple bit parts in movies. Kanner thought he was "handsome and tall" (6'5) and a "good actor" but he didn't quite fit the role the way Matt LeBlanc did.

Just before receiving the script for "Friends Like Us" (aka *Friends*), Matt LeBlanc's mom visited him in LA. He was broke and living in squalor. She begged him to move home and give up acting. He promised himself that if the audition didn't go through and he ran out of money, he would head back home and quit acting.

LeBlanc was so poor that he once saved money by doing his own dental work. After a headshot photographer suggested getting an uneven tooth filed down, LeBlanc visited a dentist and learned it would cost $80 without insurance. He went to a drug store and bought a three-pack of emery boards, and did the work himself. When he went back for the headshot, the photographer said, "They did a nice job."

After receiving the "Friends Like Us" (aka *Friends*) pilot script from his agent, LeBlanc thought it "sucked and was not believable."

The evening before the audition, an actor-friend persuaded LeBlanc to go out drinking with friends to get him into character for an ensemble comedy. Afterwards, he crashed at his friend's place and during the night went into the bathroom, passed out, and fell face-first into the toilet. He then went to the audition with a huge gash on his nose.

At the audition, LeBlanc put a "different spin" on the Joey character. Since the persona was not fully developed, he decided to portray a "dim character" like his title role in the short-lived sitcom *Vinnie & Bobby*.

At the time of the final audition, LeBlanc had $11 in his bank account. After being paid for the test reading—before knowing whether he had the role—the first thing he did was go to a restaurant for a hot meal. He was living on snacks and mooching off friends so every paid audition helped.

Initially, the creators didn't like LeBlanc's portrayal, and wanted to cast someone else. He was not a good match for their vision of Joey. But, NBC loved him, and forced the producers to reconsider.

Matt LeBlanc had six audition callbacks. It was far from certain he would get the role. His final audition paired him with Courteney Cox for a chemistry test because they were supposed to be a romantic couple. Although they had chemistry, it was not romantic in nature. Cox wanted LeBlanc to be cast as Joey because he was "so dang cute." LeBlanc also read with Jennifer Aniston.

The final audition was down to two actors: Matt LeBlanc and Louis Mandylor. Although LeBlanc received a character breakdown—Joey was a struggling Italian-American actor in NYC—Mandylor came dressed as a cowboy, complete with denim jacket, jeans, boots and hat. LeBlanc looked the competition and thought, "One of us is way off the mark. God, I hope it's you." The producers wanted Mandylor but Warner Bros. casting director Barbara Miller told them to go with LeBlanc.

Monica

At first, Monica was "darker and edgier and snarkier" (cynical, wisecracking and tough). The creators modeled the character after Janeane Garofalo and used her voice to write the dialogue.

The casting director was told to find an actress having "the attitude of Sandra Bernhard or Rosie O'Donnell and the looks of Duff" (Karen Duffy, the MTV veejay and model).

Janeane Garofalo was at the top of the audition list. She auditioned for Monica but was asked to return to try out for the role of Phoebe. At the time, the creators had a plethora of qualified actors to play Monica, but too few to play Phoebe. Garofalo decided to join *SNL* instead.

Jennifer Aniston was the top choice for Monica despite being under contract with CBS to costar in the sitcom *Muddling Through*. The producers were prepared to sign her in second position but Courteney Cox nailed the audition so the part was offered to her.

Early advertisements: Cox for Tampax in 1985, Kudrow and Aniston for Got Milk? in 1995, and LeBlanc for Cherry 7Up in 1988

Leah Remini was a finalist but knew the part was lost after seeing Courteney Cox enter the building to audition. Remini was later cast in Season 1 as a woman in labor. She is best known for playing Carrie Heffernan in *The King of Queens* (1998-2007).

At the time of her audition, Maggie Wheeler secured a recurring role in *These Friends of Mine* (aka *Ellen*), but she wanted a costarring role. Despite a quick rejection for *Friends*, she impressed the creators enough to be cast as Chandler's vexing girlfriend Janice.

Jessica Hecht auditioned but didn't get far. She was new to the industry and had never appeared in a television program. Her inexperience showed in the casting process but Hecht was later cast as Susan Bunch, the girlfriend and future wife of Carol, Ross' ex-wife. She debuted in Season 1.

Jami Gertz (*Still Standing*) was NBC's top choice because she had TV star power, having costarred in *Square Pegs* and *Sibs*. She also fit the character profile of being cynical and tough but there were too many suitable actors to play Monica and no definitive options for Rachel. Thus, network executives opted to cast Gertz for the role of Rachel.

Nancy McKeon was a finalist for the Monica role. *The Facts of Life* costar impressed the creators so it came down to her and Courteney Cox. NBC President Warren Littlefield thought it was a toss-up so he deferred the final decision to the creators. They opted for Cox because she brought something fresh to the role.

The day before her scheduled Rachel audition, Cox asked to read for the part of Monica. She felt a deep, personal connection to the role and really liked the strong character. The creators thought she was too wholesome and sweet for the part. Besides, they had settled on Jennifer Aniston as Monica.

The showrunners wanted Cox to play Rachel because they had too many strong Monica candidates so they offered her a test option deal, which would guarantee her the role of Rachel without an audition. Cox was flattered but vowed to quit the show if she was not cast as Monica.

Rachel

The role of Rachel was incredibly hard to cast. The character was potentially unlikable because she was "spoiled and whiny, and upset and crying" so she had to be portrayed as "charming and warm and modestly clueless."

Courteney Cox never auditioned for the role of Rachel. The creators approached her to audition but she insisted on trying out for the part of Monica.

When Courteney Cox refused to accept the role of Rachel, the showrunners agreed to cast Jennifer Aniston. However, since she was under contract to another series, they had to sign her in second position, which meant they still needed to cast a replacement actor as a backup.

Téa Leoni was offered the role of Rachel even though the producers thought she was too sophisticated to play the part. NBC executives were hellbent on having a big-name star to anchor the show. Leoni was interested in the part but preferred a starring role so she declined the offer. The next year she was given the lead in the sitcom *The Naked Truth* (which lasted three seasons).

After Leoni declined the part, NBC made a bold, impetuous decision—they offered Jami Gertz the role without consulting the series showrunners. The network was fixated on finding a show anchor and she was the next best option. The creators knew Gertz was not right for the part but they had no say in the decision. Fortunately, Gertz wanted a lead role so she passed.

Jane Krakowski was unknown at the time and never received a callback. "I wish I had gotten that one, ... I didn't go very far," she candidly admits. Coincidentally, while living in New York in 1982, Krakowski beat out Jennifer Aniston for the role of a 13-year-old runaway on the soap opera *Search for Tomorrow*. It was Aniston's first acting audition; she surreptitiously read for the part without her father's knowledge and thought she was a shoo-in since he starred in the serial.

Tiffani-Amber Thiessen was a hot commodity, having come off a successful stint in the *Saved by the Bell* franchise. The producers thought she was too young (20) when paired with the other castmates. She was quickly asked to join the cast of *Beverly Hills, 90210*.

Denise Richards was unknown, inexperienced, and a little too young for the role (23). She didn't get an audition callback but seven years later earned a guest role as Cassie, the Gellers' alluring cousin.

Elizabeth Berkley was beautiful and had acting experience, being another *Saved by the Bell* alumna, but too youthful (19) to play the role of Rachel.

On paper, Anita Barone had everything the producers wanted in a lead but onstage she simply did not conform to their image for the character. Although she lost the lead role, Barone was offered a recurring role as Ross' ex, Carol.

Jane Sibbett, the actress who replaced Anita Barone as Carol, also auditioned for the part of Rachel. She was offered the role but had a secret—she was over three months pregnant (though not showing). She urged her agent to be honest with the showrunners and was immediately told that it would not work out. Sibbett has absolutely no regrets about losing the role. "There's no way anybody could have come close to what Jennifer Aniston did with Rachel. She was so perfect," Sibbett said.

Melissa Rivers was age-appropriate (26) but had no acting experience so inevitably she did not make it too far in the process. She is best known as the daughter of legendary talk show host Joan Rivers.

Nicollette Sheridan (*Desperate Housewives*) was age-appropriate (31), beautiful, talented and experienced, but lacked the sweet girl-next-door look nor the convincing delivery to elevate the character to audience likability.

Parker Posey didn't get far in the audition process because she lacked experience. Her voice and delivery failed to convey sweet, adorable and lovable, which was needed.

Lisa Whelchel (*The Facts of Life*) declined an audition due to her religiosity as a devout Christian. She told her husband "this is the funniest script I have ever read and this is going to be a huge hit," but she knew the show was "going to be all about sex" so she steered clear. While Whelchel said, "I don't regret not taking that opportunity," her kids felt differently. "I remember my daughter once said, 'Are you telling me Brad Pitt could have been my father?'"

Jennifer Aniston was never told to lose 30 pounds as a requirement to being cast for *Friends*. Numerous sources have spread this false rumor. In reality, she was given this advice in 1988 while living in New York as a struggling actor. She had a callback that required her to wear a leotard and tights. She knew she was doomed. Her agent sat her down and told her the truth—she was not getting roles because she was fat. She took the advice to heart, lost weight, and the following year became the Nutrisystem Success

Story spokesmodel and appeared on *The Howard Stern Show*, having lost 15 pounds in six weeks. She eventually lost 30 pounds and began getting more gigs.

Although acting jobs were lining up, Aniston nearly quit the profession. Prior to *Friends*, she was cast in five pilots, four of which made it to the air—*Molloy, Ferris Bueller, The Edge* (with Wayne Knight) and *Muddling Through*. She was exasperated with the failed pilots and on the verge of giving up. In late 1993, she boldly approached NBC President Warren Littlefield at a gas station on Sunset Boulevard in Hollywood, and dispiritingly asked, "Is it ever going to happen?" Littlefield knew her from *Ferris Bueller* and offered reassurances that she was talented and her big break would come. Less than one year later it happened.

In the summer of 1994, Aniston was under contract with CBS for the sitcom *Muddling Through*, but NBC still wanted her to star in *Friends* so it made a venturesome decision, gambling that CBS would cancel its series. Littlefield reached a deal with Warner Bros. (WB) to allow her to appear in up to six *Friends* episodes, and promised to bankroll the cost of reshooting all her scenes using a different actress if CBS picked up *Muddling Through*. This gamble could have cost the network millions of dollars because NBC had no legal right to sign Aniston unless CBS canceled the series.

During the *Friends* photo shoot, Jennifer Aniston was excluded from a few of the shots. Since she was not officially a castmate—her contract with *Muddling Through* had not yet been resolved—NBC withheld her from some promotional shots just in case a different actor would be needed to take her place.

NBC purposely sabotaged the series *Muddling Through* so Aniston would be available to costar in *Friends*. In the summer of 1994, the network broadcast Danielle Steel telefilms opposite the sitcom to siphon viewership and crash its ratings. The tactic worked and *Muddling Through* was canceled in mid-September. At the time, four *Friends* episodes had already been filmed.

Chandler
The Chandler character was written to be the witty commentator on everybody's life as well as his own. He was an office drone, romantic blunderer, and self-proclaimed funny man who used humor as a defense mechanism. Casting required an actor to sell both the humor and insecurities of a man lacking self-confidence. The character breakdown described Chandler as "a droll, dry guy."

When the series creators and casting directors compiled a list of potential candidates, Matthew Perry's name was at the top. They thought he was great but he had already committed to another sitcom pilot. Since Jennifer Aniston was already cast in second position, Warner Bros. refused to allow the showrunners to cast another actor in the same precarious situation. So Perry was off limits.

All the actors read the same dream monologue where Chandler's penis is replaced with a phone. In the scene, Chandler gets a call on the "phone" from his mother, "which is really weird 'cause she never calls me." Series casting director Ellie Kanner played all the other roles in the audition scene. A few actors improvised lines, such as adding "on *that* line," which earned laughs but displeased the writers.

Early in the casting process, Mitchell Whitfield read for two roles, Ross and Chandler. "I went back multiple times, and then they realized Ross was the role for me," he said.

Although relatively unknown at the time, Jon Favreau was offered the part of Chandler. He didn't actually "wow" the producers with his auditions, but no one else was better. Favreau rejected the offer but later appeared in Season 3 as Pete Becker, Monica's uber wealthy UFC-fighting boyfriend.

Jon Cryer was in London performing theater when he received a call from the creators asking him to audition for their pilot. They faxed the script and he agreed to do it. Cryer read with a British casting director. The tape was packaged and mailed to LA but a few days later he was informed the producers never saw the audition because the tape was held up in customs.

NBC had signed Craig Bierko to a deal and was committed to finding a role for him in a series. Since the showrunners were having such a difficult time casting Chandler, NBC pressured them into casting Bierko for the role. They knew he wasn't right for the part, having worked with him in four episodes of *The Powers That Be*, but once again, had no control over the decision.

Craig Bierko was not committed to the show, either. He wanted a starring role, not an ensemble. He ultimately selected another sitcom where he would be the featured lead. Coincidentally, the other sitcom was called "Best Friends" (which never aired).

Prior to each callback, Craig Bierko ran lines with his friend Matthew Perry. Ironically, Perry felt the role was perfect for himself but he was not allowed to audition, so instead, he coached Bierko into the mindset of Chandler Bing. In fact, Perry advised several of his actor-friends on how to master their delivery, and a few of them advanced far into the casting process.

As an actor, Matthew Perry was a hot commodity for TV pilot projects because he had experience and was respected for his work. In late 1993, however, he was contacted by his business manager and told he was broke. He begged his agent to find him any work that was available, and what popped up was a pilot called *LAX 2194*, to play the part for a character named Blaine. Perry was desperate and accepted an offer to costar in the sci-fi sitcom. The series involved baggage handlers at LAX airport in the year 2194. The main characters sorted luggage for aliens, played by little people (midgets).

In March 1994 Perry requested an audition for "Friends Like Us" (aka *Friends*) but was turned away due to his commitment to *LAX 2194*. Six weeks later, the role remained uncast. Everyone was justifiably concerned. WB executives decided to screen the sci-fi pilot, and concluded it was terrible, so they agreed to allow Perry to audition.

At the audition, Perry didn't need a script because he memorized it while running lines with his friends. The moment he auditioned, the creators knew they found the perfect actor. The audition was on Friday, April 22nd, and he started work the following week. Perry was signed in second position but it was more a legal technicality. Although he was still committed to *LAX 2194*, WB President Les Moonves was given assurances by FOX executives that the pilot would be scrapped.

Character Development
Rachel
Casting Jennifer Aniston didn't change the manner in which the character was scripted.

Monica
The casting of Courteney Cox actually modified Monica's persona. The character was originally conceived as "darker and edgier and snarkier." The producers rewrote the role to complement her acting style. "Courteney brought a whole bunch of other colors to it. We decided that, week after week, that would be a lovelier place to go to," Marta Kauffman stated, "and more maternal."

Because Courteney Cox had been in the Bruce Springsteen video and *Family Ties*, the showrunners feared *Friends* would become a "Courteney Cox show." As far as Cox was concerned, she made her character richer than the trio had originally expected, and at the same time alleviated fears she would be the center of attention.

Monica's persona was partially modeled after cocreator Marta Kauffman—competitive, perfectionist, neurotic, nurturing, and a control freak with OCD tendencies. Courteney Cox also admits to being a lot like Monica but included some of her sisters' attributes in her overall portrayal.

In the early installments, Monica was called The Riddler by staff writers because all she seemed to do was ask questions and set up jokes. Then, a few of the writers observed Cox straightening the furniture in her pretend apartment after everyone else had gone home. (She even cleaned her costars' dressing rooms.) At that point they all decided to make Monica an obsessive-compulsive neat freak.

Kevin Bright, Marta Kauffman and David Crane in September 1994 and May 2021

Courteney Cox and Monica both possess the nurturing gene. In real life, Cox enjoyed caring for her friends and guiding them to make the right decisions. She loved to advise everyone on the best course of action, whether buying a product or planning activities.

Matthew Perry helped Courteney Cox develop Monica's personality.

Phoebe
According to the original pitch, Phoebe was "sweet, flaky, a waif, a hippie" and a goth free spirit who played bad folk songs on her guitar and dated a lot of men. The pilot episode toned down the serial dating while retaining her musical stylings and flakiness.

Phoebe's ditziness and fantastical spirituality was based in part on Marta Kauffman.

When Kudrow was cast, the Phoebe character was changed to become more spiritual. Kudrow modeled this attribute after Jennifer Aniston, who, at the time, was consumed by spiritual and New Age subjects.

Phoebe had a very tragic life story so Lisa Kudrow chose to portray it with a laid-back attitude. In her mind, Phoebe's naivete about her past traumatic life made it funny.

Phoebe's positivity was inspired by Lisa Kudrow's Vassar College friend who remained upbeat, even when her life was in disarray, e.g., she had to leave college because her parents thought it was making her atheistic, and ended up working in a nursing home. She never got down about it, ever, and could find humor in any situation.

Kudrow struggled at portraying her character during Season 3. She felt like she had deceived the producers. Matt LeBlanc comforted her and helped change her attitude.

Joey
The Joey character was envisioned as a city slicker from Chicago, perpetual horndog, womanizer, and self-involved jerk. The emphasis was on his lothario lifestyle and condescending attitude.

When Matt LeBlanc auditioned, he played the character as being rather dimwitted. The writers didn't like it at first, but it hit home while shooting the pilot when someone said, "Matt plays dumb really well." After director James Burrows suggested adding the trait to Joey's persona, the showrunners finally embraced the change and it became a major source of comedy.

In the pilot, Joey debuted as a leather jacket–wearing lothario with an outer-boroughs affect and a huge black book of conquests. Audience testing found him off-putting—a Tony Danza–type clone.

After the pilot episode was picked up, Matt LeBlanc informed the producers that Joey, as written, did not fit in with this group of companions. The showrunners retooled the character to be funnier and warmer within his circle of friends.

LeBlanc felt uneasy about Joey hitting on his friends, so he convinced the creators to have Joey be a big brother to the girls, and a lothario to all the other women in the city.

Chandler

The Chandler character's insecurities and use of humor as a defense mechanism was modeled after cocreator David Crane.

David Crane, who is openly gay, originally considered writing Chandler as gay but after casting Matthew Perry, he changed the character to a straight man often mistaken for gay. (Chandler's namesake would later jokingly accuse Marta Kauffman for ruining his life by naming a *Friends* character after him.) The producers preferred to focus on gay references, innuendos, mannerisms and stereotypes. Thereafter, the showrunners never seriously considered writing Chandler as gay.

When Lisa Kudrow first read the pilot script, she thought Chandler was gay. She was impressed with Matthew Perry's ability to portray the character as straight. Many fans assumed Chandler's sexual orientation would someday become part of an episode plot. However, in 1997 the idea was put to rest when David Crane asserted: "No, Chandler isn't gay. Nor will he be gay."

After the pilot pickup, the creators invited Matthew Perry to lunch to get to know him better. They took notice of his unique persona—sarcasm, filling uncomfortable silence with jokes, fear of talking to women, bad romantic relationships, and peculiar manner of speech by emphasizing certain words—and decided to use these characteristics for Chandler's profile.

One notable character change involved Chandler's level of nerdiness. He started out as a computer geek who liked *Star Trek* but this persona did not fit the type of character that Matthew Perry seemed adept at portraying.

Ross

David Crane admitted that his neurotic tendencies were incorporated into Ross' profile.

Ross' career was never intended to be integral to his character. His original character description read: "A paleontologist. Not that it matters." His occupation only mattered after NBC insisted that the showrunners begin emphasizing characters' workplaces to expand the number of settings in the show.

Since the Ross character was specifically written for David Schwimmer, all the script drafts already incorporated many of his traits. Thus, the writers did not need to tweak the character to comport with the actor's personality or acting style.

David Schwimmer was responsible for Ross' distinctive haircut. When cast as Ross, he was starring as Pontius Pilate in the play *The Master and Margarita*, which required a buzz cut. Since the sitcom pilot was filmed less than two months later, his hair didn't have much time to grow. To maintain continuity, Schwimmer kept the same basic style throughout the series.

Recurring Regulars

James Michael Tyler (Gunther)

Born a natural brunet, James Michael Tyler was never asked to dye his hair white for the part. It was "a happy coincidence." His friend, an aspiring hairdresser, wanted to practice bleaching hair so Tyler eagerly volunteered. Naturally, the next day he received a call to be an extra for the first season of *Friends*. Thus, for continuity, he bleached his hair every week for 10 years.

Other than the six main stars, Tyler appeared in the most episodes, but never appeared in the pilot. He was initially hired as an extra at the coffee shop but on the first day was elevated to cafe manager because assistant director Joel Wang knew Tyler worked as a barista and could convincingly operate the espresso machine. Tyler was in nearly every Central Perk scene, but his visage only appears in 178 installments. FYI: IMDB falsely lists his episode total as 150.

For the first 32 episodes, Tyler did not have a character name or speaking part. He was referred to as "Coffee Guy" on the show's call sheet. His first line was "Yeah."

In 2012 Tyler appeared as himself in Matt LeBlanc's series *Episodes*. He poked fun at the fact that he was the only former *Friends* actor that LeBlanc could get to appear on his show and claimed to have contact with all the former costars. In reality, Tyler had almost no contact with the cast since the show ended.

Tyler was often enlisted by the studio to help promote *Friends*. He appeared as Gunther in the DVD *Friends* trivia game, promoted the openings of pop-up Central Perk replica shops in London and New York, and appeared at the inaugural FriendsFest in 2015. Though often excluded from *Friends* reunion gatherings, Tyler was eventually asked to physically appear at the reunion show in 2021 but chose to attend remotely via Zoom due to health issues (he didn't want to be a "downer").

In his personal life, Tyler married Barbara Chadsey, a personal trainer, in 1995; they separated in 2003 and divorced in 2014. Shortly thereafter, he started dating Jennifer Carno, a script coordinator and production assistant, who admitted that she had no idea he was famous when they met. Their first public pronouncement as a couple was at FriendsFest in 2015. They were married on April 8, 2017.

In September 2018, Tyler was diagnosed with prostate cancer. It advanced to stage 4 and led to paraplegia (paralysis of the lower body). In a 2021 interview he stated: "My goal this past year was to see my 59th birthday. I did that. My goal now is to help save at least one life." He passed away on October 24, 2021.

Marcel

Writers Adam Chase and Ira Ungerleider suggested a narrative where Ross adopts a pet so he would appear more saucy and Mediterranean. The writers settled on two options: monkey or iguana. Jeff Strauss had been a biology major in college and contemplated becoming a veterinarian. He adamantly opposed Ross getting a monkey but the creators ignored his pleas.

Ross' pet capuchin was played by two females, Katie and Monkey. The duo have starred in films and TV shows such as *Bruce Almighty* (2003) and *30 Rock* (2006-13). Katie later became the mascot for the Los Angeles Angels and costars in the 2021 FX series *Y: The Last Man* (2021-present) on Hulu. Monkey passed away from cancer in 2020.

David Schwimmer hated working with the monkey because it always missed its mark which foiled their choreographed bits, though Marcel's trainer, Mike Morris, disputed the allegation. In addition, Schwimmer didn't like the unsanitariness of working with a monkey. Prior to each take, the simian would sit on his shoulder, eat live grubs, and rub them in the actor's hair. Finally, Schwimmer expressed discontentment that he was never allowed to bond with the pet. The trainers were very possessive. But if he had to choose a favorite, Monkey would win because she was much calmer than Katie, which made filming easier. In 1995, Schwimmer said, "I hate the monkey. I wish it were dead," and in 2021 added, "It was time for Marcel to f*ck off!"

Trained monkey actors are mercurial, prone to unpredictable rages, and untrustworthy as performers. In fact, Courteney Cox stated that the simian scared her. Head costumer Debra McGuire declared: "Marcel was just a pain in the ass. It's hard to love an animal when it's such an idiot. He was an obnoxious monkey, just not very likable." Therefore, Marcel was written out of the show after eight appearances. The other cast members did not have problems with Marcel. Jennifer Aniston "loved" the monkey and Matt LeBlanc "got along great with it."

Paul Rudd (Mike)

Casting director Leslie Litt recalled the difficult process of finding the right actor to play Mike Hannigan. "We had a casting session for that role but no one was quite it. Paul [Rudd] agreed to do a one-time meet and read with Lisa [Kudrow]. All I wrote on my notes was 'dreamy.'" He was promptly cast as Phoebe's new love interest.

Paul Rudd was originally signed to appear in only two installments, but the producers quickly recognized his chemistry with Lisa Kudrow so they continued writing stories for his character. He appeared in 17 episodes. Many fans consider him the seventh friend.

Cali and Noelle Sheldon as Emma in 2003 and taking a selfie in 2021 (age 18)

The first day on the *Friends* set, Paul Rudd thought he would be fired after rolling over Jennifer Aniston's foot with a Segway. Aniston had broken her toe and was using the transportation device for mobility. The cast was marveling at her scooter, and even Matt LeBlanc gave it a try. Rudd's test drive was not so smooth. "I spun around and rolled it right over Jennifer's foot!" he said. He didn't re-break her toe or cause any other injury, though she was not amused (neither were the producers).

The showrunners weren't sure who to choose for Phoebe's long-term love interest; it was a toss-up between Mike (Rudd) and David (Hank Azaria). Ultimately, they selected Mike because Rudd fit so well with the cast and didn't compete to become the seventh friend. According to the showrunners, "He just felt more real."

Rudd has spoken about his days on *Friends*, and admits he felt dwarfed. "In something like *Friends*, the show was about them. I was only in it for just a blip. I felt, 'I'm like a prop on this show. It's not about Mike Hannigan.' But there's a very interesting feeling to be a part of something that has that kind of profound impact on pop culture."

Maggie Wheeler (Janice)
When Maggie Wheeler (née Jakobson) first auditioned, the script made no mention of how to play the character, it merely said, "Fast-talking New Yorker." She looked at the rhythm of the language in the script, and just heard Janice's voice in her head. So she decided to go with it.

Janice debuted in "The One with the East German Laundry Detergent" (1.05). Her first words, "Oh my God," would later became her signature catchphrase, though Wheeler had not yet developed the memorable delivery and didn't speak in her trademark whiny, nasally voice. Wheeler claims she didn't have time to develop the character with only one week of rehearsal.

Wheeler was only supposed to appear in one installment but her intoxicating laugh and vexing voice resonated with viewers. She became a fan favorite so the show's producers continued inviting her back to boost ratings. Wheeler appeared in 19 episodes.

Tom Selleck (Richard)
The role of Dr. Richard Burke was not specifically written for Tom Selleck. After the staff writers plotted a story arc involving an older love interest for Monica, they had to locate an actor "appealing enough that you believe the relationship." Selleck fit their ideal guy.

Despite being a seasoned actor, Tom Selleck had to do a screen test with Courteney Cox before he was offered the role. They had instant chemistry. Curiously, he was warned to not do the show because it would look like he was "crawling back to television." He did not care what other people thought and decided to do it anyway.

Selleck was so popular that every time he appeared on the show, his first cued entrance received a standing ovation from the audience. It's a nice ego boost, but disrupts actor timing and impedes episode editing. The cast and crew had to reshoot all his opening scenes after the audience departed. Selleck appeared in nine installments and had one uncredited voice role.

Sheldon Twins (Emma)

The first twins to portray Emma were Elizabeth and Genevieve Davidson in Season 9. They were replaced by Alexandra and Athina Conley, beginning with "The One Where Rachel Goes Back to Work" (9.11). Starting with "The One in Barbados, Part 1" (9.23), Emma was played by twins, Noelle and Cali Sheldon.

The female costars loved filming scenes with the Sheldon twins because they could play with the babies backstage during breaks.

The Sheldon twins were featured in "The One with the Cake" (10.04) where Chandler and Monica videotape a segment to be watched by Emma on her 18th birthday. In the video clip, they bash the infant for sleeping all day because it caused them to miss their romantic trip. Chandler says, "Hi, Emma. It's the year 2020. Are you still enjoying your nap?" In 2020, one of the actresses who played Emma, Noelle Sheldon, poked fun at the installment by posting a message on Instagram: "Just woke up from the best nap of all time, happy 2020!!"

Cole Sprouse (Ben)

Over the course of the series, Ben Geller was portrayed by four different actors: Michael Gunderson (Season 2), twins Thomas and John Christopher Allen (Seasons 3 to 5), and Cole Sprouse (Seasons 6 to 8). Sprouse's twin brother Dylan was not part of the series. The Sprouse twins began their acting careers when they were 8 months old.

Cole Sprouse had a terrible habit of correcting the costars when they forgot their lines. Ironically, he was prone to forgetting his lines whenever paired with Jennifer Aniston because he had a serious crush on her. "I was infatuated. I was speechless. I'd get all bubbly and forget my lines and completely blank," he confessed. His crush was pretty obvious on set because he was often teased by the crew.

Cole Sprouse's favorite *Friends* episode is "The One with the Holiday Armadillo" (7.10). "I was infatuated with the costumes, and the practical effects that they had," he said.

Triplets

The infant triplets on the show were played by the Cimoch quadruplets (one girl, three boys: Alexandria, Paul, Justin and Cole). Since Phoebe had two girls and a boy, at least one of the boy quadruplets always had to play a girl.

The toddler triplets were played by Dante Pastula (Frank), Sierra Marcoux (Chandler) and Allisyn Ashley Arm (Leslie). The first two had only a couple acting credits, but no gigs since 2007. The latter (aka Allisyn Snyder) is by far the most successful actor. She starred opposite Demi Lovato in *Sonny with a Chance* and was also part of the spinoff *So Random!* Recently, she starred in the webseries *Astrid Clover* (which she created) and had a recurring role in the TV series *A.P. Bio*.

Elle Fanning (*Super 8*, *Maleficent*) auditioned to portray one of the triplets and took the rejection hard. "I auditioned for it but I didn't get it and I was like, 'I'm boycotting the show, I'm never watching this again,'" she exclaimed. "Then my sister was on it, and I refused to watch the episode. I was like, 'I am not watching this!'"

Elliott Gould (Jack Geller)

Besides James Michael Tyler (Gunther) and the six series costars, only two other actors physically appeared in all 10 seasons of the show: Elliott Gould and Christina Pickles, who portrayed Jack and Judy Geller. Ironically, Gould was instructed by his agent to reject the *Friends* role because it didn't pay enough money. He took the part because he wanted to work with director James Burrows.

Although Gould was a beloved actor on set, there was one incident that had him in hot water. In "The One with Ross's Wedding, Part 2" (4.24), the producers took unmitigated measures to ensure the ending would remain a secret. However, after returning from London, Gould went on *The Rosie O'Donnell Show* and revealed who Ross married. The producers were livid.

At one time, Kevin Bright pitched the idea of killing off the Jack Geller character and having Ross honor his father's request for a burial at sea. At the time, Bright was going through a family crisis with his father (Jackie) who was in declining health and in need of caretaking from his son. His pitch was resoundingly rejected. "Nobody wanted to kill off Elliott Gould," he admitted.

Christina Pickles (Judy Geller)

Judy Geller was based on Marta Kauffman's mother but "an extreme version of her." Kauffman felt the same familial angst as Monica: she could do nothing right to please her mother.

Guest Stars

During the first season of *Friends*, the producers had difficulty hiring big-name actors to appear on the show. Jon Lovitz, the first legit movie star to be cast, agreed to guest star because he was friends with Courteney Cox and Lisa Kudrow.

The cast and crew secured several well-known actors through friendships, romantic liaisons and work relationships. Kevin Bright was friends with Billy Crystal and Robin Williams so he roped the comedians into a cameo, and Marta Kauffman invited Jason Alexander to guest star because she was good friends with him and his wife, Daena Title. Brad Pitt was married to Jennifer Aniston at the time of his casting and Julia Roberts accepted a role because she and Matthew Perry were on the verge of a budding romance. As for working relationships, Bruce Willis guest starred after losing a bet to Matthew Perry while filming *The Whole Nine Yards* (2000), Matt LeBlanc helped secure Gary Oldman while working together on the film *Lost in Space* (1998), and Christina Applegate had worked with the executive producers on the TV series *Jesse* (1998-2000).

Once the show achieved universal acclaim, it became easier to sign *actual* movie stars. Danny DeVito was the first individual offered the role as "the oldest performer on the planet or the world's most unlikely stripper." Kathleen Turner was approached by David Crane after the producers couldn't find an actress to play the part of a transvestite, and Brooke Shields and Christine Taylor agreed to appear without first reading the script (a rarity in Hollywood).

Still others agreed because their family members were huge fans of the hit show. Susan Sarandon signed on because she and her entire family were big fans of the show. Sean Penn was watching a *Friends* rehearsal with his kids (who were *Friends* fanatics) when he was approached to appear, and Sarah Ferguson (Duchess of York) accepted an offer because her daughters were beguiled by the sitcom. Initially, Ron Leibman (Dr. Green) declined the role but his daughter insisted he reconsider so she could meet the cast.

Many guest actors experienced severe anxiety during their episodic appearance. Charlie Sheen missed his cued entrance because his legs were shaking uncontrollably so his brother, Emilio Estevez, had to be taken out of the stands to calm Sheen, rub his back, and encourage him to return to the stage. Sarah Ferguson (Fergie) was exceptionally nervous so Matt LeBlanc kept running lines with her to calm her while Matthew Perry stayed behind to offer support. Reese Witherspoon was so consumed with stage fright she quit after two episodes, Susan Sarandon had to be calmed by Matt LeBlanc prior to her entrance, and Brad Pitt flubbed his opening line. Additionally, Freddie Prinze Jr. was "totally nervous," Tom Selleck was "a little scared," Aisha Tyler felt "intimidated" by the set, and Kristin Davis was so "nervous" about her role she was "losing sleep." Two actors who felt "intimidated by the cast" include Jennifer Coolidge and Winona Ryder.

There were several disappointing guest stars. Primarily it was movie stars who failed to exhilarate the audience, such as Jonathan Silverman, Charlie Sheen, John Stamos and Jennifer Grey. Musician Chris Isaak ("Wicked Game") was a casting disaster and Sean Penn seemed dazed and confused.

Helene Marla Sherman with her sister Lisa Kudrow, husband David, and working as a sculptor

There were several potential guest stars who nearly made it on the *Friends* stage. Owen Wilson topped the list but was never asked to appear because the *Friends* writers read an interview where he admitted his "biggest fault was giving writers a hard time." Justin Theroux had an audition scheduled but chose to skip it because he wanted to sleep in that day. Justin Timberlake asked to be on the show, and even met with the producers, but they never found a way to fit him into an episode. Tom Hanks was supposed to play a male nanny but canceled at the last minute due to a delay while filming a movie, and Sting was booked to have a cameo but canceled at the last minute, so his wife (Trudie Styler) filled in on his behalf. Paul McCartney was offered the role as Emily's father in the two-part London episode but declined because he was too busy.

Stand-Ins

Stand-ins usually start their career as background extras. As their title aptly describes, their job is to stand in for an actor so the crew can set lighting and camera block. As a general rule, they do not appear on camera, but *Friends* was the exception—the episode directors occasionally gave bit parts to the stand-ins.

Kim Harris was the stand-in for Jennifer Aniston. She appeared in numerous episodes, often as an uncredited performer, but did have lines in four episodes. On the set, Harris met and then later married crew member Scott Bruza, a set dresser and artist who had paintings displayed in Central Perk. She quit acting in 2005 to assist her husband with set construction projects. Harris appeared in one installment of *Joey* and functioned as Aniston's stand-in for the movie *The Good Girl* (2002).

Actor Lisa Calderon (aka Lisa Avery) was the stand-in for Courteney Cox in 193 *Friends* episodes, from "The One with Russ" (2.10) through "The Last One, Part 2" (10.18). She was adored by the actors and made a career as a stand-in, working on several of the projects for Cox and LeBlanc, such as *Cougar Town, Dirt, Joey* and *Man with a Plan*.

Heather Sims was the stand-in for Lisa Kudrow. She had three episode appearances but only one credited. Sims later appeared in two episodes of *Cougar Town*.

As the stand-in for Matt LeBlanc, Douglas Looper was a frequent onscreen performer in *Friends*, but only credited for three roles. He had two other minor acting credits; nothing since 2005.

Joe Everett Michaels was the stand-in for Matthew Perry. He had three appearances in *Friends*, but only two were credited. Although relatively unknown in the acting world, Michaels carved a solid career as a theater producer in Los Angeles.

Body Doubles

Body doubles replace actors on camera from behind, in makeup, or during stunts.

Lisa Kudrow's sister, Helene Marla Sherman, was employed as a body double for scenes involving Phoebe and her twin sister, Ursula. Kudrow delivered all the dialogue for both characters, while Sherman functioned as the body double (viewers would see the back of her head). When both appeared in a frame, the director used a wide angle to obscure their differences since Kudrow and Sherman are not twins.

Lisa Kudrow disliked filming scenes with her sister. She felt uncomfortable and stated those scenes were the most difficult to perform. The producers decided to axe Ursula for that reason.

Extras

Television and movie scene extras can earn anywhere from minimum wage to more than $50 per hour, depending on whether they are union or nonunion, their union status, level of experience, role visibility, and physical activity requirements (e.g., swimming or ice skating). Generally, they get paid for a full day even if they are needed for only a few hours. Each *Friends* episode used 35 to 50 scene extras. Many were hired in multiple episodes, such as Andre Lachaumette who appeared in three episodes.

A few celebrities were invited to be background extras: Australian Olympic swimmer Ian Thorpe, British television host Ben Shephard, and British journalist Sarfraz Manzoor, to name a few.

The producers filled the set with friends and relatives in the series finale. Central Perk had Nancy Josephson (the creators' agent), their unidentified lawyer, Michel Stern (Lisa Kudrow's husband), and Jeffrey Klarik (David Crane's life partner). In various airport scenes the producers included their assistants, spouses and children, as well as friends and other relatives, not to mention a publicist, Pilates instructor and the show's casting director.

Series

Concept

After producing *Dream On*, which focused on one lead character, the *Friends* creators wanted an ensemble show so the stories would be spread out among many actors.

The inspiration for a coffeehouse setting occurred in December 1993. Marta Kauffman was driving along Beverly Boulevard and passed Insomnia Cafe, an offbeat coffee shop. She thought, "That's a fun reference. Sort of an over-caffeinated feel for the show." She went inside and immediately loved the eccentric patrons and esoteric surroundings.

The original pilot was somewhat different from the final version that ultimately became known as *Friends*. The concept was more dramatic. As the showrunners negotiated with studio and network executives, the series slowly evolved from dramedy to comedy.

The original series concept had four costars and two secondary characters. Phoebe and Chandler were meant to interject humor as needed. After the main actors were cast, the vision changed. "They gave us much, much more than that," Kauffman stated. "They became so central to the ensemble."

Pilot

In December 1993, Marta Kauffman and David Crane pitched the pilot concept to three networks. FOX ordered a script and NBC expressed interested so Warner Bros. started a bidding war. FOX decided to pass on the project while NBC agreed to order a pilot or risk paying a $250,000 penalty.

In preparation for writing the pilot, the creators reviewed unproduced scripts for other series, mainly *Seinfeld*. This helped the writers find their voice. It also inspired them to mirror the sitcom about nothing by creating multiple storylines with equal weight. Prior to *Seinfeld*, all sitcoms had a major plot with one or two minor subplots.

When devising characters, the creators borrowed personality traits from themselves, as well as friends, relatives, acquaintances and actors, to formulate an amalgamation of attributes that would form a loose outline for their protagonists.

The initial pilot pitch had the show being filmed with one camera, instead of three. NBC rejected this idea. In retrospect, the creators were thankful because they loved filming with an audience.

Character Names

Rachel's surname was originally Robbins. Of course, it was later changed to Green but there were spelling inconsistencies throughout the series. In most episodes it was Green (without an "e" at the end), but in a couple shows it was "Greene."

There have been many false reports that the *Friends* characters were named after *All My Children* characters: Monica (Monique Cortland), Phoebe (Phoebe Tyler Wallingford), Rachel Green (Janet Green), Ross (Ross Chandler), Joey (Joey Martin) and Chandler (the Chandler family). This is merely a coincidence. The showrunners drew from their personal lives and then picked names until one sounded right.

Washington Square Arch, Jefferson Market Library, Cooper Union and St. Paul's Chapel

Chandler was named after a college friend of Marta Kauffman. Monica was selected as a tribute to Kauffman's niece. Phoebe was named after a friend of David Crane's parents because it was a really bizarre moniker. Joey was chosen because he was an actor and the creators wanted something simple. The other main character names were random.

Pilot Changes

The initial script had nearly every scene filmed inside the coffee shop. This concerned NBC President Warren Littlefield so he recommended using the characters' apartments. The creators then rewrote the script to split the scenes between both locales.

The initial draft had Chandler living alone. Littlefield suggested having Joey as a roommate and then placing their apartment directly across the hall from Monica's tenement.

NBC didn't like the coffee shop setting. They wanted a diner like *Seinfeld*. Kauffman and Crane refused to relent. "We weren't *Seinfeld* and didn't want to be like *Seinfeld*."

The network didn't like the show format of three equally weighted storylines. Executives wanted the creators to follow the customary practice of having one dominant plot and two subplots. The creators refused. NBC ultimately acquiesced since *Seinfeld* already proved this unconventional format worked.

NBC wanted Courteney Cox to be featured as the star and the other five actors to be secondary characters. The producers adamantly objected. They wanted an ensemble and stuck to their guns.

While brainstorming the pilot concept, Warren Littlefield insisted on incorporating an older character into the series to make it more palatable to a wider age demographic. The sagacious elder character would appear in the coffee shop periodically and function as a quasi-father figure offering life and relationship advice to the youthful patrons. The creators affectionately called him Pat the Cop. He would magically appear at the most opportune times to sprinkle magical wisdom as needed.

Staff writers Jeff Greenstein and Jeff Strauss originally pitched the idea of Pat the Cop, a local police officer who would regularly visit Central Perk for coffee and conversation. The scribes named the character after an older police officer who would hang out in the movie theater where they used to work during college in Somerville, Massachusetts. The creators ultimately rejected the idea.

The next thought was an older coffeehouse owner, known as Coffee Joe. They wrote a script but the resulting draft was "terrible." They begged NBC to axe the character, and in exchange, promised to introduce older recurring characters, namely the parents of the protagonists. NBC acceded.

Show Titles

Throughout the entire process, from concept to pickup, the show title was interminably debated. In fact, literally hundreds of names were proposed, though only a handful were seriously considered.

When the initial show concept was pitched to NBC in December 1993, the seven-page treatment was titled "Insomnia Cafe." After NBC executives expressed interest in the pilot, the creators needed to change the title to avoid trademark infringements with the actual business upon which their show was based so they came up with "Central Perk Cafe" (the creators' wordplay on New York City's Central Park).

After NBC bought the pilot script, it suggested changing the focus away from the coffee shop. The creators then selected "Bleecker Street" after the Manhattan roadway where Kauffman resided during the 1980s (i.e., 77 Bleecker St.). It was a working title. But the name still didn't click to them.

The next naming idea went along with the dramedy theme of the proposed pilot and was called "Once Upon a Time in the West Village." When the concept morphed into a more humorous vibe, the elongated dramatic title did not seem to fit. After NBC ordered the pilot, the first draft of the script was aptly called "NBC Pilot Which Still Needs a Title."

After NBC President Warren Littlefield recommended Joey and Chandler be roommates that live across the hall from Monica, he proposed the title "Across the Hall." Cocreator David Crane was not enthralled with the suggestion, so he sarcastically added, "Or just have it *be* across the hall." However, since they didn't have a better title in mind, they went with Littlefield's proposal.

In early February 1994, Warner Bros. sponsored an internal name-that-show contest. The winner was David Crane's life partner Jeffrey Klarik, who proposed "Friends Like Us." This was the title when NBC received the final pilot script, and it lasted through most of April.

On March 29, 1994, ABC debuted *These Friends of Mine*, a sitcom about adults hanging out and looking for romance, starring Ellen DeGeneres. The show was given the best timeslot on television, after *Home Improvement* (#1), so it became an instant top-10 hit. Its success caused trepidation for NBC executives. Since the popular ABC show had a similar title, theme and genre, the network thought it may cause audience confusion, so it requested another name change. Ironically, one year later, in the summer of 1995, ABC renamed *These Friends of Mine* because *it* was being overshadowed by *Friends*. The rebranded series was called *Ellen*.

By the time the NBC pilot was filmed in early May 1994, the title changed again, this time to "Six of One." After the network agreed to pick up the series, they requested one final name change. The producers went back to the original title "Friends Like Us," but shortened it to "Friends."

Pilot Filming
The first table read (read-through) occurred on Thursday, April 28, 1994.

Since Courteney Cox was the only well-known actor in the cast, she made her costars nervous. In fact, the other cast members gave her professional deference and followed her lead. On the first day of rehearsal she unwittingly initiated a movement that would forever unite the cast and change the social pecking order of the thespians. Cox urged everyone to offer notes on how she might improve her performance or anything else that may benefit the quality of the program.

This selfless act changed the course of the sitcom. "There's a code with actors. Actors don't give each other notes under any circumstances," Lisa Kudrow explained. "So she was giving us permission to give her notes, and we all agreed that that would be great." Schwimmer concurred. He was energized by "the spirit of collaboration" among the cast.

Script Changes
The initial "Bleecker Street" draft in December 1993 had several script variances that did not make it into the final "Six of One" pilot in May 1994: (1) the installment starts with Monica describing how she never wants to go on another date, but reconsiders her original statement after Phoebe offers to lend her a lovely black dress; (2) Ross' crush on Rachel was the main plot (her adjustment to singlehood) and Monica's one-night stand

as subplots; (3) Ross' unrequited love was the basis for much of the pilot's comedy and its emotional core; and (4) after Chandler concludes his dream monologue, a character adds, "One word for you: therapy."

In other drafts, Phoebe did not live with her grandmother and Ross was younger than Monica. The creators also discussed Monica taking in a young pregnant woman. At the urging of Matt LeBlanc, a staffer, and director James Burrows, the showrunners finally rewrote Joey as dimwitted. In the original script draft, Monica was extremely reluctant to reconnect with Rachel because she was jealous of her wealth and upset she wasn't invited to the wedding. In fact, Monica didn't offer Rachel a place to stay and even after they became roommates, she was persistent in trying to get her to move out.

Network Run-Through

On Monday, May 2, 1994, the cast held a network run-through—wearing costumes and performing the script as if filming the installment—which was performed for studio and network executives who then offered notes on all aspects of production from makeup, clothing and set design, to dialogue, script content and innuendos (to assess if anything violated network standards and practices).

In one plot, Monica sleeps with a guy on the first date and then doesn't remember his name in the morning. NBC West Coast President Don Ohlmeyer ordered a script rewrite because it depicted her as a slut. In his mind, Joey could be a womanizer but Monica had to be sanctimonious.

The creators defended the plot so Ohlmeyer demanded they poll the audience. He then prepared a biased questionnaire to skew the results: "For sleeping with a guy on a first date, do you consider Monica to be (A) A Slut, (B) A Whore, (C) A Tramp, (D) None of the Above." Before the results were tabulated, he insisted on having Monica written out of the show. The creators laughed at the request and vehemently objected to the demand.

The questionnaire results came back overwhelmingly "none of the above" so esteemed director James Burrows persuaded Ohlmeyer to stand down. Nevertheless, to appease network executives, the creators modified the script so Monica would be emotionally invested in the relationship, and they actually preferred the rewritten version because it made the scene "smart and subtler."

After a less-than-stellar run-through, Ohlmeyer claimed he found the show confusing. There were too many characters to follow and too many storylines. He wanted the show to focus on Monica (exiling the other characters to secondary status), primarily because Courteney Cox was the only star on the show. The network was already planning on featuring her in the fall promotions. Normally, the creators would be forced to appease NBC's requests, but in this instance, Burrows, a man with plenty of power and clout, told Ohlmeyer, "Well, that's not the show I signed on to do." NBC could not risk losing the esteemed director so Ohlmeyer dropped the request.

Pilot Screening

The pilot was filmed on Wednesday, May 4, 1994, on the Warner Bros. lot in Burbank, California, in front of a live studio audience. Bright submitted the edited cut to NBC on Tuesday, May 10th, merely 72 hours before the fall schedule was slated to be publicly announced. After network executives screened the show, the overall feeling was that the pilot was out of touch with the real world.

NBC returned the pilot with one vague note from executive Don Ohlmeyer: "The opening is too slow," and then he sternly threatened, "[If] you don't cut some of the dialogue and pace it up, you're not on the air." They were given five hours to complete the task.

The creators loved the opening. They thought it was perfect and didn't want to change it. So they used a little sleight of hand. Kevin Bright spliced together a 90-second title sequence using pulls (clips) from the pilot episode and then overlaid it with R.E.M.'s "Shiny Happy People." Everything else remained intact. After Ohlmeyer viewed the new edit, he said, "Now it's right." The creators later admitted, "We didn't have to change a single word."

Famous fountains: Warner Bros. in California, and Pulitzer, City Hall and Bethesda in NYC

NBC was satisfied with the cut so the final step was to have it screened by focus groups (aka pilot testing). During this process, the network assembles a grouping of ordinary people to watch the pilot episode and provide constructive criticism (as well as stating their feelings) through a preset questionnaire. The research results concluded that the pilot was WEAK (but a high weak). In other words, the results were okay. It was not a death knell. The grade simply meant the show had potential to grow.

Pilot Pickup
A pilot pickup means the network is going to purchase the series. It can range from four episodes (the smallest pickup ever ordered, which went to *Seinfeld* in 1989) to an entire year (which is rare). Typically, networks cover their bases by ordering 10 to 12 episodes, and if things go well, they will order more later. With respect to *Friends*, NBC agreed to 12 episodes with a guarantee to air 6.

On the evening of Thursday, May 12, 2004, a mere 12 hours before NBC was slated to publicly announce its fall schedule, the creators received a call that the pilot was going to be picked up but the title had to be changed to something better than "Six of One."

The trio always liked the title "Friends Like Us," and while pondering other hit sitcoms, such as *Seinfeld*, *Taxi*, and *Cheers,* they liked the naming simplicity so they settled on *Friends*. NBC executives called the title "generic" and "a snore" but they did not have time to come up with anything better.

NBC gave *Friends* the second-best timeslot, sandwiched between *Mad About You* and *Seinfeld*, while the best position (after *Seinfeld*) went to *Madman of the People*, featuring Dabney Coleman. NBC believed *Madman* was a better show but had to eat crow upon canceling the sitcom after 16 episodes.

With a 12-episode commitment, the creators had to secure writers. They only wanted writers under the age of 40. The showrunners wanted fresh ideas and new perspectives.

Script Ideas
The showrunners researched what it was like to be a twentysomething living in the mid-1990s. Kauffman even consulted with two babysitters who cared for her children to quiz them about life as a single youth. Although the showrunners were only in their late 30s, they felt like anthropologists.

The staff writers were encouraged to use personal experiences to craft storylines, which is exactly what they did. The creators advocated collaboration among the entire creative team—writers, directors, actors, guest stars, and recurring actors—to elevate the script. Every bit, line, joke, segment and scene was dissected and scrutinized in the endless drive to make the show better.

Like *Seinfeld*, *Friends* was one of the first American sitcoms to emphasize young adult friends outside the work environment. Most viewers could identify with the characters facing life's uncertainties—finding love, searching for a career, and struggling to make ends meet. It was a universal theme that transcended cultures and milieus.

The simplistic naming of installments, e.g., "The One with..." or "The One Where..." was lifted from *Seinfeld* where all the episodes used generic titles, such as "The Opposite" or "The Conversion." The *Friends* creators merely modified the titles to be more descriptive.

Unused Script Ideas

The most shocking plot proposal was having the gang move to Minnesota in Season 5. In the storyline, Chandler is transferred for his job so the rest of the gang follows and discovers a world of "cheap apartments, friendly neighbors and subzero temperatures." The relocation was supposed to last half a season. The concept was partially devised due to criticism that *Friends* did not properly represent the racial diversity of New York City. It was also a way to conceal Matthew Perry's substance abuse issues. He could be more easily written out of scripts if he relapsed.

At the request of Walt Disney's CEO Michael Eisner, a script was written where the cast went to Disney World. In the plotline, Joey gets a summer job as a giant light bulb in the electrical parade. The gang schedules a visit but before they get there, Joey has a date with a woman who portrays Cinderella in the Disney parade. They go back to his place and have sex. Upon realizing it's midnight, she has to get the costume back or they will dock her pay. She gathers up her clothing and leaves, but Joey doesn't even know her name. In a play on Cinderella's glass slipper, the girl forgets her bra which is Joey's only clue to discovering her identity. According to Kevin Bright, "That was the story we pitched to Disney, and that's where the story ended."

Another storyline involved Phoebe being so in love with Chinese food that she attempts to marry it. This idea was unilaterally rejected. "I just find myself not caring," Kauffman would regularly respond to pitches she felt lacked an emotional through-line.

In Season 6, there was a proposal to have Rachel and Gunther become roommates. At the time, she was booted out of Monica's apartment and needed a place to live. It was finally scrapped because the arrangement seemed too contrived.

NBC executive Don Ohlmeyer censored one *Friends* storyline, namely, where Ross uses his ex-wife's menstrual pads for arch supports in his shoes and refuses to throw them out. "Overall, the network notes were almost nonexistent," David Crane stated, but this time "Don was uncomfortable with maxi pads."

Although the cast had some leeway to refuse storylines, it rarely happened and only if they could convince the showrunners. For instance, Matthew Perry objected to a plot that too closely linked his character to being gay. In the script, Chandler went to an all-male strip club because it served great tuna melt sandwiches. Perry didn't find the idea funny and asked for it to be nixed.

The creators didn't always acquiesce to cast objections. In Season 10, when the script called for Joey and Rachel to start dating, the entire cast confronted the producers to express their dissatisfaction. The top dogs refused to budge, claiming it promoted an emotional storyline for Joey's character.

Also in the tenth season, the creators crafted a plot involving Ross and Rachel traveling to Paris so he could begin to fall in love with her again. The writers didn't have enough time to develop the story arc because the final season was truncated to 18 episodes so it was canned.

Recycled Jokes

Having a character wearing two belts was used in "The One with Monica and Chandler's Wedding, Part 2" (7.24) and "The One with the Fertility Test" (9.21).

Characters purposely sitting in another person's chair was repeated in "The One Where No One's Ready" (3.02), "The One with the Race Car Bed" (3.07) and "The One with Ross's Grant" (10.06).

A character practicing dirty talk as another person discretely enters the room occurred in "The One with the Stoned Guy" (1.15) and "The One with Rachel's Dream" (9.19).

Having a character throw a glass of water in Joey's face was scripted in "The One After the Superbowl, Part 1" (2.12) and "The One with Joey's New Brain" (7.15).

Two characters going out to eat and then forgetting to pay for the meal was duplicated in "The One with All the Cheesecakes" (7.11) and "The One with Ross's Tan" (10.03).

Chandler having a tear roll down his cheek was recycled in "The One Without the Ski Trip" (3.17) and "The One Where the Stripper Cries" (10.11).

Phoebe's Songs

Lisa Kudrow did not write any songs. The *Friends* writing team penned the lyrics and she created all the melodies, including "Smelly Cat" (with help from Chrissie Hynde from The Pretenders).

"Smelly Cat" was originally titled "Smelly Dog." Episode writer Betsy Borns based the song on her pungent pooch (her dog smelled like cheese so she named it Gouda).

The tune was so popular an updated version, "Smelly Cat Medley," was added to the soundtrack *Friends Again* (1999), with artist credit to Phoebe Buffay and The Hairballs. Kudrow even performed the number live onstage with Taylor Swift at the Staples Center in Los Angeles in 2015.

Real-Life Inspirations

Two of the set's business facades were named after Marta Kauffman's parents. Dottie & Herman's bodega and Dot's Spot restaurant honor Dorothy and Herman Kauffman.

Free Being record store was named after a real-life business that Kevin Bright used to frequent in the 1970s while living in New York. Joey Ramone bought records there.

Marta Kauffman inserted the names of several ex-boyfriends into the scripts, such as Billy Dreskin and Daniel Arshack. She also used character names based on her friends, Deb Franzblau and Rona Oberman, who inspired the lesbian couple, Carol and Susan. Adam Ritter, one of Rachel's exes, was named after a friend of the creators.

David Crane often inserted his life partner's name into scripts. Many times there were references to Jeffrey or Jeffrey Klarik.

Emily Waltham's surname was taken from the city where the creators attended college. Brandeis University is located in Waltham, Massachusetts, just outside Boston.

In the pilot episode, Monica says her special feelings for Paul are much like how Rachel felt when dating Tony Demarco. The character was named after a World Welterweight Champion from the North End neighborhood of Boston. The creators learned about the boxing legend while attending Brandeis.

NBC Censors

When *Friends* debuted in 1994, NBC approved use of the word "penis" but "nipple" was taboo (until Season 2). Three years later "penis" was banned and then in Season 7 it was acceptable again.

In "The One Where Dr. Ramoray Dies" (2.18), Monica and Rachel argue over who gets to use the last condom. NBC refused to allow the characters to say the word "condom" or display a condom wrapper. Only a generic, nondescript box was acceptable.

The creators were always looking for ways to circumvent network censors. In "The One Without the Ski Trip" (3.17), Carol alludes to being intimate with Susan by removing a pubic hair from her tongue. In "The One with the Worst Best Man Ever" (4.22), Joey decorates the apartment for a bachelor party with "balloons" that are inflated condoms.

In retaliation to network censorship, the writers created a gesture to connote a swear word. Quite often the characters use the pinky-side double fist bump. As Kevin Bright noted, the staff writers created the gesture to circumvent censors, as a subtle means of saying "F*ck you!"

The original *Friends* title sequence had the cast playing cards

Directors

Director James Burrows oversaw the pilot episode en route to a total of 15 installments in the first four seasons. He later went on to direct *Will & Grace* and *Mike & Molly*.

Kevin Bright directed 54 installments. Each television season he was given first option to select the episodes he wanted to direct.

David Schwimmer directed 10 episodes. In Season 6, he asked the creators for a chance to call the shots for an installment, and they agreed. *Friends* was his first experience at directing a sitcom. He was the only costar to direct an episode, and continued directing through Season 10.

The executive producers helped several crew members gain experience directing, such as technical coordinators Dana deVally and Roger Christiansen, as well as series editor Stephen Prime. Most episode directors were selected based on availability.

Title Sequence

After the pilot was shot and edited, the *Friends* producers contemplated a title sequence to accompany the show. They had the cast sit in the coffee shop and then shot a bunch of footage of them playing cards. The title sequence was scrapped after NBC executives claimed they didn't want one.

After NBC complained that the opening scene was too slow, the producers created a 90-second title sequence using pulls (clips) from the pilot episode overlaid with an upbeat song. NBC loved the new version, but the producers were unable to license the track so they decided to write a theme which ultimately inspired them to also create an original title sequence.

The first order of business was creating a memorable logo for the series. The *Friends* logo was created by graphic designer Deborah Naysee who worked for Three Headed Monster, the company that produced the title sequence (fountain scene). She was paid for the logo but did not get another dime for its future use.

The initial plan for the title sequence involved filming on a rooftop in Los Angeles but the cost and weather considerations made it prohibitive. Warner Bros. suggested using their ranch (i.e., small movie studio), which had a park with a fountain and a row of European-style apartment buildings as a backdrop. Kevin Bright adored the location because it resembled a park in the Village. They lit the interior windows and matted a city skyline in postproduction.

The producers loved the fountain because it reminded them of Pulitzer Fountain in New York. Big Apple tour guides often claim several local fountains—Pulitzer, Cherry Hill, Bethesda, and City Hall—were used in the *Friends* title sequence. This is false. Not one scene was ever filmed in New York.

In 2019, the WB ranch was sold but the original fountain was relocated to the studio. It can be viewed by visitors during the Warner Bros. Hollywood Tour on Stage 48.

Friends title sequence in 1994 and Jay-Z's parody in his 2017 music video "Moonlight"

The _Friends_ fountain also appears in the movie _Hocus Pocus_ (1993).

The title sequence was shot a couple weeks before the pilot premiered. Filming began at 10pm on a very cold California night and lasted about four hours. (Numerous sources falsely claim it was taped at 4am.) The writers came up with a few bits for the cast to perform but most of the physical actions were improvised. The idea of dancing in the fountain came from Three Headed Monster.

The cast had to dance without the benefit of music. They actors were merely given the title to the then unrecorded theme song and told to mouth the words "I'll be there for you." Jennifer Aniston is the only cast member seen lip-syncing in the final edit of the opening credits to the pilot episode.

After a couple hours of filming, the cast began imbibing alcohol to make it feel more like a party. They quickly relaxed and ended up in the fountain, splashing around playfully. Although the water was heated through a pump, by the end of the shoot the actors were soaked, freezing and miserable. Everyone had pruney fingers.

The cast was not keen on the notion of frolicking in the fountain. According to Jennifer Aniston, it felt "sort of odd" and they only did it because they "were told to."

The original title sequence aired with the pilot on September 22, 1994. After seeing the pilot, NBC executive Don Ohlmeyer insisted on a change because, in his mind, it said to the audience: "We're young, we're hip, we're dancing in a fountain and you can't dance with us." He wanted the intro to be the final cut that was submitted in May (with only episode clips). The creators compromised by inserting clips into the fountain scene.

Kevin Bright was responsible for all title sequence edits. He added new installment clips twice a year.

Theme Song

Michael Stipe, lead singer for R.E.M., refused permission to use "Shiny Happy People" as a theme song and would not agree to perform any other tune for the show, including a duet with his friend Natalie Merchant from 10,000 Maniacs.

After Stipe's unequivocal rejection, the alternative rock band They Might Be Giants was tendered an offer to perform the _Friends_ theme song. They, too, declined. (FYI: TMBG subsequently licensed one of their songs as the theme for _Malcolm in the Middle_.)

The theme song title and chorus melody were composed by Marta Kauffman's husband, Michael Skloff, and the lyrics were penned by Allie Willis. The Rembrandts wrote the verse melody and performed the song. Kevin Bright wanted a melody and tempo similar to R.E.M.'s "It's The End of the World as We Know It (And I Feel Fine)" (#69, 1987).

The 45-second theme song was written and recorded in three days. At the last minute, the executive producers and Michael Skloff added the memorable four rapid hand claps to the track.

Shortly after _Friends_ debuted with its catchy theme song, Charlie Quinn, the program director at Nashville radio station Y107, looped the original 45-second version into a three-minute pop song. The tune went national. Although The Rembrandts' new album was finished and 100,000 advance copies had already shipped, executives at East West

Records demanded that a full-length version of the song be included on their album or it would not be released. The duo complied—a new album was issued with all the old copies destroyed—but remained resentful because the track did not fit their concept. However, it did sell a lot of albums, so for that they are thankful.

Marta Kauffman and David Crane helped write the full-length version of the song. They already had songwriting experience from crafting show tunes for musicals in the 1980s. Out of spite, the band refused to release the song as a single but surprisingly, the ditty still peaked at No. 17 on the US Billboard Hot 100 singles chart and No. 1 on the Hot 100 Airplay chart for eight weeks. It became an international hit. In Canada, it topped the charts for five consecutive weeks and was the most successful single of 1995. It hit No. 3 on both the UK Singles chart and the Irish Singles chart. In Scotland, it topped the country's Singles chart.

In 2017 *Paste* magazine had the song "I'll Be There for You" ranked No. 59 in its listing of The 75 Best TV Title Sequences of All Time. On the other hand, *Blender* magazine in 2004 ranked it No. 15 on its list of The 50 Worst Songs Ever.

Music Video

The music video wasn't shot until 1995 because it was hard to coordinate the schedules of six costars. It was filmed on *Saturday Night Live*'s Rockefeller Center stage (8H) using a white backdrop, and took three days to shoot.

Originally, the music video was highly scripted. In the story, the cast tries to attend The Rembrandts' concert and at one point they smack the duo with a frozen fish, knocking them out. The cast refused to perform the stunt so it became a basic band performance with the cast playing instruments.

The Rembrandts did not give instrument tutorials to any of the *Friends* stars, but they said Cox took her time behind the drum kit very seriously. The drummer hired for the shoot tried to give her lessons, but she said, "Pfft. I can do this."

Pilot Debut

The ages of the six cast regulars at the time of the series premiere were Lisa Kudrow (31), Courteney Cox (30), Matt LeBlanc (27), David Schwimmer (27), Jennifer Aniston (25) and Matthew Perry (25).

When Cox received her first paycheck, she bought a brand new $80,000 silver Porsche Carrera. One of the first things Matt LeBlanc did with his newfound wealth was buy a home for his mother.

Cast Camaraderie

Although the *Friends* cast was tentative at their first table read, they swiftly bonded and became a tight-knit group. The first couple years they hung out together, watched the original airing of *Friends* episodes every Thursday night at their homes, and partied at nightclubs. They even went on group vacations, such as the guys heading to London during a filming hiatus in 1996.

On set the cast was equally jocular. They teased one another when they flubbed a line, and often improvised bits to make each other laugh. During rehearsal breaks they often hung out in Courteney Cox's dressing room (it was the cleanest).

Younger guest stars were usually part of the cast clique. They felt welcome and bonded with the costars. The cast shared acting tips and production protocol. The older guest stars, however, often felt ostracized by the sextet.

Friend Pairings

Joey—Monica

When the creators pitched the pilot to NBC, the original concept had Joey and Monica hooking up in Season 1. Since these characters were the most sexual, it only seemed natural to pair them.

While casting the Joey part, the creators began to rethink the role. Joey was no longer a city slicker from Chicago; instead, he had a blue-collar working class background from an outer borough. Thus, to them, it no longer made sense to have Joey and Monica as the core couple. The change was cemented once Cox and LeBlanc tested together. They did not have good onscreen romantic chemistry.

Ross—Rachel
In the original pitch, Ross and Rachel were never meant to get together. During the pilot rehearsals, the onscreen chemistry between Schwimmer and Aniston was obvious. The creators described the pairing as "an indescribable mixture of attraction and loathing and tenderness and brutishness."

Schwimmer and Aniston admitted to their mutual crush but claim they never acted on it. The timing was not right. One of them was always in a romantic relationship. "So we just channeled all of our adoration and love for each other into Ross and Rachel," she candidly stated. "I just remember honestly saying one time to David, 'it's gonna be such a bummer if the first time you and I actually kiss is gonna be on national television.' ... Sure enough, first time we kissed was in that coffee shop!"

The initial breakup in Season 2 was supposed to be Rachel dumping Ross. Then one of the writers suggested a pros-and-cons list which made the breakup easier and cleaner.

When it came time to pen the finale, the creators considered several alternative endings. "We did talk about, with Ross and Rachel, a gray area of where they aren't together, but we hint there's a sense that they might be down the road," David Crane asserted. "But we thought, 'No, if we're going to do it, let's do it.' It's the nature of our show. It's not a show about grays. Let's deliver not just what the audience wants, but what we want, which was to see them finally together."

Joey—Rachel
The Season 10 romance between Joey and Rachel was purposely written solely to delay her romantic reunion with Ross. The decision for such an unlikely amorous pairing was made midway through Season 9.

A possible romance was alluded to in Season 8. Joey developed feelings for Rachel that she did not reciprocate. This romantic tension made their romantic coupling two years later much easier for the staff writers because it only involved establishing a storyline to make Rachel reconsider her feelings for him.

In Season 10, Matt LeBlanc was "firmly against" a Joey-Rachel romance. In his mind, Joey would never do that to a friend. It took "a lot" to convince LeBlanc to do it. In fact, the entire cast confronted the showrunners about the troubling love affair. David Crane offered reassurances that it would not be a long-term romance.

Monica—Chandler
The two characters interacted heavily in "The One Where Ross Finds Out" (2.07), where Monica functions as Chandler's fitness instructor, but the writers chose to postpone the decision to get them together. Although their chemistry was obvious, the timing was not right because the entire world was dazzled by the Ross-Rachel romance.

Serious thoughts of having Monica and Chandler as a romantic couple first occurred in Season 3 after Ross and Rachel split. Once again, the timing was not right. The creators thought their pairing would appear desperate, especially after all the emotional drama between Ross and Rachel. They did not want *Friends* to become the "Get Together and Break Up" show.

Season 4 started with the Ross-Rachel romance, but then Lisa Kudrow's unanticipated pregnancy pushed her character's surrogacy storyline to the fore. The writers just could not find the right moment for Monica and Chandler to hook up. A big reveal appeared to be the only timing that seemed perfect.

Monica and Chandler's London tryst was never meant to develop into a long-term love affair. It was meant to be a funny mistake. But then the British studio audience went insane at the sight of them in bed together. The fans screamed nonstop for 27 seconds. It totally changed the direction of the show.

The creators actually envisioned Monica and Joey becoming a stable couple in Season 5, harking back to the original pilot concept. However, after the audience embraced the Monica-Chandler pairing, the creators opted to test the waters with that relationship.

Since Ross and Rachel's romance fizzled in a blaze of bitter and cantankerous glory, the producers decided to do it differently for Monica and Chandler's love affair. "All of their fights would be light and breezy, and never have the edge that Ross and Rachel's did," David Crane said. "Principally, to make them feel different from each another."

Even though the world embraced the new couple, the creators were reluctant to keep them together so they teased the audience with a furtive romance. "We didn't want to invest too much too quickly because sometimes in a sitcom you put people together and it takes energy out of the show, and it kind of relieves sexual tension in a certain way," Kevin Bright declared. "So we wanted to see gradually how it would go with Monica and Chandler. The period of them keeping it a secret allowed us to see how much does the audience really love this."

Many believe this pairing rejuvenated the show because it was a pleasing diversion from the Ross-Rachel roller coaster romance. "Without Monica and Chandler, it ends three years earlier," says writer Scott Silveri.

Joey—Phoebe
Although the showrunners never considered a romance between Joey and Phoebe, they found the notion intriguing. Near the end of the series, Matt LeBlanc and Lisa Kudrow pitched the idea of their characters having casual sex the entire time. There would be flashback scenes to memorable episodic moments that everyone recognizes, which end, for example, with Joey and Phoebe coming out of a broom closet together. The creators swiftly rejected the idea because it didn't "fit the tone of the show."

Love Interests
Tom Selleck was introduced as the older love interest for Monica. He was only supposed to appear in three episodes but his overwhelming popularity prompted the creators to extend his contract.

Paget Brewster (Kathy) was introduced to facilitate friendship conflict for Chandler and Joey. Although she appeared in six episodes, the creators had plotted her story arc to extend longer but felt she lacked good chemistry with Matt LeBlanc, so it was trimmed.

Helen Baxendale (Emily) had her recurring role axed due to an unexpected pregnancy. The Ross-Emily union was supposed to extend into Season 5 but her maternity issue led to a whirlwind romance, expedited wedding and swift breakup, all within months.

Elle Macpherson joined the cast for a five-episode story arc as Joey's roommate, Janine Lecroix. The producers offered to extend her contract but she declined. She was living in London at the time and didn't want to travel so far for each appearance.

Dermot Mulroney (Gavin) was introduced as a love interest for Rachel but the writers' clandestine goal was to rekindle romantic feelings between Ross and Rachel. Mulroney was axed sooner than expected because he lacked romantic chemistry with Aniston.

Pregnancy Issues
When the series was first pitched to NBC, the creators never fathomed having to write pregnancy issues into their scripts. But as events arose, they opted for unconventional childbirths. The writers reminded the world that there is no right way to live our lives— having a baby is a deeply personal decision and it is different for everyone.

The first pregnancy arose in October 1997 when Lisa Kudrow informed the creators of her condition. At the time, about one-third of the Season 4 episodes were already filmed and a few more plots were projected. Thus, the first allusion to a pregnancy was not revealed until January 8, 1998, in "The One with Phoebe's Uterus" (4.11), where Frank Jr. asks his sister to be a surrogate.

Since Phoebe was not romantically involved with a man, the staff writers did not want to introduce a love interest who swiftly impregnates her, nor did they want her to be a single parent and add a baby to their milieu. The creators chose surrogacy for her half brother and giving birth to triplets because neither had been done on television before.

Since Lisa Kudrow was four months pregnant when the surrogacy storyline was first filmed, her condition had to be concealed until her fictional girth caught up to her real-life girth. Once the pregnancies were in sync, though, almost immediately, Kudrow had to start wearing padding to account for the added weight of carrying triplets. (Only one episode was shot without padding.)

The next pregnancy issue was contrived, not based on an actress becoming pregnant. It involved Rachel's unplanned pregnancy out of wedlock. The story arc was devised solely to offer the creators a grand event (giving birth) for the season finale, as well as offering hope to viewers that Rachel and Ross may reunite in the future since they shared a unifying interest, Baby Emma.

The final pregnancy focused on infertility which had always been a taboo subject for TV, and definitely not sitcom material. The *Friends* creators decided to change that belief with a lengthy story arc involving Monica and Chandler. Once again, it was a contrived pregnancy so the birth was scheduled to sync with the series finale.

Near the end of Season 9, Monica and Chandler discover they both have fertility issues. Ironically, one month into filming Season 10, Courtney Cox announced her pregnancy. This created a new dilemma. The creators could not logically incorporate her pregnancy into the series, as they did Kudrow's, because it was already established that Monica and Chandler could not conceive a child.

The producers opted to hide Cox's pregnancy. Her condition was disguised using props and baggy costumes along with special lighting and camera blocking. Despite utilizing these gimmicks, her pregnancy bump was quite visible, especially in the finale.

Sets

Monica's apartment was designed by art director John Shaffner, who modeled it after a sixth-floor walk-up he occupied in New York in the 1970s. He was especially proud of the design which had all the apartment doors opening to the living room, the focal point of the series. Shaffner applied the same concept to Joey's apartment.

Monica's bathroom was originally designed so the back wall could be removed to allow filming the apartment through the door. It was later redesigned as a false wall. Several scenes were filmed inside the bathroom so a larger swing set had to be constructed to accommodate the actors, most notably Chandler's bathing scenes in "The One Where Chandler Takes a Bath" (8.13).

When designing Monica's apartment, Shaffner included appliances and electronics that were fully functional, such as the refrigerator and television. The set's realism, however, caused many studio visitors to forget it was just a set. There came a time when visitors (friends, family, executives, etc.) had to be reminded that the set bathroom did not have functional plumbing.

None of the on-set remote controls worked; all the electronics were operated offscreen.

The golden picture frame hanging on the purple door became an iconic fixture by mere chance. It was originally placed on a side table. While dressing the set for the pilot, crew member Ricky Parker bumped the table, causing the frame to hit the ground, breaking the glass. Set decorator Greg Grande opted to remove the backing and place the frame on the door.

In Season 1, the thoroughfare outside the coffee shop was nothing more than a painted backdrop that was partially obscured with frosted windows and hanging plants. When production moved to Stage 24 the following year, the display windows were clear with an unobstructed view. Set designer John Shaffner encouraged the creators to build an entire neighborhood with business and apartment facades, and a sidewalk and roadway so pedestrians and vehicles could be added for realism. It also allowed for scenes to be shot outside Central Perk to expand the filming options.

The original Central Perk sofa was beige. Studio and network executives objected to the color so set decorator Greg Grande searched WB's property warehouse and found the iconic orange couch. But the executives still objected because there were a couple rips in the back and the arms were a little tattered. Director James Burrows argued that the couch was "absolutely believable and real." The parties agreed to have Grande mend the fringe and use a tapestry throw to conceal the largest tear.

The Central Perk espresso machine was never used on the show, but the barista had to appear knowledgeable and experienced while pretending to operate the cafe equipment. James Michael Tyler (Gunther), a real-life barista, commented that it was an obsolete coffee machine. The set designer purposely selected an outdated model because the set decorating budget was marginal.

Taping Episodes

The first season was shot on Stage 5 at Warner Bros. Studios in Burbank, California. At the start of the second season, production moved to the more expansive Stage 24 (later renamed "The *Friends* Stage" after the series finale), taking over the soundstage that was previously occupied by *Full House*. Stage 24 is purportedly haunted. It is one of the oldest stages on the Warner Bros. lot and rumors of late-night "occurrences" have been circulating for years.

Since the start of the show, the main players had duplicate names (Matts and Davids) so the crew assigned monikers to avoid confusion. Matthew Perry was called Matthew or Matty, while Matt LeBlanc was simply called LeBlanc. David Crane was referred to solely as David while David Schwimmer's appellation was Schwim.

Before filming each installment, the six costars met in a private room for a backstage huddle; no one else was present and no cameras were allowed. Schwimmer started the tradition and would always say, "All right, have a good show, love you, love you, love you, love you," as they all shared a group hug before heading onstage. One episode was especially memorable for Lisa Kudrow. Prior to filming "The One with All the Wedding Dresses" (4.20) the gang stated, "Have a great show, love you—love you, little Julian!" Kudrow was touched her fetus was included in the huddle.

The preshow huddle was skipped only once, in "The One Where No One's Ready" (3.02), due to production delays that held up the start of the shoot. "We were like, 'We're taking too long, and the audience has been waiting—let's just go,'" remembers Kudrow of that fateful decision. Shortly after filming began, Matt LeBlanc separated his shoulder. After that, they vowed never to skip a huddle.

On a typical night of filming, 500 tickets were issued but only 300 fans were seated for the show. The bleachers were raised above the stage so the audience could see the sets and actors without the cameras and crew blocking their view. Before filming and during set changes, a large black curtain with the *Friends* logo covered the stage. It was rolled upward after the cast was introduced.

After four hours of waiting in line, attendees were ushered into the studio. In the first half of the series, the episodes started taping at 6pm (the typical start time for sitcoms), which made the session extend into the early-morning hours. If the audience members became too tired, the crew would search for "fresh" bodies to fill the seats. This lengthy filming process began to take its toll on the cast. Around the fifth or sixth season they stood united to confront the showrunners and insisted on a change. Thereafter, filming started at 3pm and the audience was ushered out of the studio by 9pm.

The producers hired stand-up comedian Jim Bentley to warm up the audience before each episode taping and during filming breaks. His work duties also included meeting celebrities and dignitaries, and providing an appropriate cast introduction. The weekly entertainment included stand-up comedy, contests, singers, and free giveaways (hacky sacks, frisbees, cups, etc.).

After the audience departed, the cast would work an hour or two on pickups (reshooting scenes), which wrapped typically around 11pm. The cast and crew would usually hang around to discuss the show and eat pizza, and then the sextet would depart to Il Sole in West Hollywood.

The cast and creative team loved performing for an audience. The actors treasured the feedback to gauge their performance and the writers used it to test jokes. Each scene was shot several times with a considerable amount of rewriting between takes. If the audience didn't react to a joke while filming, the writers would huddle together, discuss ideas, and then try a new bit for the crowd.

Three to four cameras were typically used to tape an episode, totaling up to 12 hours of footage and 30,000 feet of film (i.e., over five miles), which then had to be edited to 22 minutes. Most episodes, on average, had 52 takes, 14 scenes and seven rewrites. It took 366,000 watts of electricity to light all the sets for one night of filming. In other words, that is the equivalent electrical power for 34 homes in an entire year. The series spent $1,700 a week on globes (light bulbs).

Animal Filming
All the animals used on the show were hired from Benay's Bird and Animal Rentals in Woodland Hills, California. In business since 1982, Benay's has over 100 trained bird and animal actors.

Since the show's animals could not be trained to perform on cue, the director often let the cameras roll—with the actors improvising their lines and actions—hoping to get a usable shot. Although the cast had a general framework of dialogue and comedy bits, they had to ad-lib based on the actions of the animal.

Shooting animal scenes was difficult and time consuming. The animals were oftentimes uncooperative or unruly. Filming eventually became too problematic so the pets were written out of the series.

Marcel had a tendency to disappear from the set. Everyone would have to take a 5 to 10 minute break until the monkey was located. It happened quite frequently. In "The One Where the Monkey Gets Away" (1.19), the capuchin evaded handlers and climbed into the rafters. It took 30 minutes and a lot of mealworms to lure the simian to the ground.

The chick and duck were easier to film than the monkey. They rarely evaded handlers and were used more as props to set up comedy bits. Unlike the capuchin, which was highly trained and always portrayed by the same two animals, the chick and duck were untrainable, and hence, used interchangeably without regard to gender.

Baby Filming
All scenes with newborns were preshot without an audience because the director was only allowed to use babies in 90-second intervals due to the intense heat from stage lighting. A licensed nurse stood in the background holding a stopwatch to monitor all infant filming. Real babies were only needed to show movement or for closeup shots.

When an audience was present, nearly every scene involving infants was filmed using dolls. The showrunners insisted on a live studio audience because the creative team needed the feedback to gauge dialogue and test jokes.

Filming infants and toddlers usually required hiring twins. Babies go through phases where they get fussy and do not want to be held so a backup baby was needed to make sure they had seamless filming.

Phoebe's childbirth scene used triplets. Once the babies reached age 1, the producers hired quadruplets, hoping only one infant would be uncooperative during the shoot.

During the childbirth scenes, the babies were slathered with grape jelly to represent the birthing fluid.

***Friends* cast wins Emmy Award for Best Comedy in 2002**

Location Shooting

The crew rarely ventured outside the soundstage, but when they did, it was usually on the same lot where the series was filmed, Warner Bros. Studios in Burbank, California. The most used location shoot was Hennessy Street, e.g., "The One After the Superbowl, Part 2" (2.13) (Marcel's movie set). The cemetery scene for Nana's funeral was filmed on Blondie Street. When Ross and Rachel search for Marcel, they are treading Brownstone Street. Phoebe's estranged dad lived on Midwest Residential Street, which was also the location for the Geller residence in "The One with the Prom Video" (2.14). French Street has a park so it was used for Ross' rugby match. Joey's WWI movie premiere was filmed on New York Street, and Elizabeth hitting Ross with a water balloon outside her dorm was shot on Embassy Courtyard.

The crew ventured beyond the WB lot only a couple times when the studio's business and residential streets were inadequate. In "The One with the Baby on the Bus" (2.06), the storyline had the guys riding a bus for an extended time and then chasing it. This was too much activity for the WB Studio lot so the crew went to Paramount Studios in Los Angeles, specifically Brooklyn Street.

There were two memorable filming locations: (1) Joey's big hole in the beach and the jellyfish incident were filmed at Leo Carrillo State Park along the Pacific Coast Highway near Malibu, California, and (2) Joey's movie *Shutter Speed* was filmed just north of Los Angeles at Vasquez Rocks State Park in Agua Dulce, California, in the stunning Sierra Pelona Mountains. The only full-length, on-location episode was the London two-parter.

Series Facts

There are six dots in the *Friends* logo. One for each friend.

In the series, Monica spoke the first line and Chandler uttered the last. The pilot begins with "There's nothing to tell," and the series concludes with "Where?"

The *Friends* costars unanimously voted Lisa Kudrow as the smartest of all of them.

Kevin Bright did editing, sound mixing, schedule budgets, casting of guest stars, and directing. David Crane loved doing standards and practices meetings (where network executives try to censor script content). Marta Kauffman was intricately involved with the stage activities.

In many episodes, the gang watched TV and the programs were usually old movies or cartoons. Most of the clips were from shows produced or distributed by Warner Bros., which has a massive library of movies and TV shows. Since *Friends* was produced by WB, the creators were allowed to use the clips for free. Kauffman and Crane learned about this valuable archive while producing *Dream On*, which relied extensively on clips from Universal Studios' video archive.

Marcel was the first *Friends* actor to star in a movie. Before any of the six leads could capitalized on their sitcom stardom, Marcel was cast in *Outbreak* (1995), also produced by WB. The simian's film grossed more than the sum of all the *Friends* stars' first films.

Even before Monica and Chandler became a couple on the show, Courteney Cox stated in an interview that if she had to "do" (sleep with) one of the other friends, she would choose Chandler. Interestingly, in 2021, Cox's daughter, Coco, revealed that she would prefer to date Joey.

Matthew Perry and Courteney Cox are actually distant cousins. MyHeritage ancestry discovered the pair are 11th cousins; they share the distant relatives William Osbern Haskell III and Ellen Haskell, who were married and lived in England around 500 years ago. Ellen and her two sons immigrated to America in 1635. One son, Roger, is a direct ancestor of Cox, and the second son, William, is a direct ancestor of Perry. The lineage connection is through Cox's mom, Courteney Copeland, and Perry's dad, John Bennett Perry. It also found that both actors are distantly related to Lady Gaga. Cox is a 17th cousin once removed and Perry a 14th cousin thrice removed.

The executive producers had a few odd encounters with *Friends* fans. Marta Kauffman's rabbi once stopped her in a parking lot and insisted on knowing what happened with Ross and Rachel. Kevin Bright recalled being recognized by Japanese tourists in Santa Monica who said they knew him because of the *Friends* DVD extras. David Crane said a flight attendant saw his name on a ticket and spent a six-hour flight talking to him.

Courteney Cox struggled to remember her lines and was known to scribble them on the dining table and keep an episode script in the kitchen sink. She joked, "I had so much of my dialogue within these apples," as she touched a fruit bowl on the table, and then admitted, "I have memory issues!"

There have been 11 Oscar-winning actors who have guest starred on *Friends*: Charlton Heston, Fisher Stevens, Sean Penn, Susan Sarandon, Helen Hunt, Julia Roberts, Reese Witherspoon, Jim Rash, Robin Williams, George Clooney and Brad Pitt.

Matt LeBlanc dyed his hair for the show. In the second season he started noticing gray around the temples so he began dyeing his hair black, which continued through Season 10. He tried coloring his locks at home but the project failed. The next day, he arrived at work with the back of his ears entirely black so thereafter he used the set hairdresser.

LeBlanc is often approached by new youthful fans of the hit show, who look at him and say, "What's with the gray hair? Are you Joey's dad?" Instead of using a cool Hollywood comeback, LeBlanc would blurt "Scram," which, ironically, he pointed out, "That's like what an old guy says!"

Friends TV show has been credited for helping non-English-speaking students learn the language. In 2012, Kaplan International English Colleges found that 26% of its enrolled students claimed the sitcom "helped them the most of any series in understanding the language." The list of disciples include Liverpool FC manager Jürgen Klopp, BTS band member RM, and Belgian professional golfer Thomas Pieters.

In an August 2019 court filing, Graham Chase Robinson allegedly spent "astronomical amounts of time" binge-watching *Friends* while at work, watching 55 episodes over a four-day stretch. She was also accused of embezzling money from Canal Productions, Robert De Niro's production company. In 2023, she filed a lawsuit alleging that De Niro subjected her to "years of gender discrimination and harassment" and created a "hostile work environment." The case will most likely go on for years.

Kudrow admits she was starstruck by Justin Bieber's cameo appearance at the *Friends* reunion show.

Central Perk set from its typical filming angle, and a view from the restrooms

According to Ranker, fans of *Friends* selected Chandler as their favorite character with Joey and Phoebe taking second and third place, respectively. A 2018 UK poll reached the same conclusion. However, a 2016 Comedy Central UK Twitter poll during the epic six-week FriendsFest had Ross at the top spot and Chandler a close second.

The *Friends* cast was reportedly paid $2.5M to $4M each for the reunion show in 2021. However, a knowledgeable source indicated it was closer to $5M.

As of 2021, *Friends* has been watched more than 100 billion times across all platforms, influencing everything from fashion to hairstyles.

Episodes

Season 1: 1994-95

1.01 "The Pilot" (09.22.94)

The original title of this episode was "The Pilot." Alternate titles have been given to the *Friends* pilot episode such as "The One Where It All Began," "The One Where Monica Gets a Roommate" and "The First One."

Although the orange couch and Tiffany firefly floor lamp are iconic fixtures associated with the title sequence, the lamp was not a staple on the Central Perk set. It appeared in several Season 1 installments and a couple times in Season 2 and then disappeared entirely. The set decorator admitted he never found a really good location for the lamp because it always seemed distracting.

The iconic velvet burnt-orange, tufted mohair couch from the early 1900s was found by set decorator Greg Grande in the basement of the Warner Bros. property warehouse. "Literally in the back corner, shoved under another piece, was this sofa with beautiful carved wood," he recalled. It was perfect for Central Perk. "It was probably used in an old movie," says Grande. "Over the years we've had a lot of calls from people wanting to know where to buy the couch."

When NBC insisted on introducing an older character, the creators vowed to integrate recurring characters, namely, parents of the protagonists. In fact, they even wrote an alternate pilot script with a more traditional storyline where Rachel's parents arrive just before the act break (commercial break) but the entire script was scrapped because, as David Crane acknowledged, "It wasn't good."

On the evening of filming, Matt LeBlanc had the flu with a temperature of 102 degrees. Like a true professional, he didn't cancel the taping, and no one ever noticed.

The Spanish-language TV program that the gang watches in Monica's apartment is *Tres Destinos* (*Three Destinations*), a popular American telenovela which debuted in 1993. The woman unhappy about the pipe organ is Puerto Rican actress Angela Meyer. The women on the stairs are costars Lumi Cavazos (Cristina) and Caridad Ravelo (Marcela), the latter is wearing the ill-advised jeans.

In the restaurant, Monica spits water on Paul as an expression of astonishment. This seemingly innocuous physical comedy bit had to be reshot innumerable times. Marta Kauffman frustratingly stated, "We must have done it about 140 times."

Rachel watches the wedding scene from *Joanie Loves Chachi*. Jennifer Aniston proposed using the clip because she truly loved the sitcom. As an adolescent, she would record dialogue from the sitcom on cassettes and then play them in her room, seeing what it felt like to pretend to be Joanie.

NBC insisted on removing a sequence that implied Paul, the wine guy, was getting an erection. The creators rewrote the scene and found they preferred the new version—it was "smart and subtler."

Originally, the pilot script went into more depth about Chandler's professional life. In fact, there was a scene where Rachel visits his office to work on her résumé.

In the scene where Rachel is cutting up her credit cards, the original staging by director James Burrows had Lisa Kudrow reciting her lines while crouched beneath the dining table. During a run-through, however, the creators made it clear that placing Phoebe under the table was not a good idea. Kudrow thought she was going to be fired for the mishap but Burrows accepted responsibility.

The original pilot script had a more dramatic resolution to Ross discovering his ex-wife was pregnant with his child. The producers decided to postpone the revelation to the second episode.

This episode was watched by 21.5 million viewers, making it the 15th-most-watched TV series of the week. Critics compared the show rather unfavorably to *Seinfeld* and *These Friends of Mine* (aka *Ellen*), since all three relate to friends conversing about their lives. Although David Schwimmer was praised, there was apprehension that the characters were undeveloped and the plot would not be well received by viewers.

1.02 "The One with the Sonogram at the End" (09.29.94)

This is the first appearance of Gunther. He is a background scene extra at Central Perk working behind the counter and barely visible in the cold opening.

Ross works at the Museum of Prehistoric History, which is fictional. The establishing shot is actually Alexander Hamilton United States Custom House at 1 Bowling Green, Manhattan, New York, built in 1907.

Both Anita Barone and Jane Sibbett auditioned for the role of Rachel. After not making the cut, they both auditioned for the role of Carol. However, once Sibbett revealed she was pregnant, the producer said, "Thanks, but no thanks," and cast Barone.

Anita Barone was originally cast as Ross' ex-wife Carol. After shooting her scenes, she immediately demanded that her role be expanded because she wanted a recurring role on the series. The producers refused to alter the concept for a secondary player so she quit to pursue a more full-time role elsewhere. Barone was replaced with Jane Sibbett who was a finalist for the role. Sibbett made her debut in "The One Where Underdog Gets Away" (1.09).

The Central Perk davenport received a makeover. After the sitcom was picked up, set decorator Greg Grande found the same fabric in Europe and reupholstered the orange sofa with velvet and mock tufting. He also added a piece of plywood under the cushion to keep the actors from sinking too deeply and slouching.

This is the first episode where Phoebe mentions having an unnamed twin sister that she doesn't talk to much anymore. The showrunners included this dialogue to explain Lisa Kudrow's dual appearance in *Mad About You*, which was the lead-in sitcom to *Friends*.

The ob/gyn is Dr. Oberman. The character is named after Rona Oberman, a friend of the creators. All three attended Brandeis University together and moved to New York after graduation.

In Barry's dental office, the receptionist indicates that Jason Greenspan is gagging. This is a nod to *Seinfeld* star Jason Alexander. His birth name is Jay Greenspan, and stage name is Jason Alexander. Thus, the allusion is a portmanteau of that name. Alexander and his wife (Daena Title) are close friends with Marta Kauffman.

1.03 "The One with the Thumb" (10.06.94)

Hanging in the background of Joey's apartment is a movie still of Laurel and Hardy in bed. In the scene, Stan has a toothache so he ties a handkerchief around his jaw with a knot atop his head like rabbit ears. It is from their 1928 movie *Leave 'em Laughing*.

The set decorator intentionally chose the monochromatic poster of Laurel and Hardy to symbolize the close relationship between Joey and Chandler. The comedic duo reigned over Hollywood cinema from 1921 to 1951 but their offscreen friendship was equally special as they both supported one another and remained an indispensable presence in each other's lives. In fact, when Oliver Hardy died in 1957, Stan Laurel became so lost that he refused to act in movies.

In this episode, Joey has to smoke cigarettes for a role but can't figure out how to hold one. At the time, Matt LeBlanc was a smoker. He quit in 2000 but it only lasted four years (stress from the impending series finale caused him to relapse).

Chandler was the only smoker in the series, but in real life, every member of the main cast (except David Schwimmer) was a smoker. Courtney Cox gave it up around the sixth season because she was trying to have a baby. Jennifer Aniston was a chain smoker for years and quit multiple times but it seems to have finally taken hold in 2012.

Monica mentions that a man's penis length is the same as the distance from the tip of his thumb to the tip of his index finger. This is a myth. A more accurate indicator is to compare the lengths of the index and ring fingers of a man's hand. Researchers found that men with a bigger difference tend to have longer penile length.

In the scene where the guys enter Central Perk after a softball game, Ross' Big Hitter t-shirt features the artwork of Pittsburgh artist Burton Morris. The pop art garment was part of a line he was selling at the time. When his sister moved to California, she took some shirts with her and one ended up in the hands of a production worker on *Friends*. David Schwimmer saw the design and asked the crew member, "Hey, can I wear that shirt? I think it is a great shirt for this scene." After seeing the shirt on TV, Morris spoke with Kevin Bright who then asked the artist to display some paintings on the show.

This is the first episode of blatant product placement. In Central Perk, Rachel and Joey enter with Nike cleats flung over their shoulders and the corporate logo is strategically positioned for a clean camera angle. Nike would remain a major sponsor throughout the series' run.

The exterior shot of Chandler's office is Solow Building located near Bergdorf Goodman and the Plaza Hotel. The 1974 building has 50 floors (49 floors above ground level), and is featured in *Sex and the City* (1998-2004), *Zoolander* (2001) (headquarters of Mugatu fashion empire), *Superman* (1978) and *Cloverfield* (2008) (as monster bait). The building address, 9 W. 57th St., became the namesake for the Nine West shoe store chain.

When the pilot episode was in production, NBC wanted an older seventh friend to offer wisdom to the twentysomethings. Although the creators effectively resisted the request, the character Alan represents such a character as he gives sagacious advice to convince Chandler to quit smoking.

1.04 "The One with George Stephanopoulos" (10.13.94)

As the guys are walking to the hockey game, they are on Hennessy Street on the Warner Bros. lot.

The New York Rangers hockey game is supposed to be at Madison Square Garden but it was actually filmed using the soundstage bleachers. The scene was preshot without an audience. The studio audience bleachers were often used for scenes involving sporting events, concerts and theater performances.

Four *Friends* staff writers appear as hockey arena extras. Adam Chase is seated next to Chandler holding a Rangers pennant. Next to Joey is Scott Silveri. Behind Chase to the left is Mike Sikowitz wearing a blue pullover. Jeff Astrof is in back of the guys wearing a blue Rangers sweatshirt and cap.

After Monica expresses exultation about receiving George Stephanopoulos' pizza, Rachel asks "Uh, Pheebs? Who's George Snuffalopagus?" This is a very creative *Sesame Street* reference. One of its characters, Mr. Snuffleupagus, is a giant anteater-like mammoth without tusks. He attends Snufflegarden, has a younger sister Alice, and is Big Bird's best friend.

Matt LeBlanc claims his favorite all-time "Joey" moment was the hospital waiting area scene where he repeatedly demonstrates a hockey puck coming toward his head.

Two iconic objects in Joey's apartment: Laurel and Hardy movie still and Hugsy

Monica's balcony is depicted larger than usual. The episode director needed a larger set to accommodate the girls having a lengthy conversation so the set designer made the balcony square, instead of its typical rectangular shape.

1.05 "The One with the East German Laundry Detergent" (10.20.94)

Ross' bedroom has the 1962 show bill for *The Physicists*, a surrealist play by Nikolay Akimov and Friedrich Dürrenmatt at Saint Petersburg Comedy Theatre. The artist is Igor Alexandrovich Ivanov and its imagery could be interpreted as depicting the role of a director—an anonymous hand positioning everything that appears onstage.

Maggie Wheeler debuts as Janice. When she first auditioned for the role, the script did not mention how to play the character. Wheeler explained: "But then I just looked at the rhythm of the language ... and she says: 'Here I got your socks. Mix and match. Moose and squirrel,' and I could just hear her. I heard her speak in my head. I thought, 'Okay, that's what I'm gonna do.'"

Janice debuts her vexing laugh. In preparation for the guest role, Wheeler figured her character needed a laugh because Matthew Perry was going to crack her up but admits it happened "organically during the first rehearsal." Everyone loved the chortle so they encouraged her to use it in the episode. It became her signature vocal tic.

When writing Chandler's breakup scene, staff writer Jeff Strauss was inspired by an ex-girlfriend who rapidly accelerated the relationship timetable well beyond his comfort level. It was September and she already purchased his Christmas present (Fiestaware pottery he collected) but they had only been on two or three dates. In the script, he changed the gift to Bullwinkle socks.

Friends costume designer Debra McGuire often inspired fashion trends by pulling ideas from past images that viewers might subliminally remember. For instance, the laundromat scene has Rachel wearing Lucille Ball–inspired crop pants. The retro outfit sparked a resurgence in Capri pants.

During her double date with Joey, Monica discusses the Underdog balloon escaping and floating down Broadway, but the event has not yet happened. The incident occurs four episodes later in "The One Where Underdog Gets Away" (1.09).

Around Thanksgiving 1994, while dining with his parents and partner Jeffrey Klarik, David Crane first realized that *Friends* was a success when he overheard people at the next table discussing this episode. Marta Kauffman then stated that her first realization of the show's success was after Crane told her the dinner conversation anecdote.

1.06 "The One with the Butt" (10.27.94)

This is the first episode featuring The Rachel, a layered, choppy hairstyle that became a cultural sensation, which, ironically, Jennifer Aniston loathed. She loves stylist Chris McMillan but he was also the bane of her existence at the same time because he started The Rachel, which she acknowledges was not her best look. Aniston called it the ugliest haircut she has ever seen.

Jillian Fontaine, the actress lying on the davenport in Joey's play, was Julianne Moore's body double in the movie *Assassins* (1995) and appeared in one episode of *Days of Our Lives*. Joey is later hired to portray a doctor in the fictional *DOOL* serial.

When June Gable auditioned for the role of Estelle Leonard, she played the part quite plainly and was encouraged to "go away and do something with her [character]." She returned wearing a fat suit, eating a sandwich from the delicatessen, and smoking a cigarette, which she stubbed out on the sandwich. Her performance was written into the scene but then cut due to time constraints.

The headshots lining the walls of the Estelle Leonard Talent Agency are also part of the wall of fame in the dry cleaner's store in "The One Where Paul's the Man" (6.22).

When Ross begins discussing monogamy in anthropological terms, the gang pretends to fall asleep, which became a running gag on the series. The behavior was something the cast did in real life, and it made its way into the script. They replicate the gag in "The One Where They're Up All Night" (7.12) and "The One with the Soap Opera Party" (9.20).

According to Joey, Al Pacino is the sole reason he wanted to become an actor. This was in the original pilot pitch to NBC so the creators decided to incorporate the dialogue into the script. The set decorator even added an Al Pacino *Scarface* poster to Joey's boudoir.

Although not directing this episode, James Burrows has a cameo as the movie director for Joey's butt-double scene. The extras working with the director are actual *Friends* crew members.

During Joey's naked shower scene, Matt LeBlanc is wearing baggy shorts which can be seen as a shadow on the shower wall.

1.07 "The One with the Blackout" (11.03.94)

Chandler is trapped in an ATM vestibule at Emerson Bank. The business is named after Emerson College in Boston, Massachusetts, which is Kevin Bright's alma mater.

This installment popularized the term "friend zone" in Western culture, meaning one member of a friendship wishes to enter into a romantic or sexual relationship, while the other does not.

The revelation that Monica had a crush on Joey when they first met is an allusion to the original pilot concept that paired them as the first romantic couple on the show.

One of David Schwimmer's favorite physical comedy moments was the balcony scene with the cat jumping on his back. "I can't remember in my whole actual life laughing that hard," he said. "By the way, what you see on TV, we had to cut it down. The studio audience went crazy. They couldn't stop laughing. It went on and on."

David Schwimmer is actually allergic to cats. The feline on his back is a stuffed toy that a prop department crew member discovered in the Warner Bros. property warehouse.

The writers room was consistently divided over the Paolo character, who had a purely physical relationship with Rachel. Some of the writers believed "the Latin lover" was a tired trope, while others believed it was fun and realistic. Before he became an Italian lothario, there were many discussions about giving Paolo an Inuit (Eskimo) background. However, they never thought the audience would accept a stud in mukluks (soft boots made of caribou skin or sealskin).

The *Friends* writers claim this was the first episode that had the public buzzing about the series.

This episode made Matthew Perry first realize the series was going to be a huge success. Since he didn't share any scenes with his castmates, he was able to see the show from a distance, and this fresh perspective allowed him to objectively assess the series.

Matthew Perry and Courteney Cox refer to this installment as one of their favorites. She especially loved the scene where Ross was on the balcony with a cat clambering on his back. In fact, many of the cast members rank this episode among their most treasured.

1.08 "The One Where Nana Dies Twice" (11.10.94)

Chandler's sexuality is questioned for the first time. Nearly everyone perceives him as gay, which becomes a recurring gag for the first half of the series; thereafter, he exhibits feminine qualities.

The Central Perk artwork features a group of children holding hands in a circle with the bottom child lit in blue neon. This work was in the pilot episode and remains the only one featured in Season 1. Once the series became successful, artists from around the world requested to have their work displayed, so the set decorator typically rotated the pieces every three to four episodes.

Nana has a painting on the wall in her closet which is identical to one hanging in her bedroom. It's a woman in a blue dress and hat with an attached pink accessory. Since scenes were filmed out of sequence, the set dresser inadvertently used the same piece in both locations.

When Ross attempts to retrieve a box from the top shelf of Nana's closet, Sweet'N Low packets slowly shower down upon him. A crew member is standing on a ladder with a box of packets to control the flow.

The cemetery scene for Nana's funeral takes place on Blondie Street, 411 N. Hollywood Way, on the studio lot. It was filmed on the far south side of the studio and is not a real cemetery. The WB props department has an extensive collection of gravestones.

Several sources falsely claim there is a continuity error in the establishing shots used for the Geller residence over the years. In reality, the white two-story abode was used in multiple episodes, such as in "The One Where Joey Speaks French" (10.13).

When formulating the series, the creators had trouble devising an acceptable moniker for the coffeehouse. One of the original naming ideas was Java Joe's, which is stated in this episode, on the 1939 picture with Nana and her friends, "Me and the gang at Java Joe's." The scene also alludes to the fact that Nana's life as a twentysomething parallels Monica's life over 50 years in the future.

1.09 "The One Where Underdog Gets Away" (11.17.94)

This episode is unofficially known as "The One with the Thanksgiving Lockout."

Max Wright, who plays Central Perk owner Terry, costarred with Courteney Cox in the short-lived series *Misfits of Science* (1985-86). He is best recognized as Willie Tanner in the sitcom *ALF* (1986-90). Wright was introduced to satisfy the showrunners' promise to include older guest actors in the series.

When crafting a holiday installment, writers Jeff Greenstein and Jeff Strauss suggested having one of the characters be an outspoken Thanksgiving pessimist. The writing team thought it was a perfect plotline for Chandler, and a plausible explanation for him using sarcasm as a defense mechanism.

The painful holiday divorce revelation came from the episode writers' personal lives. As friends and classmates at Tufts University, they spent Thanksgiving of their sophomore year at Strauss' parents' home in Atlanta, Georgia. That weekend, his parents decided to tell everyone they were getting divorced. It was an awkward, uncomfortable holiday as the children wrestled with the life-altering news.

Monica's storyline was based on writer Jeff Strauss' real-life experience. He had always planned and cooked Thanksgiving dinner since college, inviting his friends to share the holiday with him. Strauss told all his friends exactly where, when, and how they would be celebrating the holiday, while also cooking potatoes five different ways to appease all the fastidious attendees. Basically, Strauss was like Monica—trying to control everyone around him while also tirelessly seeking their approval.

The original apartment numbers 4 and 5 are changed to 19 and 20. The showrunners realized that Monica's tenement was presented as an upper level abode but the original numbers signified a lower level. Thus, her apartment was upped to 20, which required Joey's to be elevated to 19, since it was across the hall.

This is Jane Sibbett's debut performance after taking over the role of Carol from Anita Barone. After Barone quit in early September 1994, the producers called Sibbett's agent to offer the role to her client. Sibbett had given birth to her son Kai on September 10, 1994. The call from her agent was the next day, and she was supposed to arrive on set the following day. She told her agent: "Wow, I'm kind of sore! I don't think so." But her agent said: "Jane, this is a huge offer. They've said they'll go easy on you, and you can bring your nanny." Sibbett watched the pilot, which made the decision very easy: "I just thought, 'Oh my goodness, I have to work with this man. He is brilliant.'"

1.10 "The One with the Monkey" (12.15.94)
This installment was filmed on Tuesday, November 8, 1994, on a dreary, rainy national election night. According to Marta Kauffman, on this miserable evening, the audience was cranky so they didn't laugh at one joke the entire night.

Marcel makes his debut as Ross' pet and companion. The capuchin gained popularity as the "organ grinder" monkey of the 19th century, and today is most often recognized in movies and television shows.

Staff writer Jeff Strauss didn't like the way Marcel served as Ross' wingman and junior partner, but he was relieved that their bond was mostly depicted as an expression of a wounded spirit. When he took his children to the zoo, he was pleased to hear the zoo-keepers discussing the relatively accurate depiction of monkey behavior on the show.

This is the first appearance of Hank Azaria as David. Although he was rejected for the role of Joey, twice, he was kept in mind for a recurring role. FYI: In his preparation for both auditions, Azaria ran lines with his good friend Matthew Perry.

The first party song is "Shiny Happy People" by R.E.M. (#10, 1991). This number was the original choice as the *Friends* theme song but the group's lead singer unequivocally refused to grant permission for its use.

Janice's utterance, "Smile, you're on Janice Camera," is an allusion to *Candid Camera*, a popular and long-running American hidden camera reality television series. When the joke was revealed, victims were told the show's catchphrase, "Smile, you're on *Candid Camera*." Different versions of the show aired from 1948 until 2014.

This is the first appearance of Vincent Ventresca as Fun Bobby. He would later have a role in *Romy and Michele's High School Reunion* (1997) costarring Lisa Kudrow. The role of Fun Bobby was to act depressed because his grandfather died two hours earlier. At the time, Ventresca didn't want to audition for such a small part. "I was so young and full of myself, and I'd just done a pilot for FOX's new medical show. I thought I was the coolest person in the world," he said.

David moves to Minsk, Belarus, which, coincidentally, also happens to be the birthplace of many relatives of Lisa Kudrow. She first learned of her Belarusian roots on the series *Who Do You Think You Are?* Her ancestors were Jews from the village Illia.

1.11 "The One with Mrs. Bing" (01.05.95)
In the opening scene, as Monica and Phoebe cross the street, in the distance is one of Joey's VD awareness posters on the side of a brick building. The poster first appeared in "The One Where Underdog Gets Away" (1.09).

The scene where Monica and Phoebe distract a man who gets hit by an ambulance was filmed on Hennessy Street on the Warner Bros. lot.

Paolo's reaction to recognizing Chandler's mother on television became a running joke on the set. Between takes or just passing each other on the soundstage, the cast and crew would greet each other with the immortal words "Ahh, Nora Bing," using the same Italian accent.

While dining at a Mexican restaurant, Ross and Nora secretly kiss. According to Morgan Fairchild, in the first script draft, Nora did a lot more than just kiss Ross. The creators decided to tone it down because it seemed too salacious.

Monica's balcony defies logic and physics. The balcony changed from rectangular (most often) to square (for prolonged or intimate discussions) but the establishing shots for her building have fire escapes. Also, in some camera angles, the view outside Monica's bay window has a wing attached to her building which contradicts other exterior shots of an adjacent street.

Art director John Shaffner is well aware of the window design inconsistencies. He was initially told the creators only wanted general shots of the city so he went to New York City and came back with an armful of pictures of the tops of the sixth-floor buildings with mullion windows. But then, while editing the pilot episode, Kevin Bright needed a transition to the apartment, so a building was hastily chosen. "They found a building that had arched windows all the way across the top floor," Shaffner declared. "And I'm like, 'We don't have any arched windows.' And they said, 'Oh, well, their apartment is in the back. That's just the building.'"

The view outside Monica's kitchen window changed several times during the series. In Season 1, the backdrop was an image painted in the 1940s. In Season 2, however, the entire production moved to Stage 24, so the series had "a lot more room and a lot more money." Set designer John Shaffner built a miniature apartment building about 10 feet away from the window with bricks at about ⅝ the real size. This fake facade was even visible through the window in the hallway.

The hallway has a radiator next to Joey's apartment. In "The Pilot" (1.01) it was next to Monica's. It remained a hallway fixture until "The One with Two Parties" (2.22).

1.12 "The One with the Dozen Lasagnas" (01.12.95)

The apartment numbering returns to the original format 4 and 5, instead of 19 and 20, because this episode was filmed prior to "The One Where Underdog Gets Away" (1.09), which marked the official change of the tenement numbers.

Carol and Susan learn the gender of the baby but Ross doesn't want to know. The set decorator and costumer worked together to provide subtle hints it was a boy by having some of the characters wear blue and decorating Phoebe's office with a blue palette.

Jessica Hecht (Susan) auditioned to play Monica, but ended up with a recurring role.

After Ross leaves the apartment, Carol and Susan want to call friends and relatives to announce the gender of their baby, so Susan asks: "Who should we call first, your folks, or Deb and Rona?" Deb Franzblau and Rona Oberman were the real-life inspirations for the Carol and Susan characters.

This is the first episode to feature Phoebe's occupation as a masseuse. Her coworker, Jasmine, is played by Cynthia Mann who also played a waitress in "The Pilot" (1.01).

In the massage scene, Cosimo Fusco (Paolo) objected to his character's sexual advances toward Phoebe because it sent the wrong message—that all Italian men are sleazy guys. "What they wanted me to do was quite disrespectful," he said. The producers were able to reach a compromise so he would feel comfortable with the scene.

The scene where Rachel throws Paolo's clothes over the balcony is preceded by a shot of clothes falling onto the street outside her apartment building. To authenticate the shot, a second unit film crew based in New York City was hired to tape the segment. A crew member scaled the fire escape with bags of clothes and then dumped the garments so it could be filmed.

When Rachel and Paolo are on the balcony, the terrace is long, narrow and rectangular. A minute later, while Ross speaks with Rachel, the balcony is short, wide and square.

1.13 "The One with the Boobies" (01.19.95)

The cold opening—where Rachel is wearing nothing but a towel—was shot without an audience. The director didn't want all the noise and distraction often associated with audience members seeing Jennifer Aniston scantily clad.

In this episode, Phoebe dates a psychiatrist. Interestingly, as a youth, Jennifer Aniston wanted to be a psychiatrist. "I was always the one people would drag to one side and say, 'I've got to talk to you!'" she stated.

Fisher Stevens portrays Phoebe's boyfriend Roger. Supposedly, he had a real "attitude" on set. Aniston recalled, "I remember when we were doing a network run-through, the network and the producers would just laugh. And this person would be like, 'Listen to them, just laughing at their own jokes. So stupid, not even funny.'" She continued, "It was just like, 'What are you doing here? Your attitude, this is not what we're all about. This is a wonderful, warm place to be, and you're coming into our home and just shitting on it.'"

Stevens admitted to his misbehavior: "At that moment in my career, I had never done a sitcom before." Evidently, his script had been rewritten after he had already memorized his lines and flown to Los Angeles to film the episode. "Because that's what sitcoms did. And I didn't know that," he admitted. "I was kind of an asshole, I have to admit. 'What do you mean? So I have to relearn lines that you've written that are worse than what you'd originally written?' Yeah, I was a dick. I've rarely seen any of those people on *Friends* again, but I'm sure if you asked them about me, they would go, 'What a New York snob.'" He then issued an apology to the cast, saying, "Yeah, I'm sorry, guys. I'm sorry I was a dick to you all. I apologize. I was bad, I was wrong."

Rachel wears a fitted long-sleeve t-shirt with a monochromatic rose. She is wearing the same shirt in "The One with Two Parts, Part 1" (1.16).

In Joey's apartment, the bathroom layout evolves. In this episode the shower is opposite the door, but in other installments, the sink occupies this location. The set design was modified periodically to accommodate filming inside the bathroom or to authenticate the set. Since toilets are unsightly, the false set never had this bathroom fixture.

After Rachel observes Joey naked in the shower, Chandler races out of his bedroom to inquire about the commotion. On his bedroom wall is a 1940s Soviet Union aviation art poster with a fleet of red planes flying over a city with the slogan "Long live the strong aviation of the socialist country!"

With their presence in this episode, Joey's parents had the least number of appearances (one) on the show out of all the other friends' parents.

1.14 "The One with the Candy Hearts" (02.09.95)
Nancy Vale plays Joey's date Lorraine. She also played Samantha Thomas on *Baywatch* (and Hallie in the *Baywatch* pilot episode), which is Joey and Chandler's favorite show.

Janice debuts the "Oh. My. God" catchphrase and its signature pronunciation. The staff writers gave her the line but Maggie Wheeler (Janice) formulated the unique delivery by overenunciating each word.

The restaurant scene where Joey and Lorraine eat the same breadstick from opposite ends and then meet in the middle with a kiss is a cute recreation of the spaghetti-eating scene in the animated musical movie *Lady and the Tramp* (1995) where two dogs from opposite sides of the tracks share a plate of pasta.

In real life, Maggie Wheeler doesn't sound anything like Janice. She insists that Janice's distinct sound is based on voices she heard growing up in New York City, though it is primarily based on Fran Drescher, who perfected the nasally, high-pitched whiny voice in *The Nanny* (1993-99).

The boyfriend cleansing ritual was inspired by Jennifer Aniston during her early years in Los Angeles. When she lived in Laurel Canyon, every now and then her female friends (the hill people) would venture into the woods and form a circle filled with candles and personal mementos, hold hands, and talk. As she recalled, "I remember the first time we did it, this one girl was silent through the whole thing, and then at the end she was just weeping. She just had this huge sort of enlightening kind of experience being with these women, and it was, like, women are awesome, especially together as a group, so kind and warm and wonderful."

Four of Rachel's best fashion statements in Season 1

When the girls are performing the cleansing ritual, Rachel's t-shirt has an image of a topless woman pulling up thigh-high stockings.

Rachel burns boxer shorts belonging to Adam Ritter. He was named after a friend of the creators.

In the Japanese restaurant, the chef flips shrimp into Ross' mouth. This was not in the script. David Schwimmer suggested adding a little physical comedy to the scene.

1.15 "The One with the Stoned Guy" (02.16.95)

Chandler's storyline was based on writer Jeff Greenstein's temp job working as a claims processor for a Japanese insurance company. He despised the job but after six months his superiors wanted to promote him to a full-time position. Instead of being excited, he panicked. Greenstein was not a claims processor, nor did he ever want to be one, so the idea of progressing in a career that was anathema to his ambitions horrified him. Instead of accepting the promotion, he summarily quit.

Melora Hardin (Celia, the dirty talker) is best remembered as Jan Levinson in *The Office* (2005-13), and more recently as Jacqueline Carlyle in *The Bold Type* (2017-21).

While penning the script, Jeff Greenstein further extrapolated his Kafkaesque (bizarre) work experience by having Chandler take an aptitude test, only to discover he is best qualified to do the job he quit. Fortunately for Greenstein, this never happened to him.

While Ross is practicing dirty talk with Joey, Chandler is wearing a Blue Louie t-shirt. It is a pop art piece created by Pittsburgh artist Burton Morris to commemorate trumpeter Louis Armstrong, one of the most influential jazz figures, whose career ranged over five decades and different eras in the history of jazz.

Despite excellent weekly ratings, the producers were still looking for a big-name star to appear on the show during sweeps week. Fortunately, Lisa Kudrow and Courteney Cox both knew a comedian to fill the role. Kudrow knew Jon Lovitz from childhood—he was best friends with her older brother David—and Cox met him on the set of *Mr. Destiny* in 1988. Lovitz agreed to appear because he thought Kudrow's parents would get a kick out of seeing them on TV together.

The *SNL* star improvised several lines, such as the "tartlet" repetition, and the dropping of Sugar-O's cereal into the bowl of milk to function as life preservers for gummy bears.

1.16 "The One with Two Parts, Part 1" (02.23.95)

The establishing shot for Riff's Bar & Restaurant is actually Old Town Bar, a textbook historic Manhattan watering hole (45 E. 18th St., New York). The tavern is featured in many early episodes of *Sex and the City*. The Riff's neon sign is digitally overlaid.

The scene in Riff's bar was filmed on the Sony Television soundstage where *Mad About You* was filmed, and utilized the actual Riff's set.

This is the first appearance of Phoebe's twin sister, Ursula, who is also played by Lisa

Kudrow. The Ursula character first appeared in 1993 on the TV series *Mad About You* (ep Married to the Job). Kudrow played Ursula in 24 episodes from 1993 to 1999.

The twins storyline was purposely written to explain the presence of Lisa Kudrow in two sitcoms that aired back-to-back on Thursday night. David Crane asked *Mad About You* cocreator Danny Jacobson whether he would be amenable to a twins crossover. He said yes, so this installment was written. Crane admitted that had the table been turned, he would not have agreed to a crossover.

In the opening scene of Act 1, Ross mentions that Marcel is out of control. At this time, the entire crew was exasperated by the monkey being unruly and causing inordinate production delays. Ross' dialogue was meant to foreshadow the producers' plan to axe the pet from the show.

During an establishing shot of Chandler's office building, the hotel on the right (Plaza Hotel) is often mistaken as the Tipton Hotel, the main setting for *The Suite Life of Zack & Cody*. FYI: The exterior shots of the fictional Tipton Hotel were actually the Fairmont Copley Plaza in Boston and Vancouver Hotel in British Columbia.

During Lamaze class, there is a picture of a nude child taped to the side of the TV.

With this two-part installment, NBC introduced *Friends* to a new timeslot (following *Seinfeld*) using a unique approach. It aired this two-parter on the same night but with one installment before *Seinfeld* and the other after it. Part 1 had 26.1 million viewers, and Part 2 garnered 30.5 million.

1.17 "The One with Two Parts, Part 2" (02.23.95)

The appearance of George Clooney and Noah Wyle is often dubbed an *ER* crossover but this is inaccurate. *ER* aired from 1994 to 2009 and followed the inner workings of the emergency room of County General Hospital in Chicago, Illinois. Clooney portrays Dr. Doug Ross and Wyle is Dr. John Carter. In *Friends*, the setting is New York City, and Clooney plays Dr. Michael Mitchell and Wyle is Dr. Jeffrey Rosen.

The Clooney-Wyle cameo was a promotional stunt by NBC to interweave some of the stars from their two most popular freshman programs. The writers' unique twist was giving the doctors new identities (from their *ER* characters) which is compatible with Rachel and Monica switching names.

George Clooney met Jennifer Aniston during production week and they became friends. She still visits him and his family (wife Amal Clooney and the twins) at their Lake Como villa in Italy.

At Phoebe's birthday party, the first song is the hit "What's the Frequency, Kenneth?" by R.E.M. (#21, 1994). Kevin Bright often included the band's work in episodes because he was particularly fond of the quartet, which is the reason R.E.M. was initially chosen to perform the *Friends* theme song.

Monica reveals that Rachel had sex with Billy Dreskin on her father's bed. The creators named the character after one of their college friends. Ironically, he is now a rabbi. In 1980 Dreskin graduated Brandeis University with a music degree, and after two years in New York City, he entered Hebrew Union College–Jewish Institute of Religion. Shortly after he graduated in 1985, the musical *Personals* (cowritten by David Crane and Marta Kauffman), which he helped score, opened off Broadway at the Minetta Lane Theater. Since July 1995, Dreskin has worked as a rabbi at Woodlands Community Temple near White Plains, New York.

When Phoebe visits Ursula at work, the establishing shot has a neon sign for Riff's in the tavern window. However, the Riff's sign is a computer generated logo superimposed over the clip. When a man walks in front of the camera, the neon sign is displayed on his head.

Since the entire episode focuses on the television being stuck on Spanish audio, the tag scene airs a *Friends* segment broadcast entirely in Spanish using the actual voice-over artists hired to dub all the sitcom's episodes in Spanish-speaking countries.

1.18 "The One with All the Poker" (03.02.95)

The episode plot was inspired by director James Burrows' efforts to get the cast to play poker in his dressing room. He had the largest dressing room and encouraged the six costars to congregate there to bond. The girls didn't know how to play poker so the guys offered instruction. With the help of Matthew Perry, the staff writers recreated the dialogue and group interactions.

This episode was inadvertently written as a bottle episode—no expensive guest stars, no elaborate sets, no unnecessary secondary characters. It became a hallmark of the series starting with "The One Where No One's Ready" (3.02). Thereafter, at least one episode per year was a bottle episode.

As Ross is pining for Rachel at the coffee shop, Chandler vocalizes his signature catchphrase delivery: "Could you *want* her more?" The original script wanted Matthew Perry to emphasize the word "her" but he chose to stress the prior word. The writers learned never to italicize any word of Chandler's dialogue because Perry would always select an entirely different word to accentuate.

In Ross' abode, the decorative sword by the door is a Chinese dadao single-edge blade. The dadao ("big knife") is commonly associated with civilian militias or revolutionaries. While not a particularly sophisticated sword, the weight and balance of the dadao give it considerable slashing and chopping power, making it an effective close combat weapon for untrained troops; it was used in this role as late as the 1930s. The dadao is often used by executioners for beheadings.

Marcel incessantly plays "The Lion Sleeps Tonight" by The Tokens (#1, 1961), which is also used during the sex scene with Courteney Cox and Jim Carrey in *Ace Ventura: Pet Detective* (1994). In the movie, Ace also has a capuchin named Spike (played by Binx). In *Friends*, Marcel is portrayed by two females (Katie and Monkey). The chorus chant "Wimoweh" derives from a mishearing of the Zulu word "Uyimbube."

The TV drama *ER* was shot across the street on Stage 11 on the Warner Bros. Studio lot. While on a break, George Clooney and guest star Kristin Davis visited the *Friends* set to watch a rehearsal from the audience bleachers. She was awestruck: "I remember being blown away by their confidence level and their synergy as a group."

1.19 "The One Where the Monkey Gets Away" (03.09.95)

Costume designer Debra McGuire cites Rachel's short, plaid miniskirt with knee-high socks as one of her favorite outfits that she specifically designed for the show. The style is often compared to Cher Horowitz, the lead character in the 1995 hit movie *Clueless* starring Alicia Silverstone. However, Rachel debuted the look over four months before the film premiered.

Jennifer Aniston wasn't raving about the schoolgirl ensemble so McGuire had to use her powers of persuasion: "I remember convincing her to wear the short kilt with the knee socks. She didn't get it. She didn't understand how that could possibly be sexy and I said, 'I guarantee you that we'll get more response in this than anything else,' and we did and she was so surprised." According to McGuire, "people went berserk over that outfit."

In this installment, Marcel escapes from the apartment. Ironically, while shooting the monkey scenes, Marcel evaded handlers and disappeared into the rafters. Production was delayed over 30 minutes.

Samantha (hot blonde) lives on a different building floor but her hallway is the same set used to represent Monica and Joey's level. The set decorating crew merely painted the hallway a different color to represent another floor. FYI: Samantha lives in apartment 5, which was Monica's apartment number when the series commenced.

Joey and Chandler knock on the door of two attractive neighbors. Though enticed to go inside, they opt to proceed with their search for Marcel. The writers could not come up with a funny departing excuse. Then Jeff Astrof suggested, "We promised we'd find this monkey. If you see him, he's about yea high, and answers to the name Marcel, so if we could get some pictures of you, you'd really be helping us out." It was a left-field joke fueled by sleep deprivation at three or four in the morning.

The slow-motion sequence where Phoebe is shot by a tranquilizer dart was filmed using a special camera so it had to be preshot without an audience. The same camera is used for the slow-motion football sequence in "The One with the Football" (3.09).

The sidewalk scene where Ross and Rachel search for Marcel was filmed on Brownstone Street on the Warner Bros. lot in Burbank, California.

Chandler claims he "went to boarding school with 400 boys." Matthew Perry added this dialogue to the script using his childhood as inspiration. While living with his mother in Ottawa, Canada, he briefly attended Ashbury College, an all-boys boarding school with an enrollment of 400.

In the movie *Ed* (1996) starring Matt LeBlanc, Ed (a chimpanzee) is flipping through TV channels and stops to watch *Friends*. The episode is "The One Where the Monkey Gets Away" (1.19) where Rachel inspects Monica's shoe for monkey droppings.

1.20 "The One with the Evil Orthodontist" (04.06.95)

According to Mitchell Whitfield (Barry), one of the most awkward scenes he filmed was cuddling with Rachel on the orthodontist chair. "It was a tiny set that was filled with a ton of lights and crew members," he recalled. Of all his guest appearances, this is the one scene he vividly remembers filming.

When Jennifer Grey made her first cued entrance, the audience was dead silent—no one recognized her. Although she achieved fame with her role in *Dirty Dancing* (1987), she took an eight-year hiatus from acting and underwent two rhinoplasty procedures before appearing in *Friends*.

Jennifer Grey's rhinoplasty received sizable media attention. Surgery in 1989 corrected her hook nose but then she underwent a cosmetic procedure in 1995 which malformed her visage. "I went into the operating room a celebrity and came out anonymous," she declared. "It was the nose job from hell. I'll always be this once-famous actress nobody recognizes because of a nose job."

This is Jennifer Grey's only episodic appearance; she was later replaced by Jana Marie Hupp in "The One with Barry & Mindy's Wedding" (2.24). Many sources reported that Grey refused to return because of failed rhinoplasty or negative script references to her character Mindy having the surgical procedure, but truthfully, Grey declined to reprise the role due to paralyzing performance anxiety. She didn't like all the script changes,

In the feature film *Ferris Bueller's Day Off* (1986), Jennifer Grey played Jeannie Bueller, Ferris' sister. Coincidentally, in the television adaptation, Jennifer Aniston portrayed the same character for 13 episodes (1990-91).

After this episode, Mitchell Whitfield (Barry) would be approached by strangers on the street who would comment, "Oh, you're that jerk on *Friends*." That's when he started to think, "This thing is definitely starting to take off."

1.21 "The One with Fake Monica" (04.27.95)

This is the first episode to feature Marcel's disobedience, which relates to him humping everything in sight. It is also his final recurring role on the show. Marcel's departure was planned shortly after his first episodic appearance in "The One with the Monkey" (1.10). He was difficult on set, rarely hit his mark when filming, and delayed production, so his exit was inevitable.

Fake Monica speaks Dutch, and asks Monica, "May I have this dance?" Surprisingly, her Dutch pronunciation is accurate. Usually, in American television, the language is substituted with German.

While sitting in Central Perk, after Ross tells the guys that he has to get rid of Marcel, the trio visually demonstrates the three wise monkeys, a Japanese pictorial maxim that embodies the proverbial principle "see no evil, hear no evil, speak no evil."

While searching for a prospective caretaker for Marcel, Ross' first interview is with Mr. Baldharar, played by Harry Shearer, who costarred and cowrote the cult classic movie *This is Spinal Tap* (1984). In 1989, he joined the cast of *The Simpsons*, providing voices for Ned Flanders, Kent Brockman, Mr. Burns, Reverend Lovejoy, Waylon Smithers, Dr. Hibbert, Principal Skinner, and others.

During the farewell scene at the airport, Ross is wearing a banana lapel pin as a tribute to Marcel. The costumer thought the accessory would be a nice touch to the scene.

The woman who places Marcel in a transport cage is one of the pet handlers that works for a private company which supplies animals for productions.

During the tag scene, where Joey is auditioning for the role of Mercutio and claims his stage name is Holden McGroin, the casting directors are played by the *Friends* executive producers (David Crane, Marta Kauffman and Kevin Bright).

1.22 "The One with the Ick Factor" (05.04.95)

Twice in this episode Ross is reading *Anthropology Weekly* magazine. This is a fictitious periodical. He read the same issue in "The One Where Underdog Gets Away" (1.09).

The gang teases Monica for dating a guy who is significantly younger than her. He is a high school senior (age 17) and she is 27 years old. In real life, since 2013 Courteney Cox has been dating Snow Patrol frontman John McDaid who is 11 years her junior.

Stan Kirsch, who plays high school senior Ethan, was actually four years younger than Courteney Cox. At the time, Kirsch was 27, playing a 17-year-old. Cox was 31 years old, playing a 22-year-old.

On January 11, 2020, Stan Kirsch (*Highlander*) died at age 51 of an apparent suicide. One accomplishment was cofounding Stan Kirsch Studios, an acting school, with his wife (Kristyn Green).

This is the first time Chandler is teased for his unique word accentuation ("Could that report *be* any later?"), which is a running gag in the series. This is how Matthew Perry speaks in real life. The writers liked his comedic timing so they incorporated the vocal tic into the show, which debuted in "The One with the Butt" (1.06) ("Could she *be* more out of my league?").

After Ethan reveals his true age, Monica proclaims, "I'm like those women that you see with shiny guys named Chad. I'm Joan Collins." Joan Collins (*Dynasty*) has a storied history of dating younger men and is currently married to Percy Gibson who is 32 years her junior. The term for a woman dating a younger man is "cougar." FYI: Courteney Cox would later star in *Cougar Town* (2009-15), a comedy series based on that principle.

During the hallway tag scene, a false set was constructed to represent Joey's apartment using a privacy wall with a hanging picture. The producers decided it was not worth the time or expense to use the real apartment set for such a brief, inconsequential segment.

1.23 "The One with the Birth" (05.11.95)

This episode was originally scheduled as the season finale but director James Burrows insisted that fans cared more about the fate of Ross and Rachel than Carol giving birth.

This installment commemorates two of the creators' friends, Deb Franzblau and Rona Oberman. The lesbian couple was the inspiration for the characters Carol and Susan. They too have a child, Avery Michelle. The creators are especially proud of this episode because it features a gay couple having a child. Dr. Franzblau (portrayed by Jonathan Silverman) is named after their friend.

Coincidentally, Jonathan Silverman and David Schwimmer were classmates at Beverly Hills High School and graduated together in 1984. Schwimmer has gone on record to say that Silverman is "one of my oldest and dearest high school friends."

As Ross and Susan leave to get ice chips for Carol, Rachel enters the hospital room. In the hallway there is a directional sign which misspells nursery as "nusery."

Russian posters hanging in the guys' apartments

Leah Remini, who plays a single woman giving birth, auditioned for the role of Monica.

June Gable plays the hospital nurse who delivers a baby for Lydia (Leah Remini). She was first cast as Joey's agent, Estelle Leonard, in "The One with the Butt" (1.06) but her scene was cut.

Ross tripping on the mop bucket was not in the original script. During rehearsal, David Schwimmer suggested the comedy bit and then worked with the director to stage it.

Kevin Bright's father, Jackie Bright, appears as the janitor who opens the closet door to rescue Ross, Susan and Phoebe. As Phoebe's legs are dangling from the ceiling, his only line is: "Hey, you forgot your legs." Jackie retired as a personal manager and wanted to revive his acting career so he asked his son if he had any parts for him.

The hospital scene with the newborn was shot twice. Once with a real baby without an audience, and then with an audience using a mechanical doll borrowed from the set of *ER*. The other hospital scenes in this episode involving babies were filmed using dolls.

1.24 "The One Where Rachel Finds Out" (05.18.95)
This was originally the penultimate installment but became the season finale due to the intense media attention surrounding the Ross-Rachel unrequited love drama.

The staff writers felt the Ross-Rachel love story—his endless pining and her inexplicable oblivion—was growing stale, so they wanted to advance the plot. They discussed Ross impulsively kissing her when their taxi hits a bump in the road, and then having a long talk about the meaning behind the kiss, much like Woody Allen and Diane Keaton in *Annie Hall* (1977).

As the writers debated the Ross-Rachel storyline, Jeff Greenstein immediately thought of Jane Austen. While attending UC–Berkeley, his wife had written her senior thesis on the celebrated English novelist, and when they dated, he read all of Austen's novels. He came up with a similar plotline that involved Ross giving Rachel a cameo brooch for her birthday, only to leave on a trip to China just before she discovers his feelings for her, which she reciprocates, but by then it is too late.

After Joey's girlfriend Melanie calls him a woman, the camera pans to a replica of the bronze statue *The Thinker* by Auguste Rodin. Originally cast in 1904, the work shows a nude male figure of heroic size sitting on a rock resting his chin on one hand as though deep in thought (an image used to represent philosophy). It reflects Joey's perplexity in his new role as the giver of sexual pleasure.

All the balcony scenes were shot without an audience. A fourth wall was constructed in Monica's apartment to conceal the audience bleachers which are located directly behind the wall. Moreover, the window blinds were lowered to conceal the rafters, stage lighting and boom mics.

During the transitional establishing shot for the airport, the production song is "Take a Bow" by Madonna (#1, 1994), which addresses unrequited love and her saying goodbye.

It was chosen to portend the relationship reversal between Ross and Rachel. She now harbors unrequited love to which he is unsuspecting, and she must say goodbye as he embarks on a new love with Julie.

This was the last episode shot on Stage 5.

Season 2: 1995-96

2.01 "The One with Ross's New Girlfriend" (09.21.95)
This was the first episode shot on Stage 24 at Warner Bros. Studios. It is 21,600 square feet whereas the old stage is 14,850 square feet, one of the smallest on the lot.

A larger set meant larger dressing rooms. "The cast was so close that they had all their dressing rooms moved to one end of the soundstage upstairs," a crew member stated. However, while moving into the new dressing rooms they discovered two were noticeably larger. Thus, in all fairness and as a true ensemble, the cast "actually drew straws to see which actors would get the two larger dressing rooms, and the prized suites [were] rotated annually."

Lauren Tom pitched the humorous line where Rachel speaks slowly and loudly when saying, "Welcome to our country," to which Julie replies in the same manner: "Thank you, I'm from New York." This funny exchange was based on Tom's real-life experience. "People would speak slowly and loudly to me, and thought, because I was Asian, that I was dumb and deaf, I guess," she explained. According to Tom, fans always reference the line "Welcome to our country."

The Central Perk artwork is changed for the first time since the pilot episode. The new piece has a coffee cup with neon lights for steam.

For the first time there is a "Reserved" sign on the coffee table in Central Perk. This was added by the set decorator to address critics who expressed disbelief that the friends were always able to nab the prime seating location for every coffeehouse scene.

Matthew Perry considers the line "You have to stop the Q-tip when there's resistance" to be his favorite Chandler quip of the series.

This is the first of seven episodic appearances for Lauren Tom, and her favorite *Friends* installment. Her role in *The Joy Luck Club* (1993) influenced the creators' decision to cast her as Julie, a recurring character, with no audition required. *Friends* director Gail Mancuso suggested Tom for the part and was essential in having her cast.

2.02 "The One with the Breast Milk" (09.28.95)
Unofficially, this episode is known as "The One with Hombre Man."

For the first time, drapes are added to Monica's apartment windows. With an expanding budget for set dressing, set decorator Greg Grande was finally able to add accessories that many would consider necessities. As the show progressed, and the budget swelled, both apartments became cluttered with furnishings and knickknacks.

Joey works at Saks & Company department store. The producers included a plug for Saks because it had just signed Matt LeBlanc to a deal as their spring catalog fashion model. It is a world-famous brand name shopping destination in Manhattan; the ideal upscale department store in the city to find A-list stylists and celebs shopping any day of the week. Saks even has a stunning Instagram account featuring artsy short films about fashion.

As the Bijan for Men cologne spritzer, Joey wages a monumental war against Todd, the Hombre Man. Iranian fragrance designer Bijan Pakzad invented Bijan cologne and paid handsomely to promote his product on *Friends*.

The first customer Joey spritzes is actor Douglas Looper. He is Matt LeBlanc's stand-in.

Joel Beeson, the Hombre Man, was instructed to deliver his lines like Clint Eastwood from one of his many memorable spaghetti western movies (i.e., films made by Italian director Sergio Leone). Eastwood starred in three of Leone's films, often described as the Dollars Trilogy—*A Fistful of Dollars* (1964), *For a Few Dollars More* (1965) and *The Good, the Bad and the Ugly* (1966).

Joey's storyline parodies TV and movie westerns, starting with both spritzers dressed in cowboy outfits. The takeoff escalates during the apartment scene—where cowboy Joey sits at the counter and talks to barkeep Chandler—and concludes with the epic show-down in Saks (western theme music, newbie versus skilled gunslinger, winner gets the girl, and happy couple walks into the sunset).

According to Lauren Tom (Julie), when she filmed a scene, the studio audience would boo her—people hated that she came between Ross and Rachel. "I wasn't prepared for the amount of venom I was about to receive in a live audience," she said. "Even I was rooting for Rachel, on some level, 'cause I was a fan of the show."

2.03 "The One Where Heckles Dies" (10.05.95)
In the opening scene after credits, the gang takes turns doing impersonations of Janice. According to Maggie Wheeler (Janice), Matthew Perry could do the best impersonation of her signature voice. Speaking of impressions, Jennifer Aniston says *SNL* star Vanessa Bayer does the best impression of Rachel from *Friends*.

The photos of pets on Monica's refrigerator are from members of the crew.

When Larry Hankin's agent called about a fifth episode appearance on *Friends*, he made it seem like a sixth role was inevitable, which meant a sizable increase in pay. Hankin bought a house assuming the gig would go on. "I started to pave the driveway [but then] *Friends* took my house away," he said. "I had a house for five seconds, maybe ten. ... I was so angry." After discovering his character was being killed off, Hankin was livid and screamed at the *Friends* showrunners.

Phoebe claims she is not pulled by gravity so much as being pushed. She may be right. Einstein's General Theory of Relativity states that what we feel as gravity is actually the curvature of space-time due to the mass of the earth and this curvature is pushing us to the center of the earth.

Numerous sources claim that writer Michael Curtis has a cameo as a police officer in the hallway scene where Mr. Heckles is taken to the morgue. This is false. It's a random scene extra.

Mr. Heckles kept a journal, *My Big Book of Grievances*, to chronicle the gang's activities. This prop, as well as many objects in his abode, are meant to give Chandler a Scrooge experience—to foreshadow his future if he continues on this path. But the book is also about grievances, i.e., Monica and Rachel forging their roles as roommates, and Phoebe and Ross bickering over the legitimacy of evolution.

The nude-girl clock was discovered by the set decorator at a local swap meet.

2.04 "The One with Phoebe's Husband" (10.12.95)
In the cold opening, the pigeon doesn't fly through the window, it is dropped from above the set. The apartment set is built without a ceiling to accommodate stage lighting and boom mics. A stagehand is standing on a ladder and hanging over the edge of the wall to release the bird on cue.

According to Marta Kauffman, "There are two words you can always say in any line and it will make the audience laugh: nipple and lesbian. Works every time." Another assured hysterical reaction is when an actor botches their line and curses.

Phoebe's husband (Duncan) is portrayed by Steve Zahn. He is a lifelong military history buff and deeply regrets turning down a role in HBO's WWII miniseries *Band of Brothers* (2001), costarring David Schwimmer.

Matt LeBlanc actually appeared in soft-core porn. Prior to *Friends*, he was cast in two installments of *Red Shoe Diaries*, an erotic anthology series that ran on Showtime from 1992 to 1997. LeBlanc's last erotica role was one year before *Friends* debuted.

David Schwimmer was offered $1 million to star in a *Friends* porn parody. YouPorn, the adult film site, tendered the offer to have the actor reprise his iconic role as Ross Geller.

Julie's first grade teacher is Mrs. Cobb, like the salad. This is an inside joke referencing the three female costars who ate lunch together every day on the set and always had a Cobb salad.

Rachel queries, "What exactly is in a Cobb salad?" This was added to the script because Jennifer Aniston created a Cobb salad. A typical Cobb salad has vegetables, green salad leaves, meat, and a vinaigrette dressing. Courteney Cox once attempted to explain the concoction, "It wasn't really a Cobb salad. It was a Cobb salad that Jennifer doctored up with turkey bacon and garbanzo beans and I don't know what."

2.05 "The One with Five Steaks and an Eggplant" (10.19.95)

In the teaser, Chandler and Ross are watching midget wrestling. This is a professional sport involving little people (dwarfs). It was very popular in wrestling promotions from the 1950s into the 1970s. Many cards offered midget wrestlers, tag team, and women's midget wrestling. Slowly the sport began to wane and by the mid-1990s it evolved into comical matches and segments, not serious competitions.

While discussing his plan to deceive Jade, Chandler refers to Ross as "Tattoo" and then imitates Ricardo Montalbán's Mexican accent. This is a reference to the fantasy drama *Fantasy Island* (1977-84), a TV series starring Montalbán as the mysterious Mr. Roarke. The midget-wrestling clip was purposely used to set up the *Fantasy Island* bit because Tattoo was portrayed by 3'11 actor Hervé Villechaize.

Chandler has a Toronto Blue Jays baseball cap in his apartment, which was previously in his cubicle in "The One with the Thumb" (1.03) and executive office in "The One with Two Parts, Part 1" (1.16). It is Matthew Perry's favorite MLB team because he lived in Ottawa, Canada, as a youth. He holds both Canadian and American citizenship.

The name of the fancy restaurant is PhilloSophie. It's a play on words for "philosophy."

The concert segment was preshot without an audience because the director needed to use the soundstage bleachers for the arena seating.

At the concert, the Hootie & the Blowfish song is "I Go Blind." It was originally released in 1994 as a B-side on the band's "Hold My Hand" single. Two years later it was added to the *Friends* soundtrack and leaped to No. 13 on the US Billboard Hot 100 chart.

In the tag scene, the script called for Matt LeBlanc to answer the phone and say "Bob here." During one of the takes, he leaped for the phone, fell over the arm of the couch, and crashed into the counter before falling to the floor. The producers used this blooper in the final edit because it was funnier.

2.06 "The One with the Baby on the Bus" (11.02.95)

Ben didn't actually cry during filming. The noise was inserted in postproduction but a crying sound was used for the audience so they could understand what was happening in the scenes.

The first sidewalk scene with Joey, Chandler and Ben was filmed on Stage 24. All other street scenes were filmed on Brooklyn Street at Paramount Studios in Los Angeles.

When Joey and Chandler exit the bus, one of the women suggests going to Markel's for a drink. The bar was named after episode writer Betsy Borns' boyfriend's father.

The character Stephanie, played by Chrissie Hynde, was named after Borns' sister.

As a condition for appearing on the show, Chrissie Hynde wanted to debut the release of her latest single, "Angel of the Morning," by performing it live. The track was included on the *Friends* soundtrack album, and despite 30.2 million viewers of this episode, the song never made it into the US Billboard Hot 100 chart.

In the street scene, some random guy asks to retrieve a condom from Phoebe's guitar case. The actor is Giovanni Ribisi, who later stars as Frank Jr., Phoebe's half brother. He was only hired for this bit part but the producers liked him so much they cast him in a recurring role.

The song "Smelly Cat" premieres in this episode. Lisa Kudrow did not write the lyrics. It was a collaboration among the writers. David Crane began to sing the title and then Jeff Astrof chimed in with "What are they feeding you?" Someone else contributed the kicker "It's not your fault," and the pillars of "Smelly Cat" had been rapidly assembled.

During filming, Adam Chase was watching Lisa Kudrow perform "Smelly Cat" and he became more and more troubled. She kept stressing the word "cat" but he was sure that emphasizing "smelly" would be funnier, so he pulled David Crane aside to express his concerns. Crane was nonplussed: "You seriously want me to go out between takes, in front of a studio audience, and give her that note?" Chase panicked but held firm. Production was stopped and Kudrow was instructed. It was a tense moment on set—it is taboo to tell an actor how to perform—but it was notably funnier.

During the tag scene, Phoebe teaches "Smelly Cat" to Stephanie (Chrissie Hynde), and repeatedly instructs her on what word to emphasize. This dialogue was a last minute addition to the script to tease Adam Chase for giving Lisa Kudrow a note on how to sing the lyrics.

2.07 "The One Where Ross Finds Out" (11.09.95)
Monica functions as Chandler's exercise coach, but in real life Matthew Perry turned to Jennifer Aniston as his personal trainer to put on weight in Season 3. His substance abuse addiction caused him to lose 30 pounds, and at times he appeared dangerously malnourished.

The Central Perk logo on the main display window is readable while viewing it from both inside and outside the coffee shop. Although many sources claim this is a continuity error, it is actually legit. Since the logo is almost symmetrical, the image is readable when overlaid on both sides of the window. Astute fans will notice the coffee steam is asymmetrical and thus visible on the backside of the opposite logo.

Phoebe proclaims her boyfriend (Scott) doesn't want to sleep with her because she isn't sexy enough. Joey comforts her by saying: "Phoebe, that's crazy. When I first met you, you know what I said to Chandler? I said, 'Excellent butt, great rack.'" This line was added as an ego boost for Lisa Kudrow who felt self-conscious about her beauty and physique, especially around her female costars.

During a transition scene, Joey is watching a rabbi playing electric guitar. The jamming Jew is Yehuda Glantz, an Argentinian musician living in Jerusalem, Israel. He is the Cultural Ambassador of Latin Hebrew Music. Glantz is a multi-instrumentalist who has twice received the first-place award in the Klezmer Safed festival for his performance and compositions.

In a deleted scene, Ross tries to decide between two cats as a relationship metaphor for Rachel and Julie. Lauren Tom (Julie) revealed that fans still ask her about the cats.

Director Peter Bonerz' most memorable moment was Rachel and Ross' first kiss, so he decided to add rain effects to the scene because love and rain go together. Since it is expensive to use rain effect on a soundstage, it is often limited to poignant moments.

The producers wanted to use U2's "With or Without You" as program music for Ross and Rachel's first romantic kiss but the production team didn't secure the necessary rights in time. Instead, they chose licensed music from a library of CDs issued by the recording industry.

2.08 "The One with the List" (11.16.95)
This episode is unofficially known as "The One with the Mockolate."

The producers had no intention of having a Thanksgiving episode in Season 2 but the network strongly encouraged it. "We wrote the mockolate storyline but merely added a

Thanksgiving twist to create holiday recipes," David Crane said. Thereafter, NBC asked the creators to include a holiday-themed episode in future seasons, which they obliged.

Phoebe's song, "Two of Them Kissed Last Night," required numerous takes because the audience kept delaying production with its prolonged laughter and wild applause.

The mockolate used in the installment was ordinary chocolate. Before finally settling on mockolate, other fake products were pitched, such as cashmere-ical and pleather.

When making the list of Rachel's cons, David Crane confessed, "[It] was very difficult to come up with negative things about Rachel that felt truthful and legitimate but weren't completely damning of the character or would make Jennifer mad." The notion of her having chubby ankles came from Marta Kauffman who personally thought of herself as having this unflattering attribute.

According to writer Jeff Greenstein, Ross' pros-and-cons list was an allusion to Jane Austen's *Pride and Prejudice*. There is a parallel between Ross' major mishap and Mr. Darcy's first marriage proposal. For example, Ross emphasizes Rachel's flaws, not her positive attributes; similarly, in Mr. Darcy's overture, he spends more time focusing on Elizabeth's lower rank than asking her to marry him.

The original script did not have rain during Ross' balcony scene but the writers really wanted him to be as miserable as possible.

Ross' dedication song, "With or Without You" by U2, was supposed to be used in the prior episode but the production team didn't secure the necessary rights. However, the rights were secured for this episode. Kevin Bright figured, if they had the rights, they may as well use it.

During Ross' song dedication, the radio deejay states, "Avery, Michelle's sorry she hit you with her car." Avery Michelle is Marta Kauffman's goddaughter.

The original scripted tag scene had a guy in a hazmat suit entering Monica's apartment to remove all the contaminated furnishings. It was meant to infer that the mockolate caused an environmental biohazard. The writers decided it was a little too broad so they opted for the fishtashios segment.

2.09 "The One with Phoebe's Dad" (12.14.95)

This episode marks the first appearance of Monica's Cookie Time cookie jar. Matthew Perry stole the jar from the set and gave it to Lisa Kudrow as a wrap gift in 2004.

Gunther has his first line in the series. It is only one word. Ross asks, "Hey Gunther, you got stairs in your place?" to which Gunther replies "Yeah."

James Michael Tyler (Gunther) almost turned down the role as manager of Central Perk because his regular day job as a barista at Bourgeois Pig paid more than being a scene extra. His girlfriend Barbara Chadsey persuaded him to take the gig.

In Phoebe's grandmother's apartment, the Gladys artwork is hanging on the living room side wall. After the set was dismantled, the furnishings were stored. When the artwork was retrieved a year later, the left hand was missing and could not be located. The set decorator liked the imperfection because it made the piece eclectic which was a good fit for Phoebe's eccentric persona.

When Phoebe picks up Chandler and Joey in her grandmother's cab, a cable is attached to the rear bumper and dragging on the curb. In reality, the car was inoperable; it was pushed by stagehands and then pulled by cable for retakes. FYI: Union rules prohibit gasoline on a stage so any vehicle movement had to be done manually.

Phoebe visits her father's residence at 74 Laurel Dr. in Middletown, New York. In truth, it is a home on Midwest Residential Street on the Warner Bros. Studio lot in Burbank, California. Phoebe returns to the home in "The One with the Bullies" (2.21).

At the Christmas party, Rachel opens the door for two invited guests. They are *Friends* writers Scott Silveri and Mike Sikowitz.

Movie posters hanging in Joey and Chandler's apartment

2.10 "The One with Russ" (01.04.96)

Lisa Kudrow helped to get Thomas Schlamme hired to direct this episode because they worked together on *Mad About You*. He said that filming an episode of *Friends* was like being at The Beatles concert with all the screaming and applause.

Phoebe is wearing a printed sleeveless minidress with numerous images of Mona Lisa. The *Friends* costumer chose the print to symbolize the identity issue surrounding Ross and Russ, much like the controversy surrounding the identity of the woman posing in the *Mona Lisa* painting.

Joey is told he has to sleep with a casting agent to get a part on *Days of Our Lives*. FYI: Jennifer Aniston joined the #MeToo movement to publicize harassment she encountered in the workplace. "I've definitely had some sloppy moves made on me by other actors, and I handled it by walking away. I've never had anyone in a position of power make me feel uncomfortable and leverage that over me," she said. "In my personal experience I've been treated worse verbally and energetically by some women in this industry."

According to the closing credits, Russ was portrayed by Snaro. In reality, the actor was none other than David Schwimmer using an alias as a tribute to a friend. Schwimmer conceals his appearance with a face prosthetic for his nose, mouth and chin, along with heeled boots and a bushy wig.

The gang wagers whether Monica and Fun Bobby will break up. They also bet whether Joey will sleep with the casting director to get a part. The *Friends* writers held similar contests in the writers room so they incorporated their activities into multiple scripts.

This is the final appearance of Fun Bobby. Vincent Ventresca (Fun Bobby) still receives about $2,000 a year in residuals from his two episodic performances.

Joey is hired to appear in *Days of Our Lives* as Dr. Drake Ramoray. Interestingly, since 1985, Jennifer Aniston's father, John Aniston, has starred as Victor Kiriakis in the real *Days of Our Lives* soap opera.

When the writers penned this installment, they had no preconception which soap opera to use for Joey's big break. "NBC came to us and said, 'Please, have it be *Days of Our Lives*,'" Marta Kauffman recalled. The creators were hesitant since *Friends* was set in New York and *DOOL* filmed in California. Their preference was *One Life to Live* which filmed in New York, but NBC insisted on using its serial.

After Joey debuted on *Days of Our Lives*, the ratings dramatically improved for the real-life soap opera. In fact, the serial went from No. 6 to No. 2 in the ranking of top daytime television dramas and increased its viewership by half a million.

2.11 "The One with the Lesbian Wedding" (01.18.96)

When Joey goes into a diatribe about "smell the fart acting," the cast couldn't contain their laughter so the scene had to be reshot numerous times. Kit Harington (*Game of Thrones*) admits that he used the technique a few times during his acting career.

The head costumer added symbolism to the installment. When Phoebe enters Monica's apartment to tell the gang about Mrs. Adelman's spirit entering her body, she is wearing a large ankh around her neck, which is the Egyptian symbol for eternal life. The ankh has a cross with a teardrop-shaped loop in place of an upper bar.

Friends head costumer Debra McGuire personal life influenced the wedding attire: "My inspiration was very equestrian. For my own wedding—I was a polo player at the time, and I was really into English turn-of-the-century silhouettes. My wedding dress was kind of a riding frock, with a jacket with a bustle, a full skirt, and a top hat that kind of looked like a wedding cake. It was very equestrian, and I remember thinking that that would be a really good look for [Susan]. As for [Carol's] dress, I really just wanted it to be beautiful and feminine."

Officiating the wedding was LGBTQ rights activist Candace Gingrich, the half sister of ultraconservative Newt Gingrich, former US House of Representatives' Speaker of the House. The casting decision was intentional to malign the Republican Party's anti-gay rights stance and its "Contract with America" platform.

This was the first LGBTQ ceremony ever shown on television. At the time, the state of New York did not recognize or authorize same-sex marriage (this ruling was eventually overturned by Martinez v. County of Monroe in 2008). So its significance is undeniable when viewed in context.

NBC expected hate mail and tens of thousands of phone calls so they hired 104 people to answer complaint calls. The network received a total of 11 telephone calls and only 2 were complaints. Curiously, *Friends* received more remonstrances for Kathleen Turner's portrayal of Chandler's transgender father.

Since the lesbian marriage was a women's rights issue, the wedding had subtle suffrage references. Debra McGuire wanted to illustrate the progress made in feminism through the use of wardrobe. "That's why I went with this equestrian vibe because I thought it would reflect the turn-of-the-century feeling and people would be reminded of that time when women were speaking out to get rights to vote," she stated. The wedding dresses were both designed as turn of the century. One enthusiastic fan even hired McGuire to design an exact replica of Carol's wedding dress.

Susan and Carol were based on the creators' best friends in New York. "We didn't create them for any particular political reason or because of lesbian chic," Marta Kauffman noted. "It was just an opportunity to tell a really interesting story." GLAAD called the characters a "positive example of a gay couple on television."

There was some criticism that the wedding did not include a lesbian kiss. At the time, the major broadcast networks had an unwritten rule on the portrayal of gay characters that included sidestepping controversy by avoiding or minimizing physical contact.

2.12 "The One After the Superbowl, Part 1" (01.28.96)
The episode title "Superbowl" was purposely misspelled to prevent a trademark infringement or the need for special permission from the NFL. The league's trademark is two words. It was named by Lamar Hunt, then owner of the Kansas City Chiefs, after seeing his son playing with a Super Ball (toy bouncy ball invented in 1964).

Monkeyshine beer is a fictitious product. The TV commercial features a capuchin and beautiful, scantily clad women. In real life, as a cross-promotional tie-in to the sitcom, Central Perk Singapore brews and serves Monkeyshine lager for its customers.

Chris Isaak plays Rob Donnen, a library scheduler. The producers thought they secured a musician with massive star power so they instructed him to pause for a thunderous applause upon his first cued entrance. When he entered, Isaak was met with complete silence—the audience had no idea who he was. The creators, to this day, still consider Isaak to be the biggest casting "miscalculation."

Dean Lipson (Zoo Owner) is named after a mutual friend of writers Jeff Astrof and Mike Sikowitz.

At the library, Chandler is reading *The Little Engine That Could* by Watty Piper. It was chosen to foreshadow his desire to reconnect with a childhood classmate. Chandler is the little engine that "thinks he can" find true love with Susie Underpants.

Brooke Shields' performance impressed NBC executives so much that she was offered her own sitcom, *Suddenly Susan*, for the network's 1996 fall lineup. The series lasted four years (93 episodes).

Tennis star Andre Agassi was dating Brooke Shields at the time and visited Stage 24 to watch her live studio performance. After witnessing an intimate scene—she kisses Joey, licks his hand, nibbles on his fingers, and giggles like an insane person—Agassi rushed onto the set and berated Shields, leaving her in tears. He then drove to his residence in Las Vegas and "systematically smashed and destroyed every single trophy he had won, including Wimbledon and the US Open," according to Shields. Despite his hotheaded temper, she married him the following year but they divorced two years later.

Lisa Kudrow performs one of her favorite songs, "The Cow in the Meadow Goes Moo."

NBC aired this episode directly after Super Bowl XXX hoping to make it the "highest-grossing ad revenue day in television history." Big-name guest stars were cast to attract even more viewers and further increase advertising revenue. It ended up being the most watched night in television history with 140 million Americans tuning in.

The advertising rates for *Friends* averaged $600,000 for a 30-second spot. At the time, this was the highest rate ever for a non-series-ending sitcom episode.

2.13 "The One After the Superbowl, Part 2" (01.28.96)
All the movie-set sequences were filmed on the Warner Bros. Studio lot along Hennessy Street, which also has a back alley where Rachel and Monica hide while checking out Jean-Claude Van Damme.

In the scene where Joey shakes Phoebe and screams about the "horrible flesh-eating virus," the executive producers (David Crane, Marta Kauffman and Kevin Bright) are standing around the episode director (Michael Lembeck, seated).

Prior to agreeing to appear on *Friends*, Julia Roberts exchanged numerous faxes with series costar Matthew Perry. "There was a lot of flirting over faxing. She was giving him these questionnaires like, 'Why should I go out with you?' And everyone in the writers room helped him explain to her why," staff writer Alexa Junge detailed. "He could do pretty well without us, but there was no question we were on Team Matthew and trying to make it happen for him." After filming wrapped, the pair continued their romance offscreen and were seen on a number of dates in the first half of 1996.

Writer Jeff Astrof was a little offended by the relationship. "I remember standing with her on the sidelines. She kept saying, 'Chandler's so funny!' And I'm like, 'I wrote every one of those lines!' I felt like Cyrano [de Bergerac]," he decisively said. "Like, 'Chandler is going to date Julia Roberts and I'm going to go home to my horrible girlfriend.' That's my memory of that episode."

Susie Moss asserts that one of the actresses has a mustache that makes her look like Gabe Kaplan. In the Spanish and Italian versions, the actor's name is changed to Burt Reynolds because he is better known. In German, it is dubbed Clark Gable.

Joey seduces Cathy, the director's assistant, hoping she will help get him cast in the movie. Cathy is played by Lisa Roberts Gillan, middle sibling of Julia Roberts (younger) and Eric Roberts (older), and aunt of Emma Roberts (Eric's daughter). She was given the part because Julia demanded that her sister receive a role in the show. Gillan had small roles in nine of her sister's movies.

During the scene where Monica and Jean-Claude Van Damme walk down the street and she repeatedly asks if he can beat up certain strangers, they are passed by a man with black hair wearing a fur-collared jacket. The extra is *Friends* writer Adam Chase.

Jean-Claude Van Damme was not well respected on set. First, he showed up three to four hours late for the shoot, and second, he repeatedly tried to French-kiss Jennifer Aniston and Courtney Cox during the kissing scenes. Director Michael Lembeck called Van Damme "unprepared and arrogant."

Jean-Claude Van Damme was given very few lines because the staff writers had trouble devising jokes for him. To create "Van Damme–proof" jokes, one staff writer "would say them in a really horrible French accent, putting the emphasis on the wrong word." So, if people laughed at it, Van Damme was given the joke. One example is Van Damme's line "I can crack a walnut with my butt."

This episode became the most watched *Friends* episode with 52.9 million viewers. It still remains the highest-rated program to follow the Super Bowl.

2.14 "The One with the Prom Video" (02.01.96)

The idea for a hideous bracelet was based on Marta Kauffman's personal life. She had relatives who often wore ostentatious jewelry. She helped pick out the accessory with Marjorie Coster (aka Marjorie Coster-Praytor), the *Friends* property master. It reminded Kauffman and Kevin Bright of their trips to Las Vegas where they would see guys sitting at the card table with gaudy bracelets.

Staff writer Alexa Junge incorporated many personal experiences into the script, such as Phoebe's line about Ross and Rachel being "lobsters." It was something her husband once said to her.

Jennifer Aniston wears a prosthetic nose for the flashback scenes. Rachel's large nose was added because writer Alexa Junge believed the characters "were so good looking, you wanted to feel they had some realness in their past." Rachel then claims she had a deviated septum. In real life, Jennifer Aniston had a nose job in 2006, which she claims was due to a deviated septum. She has yet to admit having cosmetic rhinoplasty—for a slender, more natural bridge and tip—in the early 1990s, prior to *Friends*.

This is the debut episode of Fat Monica. Courtney Cox felt right at home in the makeup and fat suit. According to Matthew Perry, the first time she wore the outfit, he walked right past her on set without recognizing her.

David Schwimmer initially refused to wear the afro wig and mustache because he would look like Gabe Kaplan from the 1970s sitcom *Welcome Back, Kotter*. After speaking with the showrunners, he agreed because it enabled him to "tap into a part of himself that was very vulnerable and shy" and incorporate those emotions into his performance.

In the flashback scenes, all the costars are wearing wigs. The prom dresses came from the Warner Bros. costume stock which is a huge warehouse full of period pieces from contemporary all the way back to the beginning of time. Costumer Debra McGuire could not resist redesigning the garments to look even more hideous. She considers Monica's prom dress to be "the ugliest thing I think I've ever made, next to the [pink] bridesmaid dresses I made."

In an internet poll in May 2004, "The One with the Prom Video" was chosen as the best episode of the series, earning 1.6 million votes. Even today, many critics and fans have reached the same conclusion. In 1997, *TV Guide* ranked it No. 100 on its list of the 100 Greatest Episodes of All Time.

This is David Schwimmer's favorite episode. He liked the comedic and emotional origins of the Ross-Rachel relationship, and the verbal exchange between Monica and Chandler regarding her weight. Jennifer Aniston said it was flashbacks to Fat Monica and Rachel pre-nose job, not to mention Ross with an afro, which made her giggle most.

2.15 "The One Where Ross and Rachel...You Know" (02.08.96)

At the first table read, Matthew Perry was not happy with his storyline. "It's so stupid," he stated, but LeBlanc countered, "Yeah, but that's the brilliance!" After considering the possibilities, Perry said, "Yeah, maybe we can have fun with this." Thereafter, the pair "had a blast" doing the show.

This is the first appearance of Tom Selleck as Dr. Richard Burke, Monica's older love interest. The character was named after Karey Burke, NBC's executive VP of primetime programming, who championed the series during its fledgling days and helped persuade Craig Bierko to reject the role of Chandler, which led to the casting of Matthew Perry.

Joey and Chandler are watching *Amazing Discoveries* on television. The writers were big fans of the infomercial program so they later penned a segment featuring the show in "The One with the Metaphorical Tunnel" (3.04).

During the planetarium scene, the production song is "Wicked Game" by Chris Isaak. He guest starred in "The One After the Superbowl, Part 1" (2.12).

When Ross and Rachel are making out in the planetarium, she rolls over, gasps, and then tells him "Honey, that's okay." Ross explains it was a juice box. Relieved, she says, "Thank God!" This is a sexual innuendo regarding premature ejaculation. This segment is often excluded from the syndicated release.

Jennifer Aniston performed the topless scene in the museum without a body double. As expected, it was preshot without a studio audience.

In the scene where Ross and Rachel wake up naked in the diorama, episode writer Greg Malins portrays a priest in the museum.

In the tag scene, Chandler and Joey watch and then impersonate the title characters from *Beavis and Butt-Head*, an American adult animated series created by Mike Judge (*King of the Hill*). It aired from 1993 to 1997 and received widespread critical acclaim, particularly for its satirical, scathing commentary on society. The series was also the subject of controversy due to its violent content.

2.16 "The One Where Joey Moves Out" (02.15.96)
Product placement occurred in nearly every installment of *Friends*, though sometimes it was subtle. For instance, in Monica's apartment, Planet dish detergent is always on the sink with its label turned toward the camera. It remained part of the set in nearly every episode of the series' run.

Like many guest stars on the show, Tom Selleck was no stranger to having butterflies in his stomach before performances. "I hadn't done a three-camera live show since *Taxi*," he said. "It scared me a little. But that's the price you pay for opportunity."

Tom Selleck signed a three-episode commitment for *Friends* but during a table read he was asked to extend his contract. "They said, 'Hey, can you do a few more?' So then I did more. And I quickly realized, 'Wow, this is a big deal.'" The producers noticed the great chemistry between Selleck and Cox, and wanted to capitalize on his popularity so they repeatedly reprised his character.

The creators never expected the Monica-Richard relationship to be a serious romance. It just happened. "With Courteney and Tom Selleck ... there was no sense that was going to become a relationship with a capital 'R,'" writer Scott Silveri said. But they had such good chemistry, the producers and the writers "decided to explore it a little more."

Tom Selleck claimed the *Friends* set "was a great place to work," but less than a decade later he complained about feeling ostracized by the cast because of their close bond to one another.

Although Rachel has reservations about getting a tattoo, she opts for a tiny heart on her hip. The tattoo is a temporary drawing created by the art department. Jennifer Aniston has two tattoos: "Norman" is inked on her right foot after her beloved dog, and "11 11" is on her left wrist to symbolize two crucial dates—her birthday (February 11) and the year Norman died (2011).

2.17 "The One Where Eddie Moves In" (02.22.96)
This is the first appearance of Pat the dog. Tons of internet sources claim Pat the dog was owned by Jennifer Aniston—a good luck gift given to her from a friend on the first day of shooting *Friends*. In reality, set designer Greg Grande purchased the iconic prop

for Joey's new apartment. "The only note I got was 'Give it a little Italian flair,'" he said, referencing Joey's heritage. "I went to a store called Italy 2000 and saw this dog. It had a '70s flavor and was too funny." Thereafter, the piece took on a life of its own, being referenced and featured in multiple episodes.

While watching *Baywatch*, Joey says that Chandler is in love with Yasmine Bleeth, and then Chandler adds, "How could anyone not be in love with Yasmine Bleeth?" Although Matthew Perry was dating Julia Roberts at the time, he added this line because he had a crush on Bleeth, and used the sitcom as a public declaration of his romantic interest in her. Since he was socially gawky around women, this was, in effect, a dating loophole (à la *Seinfeld*). The ploy worked. They began dating later that year.

This is the first appearance of Adam Goldberg (Eddie Menuek). At the time, he was best friends with Matthew Perry. Although their friendship waned over the years, Goldberg bonded on set with Matt LeBlanc and they remain friends to this day. In fact, it led to Goldberg being cast in a recurring role as Jimmy Costa in LeBlanc's series *Joey*.

Adam Goldberg nearly rejected the role of Eddie because of his ego. After appearing in the 1993 feature *Dazed and Confused*, Goldberg didn't want to do television. He felt the three-episode arc on *Friends* was beneath him, and admitted to being "a little snobby," but also very grateful he reconsidered the audition.

Phoebe's music video lists the director as A. Chase, which refers to writer Adam Chase. The music label is BKC records, i.e., Bright, Kauffman and Crane, the *Friends* creators.

Elizabeth Daily (aka E.G. Daily) sings "Smelly Cat" for the music video. She will later appear in "The One with Phoebe's Ex-Partner" (3.14) as Phoebe's former vocal partner.

Phoebe's song being performed by an artist who isn't pretty enough to be commercially successful is based on the real-life scandal involving the duo Milli Vanilli (Fab Morvan and Rob Pilatus). They became one of the most popular pop acts in the late 1980s and early 1990s, selling over 10 million records, but they didn't have sufficient quality so the final mix was finished by studio performers deemed unmarketable for commercial promotion. The duo's success turned to infamy after it was discovered they did not sing any of the vocals on their records.

2.18 "The One Where Dr. Ramoray Dies" (03.21.96)

Joey rushes into Central Perk to tell Phoebe about his article in *Soap Opera Digest*. In a blooper, Matt LeBlanc tripped on his first entrance, then muffed his lines a couple more times, getting hysterical laughs from the audience. When he finally got it right, Matthew Perry purposely crashed the scene by falling on the couch, prompting another audience laugh, because he was jealous of his costar. "I was like, somebody's getting a laugh, I can't handle it, I need to get a laugh, too," he confessed.

Joey is spotlighted in *Soap Opera Digest* with the headline "Shocking Days Ahead and Three Stars of *Days of Our Lives*" (February 13, 1996). In the article, Joey asserts that he writes a lot of his own lines. This is a playful jab at recent movie stars who appeared on *Friends* and tried to ad-lib their dialogue. The producers demanded that actors stick to the script and recite the lines verbatim. Changes only occurred with prior approval.

James E. Reilly, the soap opera staff writer who kills off Joey's character, was a real-life writer on *Days of Our Lives*, as well as *General Hospital* and *The Young and the Restless*. He was the head writer for a majority of the *Days of Our Lives* installments from 1992 to 2006. Reilly died on October 12, 2008 (age 60) from complications after cardiac surgery.

Matthew Perry's severed finger is apparent when he puts his hand on Eddie's shoulder. The middle finger is significantly shorter than the index and ring finger. Perry lost the appendage at the age of 3 at nursery school when it was caught in a car door that was accidentally closed by his grandfather.

The scene where Monica and Rachel discuss who gets the last condom created a lot of on-set turmoil. "We could show the box, we could shake the box so you could hear the condom, but we couldn't say condom," Marta Kauffman exasperatingly recalls. "They're masturbating on *Seinfeld* and we can't show a condom wrapper." NBC President Warren Littlefield concurred: "What could be more socially responsible than these characters practicing safe sex?" The creators fought to include the wrapper but lost. "We felt so strongly that this was responsible television," Kauffman exclaimed.

Actor Roark Critchlow plays Dr. Mike Horton in both the *Friends* version of *Days of Our Lives* and the real-life soap opera. He starred in *Days of Our Lives* from 1994 to 2010. Critchlow also appeared in "The One After the Superbowl, Part 1" (2.12).

Dr. Drake Ramoray's death is a parody of the TV drama *L.A. Law* (ep Good to the Last Drop) which was the first series to kill off a character with an abrupt plunge down an elevator shaft. It happened to antagonist Rosalind "Roz" Shays (who was despised by viewers). The "elevator episode" ranked No. 81 on *TV Guide*'s 1997 list of 100 Greatest Episodes of All Time.

2.19 "The One Where Eddie Won't Go" (03.28.96)
Jennifer Milmore is listed as the author of *Be Your Own Windkeeper*. The literary honor was awarded to her because she was dating episode writer Greg Malins.

The empowerment book is a spoof of mystical self-help publications such as Clarissa Pinkola Estes' *Women Who Run with the Wolves* (1992) which analyzes myths, folktales, fairy tales and stories from different cultures to uncover the Wild Woman archetype of the feminine psyche.

Jennifer Aniston had the hardest time saying the line "How do you expect me to grow, when you won't let me blow." Numerous takes had to be done because she could not stop laughing.

This is only the second installment where Gunther has a line. He shares the trauma of having his television character killed off. In the original script, Gunther had no lines. During production, the creators called actor James Michael Tyler (Gunther) into their office and then handed him a new script with dialogue for his character. "It was a big surprise," he recalled.

During the goddess quiz, Phoebe retorts to Monica: "At least I didn't let some guy into the forest of my righteous truth on the first date." This is a callback to "The Pilot" (1.01) where Monica slept with Paul the wine guy on their first date.

During the goddess quiz, one question is "Have you ever betrayed another goddess for a lightning bearer?" Monica accuses Rachel of betrayal with Danny Arshack in the ninth grade. In real life, Daniel Arshack is a criminal defense attorney and cofounder of The Bronx Defenders. As a student at Brandeis University, he dated Marta Kauffman.

2.20 "The One Where Old Yeller Dies" (04.04.96)
When Chandler sports a mustache to emulate Richard, Ross quips, "Look it's the artist formerly known as Chandler." This is an allusion to musical artist Prince, known for his pencil mustache.

Matthew Perry is wearing a fake mustache for the scenes in this episode. However, the next time he sports facial hair, in "The One with the Flashback" (3.06), it is real.

The Central Perk scene where Ross prompts Ben to say, "Dada," took at least a dozen takes. In the script, after Ross says, "Can you say 'Dada'?" Ben is supposed to remain silent. Instead, the boy kept responding "Dada" which was cute at first, but vexing after numerous takes.

Chandler is sporting a Guggenheim New York t-shirt. He wears the same shirt in "The One with the Metaphorical Tunnel" (3.04). The Solomon R. Guggenheim Museum is in the Upper East Side neighborhood of Manhattan. Series costumer Debra McGuire chose the attire to remind the audience of the sitcom's Big Apple ties.

When Richard states the guys are going to watch college basketball, Monica says, "Go Vassar!" This is a shoutout to Lisa Kudrow's alma mater. She graduated from Vassar College in 1985.

Posters in Joey's apartment

Tom Selleck was a member of the USC (University of Southern California) basketball team. He holds the school record for shooting percentage—100% (2 for 2 in seven games during the 1965-66 season). In practice, when preparing for games against UCLA, he played the role of Lew Alcindor (aka Kareem Abdul-Jabbar). Selleck is 6'4 and Alcindor is 7'2.

Ben doesn't speak any lines; a voice actor was hired to add dialogue in postproduction.

2.21 "The One with the Bullies" (04.25.96)

The Central Perk bullies are portrayed by Nicky Katt (Arthur, red tie) and Peter DeLuise (Carl). Katt is known as unorthodox teacher Harry Senate on *Boston Public*. DeLuise is recognized as Officer Doug Penhall in *21 Jump Street*, and being the eldest son of actor Dom DeLuise.

Jennifer Aniston was bullied as a youth. "I was one of the kids who the others would decide to make fun of," she confided. "It was an odd period of time during fifth, sixth, seventh grades. I was a little on the chubby side, so I was just that kid."

Phoebe is ambushed by a Jack Russell terrier. The breed has its origins in English fox hunting and was first bred by Reverend John Russell in the early 19th century. It is an energetic dog that appears in many films and television series, such as Eddie in *Frasier* (the dog received more fan mail than any of the actors). The dogs who portrayed Eddie (Moose and Enzo) also starred in *My Dog Skip* (2000).

During the 1990s, the National Education Association advocated for a national day to celebrate reading across America. To support the effort, the producers featured symbols in this installment, such as a bully wearing an embroidered Grinch baseball cap and Gunther sporting a Cat in the Hat tie.

This is the first appearance of Frank Buffay Jr., portrayed by Giovanni Ribisi who also appeared in "The One with the Baby on the Bus" (2.06) in a bit part as Condom Boy.

Monica's new place of employment, a 1950s-themed restaurant with singing waitstaff, is modeled after the real-life Ellen's Stardust Diner at 1650 Broadway in Manhattan.

In the tag scene, the waitstaff dances to the 1978 hit novelty song "Y.M.C.A." which is anachronistic for a 1950s diner. Nevertheless, it was purposely included to honor Ed Debevic's, a '50s diner in Los Angeles where the waitstaff performed a dance number whenever the song "Y.M.C.A." was played.

2.22 "The One with Two Parties" (05.02.96)

The installment commences with an establishing shot of Moondance Diner. The real-life 1950s-themed diner in the SoHo neighborhood of Manhattan was highlighted in *Spider-Man* (2002) (where Kirsten Dunst's character worked) and *Sex and the City*. The famed eatery closed in 2007.

When Ron Leibman (Dr. Leonard Green) was initially offered the role of Rachel's dad, he turned it down without a second thought because he considered himself to be a serious dramatic actor, and was uninterested in doing a sitcom. His daughter, however, insisted he do it because she wanted to meet the cast. Leibman finally agreed after being told he could play Dr. Green with a slightly dark streak. He had never seen the show and knew nothing about the cast, so on his first day of rehearsal he began talking to Lisa Kudrow believing she was the actress playing his daughter.

During the party, Monica says, "You wanna push the caps until you hear them click." The writers purposely included one of Marta Kauffman's pet peeves—she was equally obsessed with pen cap protocol.

Although single in the show, Gunther is wearing a wedding ring while talking to Phoebe about leaving the party. In real life, James Michael Tyler (Gunther) was six months into his marriage to Barbara Chadsey. They separated in 2003 and divorced in 2014.

As Ross exits the party and meets Rachel's father in the hallway, he is in a suit and tie, wearing bifocals, and has a cigarette hanging from his lips. This is an homage to Jerry Lewis' classic comedy bit in *The Family Jewels* (1965) where he sports a suit and bow tie, eyeglasses and buck teeth.

At the party, Chandler's necktie has a small Cat in the Hat image near the bottom. The costumer added the clothing accessory to support the National Education Association's efforts to establish a national holiday.

2.23 "The One with the Chicken Pox" (05.09.96)

This is writer Brown Mandell's first television writing credit. She also penned "The One with Barry & Mindy's Wedding" (2.24). Mandell married comedy screenwriter Jay Kogen in 1997 and they have one son, Charlie (b. 2001), who is now a musician.

Monica's bedroom has a 1920 Portos Ramos-Pinto poster on an alcove wall. The print is illustrated by René Vincent and advertises a famous port wine. It features two lovers in profile leaning into one another with only a famous glass of the irresistible Porto Ramos between their lips. An anxious cupid awaits below with bow in hand, using the delicious drink as his arrow. This iconic image is still very much associated with the company to the present date.

Director Michael Lembeck wanted the audience to be surprised, so he staged a special guest star entrance but Charlie Sheen (Ryan) missed his cue because he was nervous. On the next cue, he entered but failed to get an ovation. Sheen was not yet a household name, and didn't become a television star until he replaced Michael J. Fox in *Spin City* in 2000. He is best remembered as Charlie Harper in *Two and a Half Men*.

Dorien Wilson (Mr. Douglas) is listed in the credits as Mr. Kogen. A different actor was originally intended for the part but then the producers decided to use a character who previously appeared in Chandler's office. During an office hallway scene, Matt LeBlanc misspeaks by calling him "Mr. Dougen" which is a portmanteau of Douglas and Kogen. FYI: Wilson was originally cast as a coworker because the showrunners liked him when he was a regular in their series *Dream On*.

While lounging in bed, Richard is wearing a t-shirt for Mallard Brand Quick Cooking Rolled Oats, M.O. Brown & Co., Minneapolis, MN. This is a fake brand and company. The costumer is using the shirt to portend Richard taking flight from his relationship with Monica in the next episode.

The tag scene where sailor Ross lifts and carries Rachel is a parody of the closing scene from the movie *An Officer and a Gentleman* (1982). In the original airing of this episode, the program song was "Up Where We Belong" by Joe Cocker and Jennifer Warnes (#1, 1982), but all future versions use an instrumental meant to imitate the duet because the producers did not want to pay for the licensing fee in syndication and DVD releases.

The creators had a few storylines they regretted, and this episode contains one of them. They felt the chicken pox narrative was underdeveloped and not an interesting plot.

2.24 "The One with Barry & Mindy's Wedding" (05.16.96)

The subplot where Joey wants to practice kissing a man for a movie role was originally a storyline about him auditioning for the role of an uncircumcised man. The rest of the group would then come up with various ways of making him look the part. The network censors felt this subplot was tasteless, and recommended changing it. The plotline was shelved for years and then revived in "The One with Ross and Monica's Cousin" (7.19) after NBC eased restrictions on episode content.

Friends costume designer Debra McGuire considers the pink bridesmaid dresses "one of the ugliest things I think I've ever made." Much to her amazement, though, the dresses were in demand. "It's so interesting how the rest of the world perceives it because there were people who wrote letters that loved them, like for real," she recalled.

When designing the bridesmaid dresses, McGuire pondered: "What would be the most hellacious outfit we could possibly put together?" In her mind, she truly accomplished the task. "We made all of it, and everything was bad: The taffeta was bad, the color was bad, the puffy sleeves were bad. It was exactly what I wanted."

Kevin Bright's father, Jackie Bright, plays Mr. Weinberg, a guest at Barry and Mindy's wedding. He is paired with Fritzi Burr (Mrs. Weinberg) who is Marta Kauffman's aunt.

In this installment, Mindy is portrayed by Jana Marie Hupp. In "The One with the Evil Orthodontist" (1.20), Jennifer Grey played the part. Grey was replaced due to numerous filming commitments.

It has always been a trademark of the series to introduce an emotional scene but then undercut it with a joke. One of the few exceptions to the rule was the Monica-Richard wedding reception breakup. Marta Kauffman regretted this ending because "it was sad, and just didn't work."

This is the final episode with The Rachel haircut.

The installment ends without a cliffhanger. This is the only season where the producers didn't include a suspenseful finale. Although some argue the Chandler-Janice reunion is a cliffhanger, the show's producers never intended such, nor did it play out that way in Season 3.

Season 3: 1996-97

3.01 "The One with the Princess Leia Fantasy" (09.19.96)

This is the only season premiere that doesn't pick up immediately after the events of the previous season finale. The fact that Chandler and Janice reunited could be interpreted as a continuation of the Season 2 finale, but it doesn't actually forward a storyline, it merely resumes their romance.

In the teaser, the gang enters Central Perk only to discover the main couch is occupied by other customers. Sitting on the sofa (from left) is set decorator Greg Grande, writers Alexa Junge, Adam Chase, Shana Goldberg-Meehan and Michael Borkow.

This is the first episode without The Rachel hairstyle and also the first time since "The One with the Blackout" (1.07) where Rachel has long hair. It even has a chestnut tint. The length remains long for four years, until "The One with Ross's Library Book" (7.07).

As Joey watches a game show on television, writer Michael Curtis has a cameo as the contestant on *Wheel of Fortune* (he's the guy who couldn't guess "Count Rushmore," as Joey adamantly posits).

Chandler is spending considerable time reading *Trout: An Illustrated History* by James Prosek. The book represents Chandler's commitment to Janice, having hooked the love of his life.

In the coffee shop, Ross and Chandler discuss the cute copy girl at the Xerox shop. This was purposely written to presage her appearance at some unspecified time later in the season. She first appears in "The One Where Ross & Rachel Take a Break" (3.15).

The series producers received a letter of praise from George Lucas, creator of *Star Wars*, congratulating them on the "great" Princess Leia fantasy.

Star Wars purists will point out that Rachel's depiction of Princess Leia with a squash blossom hairstyle and gold bikini is inaccurate. The iconic hairdo is only worn in *Star Wars: Episode IV—A New Hope* (1977), while the bikini is only unveiled in *Star Wars: Episode VI—Return of the Jedi* (1983).

3.02 "The One Where No One's Ready" (09.26.96)

This is a bottle episode, which consists primarily of the main cast with no guest stars, no elaborate sets, and no location shooting. The producers were saving money on their annual production budget so they could afford expensive guest stars or elaborate sets in future episodes. From here on, the showrunners opted to produce at least one bottle episode per season.

The joke about drinking the fat was supposed to be a one-use bit but it slowly morphed as the story developed in the writers room. The ending originally had Ross making a beautiful speech and Rachel forgiving him, but writer Ira Ungerleider said, "That isn't fun enough. We build to a conversation?" That's when drinking the fat was mentioned as a test of Ross' love.

When a staff writer suggested a storyline involving Chandler and Joey arguing over a living room chair, the creators were not on board; "it seemed so dumb to us—just give up the chair," David Crane declared. But the other writers believed so deeply about a person's investment in the chair that they convinced the showrunners to include the storyline. "It felt like one of those things you do when you're younger," Marta Kauffman stated, "and that was one of the few times we've truly felt like anthropologists on this project. Way too old to be doing this thing."

Monica's obsessive behavior is based on Marta Kauffman. "It was easy to write Monica's neurosis," the cocreator confessed. "And the writers enjoyed it."

During the scene where Joey and Chandler race to be the first to sit in the club chair, on the fourth take Matt LeBlanc tripped over a carpet and fell between the coffee table and chair, dislocating his shoulder. The audience thought the stunt was choreographed so everyone laughed hysterically. He wandered offstage, his arm visibly drooping down, and then a sickening pop pierced the silence. "In come all the paramedics, they've got to take him to the hospital, and that was the end of filming," stated David Crane. The cast had to reassemble a few weeks later—after LeBlanc ditched the shoulder sling—to finish filming the episode.

This is the only installment where the cast didn't engage in a preshow huddle. LeBlanc blamed the deviation from protocol as the cause of his on-set accident. After that, the cast always did a huddle.

David Crane and Marta Kauffman had never heard the term "going commando" before the script was written. At the persistence of the writing staff, who adamantly believed the audience would know the reference, the catchphrase made it into the show.

David Schwimmer was very concerned that Ross' tirade—ordering Rachel to get dressed and then throwing her shoes—would cast him in a negative light. The producers had to convince him to do the scene.

Staff writer Greg Malins used personal experience to create the storyline of Joey wearing Chandler's clothes. His friend Brian Boyle once sported the entire wardrobe of another friend, Sebastian Jones, who had recently moved into his apartment. When Jones came home, Boyle gestured to himself and said, "Look, I'm wearing all your clothes." Boyle's prank became Joey's revenge: "Look at me, I'm Chandler. Could I *be* wearing any more clothes?" (FYI: Both Jones and Boyle joined the *Friends* writing staff in later seasons.)

The embarrassing answering machine message was inspired by Marta Kauffman. Once, she left a very personal message for her then boyfriend Michael Skloff, but his roomie, David Crane, intercepted the recording before it reached its intended target.

Popular posters in Monica's bedroom: 1980 Winter Olympics and 1920s Portuguese wine

3.03 "The One with the Jam" (10.03.96)

Joey's sling was not originally part of this episode, but after Matt LeBlanc dislocated his shoulder while filming the previous installment, the trauma had to be explained to the audience. The staff writers settled on the story of Joey jumping on his bed and falling off, thereby injuring his shoulder.

Courteney Cox is responsible for David Arquette's guest starring role in this installment. The couple met in April 1996 on the set of Wes Craven's horror film *Scream* and started dating. When the *Friends* series began production in August, she asked the producers to cast him for the show.

The writers didn't want Courteney Cox and David Arquette sharing screen time out of fear their real-life romantic chemistry would interfere with the plotted narrative for the rest of the season. Thus, the pair remained apart except for a 15-second segment where he is on the balcony and she is in the kitchen (it is often cut for syndication).

Chandler asks Joey to choose: Xerox girl naked or big tub of jam? This is the second reference to the Xerox girl. It is meant to presage her future appearance on the series.

Monica is looking for a sperm donor and one of the contributor's forms has Joey as a specimen provider. This is a callback to "The One Where Rachel Finds Out" (1.24) where Joey participated in a fertility study that required him to deposit a specimen in a cup every other day for two weeks.

In the subway scene, Ursula is portrayed by Lisa Kudrow's real-life sister, Helene Marla Sherman. She was used as a body double in all their sibling scenes.

The creators regretted the stalker storyline, specifically trivializing such a serious and dangerous criminal act. Marta Kauffman commented, "We did a lot of rewriting to make that one work," while David Crane looked back at the episode and commented, "Really? We went with that?" The trio felt the plot was uninteresting and needed more work.

3.04 "The One with the Metaphorical Tunnel" (10.10.96)

The *Amazing Discoveries* infomercial segment was written because the staff writers were addicted to this marketing format. They often worked into the early-morning hours and would unwind by watching television, but back in the 1990s, the programming options were limited. Thus, they often viewed infomercials to discover unique products that may inspire future storylines.

Mike Levy, the real-life host of *Amazing Discoveries*, was asked to personally appear in a segment to add legitimacy and credibility to the sketch. He hosted the very popular late-night infomercial spot from 1989 to 1997. The *Friends* segment was filmed exactly like a typical infomercial to appear authentic.

Speaking of infomercials, in 1989 Jennifer Aniston was a Nutrisystem Success Story spokesmodel on *The Howard Stern Show* praising the product she claimed helped her lose 15 pounds in six weeks. She would eventually lose 30 pounds. Back in the 1980s,

Aniston was fat. "I got fat the way everyone gets fat: going nowhere, watching television, eating from the fridge, spooning from the jar, drinking from the carton. I ate too many mayonnaise sandwiches," she stated. "Mayonnaise on white bread—the most delicious thing in the world." Aniston's diet also included milkshakes and french fries with gravy.

In the opening scene in Central Perk, Chandler is reading *The Village Voice* newspaper. Founded in 1955, it was an American news and culture periodical known for being the country's first alternative newsweekly which began as a dais for the creative community of New York City. It ceased publication in 2017. The prop was added to sell the location setting of the sitcom.

Ben is overly attached to the 1995 Winter Sports Barbie. It is a fashion doll produced by Mattel, Inc. The original Barbie launched in March 1959. American entrepreneur Ruth Handler is credited with the creation, which was inspired by the German doll Bild Lilli.

There is an establishing shot for D'Agostino Supermarkets, the place where Chandler "accidentally" bumps into Janice. At its peak in the 1990s, the chain had 26 locations, but due to financial problems only 10 stores remained open by 2016. No scenes were shot inside the store.

3.05 "The One with Frank Jr." (10.17.96)
This episode features Joey's proclivity for carpentry. Matt LeBlanc actually worked as a carpenter and attended Wentworth Institute of Technology in Boston, Massachusetts, in 1985. He dropped out shortly after starting the second semester because he thought it was ridiculous to pay to do things he already knew how to do.

Yasmine Bleeth's name is on Chandler's celebrity freebie list. In real life, Matthew Perry had recently broken up with Julia Roberts so he added Bleeth to his character's freebie list because he had a major crush on her. It was a teaser to publicly profess his lust for the *Baywatch* star. FYI: They met and began dating shortly after this episode aired.

Actresses Winona Ryder and Susan Sarandon are on Ross' celebrity freebie list. They both will subsequently guest star in the series.

Isabella Rossellini was originally on Ross' celebrity freebie list but he removed her for being too international. The showrunners were looking for a well-known movie star and she was desperate for a gig. Lancôme had recently dismissed her as the face of their product line for being "too old." She was a single parent with two kids, depressed and financially distressed, so her agent jumped at the *Friends* offer. Rossellini was asked to appear without an audition.

Matthew Perry looks deathly ill as he enters Monica's apartment wearing tan pants and a white t-shirt. Season 3 was the start of his serious drug addiction. He admits that he did not remember three years of the show, somewhere between Seasons 3 and 6.

When Ross displays the laminated list of his five celebrity freebies, the names are Uma Thurman, Isabella Rossellini, Elizabeth Hurley, Vanessa Williams and Dorothy Hamill. However, a few seconds later, when Rachel reads the list, the names are Uma Thurman, *Winona Ryder*, Elizabeth Hurley, *Michelle Pfeiffer* and Dorothy Hamill. The props crew created Ross' original laminated list, which was preshot, but the writers later changed the names, resulting in the continuity error.

Writer Wil Calhoun has an uncredited cameo as the guy who is served a complicated drink order—half caff, double tall, easy hazelnut, nonfat, no foam, with whip, extra-hot latte—to whom Rachel refers to as "freak" after delivering his beverage.

3.06 "The One with the Flashback" (10.31.96)
This episode was conceived to gauge how audiences would respond to certain romantic couplings, namely ones that had not been linked together previously (Monica and Joey, Monica and Chandler, Rachel and Chandler, Phoebe and Ross). The hope was to pair Rachel and Chandler, which was the reason for the tag scene teaser. But the audience didn't react positively so the idea was shelved. The only coupling that seemed plausible was Monica and Chandler. The producers wanted to find the right time for a hookup

but the timing never worked, until the Season 4 finale.

Matthew Perry grew a mustache and goatee during a production hiatus so he asked the producers if he could keep it for the flashback scenes. They liked the idea of giving the character a different visage so they consented to the change.

Ross is not wearing a wedding ring in the flashback scenes even though he is supposed to be married to Carol at the time. The prop department is responsible for continuity.

During the 1993 flashback, the costumer dressed Joey in monochromatic black (leather zipper vest over t-shirt and jeans) to sync with his original image in "The Pilot" (1.01).

In the 1993 flashback, Central Perk was a neighborhood bar, so the set dresser took the My Goodness My Guinness poster from Joey's apartment and placed it along the back wall of the tavern.

Marissa Ribisi plays Rachel's red-headed friend Betsy. She is the twin sister of Giovanni Ribisi (Frank Jr.). In October 2007, she launched a fashion line, Whitley Kros, with her partner Sophia Banks. Marissa married musician and recording artist Beck on April 3, 2004. They have two children. On February 15, 2019, he filed for divorce after nearly 15 years of marriage.

The engagement ring on Rachel's finger is different from the one she returned to Barry in "The One with the Sonogram at the End" (1.02). The prop department was unable to reserve the ring because it was on loan to another production company.

In the 1993 flashback, Monica and Joey meet for the first time in the apartment hallway and experience an instant physical attraction, which is reaffirmed while he moves into Chandler's apartment. When the *Friends* series was originally conceived, Monica and Joey were intended to be the primary romantic couple. This scene was meant to explain why they never hooked up.

Rachel smacking the jukebox to make it play a song pays homage to Fonzie from *Happy Days*. He often performed this maneuver in the 1950s-themed sitcom.

3.07 "The One with the Race Car Bed" (11.07.96)
In Central Perk, as Ross prattles on about dinosaurs, Joey is humming the 1961 tune "Baby Elephant Walk" by Henry Mancini. The tune was written for an impromptu scene in *Hatari!* (1962) in which Dallas led three baby elephants to a waterhole to bathe. The tune's catchy simplicity made it one of Mancini's most popular works. Due to its "goofy" sound, it is often used in a humorous context.

At the start of Act 1, the gang is watching *Happy Days* (1974-84). The producers were huge fans of the sitcom during their youth so it was repeatedly referenced.

There is an establishing shot for Mattress King (on a business awning). This is a fake company. It was filmed on the Warner Bros. lot. The art department made the awning which was affixed to the storefront. The person carrying the mattress outside the store is set designer Greg Grande.

Rachel and Ross are at a restaurant waiting for her father. When he arrives, they both get up to greet him and then Dr. Green sits in Ross' chair. This physical comedy bit is recycled in "The One with Ross's Grant" (10.06).

The flower poster hanging above Monica's bed is Mikhail Avvakumov and Olga Volkova's You Are Welcome! design for the 1980 Olympic Games in Moscow. The US boycotted the Games to protest the Soviet Union's invasion of Afghanistan, which led to 65 nations refusing to participate. A large part of the Olympics promotion centered on the Soviet Union welcoming other nations to Moscow. Thus, its slogan, You Are Welcome! written in different languages, is somewhat ironic.

Joey witnesses Janice kissing her estranged husband. The producers never intended Janice to have a long-term story arc so it was planned before the season started to have her exit after a relatively brief romance with Chandler.

3.08 "The One with the Giant Poking Device" (11.14.96)

This episode reminds Marta Kauffman of how life imitates art. Shortly after shooting the storyline where Phoebe goes to the dentist, Lisa Kudrow had tooth problems and Kauffman a root canal.

The storyline of bumping a toddler's head was based on writer Adam Chase's personal experience while playing with Marta Kauffman's yearling son (Sam), who was visiting the set. Chase was tossing the boy into the air and then catching him. On about the third attempt, Sam's noggin crashed into a metal doorframe. Chase saw his career flash before his eyes and was convinced he would be instantly fired for endangering the life of his boss' son. He went to apologize to Kauffman, and she stoically replied: "I drop him on his head all the time."

Since Ugly Naked Guy is an uncredited role, many *Friends* fans mistakenly believe he was portrayed by Michael Hagerty (Mr. Treeger). He was actually portrayed by an extra named Jon Haugen. Warner Bros. asked him to keep his identity secret from the public. "They wanted everybody to have a guess who I was," Haugen said. Regarding his time on *Friends*, he added, "It was the best time in my life. I was the man."

According to cocreator Marta Kauffman, casting for Ugly Naked Guy was relatively easy. "Surprisingly, there are people who want to play Ugly Naked Guy. They do. It's just from the back, they don't have any lines, it wasn't an audition—it was just about, physically, what do we imagine."

This installment marks the first time Ugly Naked Guy appears onscreen, albeit only his torso, with his face obscured by a plant. He would have one other onscreen appearance in "The One Where Everybody Finds Out" (5.14) where his face is not shown.

Ugly Naked Guy was an extrapolation of a man that many of the writers observed living across from their apartments in the past (especially those who lived in New York City). Incidentally, the *Friends* staff writers received a letter from a woman who grew up in the building used to represent Ugly Naked Guy's tenement, and she announced that "there was, in fact, an authentic Ugly Naked Guy living across from her," and then rhetorically asked, "How did you know?"

3.09 "The One with the Football" (11.21.96)

The entire park football game was filmed on a vacant soundstage on the Warner Bros. lot. Production designer John Shaffner only had a few days to dress it. The park set has custom-made trees with autumn leaves, wired-on a few at a time, and the background building is not a painted backdrop, it's like a "real" apartment with neighborhood scene extras watching the game from the windows. The distant background utilizes a gigantic photographic backdrop of the city.

All the apartment scenes were filmed first since it would not reveal the story, and then the audience and cameras were moved to the enormous soundstage for the park scenes. Temporary bleachers were constructed to house the studio audience.

Phoebe wears a *That Girl* t-shirt to symbolize female independence and equality as the girls battle the guys in football. Also, Rachel's mother, played by Marlo Thomas, starred in the 1960s sitcom.

Joey's maroon Boston College jersey (#22) honors 1984 Heisman trophy winner Doug Flutie. BC is located in Newton, Massachusetts, which is Matt LeBlanc's hometown.

A typical *Friends* installment used three to four cameras. In this episode, the director utilized six. The soundstage was so expansive that Kevin Bright needed more equipment to get all the shots.

Marta Kauffman's two children, Sam and Hannah, are extras playing on the swing set.

The playing field is a concrete floor covered with two layers of carpet padding inverted to resemble dirt. Artificial leaves were scattered on top to create an autumn environment.

During auditions, Susanna Voltaire (Margha) passed herself off as a foreigner with an exotic accent, and it wasn't until the third day of rehearsals that the producers learned she was actually a US citizen using a fake accent. Although reputedly Dutch, Voltaire's accent was not even close.

Joey's comment, "I'm sorry, Dutch. I didn't get that last little bit," was a line the writers repeatedly quoted on set long after this episode aired.

The Geller Cup is a Danish Gjøl Troll glued onto a block of wood. It was created by prop master Marjorie Coster-Praytor. The writers loved it. After a few minor adjustments and a good polishing, it was a legitimate trophy. The staff writers never planned on having a trophy. She inspired them to rewrite the script to include the prop.

Margha was cast as a Dutch woman to create continuity between her nationality and the song "Get Ready for This" which is performed by a Dutch dance act.

At one point during the game, Phoebe is flashing her breasts to Chandler. This bit was performed in front of the studio audience. Naturally, Lisa Kudrow was wearing a bra.

The only segment not filmed in front of an audience was the slow-motion scene because it required a special camera that operates at a higher speed so when it is played back, it rolls in slow motion. Filming the football gliding through the air was the most difficult shot of the entire episode. It took 20 takes to get it right.

3.10 "The One Where Rachel Quits" (12.12.96)
Unofficially, this episode is known as "The One with the Christmas Trees" and "The One with the Cookies."

The tenant who buys cookies from the Brown Bird troop member is writer Greg Malins.

In the stairwell scene after opening credits, Ross is advising Chandler how to properly swing a racket with power, precision and panache. Interestingly, Matthew Perry was a second-ranked junior tennis player in Canada. However, when he moved to Los Angeles in 1985, he was destroyed by the competition so he set his sights on acting instead of a career as a professional tennis player.

While Ross is talking to Sarah Tuttle (bedridden with a broken leg), she is wearing a Cat in the Hat t-shirt. Series costumer Debra McGuire included the iconic Dr. Seuss image to promote reading awareness.

The old lady who berates Ross through her apartment door is voiced by Sandra Gould, aka the nosy neighbor Gladys Kravitz #2 in *Bewitched* from 1966 to 1971. She replaced her friend Alice Pearce, who died in March 1966, but only secured the role after Alice Ghostley rejected the offer. (Ghostley was later cast as Esmeralda.) After *Bewitched* was canceled, Gould reprised the role of Gladys five years later in the spinoff series *Tabitha*.

In one outdoor scene, Joey is trying to sell a Douglas fir to a Christmas tree customer. The shopper is played by Gene Crane, the father of David Crane, cocreator of *Friends*.

After Rachel learns she is hired by Fortunata Fashions, Phoebe exclaims, "God bless us, every one." This is a line uttered by Tiny Tim, a fictional character in *A Christmas Carol* by Charles Dickens, as a blessing at Christmas dinner. Dickens repeated the phrase at the end of the story, which is symbolic of Scrooge's change of heart.

Fortunata is a fictional enterprise that was established to bide time until the production company could find a corporate sponsor to function as Rachel's employer.

3.11 "The One Where Chandler Can't Remember Which Sister" (01.09.97)
Staff writer Ira Ungerleider has an uncredited voice role as the loud tenant living in the apartment above Monica and Rachel's abode.

In the third season, Matthew Perry was losing significant weight because of substance abuse issues. The show's costume designer tried to hide his slender frame by dressing him in baggy, oversize clothes, or using multiple layers, such as sports jackets, sweater vests or overcoats.

There is an establishing shot for Moondance Diner. The restaurant opened in 1933 as Holland Tunnel Diner. It seated 34 people, with six tables and 10 counter stools. Like most diners of its vintage, it was built elsewhere and transported to its site. The diner was roughly 36 feet by 16 feet.

This is the first appearance of Steven Eckholdt as Mark Robinson, Rachel's coworker. He was introduced to cause a rift in Rachel and Ross' relationship.

This installment represents the first appearance of Joey's sisters: Gina, Dina, Veronica, Mary Angela, Mary Theresa and Cookie (probably an appellation). In "The One with the Boobies" (1.13), Joey mentioned having a sister named Tina.

Joanna is mentioned in this episode but doesn't make her first appearance until "The One with the Dollhouse" (3.20). The writers wanted to signal her presence in case they decided to create a narrative that focused on Rachel's workplace.

Rachel's fashionista dreams come true when she is hired by Bloomingdale's department store. The luxury chain was chosen solely because the production company worked out a financial deal to feature the Manhattan shopping mecca. At the time, the series was already promoting the store by having its characters carrying brand bags, e.g., "little brown bag" or "big brown bag." The original Bloomingdale's store on Third Avenue is a spectacular nine-story building and great for celebrity spotting.

3.12 "The One with All the Jealousy" (01.16.97)

Since the title and plot involve jealousy, the costumer dressed many of the characters with green shades and earth tones. Gunther is literally green with envy, so at the end of the episode he wears a lime-green shirt while begrudgingly watching Rachel and Ross on the coffeehouse sofa.

In nearly every installment involving Rachel's bedroom, there is a poster for Excelsior sewing machines. The inscription is "La machine a coudre parfaite" (the perfect sewing machine). Although Rachel has no sewing skills, the set decorator chose it simply for aesthetics—he liked to use foreign prints as wall hangings.

There is an establishing shot of Moondance Diner at nighttime. After the famous NYC eatery closed in 2007, it was purchased for $7,500 and transported 2,400 miles (3,900 km) on the back of a semitrailer truck to La Barge, Wyoming, at a cost of $40,000.

Carlos Gómez (Julio) met Matthew Perry on the set of *Fools Rush In* (1997) and was told to audition for *Friends*. He then used his contact with Matt LeBlanc in this episode to land a guest role as Sam (the director) in two episodes of the spinoff series *Joey*.

As Monica's shift is ending at the diner, Julio is reading *The Flowers of Evil* by Charles Baudelaire, a poetry book dealing with themes of decadence and eroticism. First printed in 1857, it was important in the symbolist and modernist movements. The subject lays the groundwork for Julio's poem *The Empty Vase*, which describes all American women as shallow, and allows lyricism to play a central theme, most notably Monica hiring a barbershop quartet to publicly humiliate him.

Joey auditions for a fictional adaptation of *A Tale of Two Cities*. The real-life adaptation was produced on Broadway in 2008. It closed promptly after 60 performances and 33 previews. At the audition, Joey sings "You've Got to Pick a Pocket or Two" from *Oliver!* (which was another musical adaptation of a Dickens novel).

Three actors who were part of the barbershop quartet would later appear in the *Friends* reunion special in May 2021. They performed during the trivia game segment.

The Central Perk artwork features *Jump Toast* by Burton Morris. This is the first of his many paintings that were displayed in Central Perk. The piece debuted in "The One with the Race Car Bed" (3.07).

3.13 "The One Where Monica & Richard Are Friends" (01.30.97)

Unofficially, this episode is also known as "The One with the Book Spoilers" and "The One with Phoebe's Boyfriend's Shorts." In the UK and on Netflix, this episode is called "The One Where Monica and Richard are Just Friends."

Robby Benson directed this episode. In the cold open in the video store, while Monica is talking to the clerk, a wall poster for the 1977 film *One on One* starring Robby Benson is hanging on the entrance door. The set decorator added the homage to the director.

In the opening scene of Act 1, when Monica tells a store customer, "We're not judging," the DVD rack is prominently displayed. One title (bottom left) is *Beauty and the Beast* (1991), where the Beast is voiced by Robby Benson. This was a nod to the director.

Tom Selleck appears in this episode without his trademark mustache. He shaved it for his role in the comedy flick *In & Out* (1997).

Little Women by Louisa May Alcott and *The Shining* by Stephen King are central to Joey and Rachel's subplot and have hidden meanings. Three episodes prior, Joey told Rachel to quit her job at Central Perk to experience "the fear" which she now feels after starting a new job. In this episode, she experiences "the fear" by reading *The Shining*. Joey finds out that *Little Women* is too sad (and thus scary) so "the fear" he experiences relates to how the book's concept conflicts with his view of women and the code by which he lives.

While sitting in Central Perk, Ross is reading *Race: How Blacks and Whites Think About the American Obsession* by Studs Terkel. This was David Schwimmer's idea as a subtle commentary to the media that he was cognizant of the criticism regarding the lack of diversity on the show, but he personally embraced the idea of expanding his knowledge on race relations in America.

In Central Perk, Phoebe is wearing a Grateful Dead Lithuanian basketball tie-dyed tee. In 1992, Lithuania, newly independent from the Soviet Union, lacked sufficient funds to send its basketball team to the Olympics. Grateful Dead band members heard the story and took it upon themselves to raise money to get the team to the Games. To express their appreciation, the team wore tie-dyed jerseys, and went on to win a bronze medal in Barcelona.

The gang doesn't know how to tell Robert (Phoebe's boyfriend) that his family jewels are exposed, but Gunther does it smoothly and metaphorically: "Hey buddy, this is a family place, put the mouse back in the house." According to James Michael Tyler (Gunther): "That's one of my favorite Gunther moments of the whole series."

3.14 "The One with Phoebe's Ex-Partner" (02.06.97)

Actor Elizabeth "E.G." Daily (Leslie) is also a professional singer. In 1985, she appeared in the film *Better Off Dead*, singing two songs at a high school dance. The following year she released the single "Say It, Say It" (No. 70 on the US Billboard Hot 100, and No. 1 on the Hot Dance Music/Club Play chart). From 2003 to 2011, Daily did the vocals for Jake Harper in the *Two and a Half Men* theme song. She is best known as the voice of Tommy Pickles in the *Rugrats* cartoon franchise.

Leslie is playing a Taylor guitar from Daily's personal collection. The brand is used by contemporary artists such as Taylor Swift, Katy Perry, Zac Brown and Jason Mraz.

Sherilyn Fenn (Ginger) achieved fame as Audrey Horne in *Twin Peaks* (1990-91, 2017), earning Golden Globe and Emmy nominations. She is also known for her roles in *Wild at Heart* (1990), *Of Mice and Men* (1992), *Boxing Helena* (1993) and the Showtime sitcom *Rude Awakening* (1998–2001).

While in bed, Ross is reading *The Idiot* by Fyodor Dostoyevsky before he commences a war of words with Rachel about the inappropriateness of her going to a fashion lecture with Mark. Ross then commits to going with her to the presentation in a feeble effort to eliminate Mark as romantic competition. The book predicts that Ross will be an idiot in his handling of the situation.

The establishing shot for the fashion lecture is Cooper Union building, a private college in the East Village neighborhood of Manhattan since 1859. The cube artwork, *Alamo*, was placed there in 1967. It was named by the artist's wife because its scale and mass reminded her of Alamo Mission in San Antonio, Texas.

The writers spent ample time debating how to treat Ginger's disability. They loved the comedic irony of having a disabled individual break up with someone because of their "disability." In this case, Ginger breaks up with Chandler because of his third nipple.

The actress in the Cat Fresh commercial is Kim Harris, Jennifer Aniston's stand-in.

3.15 "The One Where Ross & Rachel Take a Break" (02.13.97)

A typical episode uses three cameras. This is the first time director James Burrows ever used six. He needed three cameras in the living room and three in the bedroom.

Joey asks Monica how much she would pay to see him eat an entire jar of olives. This bit was based on activities in the writers room. The staff would offer cash inducements to entice each other to eat a variety of foods, such as an entire jar of garlic pickles. This became the basis for various dares on the show, such as Ross drinking breast milk in "The One with the Breast Milk" (2.02) and him drinking the fat in "The One Where No One's Ready" (3.02).

Chloe (the hot copy girl) is portrayed by Angela Featherstone. She began her career as a fashion model, and is best recalled as the maid on *Seinfeld*, and the runaway bride in *The Wedding Singer* (1998). She has been absent from the Hollywood scene since 2016, though purportedly working on a memoir.

When the creators planned the season, Ross and Rachel were never meant to go on a break. They were supposed to stay together. But there was concern the show may grow stale, which left two options: marry or break up. They chose the latter. "It allowed us to have fun with the show and give people something to root for," Kevin Bright declared. "We were well aware the audience wanted to keep them together but when we got them together—when the first kiss happened—we go, 'Wow, the air has kind of gone out of the balloon.' There wasn't that sexual tension anymore."

Originally, there was no set plan on how Ross and Rachel would break up. The writers liked the break idea because it left the relationship ambiguous. And it paid dividends. The catchphrase "We were on a break!" became a recurring joke, and fans were in the loop about this inside joke.

A frequently used transition clip is the venerable Village Cigars located on the corner of Seventh Avenue South and Christopher Street. The sidewalk comprises Hess Triangle, a 300-square-inch mosaic with an embedded marker: "Property of the Hess Estate, Which Has Never Been Dedicated for Public Purposes." A land surveying error kept the parcel in the family, making it the smallest piece of private land in New York City.

This is one of David Crane's favorite episodes. Marta Kauffman stated that the Ross and Rachel fights were some of her favorite moments. Crane agreed, stating, "For the two of us, the emotional stuff was what sustained us."

3.16 "The One the Morning After" (02.20.97)

The blender gag—where it sprays the ceiling—was a gamble to perform live because of potential makeup or wardrobe delays. That's why Courteney Cox is wearing a hat and Jennifer Aniston has a towel on her head.

The subject of Ross cheating on Rachel was a topic of great debate in the writers room. His relationship betrayal is somewhat tempered by the break they were on. "There's a fair bit of discrepancy as to whether it was actually cheating, whether or not they were in fact on a break," David Crane explained.

The idea for Waxine came from the many infomercials at the time promoting self-waxing products. One of the writers was inspired by a segment so a script was penned using a fictional product.

After James Michael Tyler (Gunther) read the initial script, he was worried. "When I first got that script and saw what Gunther was about to do, I honestly thought I was going to be one of the most-hated characters, if not actors, in America," he said. "As an actor, I was worried it was going to ostracize the fans. But fortunately, the writers handled it well in the follow-up episodes and their break didn't last forever."

When Phoebe and Monica are screaming in pain from the leg wax, Joey and Chandler rush into the bedroom carrying cookware as weapons. Matt LeBlanc and Matthew Perry pitched the idea of having their characters carry a pot and tea kettle to defend the girls.

The conclusion to the Ross-Rachel argument was only filmed twice because it was so emotionally draining. "It's asking a lot to make them do it again and again and again. And they were both so wonderful," David Crane declared. "We couldn't come up with anything we'd want from an additional pass at the scene. It was so emotionally full." In fact, both Schwimmer and Aniston cried after it was shot.

Toying with audience emotions was a purposeful creative strategy. "We played the cruel producers because just when we bring them together, every time basically, then we take it apart," admits Kevin Bright. "As the series progressed we realized that we couldn't toy with the emotions of the audience anymore. So we moved on to other stories being the focus of the show—Monica and Chandler, Phoebe and her babies. The show started to spread out and go in different directions."

3.17 "The One Without the Ski Trip" (03.06.97)

A studio audience was not used for the highway scene since it required difficult camera angles and the use of blue screen. The scenic images were added in postproduction to create the illusion of motion, and the taxicab rocking movement was performed by crew members pushing on the vehicle to simulate driving on a roadway.

The rest-stop scenes were filmed on Stage 24 with a live studio audience. It is a swing set with abundant foliage to conceal the backstage. The set decorator added a special touch of fake snow on the concrete floor to create a winter scene since this episode is supposed to involve a ski trip.

Chandler's comment, "I thought if I littered that crying Indian might come by and save us," is an allusion to the "Keep America Beautiful" public service announcement from the early 1970s. The commercial shows a Native American in costume, shedding a tear after trash is thrown from a car window and lands at his feet. Controversy arose after it was revealed that the actor in the TV spot, Iron Eyes Cody, lied about his Native American heritage, and was actually Italian-American.

There is a noteworthy blooper that appears near the end of the final rest-stop scene: a cameraman is visible on the left side of the frame after Joey recites the line "Oh what, wait, wait a second, I mean, what are we doing? Who's going with who?" The mistake is only visible in the wide-screen format.

At the end of the episode, when the cab drives away, it is obvious the vehicle is parked and the camera is panning along the side to give the illusion of movement. This had to be done because there was not enough room on the soundstage for stagehands to pull the car since another swing set was in the way.

In the tag scene, without using any verbal cues (because of NBC censors), Carol has to communicate to Ross that she is being intimate with Susan. The writers could not craft a good innuendo so Jane Sibbett (Carol) recommended removing a pubic hair from her tongue. The writers loved it. It was the first time she pitched something that was really outrageous, and it actually made it into a scene.

3.18 "The One with the Hypnosis Tape" (03.13.97)

Gunther is revealed as a regular cigarette smoker. In real life, James Michael Tyler was a smoker.

One of James Michael Tyler's favorite quotes is Gunther's line, "Oh dark mother, once again I suckle at your smoky teat." He simply loved that Shakespearean-inspired line.

Posters in Rachel's and Chandler's bedrooms, and two custom-designed tees

This is the debut of Debra Jo Rupp as Alice Knight (Frank Jr.'s girlfriend), though she is best known for her role as Kitty Forman in *That '70s Show*. Rupp was only scheduled to appear in this one episode. In Season 4 she was given a recurring role after a surrogacy arc was created to accommodate Lisa Kudrow's pregnancy.

Marta Kauffman's voice is on the hypnosis tape that Chandler uses to quit smoking.

This is the debut performance of Jon Favreau as Pete Becker. When the character was first conceived, he was "a Bill Gates billionaire genius scientist-type" to whom Monica is not attracted. The producers and casting director had difficulty finding an actor to play Pete because they wanted "someone who was appealing enough that we liked him, so we could root for him, but on the other hand, wasn't so drop-dead male-model gorgeous that we would go, 'What's your problem?' to Monica when she didn't fall for him."

The magna doodle debuts on Joey's entry door wall. The left column has a grocery list "Buy Milk Eggs Bread" and the right has a note, "Joey call your dad."

Pete Becker's office uses an establishing shot for Brown Brothers Harriman, a high-rise at 140 Broadway in Lower Manhattan. In the foreground is Isamu Noguchi's *Red Cube* sculpture which is not actually a cube, but a distorted shape seemingly stretched along its vertical axis. His other famous artwork is *Sunken Garden* at One Chase Manhattan Plaza which decorates the main entrance to 50 Rockefeller Plaza.

The quaint Italian restaurant is Canova. The establishing shot is the real-life eatery but no scenes were filmed inside. In fact, the set interior is vastly different from the original.

3.19 "The One with the Tiny T-Shirt" (03.27.97)

Mark, Rachel's friend and former coworker, has his last appearance until "The One with Princess Consuela" (10.14), which is 165 episodes. He was first introduced to cause a breakup between Ross and Rachel, but the writers never wanted him to be a romantic interest for her, so a storyline was created to end his involvement in the series.

The magna doodle has the same message as the prior installment. In the early days, the board had no assigned artist, so occasionally it was left blank or remained unchanged.

Ross' small t-shirt with the inscription "Frankie Say Relax" is a reference to the British band Frankie Goes to Hollywood, best known for the hit "Relax" (#10, 1985). They were active from 1980 to 1987 and again from 2004 to 2007. The group's name was inspired by the intense publicity associated with Frank Sinatra's move into the film industry.

As Ross inches toward the door carrying Chandler on his back, Chandler clutches the foosball table which effortlessly slides across the floor. This cues the joke of Ross being surprisingly strong. In reality, the foosball table was resting on wheels to facilitate its seemingly trouble-free movement.

After Monica admits to having no physical attraction to Pete, he confesses: "I know I'm no Jon Bon Jovi ... or someone you find attractive." This bit was added because in May 1996, *People* magazine named Jon Bon Jovi one of the "50 Most Beautiful People in the

World." He is best known as the founder and frontman of the Grammy Award–winning rock band Bon Jovi, which was formed in 1983. In 2000, *People* awarded him the title "Sexiest Rock Star."

As Chandler is having a recliner showdown with an empty chair, behind him (in front of the world globe) is a framed photograph of actress Jennifer Milmore, who, at the time, was dating *Friends* writer Greg Malins. Although her scene in this episode was cut, it is part of the DVD version.

3.20 "The One with the Dollhouse" (04.10.97)
Since Rachel works for Bloomingdale's, the producers made every effort to promote their corporate sponsor. Establishing shots feature the main department store location, and Rachel's office has wall hangings and shelves filled with brand names, e.g., Joe Boxer, Movado, Isotoner and Bonjour. The *Friends* producers enlisted Hollywood International Placements to provide merchandise and dressing for the office set.

This is the first appearance of Alison LaPlaca (Joanna). Her character was first revealed in "The One Where Chandler Can't Remember Which Sister" (3.11). LaPlaca is known for the role of acid-tongued yuppie Linda Phillips in the 1980s TV sitcom *Duet* and its spinoff, *Open House.*

Jennifer Milmore was cast as Lauren because she was dating *Friends* staff writer Greg Malins. They met in 1993 on the set of *Daddy Dearest*, where she was an assistant to the producers and he was employed as a scriptwriter. The couple married on November 21, 1999, and have two children.

The theater scenes were filmed without an audience because the playhouse seating area is part of the studio bleachers used for taping episodes.

Phoebe makes a dollhouse out of old shoeboxes. The script called for the dollhouse to catch fire at the end of the episode. Since the producers didn't know how many takes would be required to get the desired shot, they requested six identical houses. The prop department had only three days to create the structures from scratch.

This episode offers one of the rare instances where Rachel expresses her Jewish faith by wearing a Star of David necklace. The other instances occur in "The One with Rachel's Phone Number" (9.09) where Rachel calls her grandmother "bubbe" and "The One with Princess Consuela" (10.14) where she mentions meeting a man on JewHunks.com.

Rachel Green's Jewishness was highly contested among fans until her religiosity was finally confirmed in 2011. "In our minds I guess she was Jewish," David Crane stated. "You can't create a character with the name 'Rachel Green' and not from the get-go make some character choices."

3.21 "The One with a Chick and a Duck" (04.17.97)
Matthew Perry has a mustache and goatee. In "The One with the Flashback" (3.06), he sported real facial hair and liked the look, so during a recent filming hiatus he grew it again and then asked the producers for permission to sport the visage for the remainder of the season.

The Channel 4 news report on chickens is actually archive footage from WNBC, the flagship station of NBC television network, licensed to New York City. The news anchor is Sue Simmons. She was the lead female anchor at WNBC from 1980 to 2012.

There is an establishing shot of the Moondance Diner. Despite the restaurant moving to Wyoming in 2007 and suffering severe winter damage, it reopened in March 2008 and immediately made the *USA Today* list of 51 Great Burger Joints. Unfortunately, after a decline in trade due to a downturn in the local Wyoming gas-drilling industry, the diner permanently closed in March 2012.

Since many television shows use traditional pets (dogs, cats, birds, etc.), the producers opted for unorthodox pets—a chick and duck. Marta Kauffman thought the chick and duck were a "pain in the butt" but really fun.

The animals were originally slated for one episode but the writers kept coming up with ideas to use them. The producers believed they got "so much mileage out of them" that they decided to give the pets recurring appearances.

While Phoebe and Monica discuss the eatery that Pete purchased, Phoebe is sporting the same floral blouse she donned in "The One with the Jam" (3.03) when initially being stalked by Malcolm.

While watching *Baywatch*, Chandler informs the chick: "That's Yasmine Bleeth, she's a completely different kind of chick. I love you both. But in very different ways." Matthew Perry added the line to the script because he was dating Bleeth at the time. This was the reason he named the chick "Little Yasmine." The actors broke up later in the year.

3.22 "The One with the Screamer" (04.24.97)

In the cold open, Rachel is reading *How Stella Got Her Groove Back* by Terry McMillan, a classic book about reexamining life in the face of a new romance. This foreshadows the episodic plot of Rachel's perception that Ross has moved on with his life so she needs to keep up with the Joneses. Thus, after discovering that Ross is bringing a date to Joey's play, Rachel scrambles to find one, too.

Chandler is reading *The Bear Went Over the Mountain* by William Kotzwinkle, which has all the appeal of a children's book trapped inside an adult novel. A black bear finds a briefcase containing a novel and claims it as his own. He takes it to New York, has it published, and becomes a literary success. This is meant to foreshadow Kate's career opportunity and inevitable breakup with Joey.

Tommy (Ben Stiller) verbally abuses a theater patron portrayed by Peter Bonerz, the director of this episode. He is best known for starring in *The Bob Newhart Show* (1972-78) as Dr. Jerry Robinson, though he has since become a prolific director having staged 70 different TV shows and movies.

This is the final appearance of Jennifer Milmore as Lauren. The show's producers liked her performance so much they cast her as Carrie in the sitcom *Jesse*. Milmore only has 11 acting credits on her résumé.

The magna doodle is blank. At the time, no one was assigned artistic duties so anyone with an inclination could leave their mark. The early artists were both cast and crew, such as producer Todd Stevens, gaffer (electrician) Paul Swain, and leadperson (head set dresser) Scott Bruza.

This is the last appearance of Dina Meyer as Kate Miller. She began her career with a recurring role on *Beverly Hills, 90210* from 1993 to 1994, before landing a female lead role opposite Keanu Reeves in the 1995 film *Johnny Mnemonic*. She was also Detective Allison Kerry in the *Saw* film franchise.

3.23 "The One with Ross's Thing" (05.01.97)

When Ross enters Joey's apartment, the freezer door is ajar. This was a mistake by a crew member after a scene break. The set refrigerator was fully functional and always used by the cast and crew. In this instance, a crew member failed to close the door after retrieving a frozen treat.

The magna doodle is blank. Paul Swain was not officially designated as the artist until Season 4.

Phoebe's burnt-orange t-shirt with a sunflower design is from the French fashion house Morgan. She also wore the top in "The One with the Princess Leia Fantasy" (3.01).

Phoebe visits Firehouse Engine Company 5 to break up with Vince, but first she speaks with a fireman played by Douglas Looper. He is the stand-in for Matt LeBlanc.

Kevin McDonald portrays Guru Saj. He is a Canadian actor and comedian best known as a member of the comedy troupe The Kids in the Hall, who have appeared together in a number of television, film and stage productions, most notably the TV series *The Kids in the Hall* (1988-95). He also played Pastor Dave in *That '70s Show*.

The actors who portrayed Phoebe's boyfriends, Matt Battaglia (Vince) and Robert Gant (Jason), would subsequently appear together in *Queer as Folk*. Gant was a cast regular added in season two; Battaglia was a recurring character in seasons four and five.

3.24 "The One with the Ultimate Fighting Champion" (05.08.97)

The appearance of Billy Crystal and Robin Williams was unscripted. They were working on the WB lot and visited the *Friends* set to watch a live taping. Cocreator Kevin Bright had previously worked with both comedians so he asked the duo if they would be up for an impromptu cameo. The writers quickly sketched the outline for a scene where Tomas (Williams) discovers his wife is having an affair with Tim (Crystal).

Most of the cold opening dialogue was ad-libbed, including Matt LeBlanc's interruption, Crystal's annoyed reaction, and his comeback telling Joey to mind his own business, as well as Courteney Cox's line, "I really can't remember," at the end of the segment.

Although Robin Williams and Billy Crystal are polished comedians, their improvisation required four takes to get it in the can.

Chandler gets butt-slapped by his boss as a compliment for his job performance, much like football players express praise for one another. One of the writers had a friend who experienced the same odd workplace behavior which became the basis for this storyline.

Christine Taylor was the only actress considered for the part of Bonnie. She jumped at the opportunity. "I got the call saying, 'Hey, do you wanna do an arc on *Friends*?' I said, 'Absolutely, hands down. I don't even need to read it.'" Her acting career really picked up after her episodic performance.

While attending the fight, Ross purchases a large cup of soda (Big Gulp). This prop was a tribute to *Friends* writer Greg Malins who came to Stage 24 every day with a Big Gulp Diet Coke.

This is the last guest appearance of Jon Favreau as Pete Becker. He was vexed at how the writers crafted his character as a "sweet but geeky overgrown kid" so he demanded that Pete be made "cooler." Although the writers obliged by creating the UFC plotline, they also axed him from the show.

Due to the unanticipated early departure of Jon Favreau, the producers asked NBC for permission to produce an additional episode so they could pen a new cliffhanger season finale. Favreau was supposed to propose marriage to Monica in the finale. When he was axed, the writers came up with the storyline where Chandler tries to prove to Monica that he is boyfriend material.

3.25 "The One at the Beach" (05.15.97)

Phoebe was the first fictional character to use the acronym BFF (Best Friends Forever) on national television. The term became so popular it was added to some international dictionary databases, such as Cambridge and Oxford, and is still widely used today.

The beach house was actually a stage set filled with sand. "It took forever to get rid of all that sand on the stage," recalls set designer John Shaffner. "There's probably still sand on Stage 24."

The photographs on Phoebe Sr.'s refrigerator are personal photos from crew members.

Joey's mermaid sand figure, supposedly constructed around him as he slept, was not actually made of sand. It's a mold created by the art department and then painted to create the desired effect.

All the while Bonnie complains about sand in her hair and contemplates shaving her head, Rachel is reading *The Last Thing He Wanted* by Joan Didion, an exploration of US politics. It's the title, not the content that functions as the precursor to Rachel's plan to reunite with Ross by causing friction between him and Bonnie. Shaving Bonnie's head is phase one, and then confessing her love to Ross is phase two. Ross is truly content with Bonnie so Rachel's interference is the last thing he wanted.

After shaving her head, Bonnie is shown with a towel around her neck. Christine Taylor (Bonnie) is wearing a skullcap so the towel hides the fact that it is not attached to her neck. Rather than spending extra time to affix the cap, the producers opted to cover it with a towel. In fact, all of Bonnie's bald scenes were preshot. There wasn't enough time between takes for the makeup artist to attach a skullcap, which can takes hours, so it had to be preshot without an audience.

The Season 3 finale ends with a cliffhanger—Ross must decide whether to date Bonnie or Rachel, which is represented by two bedroom doors he is standing between in the hallway. The producers were in a similar dilemma. At the time this episode was written, they had no idea which woman he would pick so they waited until the summer hiatus to decide.

Season 4: 1997-98

4.01 "The One with the Jellyfish" (09.25.97)

Nearly all the hairstyles changed since the Season 3 finale, even though this installment takes place on the same weekend. Rachel returned to a light brunette with blonde highlights, a look she keeps for two seasons. Ross' hair is longer and has more body, while Chandler's hair is somewhat longer, especially on the sides, and tinted a lighter shade. Meanwhile, Teri Garr (Phoebe Sr.) has a shorter, poofier bob.

Courteney Cox's new hairdo was the only style that raised an objection from the show's producers. She arrived on the set with a sleek bob and streaks in her hair from a role in *Scream 2*. The producers asked Cox to dye her hair but did not require her to wear a wig. For continuity, they had her wear a hair topper styled in a back bun. This served as a transition to the next episode where her bob debuts.

Two scenes—Joey's big hole on the beach and Monica's jellyfish sting—were filmed at Leo Carrillo State Park along the Pacific Coast Highway near Malibu, California. Only the three relevant costars traveled to the beach. The other beachgoers are bystanders, not paid extras.

In the beach scene, where Monica and Chandler are looking down to talk to Joey, the blue sky with clouds is a painted backdrop. This segment was filmed on Stage 24 with the actors on a platform.

Monica and Chandler's monologue of the jellyfish incident was homage to the film noir genre, known for themes of pessimism, fatalism and menace. The term was originally coined by a group of French critics to describe American thriller or detective films made in the period from 1944 to 1954 and the work of directors such as Orson Welles, Fritz Lang and Billy Wilder.

Rachel's bedroom contains a film noir poster over the headboard. This wall poster was included in the scene to juxtapose the jellyfish monologue. The bedroom poster debuted in "The One Where Dr. Ramoray Dies" (2.18). It's a print of Kirk Douglas and Lizabeth Scott from *I Walk Alone* (1947).

After Ross and Rachel have their fight and he storms out, Rachel states, "Just so you know. It's *not* that common, it *doesn't* happen to every guy, and it *is* a big deal!" This is a reference to premature ejaculation. The original line was, "Well, one time, when you prematurely ejaculated, I told you it was okay and it wasn't." The writers then molded it from there. This joke is a direct nod to "the juice box moment" in "The One Where Ross and Rachel...You Know" (2.15).

4.02 "The One with the Cat" (10.02.97)

The plotline of a stray cat being Phoebe's reincarnated mother was inspired by Marta Kauffman's life. She pitched the idea shortly after her mother passed away and it was not just a fantastical concept, it reflected real feelings she experienced at the time. The pitch should have been shot down at the first table read, but nobody felt comfortable saying "No" to her under the circumstances.

The yellow cupboards above Monica's refrigerator were lowered and widened in Season 4. Since the kitchen was getting a makeover, the set designer wanted to make the area above the refrigerator more visible. The new cupboard backdrop was designed for better product placement. Since the series was starting to get serious interest from corporate sponsors, the showrunners decided to make the set more accommodating.

In Monica's apartment, the 1950s Westinghouse refrigerator is replaced with a 1950s International Harvester, rounded top with copper-colored decorative strip beneath the door handle and extending across the door.

Monica has a bob haircut. Although this style was created for a movie role, Courteney Cox was jealous of all the attention Jennifer Aniston was receiving for her haircuts so she frequently tried new hairstyles in an effort to create media buzz about herself.

The first time the burglar exits the apartment with a boom box, the magna doodle reads "Spam to the world!" After the apartment burglary, it reads "Thanks for all your stuff!"

The home burglary storyline was written so the set decorator could replace the black recliners. According to Mikel Neiers, the director of photography, the chairs were like black holes for lighting on the set. "The black in the original chairs would absorb more light than the objects near them on the set, making them more difficult to set lights for," explained producer Todd Stevens. "Apparently the crew tried to make them work, but ultimately they had to be replaced."

At the end of the episode a title card is inscribed "Dedicated to the memory of Dorothy Kauffman." She is Marta Kauffman's mother who passed away in September.

4.03 "The One with the 'Cuffs" (10.09.97)
Ross is the only character who isn't intricately involved in a narrative. The writers didn't want a fourth story and couldn't think of a way to incorporate him into the other characters' plots.

Some sources state the exterior establishing shot used as the Gellers' home is the same residence for Tony Soprano's mother in *The Sopranos*. This is false. Although close in appearance, the Gellers' home doesn't have the gable facing the road.

The magna doodle drawing has a big smiley face with two eyes, thick eyebrows, button nose and rosy cheeks. The message board is now attached to the wall on the right side of the entry door.

The encyclopedia salesman is played by Penn Jillette, of Penn and Teller fame, a pair of magicians and entertainers headlining in Las Vegas at the Rio. FYI: The ring finger on his left hand has a red nail. When Jillette first began performing, his mother told him to get a manicure because people would be looking at his hands. The red fingernail is in memory of her.

Joanna's office contains a secret nude photograph. In the wooden cabinet with glass doors, on the second shelf from the top, there is a framed photo of a topless woman. The picture is visible after Chandler retrieves his pants from a wall hook and utters the words "I'll make something up."

Rachel offers to make Chandler a legend—this generation's Milton Berle (1908–2002). Berle was a comedian and actor who married four times and purportedly had a large penis, hence, her comment about boosting Chandler's reputation with the ladies.

Central Perk's back wall features a neon light of children in a circle. The piece returned after a lengthy two-year hiatus in storage. It was the original artwork in the pilot.

4.04 "The One with the Ballroom Dancing" (10.16.97)
The writers included dialogue about rent control to address TV critics who complained that Monica could never afford her expansive New York apartment on a waitress salary. The *Friends* creative team were mostly from New York and familiar with rent control.

Michael Hagerty, the building superintendent (Mr. Treeger), knew Matthew Perry long before they worked together on *Friends*. They both frequented the Formosa bar in Santa Monica, separately, but would often spend time chatting. Hagerty referred to Perry as being "precocious but very interesting."

An often used transition clip features Washington Square Arch. It is a marble Roman triumphal arch in Washington Square Park, in the Greenwich Village neighborhood of Lower Manhattan. Designed by architect Stanford White in 1892, it commemorates the centennial of George Washington's 1789 inauguration as President of the United States, and forms the southern terminus of Fifth Avenue.

The transition clip to the bank scene spotlights St. Paul's Chapel, an Episcopal parish for Trinity Church, at 209 Broadway. Built in 1766, it is the oldest surviving church building in Manhattan, and one of the nation's finest examples of Late Georgian church architecture. When St. Paul's Chapel remained unscathed after the September 11, 2001 attack and collapse of the World Trade Center behind it, the chapel was subsequently nicknamed "The Little Chapel That Stood."

When Chandler and Ross attempt to close their bank accounts, there is a red, white and blue flag behind the banker's desk. Many sources claim it's the California state flag (where the show's taped) and not the New York state flag (where the show's set). FYI: It's the New York City flag.

EJ Callahan, the massage client (Mr. Simon) who enters the room with Phoebe's boss, is the same actor who portrays Al Zebooker, the guy who eats paper in "The One Where Estelle Dies" (10.15).

4.05 "The One with Joey's New Girlfriend" (10.30.97)

In the cold opening, Rachel is reading *Anthem: An American Road Story* by Kristin Hahn and Shainee Gabel. Jennifer Aniston unabashedly promoted the book (released August 1, 1997) because it was coauthored by her friend Kristin Hahn. *Anthem* describes the authors' road trip, including encounters with actor Robert Redford and writers Hunter S. Thompson and John Irving.

This is the first appearance of Kathy, played by Paget Brewster. At the casting audition, Brewster believed she was the "runty alternative" who didn't have a chance at getting the part. Matthew Perry later told her that the producers knew she was right for the role the moment she called herself a "runt."

Casting the role of Kathy was difficult. "We held auditions. It was kind of like casting for the pilot," Kevin Bright said. "We looked and looked, and she came in at the end and ended up being terrific."

Brewster spent her first two weeks working on the show believing she would be fired and the part would be recast with a better looking actress. She appeared in a total of six episodes. Brewster is best known as Emily Prentiss on *Criminal Minds*.

Kathy was introduced to create conflict between the roommates and develop a plotline that tested Joey and Chandler's friendship.

Ross debuts an alternative means of using the swear finger—the pinky-side double fist bump. Each character (except Phoebe) used the gesture at least once. The hand signal was created to circumvent network censors. It also became an in-joke that only *Friends* fans would understand.

The magna doodle has cartoon drawings of a duck, tree, and cow (uttering "Moo").

Joey, Chandler, and Kathy visit the Irish bar Nicky St. Hubbins, in Manhattan. The bar name was used for the short-lived four-episode sitcom *Misery Loves Company* (1995) where four unlucky-in-love buddies hang out at a sports bar operated by its namesake. In the TV drama *Castle*, the same stock footage was utilized to represent McCormack's Pub & Restaurant in New York.

4.06 "The One with the Dirty Girl" (11.06.97)

This episode is the acting debut of Rebecca Romijn (Cheryl aka Dirty Girl). She went on to portray Mystique in the *X-Men* films. Her only other acting role was appearing in the music video "Please Don't Go Girl" (#10, 1988) by New Kids on the Block.

Chandler is holding *The Velveteen Rabbit*, which he wants to wrap as a gift for Kathy. This is the first time the book is cited, which is Kathy's favorite. There is no mention of it being Chandler's favorite; that fact is later revealed in "The One with the Halloween Party" (8.06).

The Velveteen Rabbit by Margery Williams is essential to the love triangle subplot. The book plotline involves a rabbit toy that comes alive thanks to the love of a child. It's a metaphorical harbinger of romantic developments between the *Friends* characters, i.e., although Kathy is dating Joey, she only comes alive with the love of Chandler.

Prior to *Friends*, Brewster had only one acting credit so her first day on set was fretful. She was intimidated because the cast was so famous and it was the biggest television show in the country. The actress ended up hiding in her dressing room. "It was my first real acting job. I remember so little because I was so scared," Brewster recalled.

In the scene where Monica and Phoebe cater a funeral wake, two different high-rises are utilized for the establishing shots of Mrs. Burkart's condominium. The editor wanted to show a notable time lapse by incorporating a dusk clip, but he didn't have stock footage for the same high-rise.

Rachel is doing a crossword puzzle in Central Perk and joyously exclaims, "I did it! Oh, I finished it! I did it all by myself! And there's nobody to hug." Gunther quickly sprints from the backroom and falls flat on his face behind the sofa. Actor James Michael Tyler recalls the scene: "There was a pad there, but I had to take a dive. And the night before, I had fallen and cracked a rib on the side I had to fall on, so after about five takes of that, that was a little bit painful."

The magna doodle reads "Yo Fuff ... Where's G-Daddy? signed LSB." Although meaningless to viewers, it's a personal message among crew members.

4.07 "The One Where Chandler Crosses the Line" (11.13.97)
The uncut DVD features an extra subplot where Rachel starts dining out by herself. She enjoys it so much that she blows off a date with a doctor. Later, she reconsiders dating him, but he is no longer interested after he observes her dining alone. Chandler concurs with the doctor, and once stated, "I totally judge any woman I see eating alone [because] there is obviously something wrong with her if she is eating by herself."

Ross is not actually playing music on the keyboard. The instrument's sound effect was added in postproduction to correspond with his key strokes. Versions of his "wordless sound poems" were piped to the audience so they could understand the scene.

When Ross performs his "music" in the apartment, Jennifer Aniston cannot contain her laughter so she covers her mouth with her hand. She was laughing in every take, so it could not be edited.

Chandler and the duck are watching *Baywatch* with a clip of Yasmine Bleeth jogging on the beach. He then comments to the duck: "Yeah, I know what you're thinking. Yes, yes, your breasts are just as firm and juicy." Matthew Perry added the dialogue to the script and then specifically requested a clip of Bleeth be shown because they were dating at the time.

Building superintendent Mr. Treeger leaves a message on the magna doodle: "Clean up the duck feathers in hallway! Treager." First, Treeger would not misspell his own name. There is no "a" in Treeger. Second, in "The One with the Ballroom Dancing" (4.04), Mr. Treeger insinuates that pets are prohibited in the building. Thus, he would not condone this rule violation (unless he is still grateful for Joey giving him dance lessons).

After Chandler and Kathy kiss, the magna doodle changes to "I Love You, Man!" with a cartoon drawing of Chandler. The message expresses his guilt and foreshadows the test of his and Joey's friendship in the next episode.

The creators anticipated a longer story arc between Joey and Kathy but quickly realized the characters lacked romantic chemistry, compared to Monica and Richard or Phoebe and Duncan, so the writers planned an expedited breakup. The female costars lobbied the producers to extend Brewster's contract but the decision had already been made.

4.08 "The One with Chandler in a Box" (11.20.97)

Secret Santa was a huge event in the *Friends* office. Every Christmas the writers had a drawing; it was one of the fun highlights of their year. And that's how it became part of this episode.

When Joey goes into Central Perk and asks Gunther if he has seen Chandler, the glass pastry dome has a russet potato in it. In early years of the show, the *Friends* crew had a little rag doll they used to hide in and around some of the sets as a personal Easter egg hunt. In the latter years, they used props (potato, M&M doll, etc.) as a challenge to the crew to find.

The writers debated whether to revisit the Richard Burke saga. David Crane thought a story using Richard's son was an exciting twist. The problem was how to introduce the subject. "We spent a lot of weeks talking about how you get her attracted to Richard's son and have it not be completely gross," Crane explained. "And then we hired Michael Vartan." The actor is best recognized as Michael Vaughn in *Alias* (2001-06).

While filming the entire Thanksgiving scene in Monica's apartment, Matthew Perry was actually inside the box. He didn't seem to mind it too much even though he spent many hours entombed. Before doing the confinement scene, Kevin Bright had to be positive that Perry wasn't claustrophobic and that he would agree to do it for the entire time.

A tremendous amount of food is prepared for holiday installments. Every time a scene is reset for the next take, all the food on the table is replaced. Kevin Bright joked, "Usually there is enough food to feed a small army." After the show, the leftovers were given to a homeless shelter.

Caterers specializing in on-camera food are hired to cook the meal. It is heated in ovens on the soundstage, and then the prop department sets the plates and table. The actors actually eat the food so it must be edible; their facial expressions must correspond to the scene, not to the taste of the food.

The final segment—where Chandler chases after Kathy—originally involved a giant train station with a grand finale where he finds her and they reunite. After realizing the cost associated with such an endeavor, the producers opted for the cheapest option—talking about it in the apartment.

4.09 "The One Where They're Going to Party!" (12.11.97)

The magna doodle is uncharacteristically blank.

The head of the hiring committee (Mr. Posner) is played by Richard Fancy, who is best known as Mr. Lippman in *Seinfeld*. He also had recurring roles in *It's Garry Shandling's Show* as network supervisor Mr. Stravely, and *The Wonder Years* as Kevin Arnold's high school principal, Dr. Valenti.

When Phoebe is looking at the *Chelsea Reporter*, Monica says her review is on the back page. Phoebe is reading the front page of a folded newspaper, but instead of going to the back page, she flips the newspaper and starts reading the bottom of the front page.

As Rachel is packing her desk, the background wall has a poster for Tag watches. This set dressing became the inspiration for naming her assistant in the seventh season.

Joanna's death did not go over well with the audience. When the scene was filmed and her death was announced, the audience went silent and did not laugh at anything the rest of the night. David Crane acknowledged that they didn't do death well in the series, except the grandmother's demise in "The One Where Nana Dies Twice" (1.08).

4.10 "The One with the Girl from Poughkeepsie" (12.18.97)

One of Ross' girlfriends lives in Poughkeepsie, New York. The writers chose the city as a shoutout to Lisa Kudrow (Phoebe) who is an alumna of Vassar College in Poughkeepsie.

Phoebe complains that "Rachel" doesn't rhyme with anything good, so Monica tells her that Rachel's dad used to call her Pumpkin. This word actually has fewer rhymes than "Rachel." FYI: The only word in the English language with no rhyme is "orange."

Monica is supposedly employed at Allesandro's but the establishing shot is Blue Lou's Rhythm, Ribs & Blues, 1510 E. Carson St., Southside Flats, Pittsburgh, Pennsylvania.

The restaurant scene where Joey repeatedly pats Monica's breast, claiming her apron is still smoking from the kitchen fire, was choreographed with the director, and Courteney Cox was fine with the physical contact.

The magna doodle image has a Christmas tree with the text "Our Christmas Tree" and underneath is "Put Present Here" with arrows pointing downward.

The woman on the train claims Montreal is "just a two-hour ferry ride to Nova Scotia." Truthfully, no passenger ferry service exists between Montreal and Nova Scotia (they are connected by road). Regardless, the trip would take much longer than 2 hours (e.g., to Amherst is 90 minutes by plane, 11 hours by car, and over 18 hours by train).

When Ross is talking to the Canadian woman, they are supposed to be in Montreal but a reflecting blue light in the train window indicates "Penn Station" which would never be a sign in a Montreal train depot. Penn Station is the main intercity railroad station in New York City and the busiest in the Western Hemisphere, serving more than 600,000 passengers per weekday as of 2019.

4.11 "The One with Phoebe's Uterus" (01.08.98)

In October 1997, Lisa Kudrow told the showrunners that she and her husband, Michel Stern, were expecting their first child. At the time, about one-third of the episodes had been filmed and other narratives were projected through December, which is the reason Phoebe's surrogacy plan was not revealed until January 8, 1998 (in this episode).

When Lisa Kudrow told the creators about her pregnancy, they embraced the life event. "They said, 'Look, we hate those shows where the actor is pregnant and then everyone is pretending they're not. You're going to be seven months pregnant by the time we're done so it's going to be hard to hide so let's just come up with a storyline,'" she recalled.

The writers had lengthy discussions on how to explain Phoebe's pregnancy. She wasn't dating anyone so there wasn't enough time to introduce a love interest, and the creators did not want to have a baby complicating the series. They wanted the pregnancy to be "huge, like comedically funny" so they came up with her having triplets, because it had never been done on TV, and they liked the idea of her carrying her brother's children.

In the museum lunchroom scenes, Sherri Shepherd plays a tour guide. She costarred in *Suddenly Susan* (1997-2000). After the sitcom was canceled, she took a temp job as a legal secretary working for David Schwimmer's father.

After being cast, Shepherd sent out a promotional postcard to her friends and industry colleagues with a photo and the message: "*Friends* finally got some color this week," a jab at the executive producers for the show's lack of racial diversity.

Women's health sites claim Monica's seven erogenous zones include the ears, lips, neck, breasts, buttocks, inner thighs and vagina. Chandler's surprised reaction is most likely to the ears.

After Ross, Joey, and a coworker remove their coats in the lunchroom, three museum employees reveal their names (Ted, Andrew and Scott), which is a nod to *Friends* writers Ted Cohen, Andrew Reich and Scott Silveri.

In the tag scene, Rachel is reading *Anthem: An American Road Story*, which is the same tome she peruses in the opening scene of "The One with Joey's New Girlfriend" (4.05).

4.12 "The One with the Embryos" (01.15.98)

According to David Crane, the story arc of Phoebe carrying Frank and Alice's babies was considered "risky." When the storyline was first discussed, their primary concern was whether it was "too crazy." The showrunners worried where to draw the line regarding Phoebe's eccentricities.

The chick and duck were utilized "as a spark" for the main plot of this episode but the script was not written as a means of getting rid of the fowl. The pets were just the setup for the contest. The staff writers loved the flexibility that the pets provided for the show. They would simply appear and disappear as needed for a comedy bit.

The producers found it difficult to get Giovanni Ribisi to reprise the role as Frank Jr. on a long-term basis because he had numerous movie commitments. A similar situation occurred with Debra Jo Rupp after she was named a costar in the fledgling FOX sitcom *That '70s Show*.

The idea for using trivia questions to decide the apartment contest winner was partially based on a real-life game that writer Seth Kurland watched his friends play.

According to Kevin Bright, the apartment contest is one of the most favorite events on *Friends*. It was actually turned into a board game in Europe. Some fourth season DVDs included the interactive game "Who Knows Whom Best?—Ross's Ultimate Challenge." It utilized clips from the show for the answers, allowed viewers to choose a team (boys or girls), and even had participants call the coin toss.

The "Miss Chanandler Bong" joke was inspired by an incident from Kurland's childhood when his surname was misspelled on an address label.

For the longest time, the staff writers could not decide on a name for the gay burlesque show. According to David Crane, it changed "about a million times." On the evening of filming, the writers continued to pitch different ideas to generate a better response from the audience. They finally settled on Viva Las Gaygas. This is a play on words from the 1964 movie *Viva Las Vegas* starring Elvis Presley and Ann-Margret. The film is regarded by fans and film critics as one of Presley's best.

The tag scene where Rachel opens a kitchen drawer, only to be aghast at what's inside, was based on the writers room. "There's a drawer in our writers room that has things in it that have been there since the second season," David Crane candidly admitted. "I'm afraid to open that drawer."

In 2009, "The One with the Embryos" ranked No. 21 on *TV Guide*'s list of TV's Top 100 Episodes of All Time. In a 2018 oral history, *TV Guide* voted it the series' best episode: "*Friends* at its peak, a lightning-in-a-bottle gem." Courteney Cox and Matt LeBlanc both picked this episode as their favorite.

4.13 "The One with Rachel's Crush" (01.29.98)

Dana deVally directed this installment. She usually worked as a technical coordinator, which is a job handling reports, customer quotes, and technical documents, as well as communicating scheduling changes and relevant infrastructure shifts to staff.

While sitting in Central Perk, the gang converses about celebrities who fell in love while starring together in movies. This was written for Courteney Cox's benefit. In April 1996 she met and fell in love with David Arquette on the set of *Scream*.

Rachel was intentionally demoted at Bloomingdale's so the writers could introduce Mr. Waltham, her new supervisor. In the next installment, he wants Rachel to entertain his niece, Emily, who is slated to be Ross' latest fiancée.

Tate Donovan (Joshua) was initially considered for a lengthier story arc because, at the time, he and Jennifer Aniston were engaged to be married. They had been romantic for three years. However, by the time Donovan received the *Friends* offer, the couple was in the midst of a breakup.

The theater lobby has several theatrical posters, real and fictional. *Dreamgirls* debuted in 1981 and *Nunsense* in 1985. The fictional play *The Milkman is Coming* is meant to presage Kathy's infidelity. It's an allusion to the old gag involving the housewife having an affair with the milkman.

The origin of Joey's famous pickup line is unknown. According to David Crane, it was someone in the writers room, but "it wasn't introduced as a catchphrase. It was a line, and then it became a catchphrase as it went along." It ranked No. 4 in *TV Guide*'s 2005 list of TV's 20 Top Catchphrases.

Matt LeBlanc confessed that during the *Friends* years he used Joey's pickup line at the bars. When his daughter was younger she started saying: "How are you doing?" He tried to tell her it's "How you doin'?" but she told him that "No, in fact, it should be 'How are you doing?'"

As Monica is twirling in circles atop the floor sanding machine, a stagehand is behind the door holding the cord to make sure it properly wraps around her.

Actress Paget Brewster didn't want Kathy to be written out of the series for cheating on Chandler. She tried to persuade the creators to have her character tour in a play out of country. The showrunners were not persuaded by her plea and decided to stick with the original narrative as written.

4.14 "The One with Joey's Dirty Day" (02.05.98)

Phoebe is supposed to be one month pregnant but it is obvious from her girth, mainly sitting by the foosball table in the cold opening, that she is quite pregnant. In real life, Lisa Kudrow was five months pregnant at the time of filming in early January 1998.

Phoebe is holding a box of prop crackers designed to connote Premium saltines. Many sources indicate this is blatant product placement but it is actually shrewd subterfuge by the art department for creating a false association with a well-respected brand.

The magna doodle image is inexplicably removed from the door in Joey and Chandler's apartment. This is the first (and only) time it is missing from the apartment since its debut in "The One with the Hypnosis Tape" (3.18). The resident message board artist accidentally left the prop in his office.

Joey's new apartment has a 1920s Bieres de Chartres (Chartres Beers) wall poster on the secret-closet door. In his old abode, the poster was barely visible hanging to the left of his bedroom door. Created by obscure artist AK Girenel, it depicts a waiter drinking the beer he is supposed to be delivering to patrons. Chartres is a commune and capital of the Eure-et-Loir department in France. It is 56 miles (90 km) southwest of Paris. The historic city is famous for its Gothic cathedral, mostly erected between 1193 and 1250.

This episode marks the first appearance of Helen Baxendale as Emily Waltham. She will meet, have a whirlwind romance, and then marry Ross all within 10 episodes. The staff writers anticipated a lengthier story arc as they mapped out the season but Baxendale's unexpected pregnancy forced them to accelerate the relationship timeline.

The strip club scene was preshot without a studio audience because one of the dancers performed topless.

4.15 "The One with All the Rugby" (02.26.98)

This is the last episode directed by James Burrows. He directed 15 *Friends* installments beginning with the pilot episode in 1994.

Janice became such a fan favorite that the showrunners kept her appearances secret. They wanted her unexpected entrance to electrify the crowd so they could capture the uproarious applause on tape. "It was sort of a rock star moment," she said. "They would keep me hidden—I could barely come down to get a donut. I had to stay in my dressing room until the last moment and then they'd secretly move me from behind the set to the right spot and they'd keep a black screen so the audience couldn't see me until I made my first entrance. I will never have anything like that again. It was incredible."

Establishing shots for the museum (US Custom House) and Allesandro's (Blue Lou's)

In Monica's new apartment, Rachel is holding a Jones soda bottle. In a shameless act of product placement, Jennifer Aniston purposely positions the bottle after being advised by a crew member to turn it to face the camera.

After Chandler and Janice enter Monica's apartment, Phoebe is reading *What to Expect When You're Expecting*. The producers wanted viewers less familiar with the sitcom to know that Phoebe was pregnant, not gaining weight unexpectedly.

The magna doodle reads "Nice Nails Chandler!" referring to the cold open scene where he receives a manicure.

Monica is reading *Like a Hole in the Head* by Jen Banbury as a commentary on her odd obsession—she has to solve the light switch mystery like she needs a hole in the head. The book was released just days before this installment was filmed, and can be seen in several *Friends* episodes. Some sources falsely claim the author as James Hadley Chase from his 1970 novel of the same name.

This episode marks the end of Janice and Chandler's on-off relationship. Actress Maggie Wheeler often cites this episode as one of her favorites. "I have many favorite memories, moments and episodes—15 Yemen Road. I love that episode."

The tag scene is a clever spoof of the popular 1960s sitcom *I Dream of Jeannie*. Phoebe believes her blink and head bob (à la Jeannie) is causing the television to malfunction.

4.16 "The One with the Fake Party" (03.19.98)

While filming *Friends*, Helen Baxendale was also costarring as Rachel Bradley in the UK dramedy *Cold Feet* (often regarded as the British *Friends*). Her pregnancy during Series 4 meant that Bradley's infertility had to be abandoned and the rest of the arc rewritten. Similarly, in *Friends*, Baxendale's pregnancy forced the producers to rewrite the ending for Season 4 and reformulate Season 5.

Patsy Kensit was originally approached to play the role of Emily but turned it down. She blames her decision on being a hopeless romantic (at the time she was married to Oasis frontman Liam Gallagher). Kensit admits she was so desperate to make their turbulent relationship work that she turned down the biggest opportunity of her life.

The Central Perk artwork features a Burton Morris original, *Coffee Break* (large cup of coffee with steam rising above), which was specially made for the coffeehouse milieu.

Joey struggles to fasten Rachel's zipper and then repeatedly brushes her black dress, touching her hips and ass. This was rehearsed with the director and Aniston approved the physical contact.

In a DVD extra, when the gang is playing spin the bottle, during Chandler's spin, the bottle lands on him and he says, "Story of my life." He spins again and the bottle lands on Joshua (which means they are supposed to kiss) so Chandler retorts: "Story of my father's life."

Above the headboard in Chandler's bedroom is the baseball print *America's Greatest GAME 1931*. The set decorator chose the photograph as juxtaposition for the game that Rachel is playing to win Joshua's affection. This print will later appear in Rachel's office at Ralph Lauren.

Rachel and Joshua nearly kiss in the hallway and then seek privacy in her apartment. In real life, actors Jennifer Aniston and Tate Donovan were in the middle of a protracted breakup which made their romantic scenes insufferable.

4.17 "The One with the Free Porn" (03.26.98)

In the cold opening, Joey and Chandler are watching the porn movie *On Trial 2: Oral Arguments* (1991). Several scenes are repeated throughout the episode because Warner Bros. didn't want to pay extra for airing multiple segments.

In the opening scene after credits, porn legend Ron Jeremy has a cameo in one of the adult films where a woman is putting shaving cream on his chest.

Phoebe's ob/gyn is Dr. Oberman. The surname was used in many episodes as a tribute to Rona Oberman, a friend of the creators.

Chandler mentions seeing *In & Out... and In Again*, which is a porn parody of the 1997 comedy film *In & Out* starring Tom Selleck, who played Richard Burke in *Friends*.

When Chandler and Joey enter the apartment to watch cartoons, Monica is sitting on the couch and reading *Like a Hole in the Head* by Jen Banbury. This was meant as a commentary on the female perspective regarding free porn. Her belief is that the guys need porn like they need a hole in their heads.

Phoebe's demonstration of a knife cutting an aluminum can is homage to Ginsu knife infomercials which first aired in 1978. The *Friends* writers were infomercial fanatics so they included the product in the narrative. The brand gained notoriety in 1993 after Lorena Bobbitt used a Ginsu kitchen knife to sever her husband's penis while he slept.

As Phoebe discusses her relaxi-taxi idea, Chandler and Monica are cuddling on a club chair, even though they are not dating and the sofa is unoccupied. This was purposely choreographed to foreshadow the couple hooking up in London.

There is product placement for Toblerone in anticipation of the season finale in London.

Due to the success of *Friends*, a porn movie was made to parody the show. *Friends: A XXX Parody* (2009) has a fountain scene title sequence with a catchy theme song ("these friends go all the way / these friends love to screw") and Rachelle (Rachel) even flashes her breasts. The movie parodies several episodic themes: (1) Russ (Ross) enters Canoga Perk (Central Perk) to proclaim his wife is lesbian, then Carol and Sandra (Susan) want a three-way; (2) Moanica (Monica) and Sandler (Chandler) are getting married and doing it all over the place; (3) Freebie (Phoebe) and Joe (Joey) have sex; and (4) the girls plan a bachelorette party where the stripper is Naked Guy (Ugly Naked Guy).

4.18 "The One with Rachel's New Dress" (04.02.98)

Monica only appears in two scenes. The writers could not come up with a legitimate way to insert her into the storylines so she was relegated to a supporting role.

Joey declares that Chandler is a stupid name—it's kind of like chandelier, but it's not. Since the character Chandler was named after a friend of the showrunners, they hoped he didn't take offense when Joey listed multiple reasons "Chandler" is a terrible name.

Joshua's father (Mr. Burgin) is played by John Bennett Perry, who is Matthew Perry's dad. They didn't share a scene together so most viewers never noticed the resemblance.

In Joshua's parents' condominium there is a bust on a side table in the corner of the living room. In a few shots the eyes glow red, but only when Joshua and Rachel are in the same frame. This was a prank by one of the crew members. Much like their game of hiding props, crew members enjoyed clowning around with one another by changing the set dressing to see if anyone would notice.

In Central Perk, the Tiffany firefly table lamp behind the bar is the same fixture present at the London wedding reception in "The One After Ross Says Rachel" (5.01). However, this is an entirely different lamp than the one utilized in the title sequence and Central Perk decor in Seasons 1 and 2.

Tate Donovan found it rather challenging to film romantic scenes. As he recalled, it was tricky to act like he was falling in love when he and Aniston we're actually breaking up.

4.19 "The One with All the Haste" (04.09.98)

Joey's neighbor sings "Morning's Here" using the melody from Chuck Mangione's jazz-fusion hit "Feel So Good" (#4, 1978). The staff writers often jammed to the song on their boom box during sunset. Sometimes their dinner order would arrive at the same time so they would launch into a Mangione-inspired song: "The food is here, the food is here." Their ad-libbed lyrics inspired the "Morning's Here" song for this episode.

The magna doodle has the phrase "Whasup!? Bro?" This was a popular expression in the late 1990s that achieved international recognition after the release of a Budweiser television ad. The spot first aired during *Monday Night Football* on December 20, 1999. The three-year campaign ran worldwide and changed pop culture. The phrase itself is a slurred variation of "What's up?"

Ross' newly pierced ear is not actually pierced. David Schwimmer is wearing a clip-on earring. FYI: His left ear was pierced for his high school senior year class photo in 1984.

Phoebe uses the same magician's deck of cards that Rachel used in "The One with All the Poker" (1.18).

The stagehands spent two days moving furniture back and forth to know exactly where everything was going to hang, what pieces had to be moved, etc. On the night of filming, they had to perform the entire apartment switch during a 30-minute wardrobe change.

After Ross announces that he and Emily are getting married, Phoebe asks "Oh, are you pregnant, too?" This was an inside joke for Helen Baxendale (Emily) who was over two months pregnant.

In the original script, Rachel proposed marriage to Joshua immediately after Ross and Emily became engaged. After shooting the first engagement sequence, the audience was remarkably doleful so the producers moved Rachel's scene to the next episode to give fans sufficient "recovery time."

4.20 "The One with All the Wedding Dresses" (04.16.98)

During a late-night writing session, someone told Greg Malins that his fiancée was on the phone so he immediately exited to speak to her. After he left the room, staff writer Michael Borkow declared, "Huh. Wapah!" All the writers turned to him, confused. He responded, "You know, he's running out to take a phone call. He's whipped. Wapah!" This became Chandler's bizarre sound effect.

Emily's bridal gown is different from the one she wears at her wedding. That's because the nuptials were actually filmed five weeks later and Helen Baxendale's pregnancy and expanding girth made the dress unusable. Since the series costumer did not have time to make alterations because she was designing all the other bridal attire, an alternate gown was chosen for Emily.

Since Lisa Kudrow was nearly seven months pregnant, finding a wedding dress to fit wasn't easy. Series costumer Debra McGuire did not have time to design a dress so she scoured thrift shops in the LA area to no avail. But then she got lucky. Casting director Leslie Litt's mother and sister owned Lili Bridals on Ventura Boulevard and McGuire was able to acquire a suitable dress at their boutique.

Thea Mann, the sleep clinic worker, is Lisa Kudrow's cousin. She is known for *Celebrity Name Game* and *Bounce*. Prior to acting, she worked at Stephanie's eatery in New York.

Rachel is wearing a wedding dress similar to the one she sported in "The Pilot" (1.01) because the series costumer was unable to find the original gown in the WB costume warehouse. "We had no idea that *Friends* was going to be a huge hit," Debra McGuire explained. "It would've been great to have multiples of that dress. ... But I mean, how could we have known?"

This is the final appearance of Tate Donovan as Joshua Burgin. The original story arc had a season-ending cliffhanger where both couples, Ross-Emily and Rachel-Joshua, are engaged to be married but only one follows through. Once the creators discovered Jennifer Aniston and Tate Donovan were no longer dating, he was axed from the show and a new cliffhanger was formulated.

4.21 "The One with the Invitation" (04.23.98)

This is the first clip show on *Friends*. The writers wanted to focus their attention on the season finale so they duped their audience by pretending to produce a real episode.

When Ross and Emily walk into his apartment, the wall poster is *Russian Thinker* by A. Lebedinsky and S. Shukhman, two relatively unknown artists. It depicts a young man studying with the tagline: "To build you need to know, to know you have to learn." The 1958 print was made during key Soviet events: launch of the Sputnik satellite (1957) and its first manned orbital flight (1961).

Due to her pregnancy, Helen Baxendale asked the showrunners to film her first seven episodic appearances over a seven-week period to limit transatlantic flights. Naturally, the producers were accommodating. Afterwards, she returned to London to await taping of the season finale a month later.

According to the wedding invitation envelope, Rachel's residential address is 545 Grove St. #20, New York, NY 10001. The real-life apartment building used for the establishing shot is 90 Bedford St. (at the Grove Street intersection).

Ross addresses the invitation envelope to "Rachel Greene." In most episodes, her name is spelled Green (without an extra "e"). The writers and crew members were inconsistent in their spelling.

Throughout the series' run, Joey's living room featured the French poster *Les Mystères de New-York* (1915) presumable by Charles Tickon. Written by Pierre Decourcelle, it is a re-edited adaptation of three chapters from the American serial *The Exploits of Elaine* (1914). The French series screened weekly in theaters between December 1915 and May 1916, and his written version of the story was published in the French newspaper *Le Matin*. It was one of the first cross-promotional campaigns.

The six costars revealed a few backstage secrets about their acting propensities: (1) first to flub their lines (Kudrow), (2) biggest flirt (Aniston and Schwimmer), (3) biggest thief (Aniston), and (4) most emotional (Aniston).

Out of 236 *Friends* episodes, this installment is most often ranked as the worst.

4.22 "The One with the Worst Best Man Ever" (04.30.98)

The writers loved creating dialogue to depict Phoebe's sporadic mood swings. She was given carte blanche to say foul things to other people, which is normally a script writing faux pas, but her pregnancy made the conduct excusable.

The magna doodle reads "Big Chief Ain't Got No Fire Water" to indicate that the guys need alcohol for Ross' bachelor party. The wording also alludes to The Wild Magnolias' 1975 song "(Big Chief like Plenty of) Fire Water."

The *Friends* creators talked extensively about the struggles they had incorporating adult material into the show, given that NBC wanted to keep it family-friendly. Words such as "condom" and "nipple" were often excised from scripts, and even condom wrappers were verboten. In this installment, the producers discovered a clever way to circumvent this restriction by decorating Joey's apartment with inflated condoms.

In the uncut DVD, the tag scene in Central Perk has Ross confessing that he has his grandmother's wedding ring because presumably Monica would never need it. Monica then tells Emily the ring spent two days in a duck's colon. In syndication, the tag scene has the duck swimming in a bucket to "Sailor's Hornpipe," a traditional melody. It is a linked dance with origins in the British Royal Navy. The catchy tune was part of *Popeye* cartoons beginning in the 1930s, usually as the first part of the opening credits theme, which then segued into an instrumental of "I'm Popeye the Sailor Man."

Helen Baxendale is credited in this installment, despite only appearing in the tag scene (which is excised in syndication). The sequence was previously filmed as part of another episode. Her segment was cut so the producers would not have to pay her royalties for each syndicated airing.

4.23 "The One with Ross's Wedding, Part 1" (05.07.98)

Nearly a year prior to this installment, during the summer hiatus of 1997, the *Friends* producers were contacted by Channel 4, the British first-run broadcaster of the series, with a proposal to film an episode in London. The producers loved the idea but needed a believable storyline to justify the entire gang traveling abroad. When they decided on a wedding for Ross, they made his girlfriend a London resident visiting New York for two weeks, which commences a tornadic romance. The creators already planned on having Ross marrying the hot copy girl (Chloe) in the Season 4 finale, so the narrative only had to be tweaked a little to have it apply to Emily.

The gang stays at London Marriott, which was the actual hotel utilized by the cast and crew while filming in England. This was part of a paid promotion. The accommodations were free in exchange for promoting the hotel throughout the double-length episode.

By the time the cast left for London, Lisa Kudrow was nearly eight months pregnant so her doctor advised her not to travel. She gave birth on the day this episode originally aired in the US.

This installment was filmed in three pieces: on Stage 24 in Los Angeles, on the streets of London, and on a Wembley soundstage in front of an audience of 500 people. Each episode was filmed three times using three different audiences. People lined up for six to seven hours in the rain for a chance to see a live taping.

Joey and Chandler standing outside the London Marriott was the first scene filmed in London. They were originally going to visit McDonald's (fast food eatery) but the scene was replaced with Joey "going into the map."

Location filming was based on convenience and proximity, which included combining locations as much as possible. For example, after Joey and Chandler visit Westminster Abbey, the film crew simply moved to the other side of the landmark to shoot a scene with British royalty.

Ross and Emily's wedding was held at St. John's Church in Wapping (east London). Set designers built a fake exterior to resemble a construction site. The interior was a studio-constructed set.

The open-top double-decker bus segment involved the crew riding around London and ad-libbing bits for the camera. In back of Matt LeBlanc and Matthew Perry are Marta Kauffman (cocreator) and Adam Chase (writer), and behind them are Michael Borkow (writer), Robin Siegel (makeup artist) and Kim Harris (stand-in for Jennifer Aniston).

There was originally an entire scene where Rachel reupholsters a couch in an effort to get over Ross. "It just wasn't funny," admits writer Greg Malins. The scene was replaced with Joey's references to "London, baby!" (wordplay for the US saying, "Vegas, baby!").

British millionaire Richard Branson offered 75 first-class tickets for the cast and crew via Virgin Atlantic airline to film an episode in London, provided he could be a guest on the show. Branson was given the part of a street vendor who cajoles Joey into buying a Union Jack hat.

When selecting a celebrity cameo, the producers perused a long list of famous British people, but they wanted royalty because it's something unique to their culture. Luckily, Sarah Ferguson (Fergie) was available and willing to do it. Kevin Bright thought she was hysterical.

Chinese advertising posters used in the early 20th century

Fergie agreed to the role because her daughters, Eugenie and Beatrice, were obsessed with *Friends*. Although "coaxed into the appearance by her daughters," the brief cameo actually helped mitigate some of the animosity toward her in Britain. "At a time when Fergie-bashing had become a national pastime, *Friends* was a welcome relief," said the Duchess of York.

4.24 "The One with Ross's Wedding, Part 2" (05.07.98)

The title sequence is exclusive to this episode. It features only one shot from the original fountain scene, and the remaining footage uses clips from the double-length episode of Ross' wedding.

The housekeeper scenes were originally shot in LA using Megan Mullally (*Will & Grace*) but when June Whitfield became available, the creators had to hire her for the role.

Numerous British actors were spotlighted: June Whitfield as the housekeeper, Jennifer Saunders as Emily's stepmother (Andrea Waltham), Olivia Williams as the bridesmaid (Felicity), and Hugh Laurie as the brash passenger sitting next to Rachel on the plane.

The British actors gave guidance to the *Friends* staff writers on proper local vernacular. Naturally, the script was written from an American perspective so the dialogue had to be changed to comport with British culture. For example, in the brief scene where Mrs. Waltham hangs up on Phoebe, Jennifer Saunders changed her line from "I'm going to hang up," to "I'm going to have to cut you off."

During a restaurant scene, a drunken gentleman confuses Monica for her mother. This was based on Marta Kauffman's personal experiences. It happened to her all the time. For instance, while on vacation with Jason Alexander and his wife, Kauffman was asked if she was his mother. In addition, when in public with her teenage daughter, Kauffman was repeatedly asked if she was the grandmother.

When Monica appeared from beneath Chandler's comforter, the two actors had to hold their position for 27 seconds while waiting for the studio audience to stop howling and shouting. The big reveal was performed for three different London audiences and their reaction was the same each time. Writer Scott Silveri stated, "It was a combination of a laugh, gasp, cry and shriek."

Despite the lively audience reaction, the creators were tentative about keeping Monica and Chandler as a couple. "The fear was that we'd jump the shark," David Crane said. Marta Kauffman added, "We really did not think it would go on. We thought it might go on for a few episodes." In fact, the showrunners played it casual for several months to monitor audience reaction.

In an airplane scene, Rachel is talking to a guy holding a book. The passenger is writer Greg Malins (wearing glasses). He started working for Kevin Bright as a runner when he was 17 years old. It's an entry-level job helping out wherever needed; it can vary from office administration or crowd control to cleaning up locations and public relations.

On the plane, Malins is holding the book *Like a Hole in the Head* by Jen Banbury. The title is meant to signify the consequence of Rachel's plan to ruin Ross' wedding.

Originally, it wasn't scripted for Ross to say the wrong name during his wedding vows. The idea arose during rehearsal when the actors were running lines. David Schwimmer said, "Rachel, the taxi's here," instead of his given line: "Emily, the taxi's here." At that moment, writer Greg Malins turned to David Crane and said, "That's what happens."

The episode received good critical feedback in the US on its first broadcast, and is often cited as one of the series' best installments; however, many British viewers regarded the episode as an ill-informed and patronizing caricature of the UK and its people, causing the episode to be unofficially labeled "The One Where They Insult the English."

Season 5: 1998-99

5.01 "The One After Ross Says Rachel" (09.24.98)
The opening wedding scene was filmed on April 10, 1998, when the cast and crew were shooting the double-length season finale in London. It was filmed without an audience.

When Ross tells the wedding guests they should be dancing, the couple standing at the buffet table are Tom and Sue, the well-educated friends of Mike's parents in "The One with Ross's Inappropriate Song" (9.07).

This is the first time Phoebe uses her alias Regina Phalange. She claims to be a doctor so she can explain to Emily's stepmother the reason Ross uttered Rachel's name during his wedding vows. According to Dr. Phalange, Ross forgot to take his brain medicine.

Chandler's teeth are noticeably different in this installment. During the summer hiatus, Matthew Perry added six porcelain veneers to his top teeth.

Ross and Emily's marriage was supposed to be a longer story arc but Helen Baxendale's unexpected pregnancy with her daughter Nell Marmalade (b. 9.13.98) caused the staff writers to change their vision for Season 5. Baxendale did not want to reside in the US throughout her pregnancy and couldn't travel shortly before or after the birth. The staff writers were unable to craft a convincing storyline to explain her absence so she was written out of the show, having only three cameos during Season 5.

The first four seasons were preoccupied with the "will they, won't they" relationship of Ross and Rachel, but thereafter a different relationship took center stage—Monica and Chandler. Staff writer Scott Silveri believes that *Friends* might have finished a few years earlier had the showrunners not advanced this relationship.

5.02 "The One with All the Kissing" (10.01.98)
When Joey is in the bathroom doorway talking to Chandler, who's soaking in the tub, the camera angle has a rare glimpse at the fourth wall of the guys' apartment. However, between edits there are different wall hangings, e.g., a blue light fixture versus a black-and-white picture.

This is the first installment where the opening title sequence is reduced from 45 to 35 seconds. It was purposely done to add 10 seconds of run time to the show.

The opening scene of Act 1 has the gang repeatedly referencing their London experience which infuriates Phoebe. This scene was inspired by real events. Since Lisa Kudrow was unable to join the cast in London, she had to endure all the anecdotes of her castmates' travel abroad. She was frustrated hearing about everything she missed out on. Thus, the writers added dialogue to express her discontent.

The *Friends* production company was paid to advertise Boddingtons beer. At the time,

Boddingtons Brewery was only a regional brewery in England, but after its exposure on *Friends*, the brewery earned international recognition and sales spiked. Its beer brands are now owned by the global brewer Anheuser-Busch InBev.

Rachel recapitulates her horrible vacation in Greece. Coincidentally, Jennifer Aniston visited Greece when she was 6 years old. Her family vacationed there in July 1975 when her father relocated to pursue a medical doctor degree. Meanwhile, for a year she and her mother lived in Pennsylvania at her grandparents' home. When her father's medical pursuit failed, he returned to acting and the family moved with him to New York.

When Monica says, "Here's all of us at the Tower of London," the photo is correct. After Phoebe finishes defacing the picture, the image changes to Westminster Abbey.

Rachel returns from a date wearing a strapless midi silhouette with embroidered floral jacquard and high slit. This elegant dress receives more positive comments than any other garment worn on the show.

5.03 "The One Hundredth" (10.08.98)
This episode is also known as "The One with the Triplets."

Lisa Kudrow was no longer pregnant by the time this installment was filmed. Her son Julian was born on May 7, 1998, thus her belly is a prosthetic.

The show's producers wanted to mark the landmark 100th episode with a major event, so concluding the surrogacy narrative was a perfect fit. Marta Kauffman was pleased at the timing—100th episode, a birth, and broadcast during sweeps week—it's the network equivalent of a trifecta.

Staff writer Greg Malins pitched the idea of an obstetrician offering a wide array of facts about Fonzie from *Happy Days*. The other writers loved the proposal but Kauffman and Crane were skeptical; to them, it made no sense at all. Nevertheless, the showrunners acquiesced because Malins and the other writers were so enthusiastic about the idea.

After Joey exits the elevator carrying a basket, the guy in the elevator drinking coffee and wearing a lab coat is production manager Rick Allen. Next to him in the green shirt is Kevin Bright's best friend from high school, Matthew "Matty" Mullany.

Doctors Oberman (TJ Thyne) and Franzblau (Jonathan Silverman) are actually named after Rona Oberman and Deborah A. Franzblau, friends of the creators.

The main episode subplot involves Monica and Chandler discussing their relationship. The writers felt they needed an additional subplot, something fun and humorous, so they chose Joey going through a parallel experience to Phoebe's pregnancy, except he is "giving birth" to a kidney stone. Marta Kauffman's father had kidney stones so she used his experience to craft the plot. David Crane felt the audience never really grasped the analogy between giving birth and expelling kidney stones.

The doctor's protracted pronunciation of "kidney stooones" became a preferred catch-phrase in the writers room. Moreover, Matt LeBlanc and Matthew Perry had a difficult time doing the kidney stone diagnosis scene because they cracked up every time actor Iqbal Theba spoke those words.

Chandler propositions a nurse (Heidi Beck), who ignores him and then exits the birth room. Beck is an actual nurse hired to oversee the delivery. All scenes using real babies require a qualified nurse to be present, either on set or just off camera.

To prepare for writing the labor and birthing scenes, Marta Kauffman watched a video-tape of her cousin giving birth.

Earlier scripts had Phoebe insisting on keeping the babies, but the producers thought a sentimental sendoff would be better, to keep it dramatic. "When we get to the speech at the end, we realized we're better off with just saying goodbye," recalls David Crane.

Joey's kidney stones stored in a vial are actually Tic Tacs. Kidney stones are typically yellow and misshaped like spiky rocks, which makes them so painful to pass.

The birth scene filming uses actual triplets. The director wanted to make the birth real, yet keep it comedic, so there is no umbilical cord or other technical aspects of birth. The babies are covered with grape jelly to represent birthing fluid.

Since *Happy Days* never aired in Spain, all the Fonzie references were changed to *Star Trek*. Thus, Dr. Harad proclaims to be a Trekkie, the triplets are born on Spock's half birthday, and Kirk once dated triplets.

5.04 "The One Where Phoebe Hates PBS" (10.15.98)

In the scene where Ross is excited that Emily answered the phone, he hands a lamp to Chandler. This bit was unscripted. David Schwimmer inadvertently handed the prop to Matthew Perry which explains his confused reaction. The producers liked the ad-lib so it was used in the final edit.

Londoner Helen Baxendale (Emily) became pregnant in mid-December 1997 so she was unable to travel to film her scenes in Season 5. Thus, she taped her scenes in London and hid her condition. In this episode, she is wearing a baggy nightshirt and the camera is framed to shoot above the waist. In a later scene, she is lying beneath the covers.

To save their relationship, Emily tries to convince Ross to move to England. In a deleted scene, he frantically tries to convince Susan and Carol to move to London so Ben could come along. That one scene would have done wonders in proving to the audience how much Ross loved Ben and that he would never leave his son behind. Instead, viewers raised concerns that Ross was a bad parent since he infrequently spent time with his son, seeing him only a couple times per year.

The establishing shot for the telethon is Unitel Video Studio 55, in Manhattan. From 1969 to 1993 it was home to Children's Television Workshop which produced *Sesame Street*, hence Phoebe's reference to the show. In 1999, Unitel filed for bankruptcy.

While the chick and duck are watching television, an installment of *Emeril Live* is airing with the chef preparing duck. When Chandler notices the program, he rushes to turn off the TV and then scolds the fowl: "How many times have I told you guys, you never watch the cooking channel!" The production staff had some difficulty finding a cooking show clip where they were preparing duck.

The magna doodle reads "Evil Joe" in large letters with flames below. It is purportedly written by Phoebe suggesting that Joey is the devil after he contends there is no such thing as a selfless deed.

5.05 "The One with the Kips" (10.29.98)

Dana deVally directed this episode. She was a technical coordinator on *Friends* for 92 episodes from 1995 to 1999, as well as *Veronica's Closet* and *Jesse*, which happen to be two other TV shows created by the executive producers of *Friends*.

When Joey falls asleep on the toilet, it is on the left side of the bathroom in full view. In "The One with All the Kissing" (5.02), the toilet is on the right side behind the door, and in "The One with the Boobies" (1.13) it is substituted with a bathtub. The set designer often changed the bathroom layout as needed for each episode.

Ross is consuming Pepto-Bismol to calm his upset stomach. He drinks from a bottle in Monica's abode, and then later places it on the coffee table in Central Perk while talking with Rachel. This is blatant product placement for Procter & Gamble, the manufacturer. Pepto-Bismol's trademark pink liquid is also plugged in "The One with Barry & Mindy's Wedding" (2.24).

This episode's comedic setup is a callback to "The One the Morning After" (3.16) where Rachel and Ross argued in the living room while the gang eavesdropped from a bedroom and satiated their hunger by eating an organic leg waxing product. The current episode has the same premise but the staff writers added an allusion to the earlier episode by revealing that Joey stashed a survival kit under the bed in case the same scenario ever occurred again.

The transition shot of Atlantic City at night is the actual city, and the establishing shot of Chandler and Monica's hotel is the real Resorts International Hotel Casino in Atlantic City, New Jersey.

The magna doodle is inexplicably blank. This only occurs in a handful of episodes.

There is an establishing shot featuring Washington Square Arch. It stands 77 feet (23 m) high and is constructed of white Tuckahoe marble to copy Roman Triumphal Arches, which are iconic monuments the Roman emperors built all over the empire to celebrate a victory or event.

5.06 "The One with the Yeti" (11.05.98)
The magna doodle has the word "WHY" in big, bold letters, expressing Joey's growing frustration in trying to keep Chandler and Monica's tryst a secret from the gang.

George Newbern plays Danny the Yeti. He is known for voicing Superman in many DC animated features. FYI: Yeti, Beast Boy, and Bigfoot are all minor fictional characters in the DC Comics universe.

Rachel describes Danny as a "crazy-eyed, hairy beast man ... like a bigfoot or a yeti!" In Himalayan folklore, the Yeti or Meh-Teh is an apelike creature purported to inhabit the Himalayan mountain range in Asia. It is similar to the Abominable Snowman in western popular culture.

The first two times that Monica and Rachel visit Danny's apartment, the entire corridor wall wobbles as he closes the door. It was poorly constructed with inadequate braces.

When Danny opens his apartment door, there is a privacy wall directly behind him with a black-and-white picture of a steamship. The print is hanging in a different location between the first and second visit.

This is the last physical appearance of Emily; she has one final voice role in "The One with the Ride-Along" (5.20). Her scenes were taped shortly after Helen Baxendale gave birth so the actress is still carrying baby weight. Thus, she was filmed with closeups or curled up on a club chair.

Helen Baxendale was invited to reprise the role of Emily in Season 10 but declined so she could star in the West End play *After Miss Julie*. In reality, she could not handle the intense tabloid scrutiny. The media attention during the London episode in 1998 was unbearable and she knew it would be worse during the final season of *Friends*.

5.07 "The One Where Ross Moves In" (11.12.98)
Inside the coffeehouse, Monica is reading *Practical Intuition in Love* by Laura Day, which was released on October 7, 1998, shortly after this episode was filmed. Courteney Cox received an advance copy so she brought the prop to the set to promote the book. She and Jennifer Aniston are huge fans of the mystic, self-help author. They even attended a book signing, along with Reese Witherspoon, to support their friend.

The book title is intended to foreshadow Rachel's lack of practical intuition in love. She spends the entire episode hatching a romantic plan of playing hard to get, despite the fact that Danny expresses no romantic interest in her.

The magna doodle scribbling reads "No Girls Allowed" which refers to the fort Joey built using Ross' storage boxes, and the fact their apartment has become a serious bachelor pad now that Ross moved in.

In the scene where Rachel hides behind the entry door to avoid being seen by Danny, she visibly shakes her hand as if in pain. Jennifer Aniston actually injured her hand performing this scene so her reaction is genuine, and not a scripted response.

Danny's housewarming party utilizes the hallway set for Monica and Joey's apartment. Tenement levels usually have the same floor plan, so in an effort to save construction costs, the crew simply repainted the old set. Eagle-eye fans will recognize furnishings in both main apartments through the door cracks.

The magna doodle has a smiley face with the word "Happy" next to it. This was meant to represent Ross' elation for having a home after being evicted from his last abode.

In the tag scene, Chandler enters the apartment as Joey and Ross are playing Cowboys and Indians. While shooting the scene, David Schwimmer and Matt LeBlanc decided to play a prank by exiting the fort and simultaneously pulling up their zippers at the exact moment that Matthew Perry walks into the abode to witness the act (implying they were having sex in the fort).

5.08 "The One with All the Thanksgivings" (11.19.98)
Many fans refer to this episode as "The One with the Thanksgiving Flashbacks."

While discussing story ideas, the writers originally settled on "a bunch of little pieces" or vignettes to represent the installment. When someone finally said, "What if it's the worst Thanksgivings," the creators knew they had their hook and the story evolved from there.

The crew only had five days to create seven time periods, which included Phoebe's past lives in the Civil War (her arm blows off) and WWI (her arm blows off again). Her past life experiences were inspired by the 1978 "Julia Child" skit on *SNL* where Dan Aykroyd dressed as the famed chef to parody a real-life incident where she cut her finger during a live cooking segment. Aykroyd took the gag a step further by severing his finger which caused blood to spray everywhere.

A rubber-and-foam turkey prop was designed so Joey and Monica could easily place it over their heads. A weaving, invisible to the audience, was placed in the middle of the bird to allow the actors to see.

Matthew Perry grew a goatee during a filming hiatus and really wanted to keep it for the episode. Thus, the 1992 flashback has him rocking real facial hair. David Schwimmer's mustache is fake.

Jennifer Aniston wore a prosthetic nose for her flashback scenes.

Chandler's 1987 coiffure was modeled after A Flock of Seagulls' lead singer, Mike Score. In fact, the script specifically refers to Chandler's hair as "A Flock of Seagulls haircut." The new wave band is best known for their hit "I Ran (So Far Away)" (#9, 1982). Actor Matthew Perry is wearing a wig for the flashback scenes. His hair was too short to be styled with long, sweeping locks.

The physical comedy bit where Monica sits on the sofa causing Chandler to bounce in the air was suggested by Matthew Perry during filming.

The segment where Monica severs Chandler's toe was preshot. The original scene had sound effects of his shoe being slashed, and the crunch of a toe, but it was a little too graphic so Kevin Bright opted for Alfred Hitchcock's *Psycho* score to create the allusion.

Chandler's severed toe was inspired by Matthew Perry's childhood trauma of having his right middle finger severed by a car door. The writers needed a pivotal injury to justify Chandler's animosity a decade later so a severed appendage seemed to fit. Nonetheless, they didn't want to focus on Perry's real-life disfigurement so a toe was used instead.

When Chandler is carted into the hospital, the paramedic is played by Douglas Looper, the stand-in for Matt LeBlanc. He also appears as an injured soldier in the tag scene during the Thanksgiving 1915 flashback.

5.09 "The One with Ross's Sandwich" (12.10.98)
After Rachel finds Monica's razor in Joey's bathroom, Joey claims he shaved his legs for a role in a play. Matt LeBlanc actually shaved his leg for this episode. No leg double or prosthetic covering was used in the making of this scene.

In the literature night class, the assigned book readings are *Wuthering Heights* by Emily Brontë and *Jane Eyre* by her older sister Charlotte Brontë. Both novels were originally published in 1847. The former depicts unfulfilled love as pain—love is not sufficient for happiness and if anything, stirs up more agony. The latter is a quest to be loved, not just romantic love, but a sense of value and belonging. Each novel was chosen for its thematic relevance to Monica and Chandler. They realize their love is pain by keeping it a secret and cannot find complete love until they reveal it to the world. Only then will they be fulfilled.

Writers Andrew Reich and Ted Cohen tapped into their childhood memories to create the Thanksgiving sandwich. "Everyone could relate to loving that leftover sandwich, and it being one of the best parts of Thanksgiving," said Cohen. This inspired Ross' fixation.

Ross' leftover Thanksgiving sandwich is dubbed The Moistmaker, though the episode writers do not recall exactly where the moniker came from.

Reich and Cohen admitted that their least favorite part of the episode is the pigeon cutaway scene. They thought it was the best way to rescue the story from seeming insane. "We had to get out of that scene, but there was always something that feels not great about cutting outside and seeing those pigeons flying off," Reich stated.

The establishing shot for Ross' employer, the Museum of Natural History, is the same building used to represent his employment at the Museum of Prehistoric History in "The One with the Sonogram at the End" (1.02). It is actually the Alexander Hamilton United States Custom House at 1 Bowling Green, Manhattan, New York, built in 1907.

Ross' boss, Mr. Ledbetter, is named after the 1992 Pearl Jam song "Yellow Ledbetter." Kevin Bright was a fan of the grunge band so the track was included in the series finale.

While fabricating a story about sleeping with Monica, Joey slaps her on the butt twice. This was ad-libbed during rehearsal and incorporated into the show. He replicates the bit with Phoebe in "The One Where Rachel Has a Baby, Part 1" (8.23).

5.10 "The One with the Inappropriate Sister" (12.17.98)
The magna doodle has the word "SHOOT" which pertains to Joey and Chandler playing the game Fireball. Later, there is a stick person standing next to a Christmas tree with presents underneath, which relates to the holiday theme of the episode. Finally, there is a desert island with a palm tree in the center surrounded by water and full sun above. This is a metaphor for Joey being stuck in the middle of Ross and Chandler's argument.

Hugsy makes his first appearance, sitting on a barstool beneath the dartboard in Joey's apartment. The toy is barely accessorized—it has a red scarf but no vest or goggles.

In the cold open, there is a racing poster hanging in Joey's bedroom. The Danish print celebrates a double victory by Mercedes-Benz cars (driven by Juan Manuel Fangio and Karl Kling) during the French Grand Prix (later Formula 1) in 1954.

This episode debuts the mannequin in Joey's apartment. It is located behind the couch in a Santa hat and button-down shirt with a gold garland string around the neck. The set decorator thought it would be an eclectic addition to the abode but quickly realized it was ill-suited for Joey and Chandler. It's removed after "The One with the Ball" (5.21).

Danny's apartment corridor is different from "The One Where Ross Moves In" (5.07). A new swing set was built because the main hallway was already being utilized in other scenes. Danny's corridor was designed radically different than the main one because the series set designer thought viewers would be confused if the two hallway sets were identical. When his sister opens the apartment door, the floor plan is open with no wall for privacy. In "The One with the Yeti" (5.06), a privacy wall was built because it was a false set; there were no living quarters since no scenes were filmed inside the tenement.

5.11 "The One with All the Resolutions" (01.07.99)
Friends writer Adam Chase went to an upscale clothing store with a female friend who suggested a pair of expensive leather pants which he tried on to impress her, and then bought the trousers after a beautiful store clerk said the pants looked great on him. He paid $600 for trousers he would likely never wear. This became the inspiration for Ross' clothing purchase.

The other writers expanded on the initial idea and wondered what might happen if Ross were to get stuck in the leather trousers. This led to him utilizing a variety of bathroom products in a futile attempt to pull them up.

The Central Perk coffee table has an issue of *LOOT*. This is the first episode to feature the weekly periodical. *LOOT* is one of the UK's top free classified advertising publishers. The issue was brought to the US by a crew member after filming the London episodes.

Phoebe admits, "I don't know the actual names of the chords but I made up names for the way my hand looks while I'm doing them." The unique chord names were purposely written to poke fun at Lisa Kudrow's limited musical knowledge. The writers added the actual chord names she used in real life: bear claw, turkey leg and old lady, and then added a few of their own, such as tiger, dragon and iceberg.

The bathroom scene is one of David Schwimmer's favorite physical comedy moments. Ross hitting himself in the forehead with a hand full of lotion was purely accidental. It was included in the final cut because the producers thought it was so funny.

Shooting Schwimmer's bathroom scene was complicated to film. "We had to shoot that a thousand times, he had to do it over and over again," said costumer Debra McGuire. Most scenes are filmed three to four times but this time it was different. "We do scenes multiple times on a sitcom, but we knew when we did that scene that it was going to be complicated with him shimmying in and out," she thoughtfully recalled. "He was a good sport nonetheless because it was extremely difficult."

This is one of Matt LeBlanc's favorite episodes. Decades later he admitted that he still cracks up at the sight of Ross in the bathroom trying to pull up his leather pants.

5.12 "The One with Chandler's Work Laugh" (01.21.99)
Chandler enters Central Perk wearing a dark-blue tie. The neckwear was designed by Burton Morris and produced by Pittsburgh's clothier Charles Spiegel. Morris' colorful line of clothing accessories debuted in October 1996 and were often worn by Chandler.

Lisa Kudrow suffers from ornithophobia (fear of birds) so it took considerable coaxing to get her to agree to hold the chick. She held the chick because she was especially afraid of the duck.

The tennis match was preshot without a studio audience since it involved constructing a court on the soundstage. A large, black canvas tarp covers the concrete soundstage to make it resemble an athletic club setting.

This episode panders to a corporate sponsor. The entire tennis match is basically a Nike ad. Even after the tennis outing, Chandler is wearing a blue Nike jacket with white logo, and then relaxing on a recliner in white Nike sneakers with gray logo outline.

Monica and Chandler intentionally lose the doubles tennis match. In real life, Matthew Perry was a second-ranked junior tennis player in Canada. After moving to Los Angeles in 1985 he was crushed by the US competition so he quit the sport to focus on acting.

The magna doodle message is "Joey, Call Kim" with a smiley face. Later on, it reads "J— Kim called Again!" This was written by crew member Scott Bruza to his girlfriend Kim Harris, the stand-in for Jennifer Aniston.

Of all her grand entrances, Maggie Wheeler considers this installment "the grandest of them" because nobody was expecting her to walk through that door. "So, when I made that entrance, the whole place went nuts ... the laughter was insane," she recalled. In fact, the entire cast started to crack up. In the final edit, Wheeler can be seen raising a scarf over her face to conceal her laughter.

5.13 "The One with Joey's Bag" (02.04.99)
The man purse was first popularized in *Seinfeld* (ep The Reverse Peephole) where Jerry uses the European carryall to store his girlfriend's purse contents. Of course, his man purse was markedly smaller like a typical woman's purse, not big and bulky like Joey's satchel.

Some fashionistas credit Joey for popularizing the man purse (or satchel). The fashion accessory, once relegated to bike messengers, is now accessible to the masses.

Joey's mock credit cards are MoosterCard and VASA. The producers didn't want to pay licensing fees associated with displaying the official MasterCard and VISA credit card logos so they turned it into a joke related to Joey being destitute.

Bob Balaban plays Phoebe's estranged father, Frank Buffay Sr. He is best remembered as Russell Dalrymple in *Seinfeld*. He also appeared in the 1999 movie *Three to Tango* costarring Matthew Perry.

Joey's audition was preshot because the set utilizes the studio bleachers.

In the final scene before closing credits, a bottle of Virgin Cola is prominently positioned on the coffee table in front of Monica. The brand was available in the UK from 1994 to 2012 (and US from 1998 to 2001). Virgin Group founder, Richard Branson, previously appeared on *Friends* and was a fan of the sitcom. The producers included the product placement as a thank you to Branson for his generosity in supplying free air travel to London to film two *Friends* episodes.

5.14 "The One Where Everybody Finds Out" (02.11.99)
The staff enjoyed writing this script because it was challenging. Marta Kauffman noted, "We wanted to see how many twists we could make without getting confused."

After Phoebe observes Monica and Chandler getting naked in the apartment across the street, she screeches, "My eyes! My eyes!" This is a callback to "The One with the Butt" (1.06) where Chandler utters the same line after witnessing Joey applying moisturizer to his buttocks.

Before delivering the aforesaid line, Lisa Kudrow asked Matthew Perry for permission to mimic his character's vocal style. He said, "Yeah, go for it." Jennifer Aniston remarked, "Matthew required us to ask permission when we borrowed Chandler's cadence."

In early script drafts, Phoebe was really mad and vindictive after learning about Monica and Chandler's secret relationship. The idea was abandoned because "it didn't feel right or funny." It only became hilarious after the writers came up with the hook "they don't know that we know they know we know" and the game of chicken between Phoebe and Chandler at the end.

Ross' struggle to find an apartment in New York was based on the executive producers' personal experience while residing there in the 1980s. "Finding an apartment was the hardest thing, especially one that you could afford," recalled Marta Kauffman.

This is the first time Hugsy is prominently featured in an episode. While walking on set, the stuffed toy caught the attention of writer Alexa Junge, who decided to incorporate the penguin pal into a script. Hugsy "guest stars" in other TV shows, such as *Boy Meets World*, *Everybody Loves Raymond*, *8 Simple Rules* and *Spin City*. It became a gag—the TV version of Where's Waldo? but with Hugsy.

Ugly Naked Guy is clutching a Big Gulp as he opens the apartment door. Kevin Bright added the prop in honor of writer Greg Malins who came to work every day with a Big Gulp Diet Coke.

"Casting for Ugly Naked Guy was an interesting process," said Kevin Bright. "He doesn't actually say anything so it had to be based upon somebody who's big and willing to get somewhat naked. It wasn't a long casting session. Four or five guys came in. They auditioned in boxer shorts because we had to see how they looked." In the naked scenes, the actor was wearing boxer shorts.

This is Ugly Naked Guy's final appearance and the last mention of the character. In the uncut DVD version, there was a scene where naked Ross sips tea and converses with Ugly Naked Guy. The writers were concerned that David Schwimmer would disapprove to stripping down to his boxers, but much to their awe, he was "all in for the scene."

When Phoebe performs her erotic dance for Chandler, Lisa Kudrow is actually dancing without music. The instrumental cue was added in postproduction. This is a common practice because if "the music is married to the dialogue," it may interfere with vocal clarity and create editing issues. Phoebe's dance was choreographed by Lisa Kudrow.

A classic segment has Joey using one hand to nonchalantly unbutton Phoebe's blouse. During filming, Matt LeBlanc attempted the trick about a dozen times to no avail, so when it finally worked, Lisa Kudrow was stunned and laughed out of character, which required the scene to be shot again. The audience cheered rhapsodically because they had to endure a dozen takes to get it right, which makes Joey's line, "Not my first time," so hilarious and much more memorable.

During Chandler and Phoebe's slow dance, Matthew Perry places his right hand on her hip and then immediately switches to using his left hand. "He switched hands because there was a whole big thing for camera, which hand it should be. So he put the wrong hand on first and switched suddenly," Marta Kauffman recalled. "You don't even quite know why, it's just very funny."

5.15 "The One with the Girl Who Hits Joey" (02.18.99)
In the teaser, Ross hugs Joey and Rachel in the doorway. During one of the takes, her wrist is crushed by Joey's hand. After they separate, she shakes her injured wrist and mouths "Oww." Jennifer Aniston's pained reaction is real, and not part of the script.

The Central Perk artwork is *Lady Liberty* by Pittsburgh-native Burton Morris. Courtney Cox also has ties to the city having dated Pittsburgh-born actor Michael Keaton from 1989 to 1995.

Series set decorator Greg Grande tried a new look by adding designer throw pillows to the Central Perk sofa. The pillows first appeared in "The One with All the Resolutions" (5.11), but the new addition did not last long before he returned to the original single-fabric complementary accessories.

Soleil Moon Frye plays Katie, Joey's punch-happy girlfriend. She is best remembered for her titular role in *Punky Brewster* (1984-88). Frye began her career as a child actor at the age of 2, and six years later beat out 3,000 applicants for her defining role.

In this episode, Ross' apartment has several design flaws. First, the door number is 3B, but in the prior episode it was 201, and in the future there is no number at all. Second, the numbering system is illogical. Ross is 3B but across the hall is 3R. Finally, there is an apartment located across the hall but in the prior episode it was nonexistent.

In preparation for a breakup with his girlfriend, Joey wears six sweaters to cushion the blow from Katie's punches in case she doesn't take the news well. The costume designer specially created this bulky garment using a fat suit. It has numerous clothing items stitched together with a back zipper overlaid with a sweater. Joey is wearing a dickey to conceal the fat suit underneath.

After Howard's party, Ross is sitting in his apartment eating Snak King Brand Cheese Puffs while Phoebe is holding a bag of Keebler CHEEZ-IT Party Mix. To avoid paying the manufacturers, the brand names were distorted. Snak King is actually "Shak Kino" and CHEEZ-IT is "HEEZ-I."

5.16 "The One with the Cop" (02.25.99)
In the cold opening, as Chandler and Joey are doing a crossword puzzle with Monica, the paper has an ad for Paul Reiser's 1997 book *Babyhood*. The producers included the promotion as a nod to the comedian for allowing Lisa Kudrow to play Ursula's twin.

In the DVD version, while helping Ross move a couch upstairs to his apartment, Rachel references news anchor Jane Pauley from *Dateline* as being the only woman she would ever kiss. This is a fact error. She kissed Monica for one minute and a sorority sister in college. FYI: Pauley has twins (boy and girl) born in 1983 named Ross and Rachel.

Writer Andrew Reich remembers visiting a friend named Katie who lived in a walk-up apartment with a very narrow staircase. When he got up to her apartment, he noticed she had an oversize sofa and wondered just how she managed to get it up the stairs. He brought this mundane observation back to the writers room, where it mutated into the classic "Pivot!" scene.

The uproarious "Pivot!" scene is one of David Schwimmer's top-three favorite physical comedy moments in the series.

House Beautiful magazine describes the Pivot! scene as "iconic," but filming it required multiple takes. Every time David Schwimmer yelled "Pivot!" his scene costars burst into laughter. According to Matthew Perry, he's never laughed so much in his life. Several outtakes were added to the season-ending blooper reel.

Mathematician Caroline Zunckel calculated the best way to maneuver the sofa upstairs. She ran 10,000 simulations to produce an equation and methodology. It turns out Ross was correct to order his helpers to "pivot" but it was a lack of "tilt" that led to the sofa getting stuck.

In the uncut DVD version, Rachel accidentally pulls the fire alarm causing the tenants to sprint downstairs, breaking Ross' couch in half. This explains its damaged condition when he returns the davenport for a refund in the tag scene.

5.17 "The One with Rachel's Inadvertent Kiss" (03.18.99)

An issue of *Shout* is on the Central Perk coffee table. It's a bimonthly UK magazine for tween and teen girls featuring articles on fashion, celebrities, beauty, true stories and embarrassing moments. A crew member brought it back from London for his daughter and then added it to the set dressing.

Ross' apartment has no number on the door. The set designer removed the number so Joey would keep knocking on Ross' door. Joey may be dimwitted, but even he would notice the same number and stop revisiting Ross' apartment. Thereafter, the producers decided to keep the designation a mystery in case they needed it for future episodes.

Monica is reading *To Kill a Mockingbird* by Harper Lee. The mockingbird represents the idea of innocence, so to kill a mockingbird is to destroy innocence. In this installment, Phoebe meets Gary the cop and they start dating. Just four episodes later, she dumps him after he callously and insouciantly kills an annoying bird. His behavior effectively destroys Phoebe's innocence.

In the DVD version, after exiting the second interview, Rachel tells the next candidate, "If you're going in there to see Mr. Zelner, I hope you're ready to put out!" (sleep with him) to which the applicant enthusiastically responds, "I am!"

Chandler offers cardboard cutouts of Pamela Anderson and Yasmine Bleeth to convince Ross that Monica and Rachel are watching his impressions. The staff writers used the props to lampoon Matthew Perry. In 1997, while romantically pursuing and then later dating Bleeth, Perry added flattering dialogue and images of her in several installments. Since the couple had been broken up for nearly two years, the writers felt Perry was fair game for an inside joke by resurrecting her memory.

5.18 "The One Where Rachel Smokes" (04.08.99)

David Crane tried to stop this installment from airing because he felt the plotlines were weak and the actors' performances suffered because of it. He asked NBC for one week to improve the episode but NBC refused. Thus, it was aired without changes. Crane still considers it the show's weakest episode.

There is blatant product placement for Act II Light Butter popcorn on Monica's dining table. The bag is purposely positioned for the camera after Rachel complains to Monica and Chandler about being excluded from office decisions because she doesn't smoke.

The Chinese poster in Kim's office also appears in Carol and Susan's abode when Ross asks them to move to London in the DVD version of "The One Where Phoebe Hates PBS" (5.04). It's a 1920s Chinese Nanyang Brothers Tobacco Company cigarette ad poster.

In the uncut DVD version, there is a birthday party segment where Chandler is rifling through a purse looking for cigarettes when he is busted by Monica. She presents an ultimatum: cigarettes or her. He chooses Monica but implies the reason is due to the cigarettes being menthol.

In the aforementioned sequence, Chandler is holding a pack of Morley cigarettes. The brand has been featured in hundreds of movies and TV shows. It first appeared in the movie *Psycho* in 1960 and the TV series *Naked City* in 1961. As of 1998, tobacco advertising was banned in both films and TV so Morley became the preferred prop brand. Its packaging resembles the original packaging of Marlboro. The name "Morley" is a play on "Marleys," a nickname for Marlboro cigarettes. Morley cigarettes appear in other *Friends* episodes where a character is smoking.

Despite Rachel's reluctance to smoke, in real life Jennifer Aniston was a chain smoker. She publicly announced her intention to quit in the past and even turned to hypnosis. Finally, in 2011 she did it and attributes her success to yoga.

This episode marks the final appearance of Charlie and John "Jack" Allen as Ben. They would be replaced with Cole Sprouse in Season 6.

5.19 "The One Where Ross Can't Flirt" (04.22.99)
This is a bottle episode with only three sets and two minor day players (actors).

While the group is watching Joey's scene on *Law & Order*, there are several TV screen closeups that reflect into the living room. As Joey is carted out in a body bag, the image shows an empty living room—the davenport is visible but no one is seated. The *Friends* cameraman shot the image of a blank TV screen so the *Law & Order* episode clip could be digitally overlaid in postproduction.

Joey's grandmother mentions *Capricorn One*, which costars Elliott Gould (Jack Geller) and James Brolin (the biological father of Phoebe's imaginary baby). It also costars Telly Savalas (*Kojak*), who was Jennifer Aniston's godfather.

During Ross' awful flirtation with the pizza girl, Chandler declares, "Oh, the Humanity," which is a reference to a newsreel quote from the Hindenburg disaster in 1937. When radio reporter Herb Morrison saw the airship burst into flames, he exclaimed "Oh, the humanity!" (meaning, what terrible human suffering).

Joey's videotaped hostage scene is taped over Chandler's performance of David Bowie's "Space Oddity" (#15, 1973). Joey sings the song in "The One After Vegas" (6.01).

Chandler's singing performance is very recent in time because the videotape shows a mannequin in the living room, which first appeared in "The One with the Cop" (5.16).

5.20 "The One with the Ride-Along" (04.29.99)
The ride-along plot derived from a US Supreme Court case pending at the time which gained national media attention. The issue was whether a ride-along violates personal privacy. The Court concluded that allowing journalists or photographers to enter and film private homes during a police ride-along is a violation of the Fourth Amendment.

When Chandler sniffs a sandwich, Joey claims that "half the taste is in the smell." After numerous studies on the subject, researchers found that the nose accounts for 75% to 95% of the taste.

In Ross' apartment, underneath the money is PlayStation's videogame *Rally Cross*. The guys loved to use PlayStation for gaming during rehearsal breaks.

Ross' desktop features a phrenology bust. Phrenology is a pseudoscience which involves measuring bumps on the skull to predict mental traits. Developed by German physician Franz Gall in 1796, the discipline influenced psychiatry and psychology during the 19th century. His belief that character, thoughts, and emotions are located in specific areas of the brain is viewed as an important historical advancement toward neuropsychology.

This is the last guest appearance of Helen Baxendale as Emily Waltham, though only in a voice role. She is credited as a "Special Guest Caller" in this episode.

Two of the most recognized French posters in Monica's apartment

In the DVD version, there is an extra segment in Ross' apartment where Rachel is trying to recreate Emily's answering machine message. While practicing accent and cadence, she inadvertently utters her own name instead of Emily's. This is a parody of "The One with Ross's Wedding, Part 2" (4.24) where Ross accidentally says "Rachel" while reciting his vows to Emily.

5.21 "The One with the Ball" (05.06.99)

The gang tossing a ball back and forth was inspired by real-life activities in the writers room. During work breaks, the staff writers would entertain themselves with antics like tossing a small football back and forth for hours without dropping it. This rather insipid ritual turned into a storyline.

During long days at the studio, the staff writers would relax by playing videogames or watching the latest installment of *The Osbournes* (2002-05). The reality show followed the daily activities of Black Sabbath rocker Ozzy Osbourne, manager-wife Sharon, and two of their children—Jack and Kelly.

Another fun activity in the writers room was Taste Test Wednesdays where an assistant was sent to the local grocery store to purchase, for example, every brand of plain potato chips. The writers would try each variety and vote for their favorite, and then the best potato chip would be declared.

When Chandler visits the precinct, the blackboard has names written in blue chalk. All the names refer to, or are fictional characters from, Stanley Kubrick movies—Redrum, Quilty, Barry, Strange, Love, Ripper, Mandrake, Buck, Turgidson, Dimitri, Kissoff, Dim, Hal, Dax, Alex and Humbert.

Monica starts sneezing and blames Rachel's hairless cat. Amazingly, hairless felines are not hypoallergenic. Cat allergies involve a reaction to proteins in the cat's saliva, urine and dander. People with allergies have oversensitive immune systems which cause an allergic reaction in the body.

When Rachel is on the sidewalk trying to sell her cat, the feline hissing sounds were not part of the original taping. They were added in postproduction.

This is the final appearance of Michael Rapaport as Gary. He previously worked with David Schwimmer in *NYPD Blue* (ep Brown Appetit) and the 1996 film *The Pallbearer*.

5.22 "The One with Joey's Big Break" (05.13.99)

In the teaser, Rachel is flagrantly displaying an issue of *Newsweek* magazine with the headline "Health for Life: What Every Woman Needs to Know" (spring/summer 1999). Contrary to some reports, the woman on the cover is not Andie MacDowell.

While the gang is sitting in Central Perk, Ross is reading *The Alchemist* by Paulo Coelho, which is meant to foreshadow his marriage to Rachel. The book's central message is about self-discovery and to follow one's dreams—which is exactly what Ross and Rachel do, albeit drunkenly, but it is their true subconscious desire.

Chandler complains that all he ever hears is "Richard, Richard, Richard." This dialogue is meant to signal Richard becoming a wedge in Monica and Chandler's relationship.

After Chandler is ejected from the vehicle, a wide-angle view of the bridge features cars and vans moving in reverse. This is due to an error when inserting the image as part of postproduction editing.

Joey's movie, *Shutter Speed*, is purportedly being shot outside Las Vegas, but in reality it was filmed at Vasquez Rocks State Park, 10700 Escondido Canyon Rd., Agua Dulce, California. The location is used in numerous films and TV shows, such as *Star Trek V: The Final Frontier* (1989), *Star Trek* TV series (aka Gorn Rock to Trekkies), and *Austin Powers: International Man of Mystery* (1997).

There is further proof that Joey is not in the Las Vegas desert: the presence of saguaro cacti. The plant is only native in the Sonoran Desert, not the Mojave Desert where Las Vegas is located.

Coincidentally, the Season 2 premiere of the spinoff *Joey* began with a two-part episode, "Joey and the Big Break," which was named after this *Friends* installment. Unlike the *Friends* episode, where Joey's movie gets delayed and then canceled, in *Joey* the movie is made but he is later fired.

5.23 "The One in Vegas, Part 1" (05.20.99)
The Las Vegas setting was intentionally chosen by the producers to commemorate the cast's September 1994 trip to Caesar's Palace before they were famous. Director James Burrows wanted the cast to bond and anticipated the series being a hit, so he treated the cast to an evening of dining and entertainment which he dubbed "their last night of anonymity." He borrowed the Warner Bros. private jet, paid for dinner, and even fronted them gambling money.

Rachel takes advantage of being alone by getting naked in her abode. Jennifer Aniston did the sequence herself. The scene was written as an inside joke because Aniston was dating Brad Pitt at the time and he was known for walking around his home in the buff.

No sequences were filmed in Las Vegas. The casino was actually a massive stage set. To accommodate the expansive set—with casino, gift shop and hotel room—the crew had to dismantle Central Perk.

In the first airplane scene with Ross and Rachel, he is holding *Time* magazine with the headline "The Attack" from April 5, 1999 (vol. 153, no. 13). This is meant to forewarn viewers of Ross and Rachel's game of trying to embarrass each other.

On the airplane, Rachel is perusing *High Fidelity* by Nick Hornby. In the novel, a man reexamines his failed relationships and realizes his fear of commitment compels him to pursue other women, so he gets in touch with a former girlfriend and makes a token allegiance to her. The book portends Chandler's effort to overcome his fear of commitment by agreeing to get married, and then (two episodes later) suggesting cohabitation.

Thomas Lennon portrays a blackjack dealer who is also Joey's hand twin. Lennon and Matthew Perry costarred in the movie *17 Again* (2009) and the television reboot of *The Odd Couple* (2015-17).

While playing craps, Monica hugs a man wearing a multicolored button-down shirt. The casino patron is *Friends* writer Adam Chase.

This is one of director Kevin Bright's favorite episodes.

5.24 "The One in Vegas, Part 2" (05.20.99)
The little boy who laughs at Rachel's mustache is AJ Foster. Since it was his first role as an actor, Foster's parents were hired to walk behind him in the scene. Kevin Bright

was so thrilled with the performance that he took Foster into the set gift shop and told him he could have anything he wanted. He chose a squirting slot machine toy.

After Ross and Rachel arrive in Las Vegas, Phoebe asks if they were at a costume party because of Rachel's mustache and beard. In the original version, Phoebe assumes Ross' costume is Bob Saget. In the German version, she claims he is portraying Tom Selleck (aka Richard Burke in the series).

While Monica is playing craps, the man directly to her right in the multicolored button-down shirt is writer Adam Chase. As Joey approaches the blackjack dealer and asks if she has seen his hand twin, the two men seated are *Friends* set decorator Greg Grande and writer Greg Malins.

When Monica and Chandler roll dice for the last time—wagering to get married if she throws a hard eight—one die jumps off the table yet inexplicably lands underneath it.

While using the alias Regina Phalange, Phoebe describes herself as a "businesswoman in town on business," which is an allusion to *Romy and Michele's High School Reunion* (1997) where Michele (Kudrow) prattles on about being a businesswoman who has to be in Tucson for a business thing.

The exterior business sign for A Little White Chapel lists two celebrities: Joan Collins and Michael Gordon. Collins is best known as Alexis Colby in *Dynasty* (1981-89) which made her an international star. In 2015 she was made a Dame by Queen Elizabeth II for services to charity. Gordon was a stage actor and stage-film director. His grandson is actor Joseph Gordon-Levitt (*3rd Rock from the Sun*).

In 2002, *TV Guide* named Ross and Rachel's drunken matrimonial union as the No. 1 *Friends* moment.

Season 6: 1999-2000

6.01 "The One After Vegas" (09.23.99)

To save on expenses, the smaller casino sets constructed for the previous installment were left standing over the summer hiatus. This allowed the production team to resume filming on the Las Vegas sets. Of course, it still required razing the casino to assemble Monica's apartment and Central Perk.

Each scene was shot a number of times with a surprising amount of rewriting between takes. For example, Chandler's line: "I don't think they're as much dating as they are drunk," bombed in front of the audience so after seven minutes of brainstorming ideas, Matthew Perry came up with a better line: "I don't think they're as much dating as they are two bottles of vodka walking around in human form." Since it's not a fantastic one-liner, it is often cut in the syndicated version.

In the cold open, Phoebe proclaims, "It's not like you're married everywhere," implying she was once married in Vegas. The staff writers were worried the audience would not understand the inference so during a break in taping they took a vox pop (poll) of the crowd. It was this immediate feedback that helped improve the show. (And, yes, they understood the implication.)

This is the first installment after Courteney Cox and David Arquette were married so the creators honored the occasion by having the name "Arquette" added to the surname of the cast and showrunners in the opening credits. Since Cox legally changed her name to "Cox Arquette," the opening credits were symbolically changed to show that marrying one of them is like marrying all of them.

Customarily, the cast credits roll alphabetically because it's an ensemble show with no headliner. In honor of Cox's marriage, though, her name appears first, and thereafter the credits roll alphabetically.

Starting with this episode, Courteney Cox is credited as Courteney Cox Arquette for the rest of the series. She modified her stage name to "Cox Arquette," but as of 2004, her marriage became rocky, so three years later she dropped the name Arquette.

***Friends'* fashions were worn on *Buffy the Vampire Slayer* (top row and bottom left) and even Rachel duplicated her outfits in Season 1 (eps 4 and 19)**

Phoebe wears her hair in a bun because the producers didn't know how to handle Lisa Kudrow's new bob hairstyle. They needed time to decide if they liked the new look and whether it fit her character. Kudrow had it cut for the movie *Hanging Up* (2000).

One criticism of this episode is the omission of ink on Ross and Rachel's faces since it is supposed to be indelible. The writers debated three options: leave it, delete it, or fade it. Marta Kauffman wanted it faded but the other staff writers wanted it gone, so the group consensus prevailed.

Once Joey discovers he's at a buffet, he declares, "Oh, here's where I win all my money back." This line was not part of the original script. The staff writers brainstormed the line between takes.

During Ross and Rachel's argument in Monica's apartment, Rachel's original line was "Ross, stop saying the word marriage. Ross, stop, listen. If you don't get this annulled, I will." During a filming break, the writers huddled to discuss a better line and came up with this: "Ross, this is not a marriage, it's the world's worst hangover." *Entertainment Weekly* called it the best line of the episode.

At the end of Act 2, there is a title card dedication: "For Courteney and David, who did get married" to commemorate the marriage of Courteney Cox and David Arquette.

6.02 "The One Where Ross Hugs Rachel" (09.30.99)
Lisa Kudrow begins wearing a wig which will last throughout the season. Her real-life hairstyle was a bob but the producers didn't feel it was a suitable cut for her character. The opening scene in the cafe was filmed the prior week and functions as a lead-in to this episode's storyline.

Chandler tells Monica that when it comes to sweets, Joey is surprisingly strict. But in "The One with the Kips" (5.05), he claimed that Joey left Rolos all over the apartment. In the last couple years of the series, Matt LeBlanc approached the producers "to go easy on some of the Joey food jokes." The staff writers ignored the request because, as Kevin Bright said, "It's a really rich area to go to [so] we just keep coming back there." LeBlanc was facing media scrutiny for his weight gain.

When Monica finally clarifies the cohabitation plans—meaning that Rachel must move out of the apartment—Rachel is reading *Like a Hole in the Head* by Jen Banbury. The book title is intended to express her feelings about the new living arrangement.

Alex Kapp Horner (Stephanie, the cafe woman who would date Ross but not while he is married) is best known as Lindsey (one of the mean moms) in *The New Adventures of Old Christine* (2006-11). Horner first gained notoriety for being the girlfriend of Preppie

Killer Robert Chambers and breaking up with him just hours before he murdered his other girlfriend (Jennifer Levin) in Central Park in 1986.

The magna doodle has a cat chasing a mouse with a hill in the background. This image represents the episode plot where the living arrangement is a cat-and-mouse game.

In honor of Caesar's Palace allowing the past three installments to feature its hotel and casino, the set decorator added gratuitous product placements, such as the Caesar's Palace Las Vegas Keno card holder above Joey's stove.

6.03 "The One with Ross's Denial" (10.07.99)

Phoebe rejects Rachel's request to be roommates by claiming that she already has one (Denise). However, Denise doesn't exist. It's a writer's joke so Phoebe won't be the "bad friend" who doesn't want Rachel as a roomie. In "The One with Joey's Porsche" (6.05), as Rachel is on the verge of homelessness, Phoebe changes her mind and asks Rachel to move in with her. Phoebe then claims Denise moved out and won't be back until the 26th of December.

Phoebe claims "Ninety percent of a woman's pheromones come out the top of her head." If truth be told, pheromones in humans may be present in bodily fluids such as semen or vaginal secretions, urine, breast milk, and potentially saliva and breath, though most attention thus far has been directed toward axillary (armpit) sweat.

To the left of the entry door in Joey's apartment is an old tin sign: "When he wears 'em, Shoeless Joe Jackson Wears Selz Shoes, Make Your Feet Glad" which was the 1920s advertising slogan for Selz-Schwab & Company of Chicago. The Elgin, Illinois, factory closed in 1929. Jackson is considered one of the greatest baseball players of all time, though often falsely associated with the Black Sox Scandal, in which members of the 1919 Chicago White Sox participated in a conspiracy to fix the World Series.

Ross' apartment decor properly reflects his personality. Peppered throughout are nods to his paleontology career with fossils and archaeological figures on shelves, side tables and walls. Although some items were found in the WB prop warehouse, most articles were acquired by the set decorator at flea markets, swap meets and secondhand stores.

The Central Perk coffee table contains a location-appropriate book that remains present for years: *The Coffee Book (The Coffee Connoisseur's Cookbook)* by Jacki Baxter which features recipes using coffees from several countries. There are tasting notes for coffee varieties so the reader can recognize and choose the right one for every occasion.

The magna doodle has an island with palm trees, shark in the water, and a man sitting in a boat. It is a metaphor for Ross being in denial about his feelings for Rachel. Either decision—to suppress his feelings or act on them—has dire consequences: one option has him alone on an island and the other has him facing the shark (i.e., Rachel's wrath once she discovers they are still married).

6.04 "The One Where Joey Loses His Insurance" (10.14.99)

When Ross tells Rachel: "You complete me," this is a direct reference to the movie *Jerry Maguire* (1996). Ross was attempting to convince Rachel to move in with him by using a magnetic bottle opener—the one thing he doesn't have in his apartment—as a metaphor for them being perfect for one another.

Ross is offered a teaching position at New York University (NYU). The campus is near Washington Square Park, which Phoebe claims to be a good place for street performers. Her statement is correct. The presence of street performers has been one of its defining characteristics. For many years, people visiting the park have mingled with the buskers, performers, musicians and poets.

On the Central Perk coffee table is *Blue Dog* by George Rodrigue, an inspirational tale of the Cajun character known as Blue Dog (Rodrigue) and its master with paintings that tell a story about love, art and human nature. The coffee table also features Rodrigue's *Blue Dog Man,* a pop culture book with 70 paintings and details about the legends and inspirations behind his creation. All his book cover images are paintings created by the author and periodically hang in the coffee shop.

Monica's apartment has a unique decorative chest inscribed with an original poem from *On Dante Alighieri* by Michelangelo Buonarroti (aka Michelangelo). The transcription is "From heaven his spirit came, and robed in clay, the realms of justice and of mercy trod, then rose a living man to gaze on God." Several scholars claim he is the greatest artist of all time. He is most known for the *David* sculpture and painting the ceiling of the Sistine Chapel.

In Joey's first audition, where he has a surprise for a little boy, the casting director is played by Kim Harris, Jennifer Aniston's stand-in.

Joey's third audition is for the part of Dying Man. The casting director is portrayed by Joe Everett Michaels, Matthew Perry's stand-in.

In the DVD version, Rachel uses a fake Irish accent for a prank call to Ross, stating: "This is Dr. McNeely from the Fake Accent University. We'd like you to come on board with us full time."

6.05 "The One with Joey's Porsche" (10.21.99)

Monica mispronounces "Porsche" in "The One with All the Thanksgivings" (5.08), but Joey properly enunciates it as "Por-shuh" in this episode. Many people believe the "e" is silent but it is actually pronounced.

Season 6 was a banner year for the show's producers shamelessly selling out the series for lucrative side deals with corporate sponsors. This episode is second only to "The One with the Apothecary Table" (6.11) in its blatant brand integration. Besides the car, there were egregious product promotions using Porsche attire and accessories (jacket, t-shirt, cap, fanny pack, pants, logo keychain, etc.), and repeated references to the brand.

Chandler offers the triplets a toy named Krog, a fictional action figure. It is actually a modified He-Man action figure from *Masters of the Universe*. The *Friends* art department repainted the toy and added curly horns and accessories, such as a sonic blaster. The producers could not get permission to use a brand-name action figure because of the episode's negative portrayal of the toy as being unsafe.

Much like Joey, Matt LeBlanc is an avid car enthusiast. He has a massive automobile collection that includes numerous Porsches, e.g., 2016 911 R and 1988 911 Carrera (964), which he acquired in 2016 after becoming the new host of BBC's *Top Gear*.

Matt LeBlanc is a dedicated Formula 1 enthusiast. He has substantial knowledge and experience behind the wheel and has enough chops to be considered a professional race car driver, according to HotCars.

Leslie is the missing baby but when she is shown sitting in the drawer, there is a brief shot of male genitalia. Since the triplets were portrayed by quadruplets (one girl, three boys), at least one of the boy quadruplets had to play a girl.

In the tag scene, Joey's Porsche is covered with a tarp before a teenager dives onto the car, revealing cardboard boxes underneath. The producers debated whether the joke was worth the cost because constructing the cardboard shell cost thousands of dollars.

In honor of the *Friends* reunion special on May 27, 2021, Porsche publicly announced a new Porsche edition on its Instagram. "Could we BE any more excited about the Friends reunion? So much so, in fact, that we present: the Porsche Tribbiani edition. Careful, she's sleeping. #FriendsReunion."

6.06 "The One on the Last Night" (11.04.99)

David Schwimmer directed this episode, the first of 10 over the next four years.

This is a bottle episode because it uses a single set and no guest stars. It is one of the few *Friends* installments featuring only the main cast with no day players. Kevin Bright believes these types of episodes were some of the best of the series.

An early transition clip features the Washington Square Arch. Its piers stand 30 feet (9.1 m) apart and the arch opening is 47 feet (14 m) high. The iconography of the Arch centers on images of war and peace. On the frieze are 13 large stars and 42 small stars, interspersed with capital "W"s. The spandrels contain figures of Victoria (goddess of victory), and the inscription on the attic story reads: "Let us raise a standard to which the wise and the honest can repair. The event is in the hand of God—Washington."

The magna doodle drawing is a nighttime scene with a hill containing a saguaro and a wolf howling at the crescent moon. This represents the final night Joey and Chandler will spend together to howl at the moon. It also applies to the girls' last night alone.

When Monica enters the bedroom and sees Rachel unpacking, on the bed is a LoveBug stuffed toy that Ross gave to Rachel in "The One with All the Jealousy" (3.12).

In Ross' apartment, the kitchen door push plate is on the left (opens right) but in later episodes it's on the right (opens left), which is especially noticeable in "The One with the Male Nanny" (9.06).

6.07 "The One Where Phoebe Runs" (11.11.99)
In the scene where Phoebe and Rachel are recording an outgoing answering machine message, they are not actually recording their voices. Their voices were prerecorded for the audience then altered in postproduction to sound like a taped message.

Model Elle Macpherson debuts for a multi-episode story arc as Joey's roommate, Janine Lecroix. She later confessed that had she known how popular and iconic the show was, she probably would have chickened out and turned it down.

The role of Joey's roommate was not written specifically for Elle Macpherson. The script called for a "gorgeous roommate." The showrunners put out feelers to casting agencies to see who might be interested in playing the part, and Macpherson accepted, which thrilled the staff. Her appearance had nothing to do with an earlier episode, "The One with the Princess Leia Fantasy" (3.01), where Chandler mentioned that her image pops into his head during sex.

The magna doodle image is a truck stuck on a mound of dirt with two guys, one in front of the vehicle and the other in back, and the word "Oops!" scrolled across the top. This is an inside joke for crew member Paul Swain because he drove his truck into a ditch and it had to be pulled out.

This is the first and only time that Monica and Chandler are called Mondler. The writers were trying to create a moniker the media would embrace to hype the characters, but it never panned out. The other primary couple, Ross and Rachel, were referred to by many fans as Roschel but this was never spoken in the series.

On the side wall in Phoebe's living room is a poster of a woman holding a parasol while lounging in a canoe with her red crop top partially unbuttoned, exposing one breast and nipple. It is a risqué advert for The Great Eastern Dispensary LTD (c. 1930s). Starting in the 1920s, this Shanghai enterprise began making medicines and advertising its wares, propelling it to become one of the most famous and influential dispensaries at the time.

In the final scene of Act 2 where Rachel is jogging by herself, many sources claim the background building is the Museum of Natural History, where Ross works. This is false. It is the same location as all prior jogging scenes—New York Park on the Warner Bros. Studios lot. The cast never shot on location in New York. The crew did some backplate shots but never filmed any scenes there.

6.08 "The One with Ross's Teeth" (11.18.99)
Ross' plotline was inspired by Matthew Perry having porcelain veneers attached to six of his top teeth in the summer of 1998. Of course, to conceal the obvious insinuation, the writers had Ross use a teeth whitening gel. Porcelain veneers are made in a laboratory and then bonded on the teeth using a composite resin. The procedure often requires two separate visits. The first appointment has the dentist trimming a tiny amount of enamel off the teeth.

Since Janine Lecroix (Elle Macpherson) is Australian, the writers wanted to incorporate at least one famous Aussie artist to legitimize her backstory. They settled on Australian-born photographer Anne Geddes whose art books have been published in 83 countries, translated into 23 different languages, and sold more than 18 million copies. She also sold 13 million calendars.

The portrait of a baby that is hanging in Joey's apartment is the work of Anne Geddes, world famous for her stylized depictions of babies and motherhood. The one featured in this episode is titled *Waterlily*.

Joey's line about the gang sitting in Central Perk at 11:30am on a Wednesday was a subtle jab at the media for making an issue of this fact and questioning the realism of the show.

Phoebe is wearing a multicolored top with pink sleeves. It is the same "birthday cake shirt" that Willow wore in *Buffy the Vampire Slayer* (ep Wild at Heart) which aired nine days earlier on November 9, 1999. *Buffy*'s costume designer, Cynthia Bergstrom, often borrowed clothes from the *Friends* wardrobe department because she was tight with its head costumer, Debra McGuire.

This is the third episode of the sixth season with blatant brand integration. In Central Perk, Rachel is holding a Ralph Lauren Country catalog that is purposely positioned for the camera. The back cover has an advertisement for Polo Country, which is another Ralph Lauren collection.

Clothier Ralph Lauren makes his only *Friends* guest appearance during two very short elevator scenes with merely two words of dialogue: "Hi Kim." It didn't take long for the show's producers to realize Lauren couldn't act so his dialogue was limited.

Ralph Lauren paid a hefty sum to the production company to advertise brand names, feature him in a cameo, and hire Rachel as an employee of the company. The marketing gimmick paid off. A study on product placement found that "As the show scored a big success around the globe, there was a significant impact on brand recall."

This episode is dedicated to Gail Joseph, an NBC publicist who passed away less than three weeks before the airing of this episode. The title card reads: "In Loving Memory of Gail Joseph."

6.09 "The One Where Ross Got High" (11.25.99)

Joey and Ross playing a videogame was inspired by the thespians. The male leads often spent free time gaming in their dressing rooms (*Super Mario Bros.* was their favorite). In the scene, the videogame is a preloaded sequence and the actors just pretend to play by randomly pushing buttons so they can concentrate on acting. The videogame they are "playing" is *Twisted Metal 2: World Tour* (1996) on Sony PlayStation.

The magna doodle sketching has an astronaut holding a US flag freshly planted in the lunar surface. There are also craters, a space capsule, and a view of Earth in the background. This is a tribute to the 30th anniversary of the lunar landing.

The creators were aware of how stories may impact public perception of the characters, especially as it pertained to them engaging in illegal activities. "That's never crossed our mind in this episode," Kevin Bright confessed. "Our feeling was, if you went to college and you went through that time in your life where there was experimentation, it's not unreasonable to understand that somebody at one point may have smoked marijuana. I think this makes the characters more relatable and real, rather than damn them."

NBC executives did not have a quandary with Ross smoking pot because it was in the distant past. "We weren't saying that Ross smokes marijuana now or that he still thinks that it's something right to do. We didn't have the character comment on it in that way," Bright added. Moreover, despite broadcasting at eight o'clock, NBC had no objection to the content being viewed by children.

Rachel makes an English trifle which ends up being half shepherd's pie. As the writers debated which dessert to serve, someone suggested trifle, which started a disagreement whether it was a pudding dessert or meat entree. "You have to understand, back then there's no internet and there weren't a lot of cooking shows on TV," Greg Malins stated. Their mutual confusion became the inspiration for combining a dessert and entree into one disgusting amalgamation.

Although Rachel's dessert concoction is an iconic moment in television, the producers initially rejected the idea as being too outlandish.

Having meat in the middle of Rachel's dessert is an obvious error, which would require her to flip back and forth between recipes. But it was an intentional mistake because otherwise the guests could have removed the top layer of meat and vegetables to eat the edible trifle portion.

When the cookbook pages are stuck together, Joey accuses Chandler as the wrongdoer (insinuating masturbation). David Crane thought this was one of the dirtiest jokes on the show. The bit was not in the original script; it was added during production week. Of course, the comedy is a stretch since typically an adult magazine would have pages stuck together, but in this case it's a cookbook.

In the scene where Ross stuffs his mouth with dessert, David Schwimmer couldn't stop laughing so they had to film another take. He spit the food on a plate and prepared to stuff his mouth again. As they roll the scene, LeBlanc unwittingly scraped Schwimmer's masticated food onto his plate and instructed the crew he was ready to go. They filmed the scene and LeBlanc ate all of Schwimmer's discarded food. No one said a word about it until *after* the scene wrapped.

This is Elliott Gould's favorite episode.

"The One Where Ross Got High" is always on a top-20 list of the best *Friends* episodes. There are 10 Thanksgiving-themed episodes (one for each season) and this installment is most adored by fans.

6.10 "The One with the Routine" (12.16.99)
Although Monica and Ross are Jewish, the gang is decorating a Christmas tree in her apartment. The creators stated that the siblings' father was Jewish, not their mother, so they incorporated elements of Christmas and Hanukkah into their celebrations. This interfaith concept was based on Kevin Bright's life where he is Jewish and his wife is not, so their family celebrated both holidays.

After Chandler realizes that Phoebe and Rachel discovered a private stash of porn in his closet, he awkwardly utters, "Okay, that didn't just happen," and then mimics Jeannie from the 1960s sitcom *I Dream of Jeannie* by waving his hands and snapping his fingers to make himself disappear. He repeats the motion after Rachel again mentions finding porn in his new closet.

Courtney Cox and David Schwimmer diligently practiced the dance routine for two days before filming the memorable scene. The dance moves were choreographed by Robin Antin, founder of the modern burlesque troupe The Pussycat Dolls. Antin also worked with Paris Hilton, Anastacia, Pink, The Offspring and No Doubt.

Courteney Cox and pop singer Ed Sheeran recreated the dance routine and posted it on Instagram as a tribute to fans following the much anticipated *Friends* reunion in May 2021. Though not as polished as the original, the Grammy Award–winning singer was in sync with Cox until she jumped into his arms, taking them both to the ground.

After the director starts the countdown at 10, the shot goes to Joey with his thoughts overdubbed. When the countdown hits 7, he begins expressing his inner thoughts. The monologue lasts nine seconds and then the countdown resumes with three seconds left.

When the director yells "Cut!" and Joey screams "Nooo!" the camera angle switches and he is again mouthing the word "Nooo!" without sound.

After Chandler states that finding the presents early is not what Christmas is all about, Rachel refers to him as Linus, which pays homage to *A Charlie Brown Christmas* (1965) where Linus' monologue ends with the line, "That's what Christmas is all about, Charlie Brown." The famous speech was nearly axed from the telefilm because the producers resisted including a Bible verse (Linus recites the Gospel of Luke) but creator Charles M. Schulz insisted on using the quote.

6.11 "The One with the Apothecary Table" (01.06.00)
This installment is unofficially known as "The One with the Pottery Barn" and "The One with the Product Placement."

This is the final guest appearance of Elle Macpherson as Janine Lecroix. The producers invited her to appear in more installments, but she declined the offer. Macpherson did confess that working with LeBlanc had its perks. "Great working partner," she noted. "Good kisser."

Entertainment Weekly ranks this episode No. 1 on their Best Product Placements list for the show. It is basically a 22-minute Pottery Barn advertisement. The brand name is mentioned 18 times. Even the Pottery Barn logo is affixed to the furniture store window.

The financial arrangement between Pottery Barn and Warner Bros. has never been disclosed, but WB executive Peter Roth claimed the deal was necessary to "offset the high cost of production." Pottery Barn donated pieces for the episode but denied paying for the promotion. Patrick Connolly of Williams Sonoma (owner of Pottery Barn) stated it's "the gift that keeps on giving" because "the phones light up with catalog requests every time it airs in syndication." In truth, Pottery Barn paid for the plug.

The apothecary table was a real furnishing sold by Pottery Barn at the time. Production designer Greg Grande went to the local store and asked if he could use it for an episode. They gave him carte blanche to shop for anything he wanted. A fair amount of the small pieces in Phoebe's apartment—e.g., partition wall, ornamental birdcage, and tchotchkes (trinkets)—and a couple larger items like the Sahara desk (along wall by kitchen) and Parker console table (along back living room wall) were all from Pottery Barn.

On July 30, 2019, Pottery Barn launched a 25th anniversary *Friends*-themed collection that included an apothecary table; however, it did not sell for $150, it cost $1,099. The entire collection had mugs, pillows, and wall art featuring iconic dialogue, catchphrases and images from the series.

This episode was cited in a study of product placement in television. Brand the Change found that frequent use of a brand name in a sitcom can have a profound impact on the brand and its product. In fact, it can increase brand awareness from 20% to 43%.

6.12 "The One with the Joke" (01.13.00)
Ross has a joke published in *Playboy* Collector's Edition (January 2000). In the actual issue, the first cartoon has nothing to do with monkeys; instead, it is a gag about Prince Charming reviving Snow White by sleeping with her, but she's "faking it."

The magna doodle has an armed hunter flipping a treat to an eight-point buck. Crew members went deer hunting during their production break so they commemorated the event with a sketch.

This is the first appearance of the stuffed toy Marvin the Martian (on Joey's couch). It is an extraterrestrial cartoon character that originated in the 1948 Bugs Bunny cartoon *Haredevil Hare,* and appeared only four more times between 1952 and 1963. Marvin's design is based on the Hoplite style of armor usually worn by the Roman god Mars. The set dresser introduced the stuffed toy hoping it would attain popularity like Hugsy but it never caught the attention of the writers.

In the Central Perk scene where Joey asks everyone for their drink order, the gentleman sitting at a small table by the window (with the woman who orders ice water) is Matthew Mullany, Kevin Bright's good friend from high school.

Gunther declares he's going out for an hour to have his hair dyed. Joey then comments that he likes Gunther's natural hair color. This is an inside joke because James Michael

Tyler (Gunther) is a natural brunet and dyed his hair blond every week for 10 years.

After Chandler explains the origin of the joke to Monica, he crosses his ankles twice. It is a bit used by a number of pantomimes and TV show comedians, such as the British comedy sketch show *The Morecambe and Wise Show* (ep Richard Briers & Diana Dors).

6.13 "The One with Rachel's Sister" (02.03.00)

The creators specifically targeted Reese Witherspoon to play Rachel's sister. "We were obviously big fans of her. Anybody who saw her in *Election* would just say, 'Oh my God, yes, get her!'" said David Crane. And Witherspoon wanted to appear because she was a massive *Friends* fan so she made herself available. "I would not stop watching *Friends*," she said. "They were my friends and there was no taking me away from my friends."

Despite Witherspoon's long list of accomplishments, she was ill-prepared for working in front of a live studio audience which left her overwrought with stage fright. Thankfully, Jennifer Aniston unhesitatingly stepped in to calm Witherspoon's nerves and from there the pair became fast friends.

The Central Perk artwork is a montage of eight cups of coffee by Burton Morris. It is a different painting from the cold opening because that scene was shot for inclusion in another episode.

As Rachel attempts to convince Jill that Ross is undatable, she is perusing *The Art of Happiness* by Dalai Lama. This is an ironic juxtaposition. Rachel's art of happiness is Machiavellian (the end justifies the means), which is opposite of Dalai Lama's tenets.

Monica is extremely ill but horny. While trying to entice Chandler into the bedroom, he is reading *Rebuilding the Indian* by Fred Haefele, the biography of a man rebuilding a motorcycle and his life. The book foreshadows Chandler's efforts to rebuild his life with Monica beyond the tribulations related to her illness and current sexual repulsion.

Lex Arquette (aka Alexis Arquette) makes a quick cameo as the patron receiving a free birthday muffin before Gunther chastises Joey and revokes his complimentary birthday muffin privileges. At the time this episode aired, she was Courteney Cox's sister-in-law.

The nude scene where Monica disrobes to entice Chandler by slathering vapor rub on her chest is performed by Courteney Cox's stand-in, Lisa Calderon (aka Lisa Avery).

The uncut DVD version has a different tag scene. Chandler is looking for something to eat but the refrigerator is empty. Joey is then seen attempting to give a Central Perk customer free food from Monica and Chandler's icebox. The female patron is played by Cheryl Hines, best known as Cheryl David in the HBO series *Curb Your Enthusiasm*.

6.14 "The One Where Chandler Can't Cry" (02.10.00)

In an early Central Perk scene, Phoebe's porn-star fan is played by Larry Joe Campbell, who is best known as Andy (Jim's brother) in *According to Jim* (2001-09).

The storyline of Ursula being a porn actress was inspired by an episode of *Mad About You* (ep The Final Frontier). In the show's series finale on May 24, 1999, a flash forward segment, set in the year 2021, reveals that Ursula is elected governor of New York after a successful career as a porn star.

Douglas Looper, the vampire in *Buffay the Vampire Layer*, is credited in four *Friends* episodes. He is the stand-in for Matt LeBlanc. Looper has only two other minor acting credits, nothing since 2005.

As Rachel watches the porn video, she notices a tattoo on Ursula's ankle. In real life, Jennifer Aniston has the tattoo "Norman" on her right foot in honor of her beloved dog who died at the age of 15. It was her first tattoo. She had it inked in 2011.

Set decorator Greg Grande appears in Central Perk during the last scene of Phoebe's narrative. As she and Joey discuss her collecting Ursula's residual checks, Grande is the stranger berated by Phoebe after he recognizes her visage from the adult films.

This is the final appearance of Reese Witherspoon as Jill Green. She was supposed to have a six-episode story arc but quit after two. Her unexpected departure caused mass hysteria in the writers room as everyone scrambled to rewrite scenes and storylines to accommodate her departure.

Numerous sources claim Witherspoon didn't reprise her role because she and Aniston clashed on set. This is furthest from the truth. The pair became good friends from day one and remain close. In fact, they costar in the Apple TV series *The Morning Show*. She has declared, "Aniston is a very strong and welcome presence in my life." Witherspoon declined the *Friends* offer because she did not enjoy live audience performances. She admitted to being "scared and too nervous."

The adult movies are parody titles of popular films and television programs: *Buffay the Vampire Layer* (TV series *Buffy the Vampire Slayer*), *Inspect Her Gadget* (animated TV series *Inspector Gadget*), *Sex Toy Story 2* (animated film *Toy Story 2*) and *Lawrence of A Labia* (iconic film *Lawrence of Arabia*). In "The One with the Free Porn" (4.17), Chandler and Joey watch *Good Will Humping* (drama film *Good Will Hunting*) and *In & Out... and In Again* (comedy flick *In & Out*). "They had a few other titles the writers came up with that they couldn't use on TV," James Michael Tyler said. "I don't remember any offhand, but I know the ratings people would not let them get away with it on network TV."

6.15 "The One That Could Have Been, Part 1" (02.17.00)
Every year the network asked the producers to film at least one double-length episode. Usually it was for the season finale but NBC wanted a special event for sweeps week, something with an advertising hook to attract viewers. The writers devised an alternate reality theme—each character can change one thing in their life but they must live with the decision no matter the consequence.

David Schwimmer came up with the unique pronunciation of karate [kar-ah-TAY].

This is the only episode with an entirely different title sequence. The producers decided to recreate the iconic fountain scene to give the impression that this was the way life really went for the gang. Each character is portrayed in their alternate reality persona with clips from nonexistent installments. The syndicated version uses the original title sequence with a tag scene of Fat Monica dancing.

The alternate title sequence was shot immediately after taping this episode. Courteney Cox was already in the fat suit and didn't need any costume or makeup preparation for the fountain shoot. The cast and crew were on the Warner Bros. ranch shooting until one in the morning.

Phoebe's alternate universe hairstyle is Lisa Kudrow's actual cut. In Season 6, she had to wear a wig because the creators thought her bob was too short for her character.

Monica's fat suit was very uncomfortable because Courteney Cox became unbearably hot inside the contraption. The costume didn't breathe so it trapped body heat, which was compounded with clothes, physical exertion and stage lighting. The end result was insufferable misery.

Matthew Perry devised the physical comedy bit involving Monica sitting on Chandler's hand and crushing it while they are waiting outside Phoebe's hospital room. Perry often added bits to scenes that paired him with Fat Monica.

During Joey's behind-the-scenes tour of *Days of Our Lives*, he says, "Hey, old man!" The old man is a real crew member. In fact, all the stagehands are *Friends* crew members.

During Joey's studio tour with Rachel, the fictitious *Days of Our Lives* backstage is in fact the backside of the regular sets being used for filming this episode. A couple of the extra flats (painted backdrops) were added to make it look like a soap opera set but a vast majority was the way it looked on the *Friends* set.

This episode marks the debut of Cole Mitchell Sprouse as Ross' son, Ben. Sprouse was cast after a solid performance in *Big Daddy* (1999) starring Adam Sandler. Since Ben was getting older, the producers needed a genuine actor who could handle the comedy and perform in front of a crowd, because it is often difficult for kids to perform properly and not be distracted by the circus atmosphere of a live studio audience.

Rachel's hot-pink faux fur is a fashion sensation according to most experts in the field. The outfit came from *Friends* costumer Debra McGuire's personal wardrobe collection.

After Rachel exclaims, "Oh, my God. You're a 30-year-old virgin!" Monica replies, "Say it louder, I don't think the guy all the way in the back heard you!" The patron in the back responds, "Yeah, I heard it." He is *Friends* writer Adam Chase.

This is the first episode where a fictional *Days of Our Lives* scene was shot on Stage 24. When Joey previously appeared on the soap opera in Season 2, his scenes were filmed at NBC Studios in Burbank on the actual *Days of Our Lives* set, using their cameras.

When Rachel is watching *Days of Our Lives* on television, the scene was purposely shot in video—the way daytime serials are actually filmed—so the shot would be authentic.

6.16 "The One That Could Have Been, Part 2" (02.17.00)
David Schwimmer loves physical comedy and specifically requested something physical to do for this episode. The writers obliged by adding the karate element.

The producers were huge fans of *The Archie Show* (aka *The Archies*) and *Speed Racer* (Japanese comic) so there are numerous allusions to them throughout the series (jokes, posters, t-shirts, etc.), even though many viewers may not know the cartoon characters. According to Kevin Bright, "If it rings a bell with all of us who work on the show, that's what we use as our barometer."

While trying to seduce Roger, Monica is wearing a scarf around her neck because the prosthetic double chin was bulky, heavy, and difficult to conceal. She also wears a scarf later in the episode (the day after sleeping with Chandler) for the same reason.

Even Carol and Susan are given alternate realities by swapping hairstyles—Susan's hair is straight while Carol's is curly. Normally, Susan has frizzy hair and Carol's is straight.

Jessica Hecht (Susan) was pregnant with her daughter, Stella Rose (b. 2000), during the filming of this installment. Hecht is married to Adam Bernstein, and they have one other child, Carlo (b. 2002).

In the alternate *Friends* reality, the ring on Rachel's right hand is the same jewelry she wears in the normal *Friends* universe. Jennifer Aniston owns the ring; it is not a prop.

Rachel falling off the couch while drunk was Jennifer Aniston's idea. She pitched it to the writers during rehearsal. They liked the way it looked so it was added to the scene.

When Rachel walks into the bedroom and busts Barry in bed with another woman, the mistress is Lisa Calderon (aka Lisa Avery), Courteney Cox's stand-in.

When Phoebe announces she is having a second heart attack, a coworker states, "Hey Pheebs! How's it going?!" The coworker is played by Cox's stand-in, Lisa Calderon.

The outcome of the alternate reality is, for the most part, the same as the real *Friends* universe: Ross' wife is lesbian with Susan as her lover, Monica and Chandler become a romantic couple, Rachel is single (after Barry cheats on her), Phoebe plays at Central Perk, Joey is an actor and a lothario, Chandler has a promising career (albeit a different profession), and there may be a Ross-Rachel romance.

6.17 "The One with Unagi" (02.24.00)
This episode is also known as "The One with the Mix Tape."

Unagi is a freshwater eel. "Zanshin" (literally "remaining mind") is the word closest to the concept Ross is trying to convey. It is a state of awareness (relaxed alertness) in Japanese martial arts.

Louis Mandylor (Carl) was a finalist for the role of Joey. He was cast ironically for the role of Carl since he was playing Joey's identical twin.

In Phoebe's apartment, Gladys has blonde hair and a blue dress, but in prior episodes she had black hair and a red dress. The set decorator occasionally changed Gladys' hair and dress colors to comport with the tone or mood of a scene.

Maggie Wheeler has a voice-only cameo as Janice where she leaves a special birthday message and song on Chandler's mixtape. Season 6 is the only season where she does not physically appear.

In the tag scene, Ross observes two women from behind whom he mistakes for Phoebe and Rachel. The doppelgangers are actually the stand-ins for Lisa Kudrow and Jennifer Aniston, i.e., Heather Sims and Kim Harris, respectively.

In Central Perk, Rachel and Phoebe sit on a couch by the window because their usual spot on the main sofa is occupied. Rachel complains that she can't stand sitting there. This is a rare instance where the sofa is occupied. It also happens in "The One with the Princess Leia Fantasy" (3.01) and "The One Where Chandler Gets Caught" (10.10).

All reviews rank "The One with Unagi" as a top-20 *Friends* episode.

6.18 "The One Where Ross Dates a Student" (03.09.00)
Ross enters Monica's apartment and raves about his teacher evaluations. Even though Ross is not a real-life professor at NYU, that didn't stop NYU students from evaluating his performance on RateMyProfessor.com, posting fake reviews of his teaching style and course load. Surprisingly, his marks are quite high. FYI: Famous NYU alumni include Cole Sprouse, Dakota Fanning, Angelina Jolie, the Olsen twins and James Franco.

This is the first guest appearance of Alexandra Holden as Elizabeth Stevens. After her first audition, she received a callback to do a "chemistry read" with David Schwimmer. Holden was terrified because the show's producers told her to come in looking "as hot as possible." She remarked, "I didn't know what to do with that information. It sent me into a tailspin. I stayed up all night trying to figure out what to wear. ... Now that I'm older I wouldn't be happy getting that message."

In Phoebe's apartment, Gladys is bald and wearing a blue dress. The figure's baldness represents the fire destruction, even though the artwork was unscathed from the blaze.

Ross' colleague Burt is exiting Dot's Spot restaurant. This is the same location where Monica has a dinner date with Chip Matthews in "The One with the Tea Leaves" (8.17). The eatery is named after Marta Kauffman's mother, Dorothy "Dot" Kauffman.

In one segment, Rachel is wildly throwing wet paper towel wads at Joey's entertainment unit. As she declares, "I love it at Joey's," Matt LeBlanc is lip-syncing her line.

The number and placement of paper towel wads that are sticking to the entertainment unit changes after Phoebe enters the apartment and interrupts their game.

The magna doodle sketch has a winged pyramid blasting off (and fire below) topped with the Eye of Providence and two asps slithering around.

6.19 "The One with Joey's Fridge" (03.23.00)
The magna doodle sketch has two upside down skateboarders on a steep half-pipe ramp with the sun blazing above. It's an inside joke for the stagehands after an unforgettable skateboarding wipeout.

Joey claims his parents bought the fridge when he was born, but in "The One with the Flashback" (3.06), the appliance was already in the apartment before he moved in, so it is either owned by Chandler or the landlord. Typically, in New York, the landlord owns and replaces the appliances.

Chandler mentions that Rachel's date to a charity ball must have at least $50 (to rent a tux), to which Joey remarks, "Ooh, so close," meaning he doesn't have the money to be her date to the ball. Coincidentally, when Matt LeBlanc was cast for the role of Joey, he only had $11 to his name.

Spanish posters sprinkled throughout various office, home and restaurant sets

Phoebe competes with Monica and Chandler to find a date for Rachel. In the real world, Jennifer Aniston is a matchmaker. "I'm really good at bringing people together. I'm like an alchemist with people," she confided. "I love introducing people to people I know."

Ross is constantly teased for dating someone much younger than him. In real life, David Schwimmer reeled in a much younger bride, Zoe Buckman, who is 19 years his junior. The couple married in 2010 and divorced seven years later.

Rachel said she met Sebastian at a newsstand as they both reached for *Field & Stream* magazine. She is holding a real-life issue with the headline "Deep Trouble" (February 2000), which is meant to portend unexpected friction in the competition to find Rachel a date for the charity event.

In the uncut DVD version, when the gang is on the sofa in Central Perk talking about spring break, Joey blames Elizabeth for breaking his fridge.

Ross and Elizabeth spend spring break in Daytona, Florida, where their escapades are broadcast on MTV. In reality, *MTV Spring Break 2000* was stationed in Cancun, Mexico.

6.20 "The One with Mac and C.H.E.E.S.E." (04.13.00)

This is another clip show episode. The *Friends* creative team was lazy and shortchanged their audience—a pattern of condemnable behavior they repeated each season until the series concluded. Since the producers did not know when this episode would air, they intentionally wrote a generic plotline devoid of any chronological context or character relevance. In other words, the installment could be inserted between episodes without impacting past or future narratives.

Like most clip shows, this episode was produced after the season finale. The creators purposely delayed production so the writers wouldn't waste their time and effort on an irrelevant installment.

This is the first and only episode to explicitly mention the magna doodle, and feature it in a plot.

When Joey and Phoebe are running lines for his audition, the script they are holding is the actual *Friends* script for this episode.

Rachel's hair is noticeably longer than the previous episode. Jennifer Aniston has hair extensions because she starting shooting the movie *Rockstar* (2001), which required her to have long hair. This episode was filmed over two months after the prior episode.

A clip of Paolo grabbing Phoebe's ass is featured in this episode. Cosimo Fusco (Paolo) reflected upon his *Friends* stint and its international success: "I can work in the most exquisite film, but the minute people find out I was Paolo, they're like: 'Oh my God!'"

Born in Matera, Italy, Fusco was educated in Los Angeles, Rome and Paris. His works include *Gone in 60 Seconds*, *Coco Chanel*, *Angels & Demons* and *The Man Who Invented Christmas*. Fusco speaks Italian, English, Spanish and French, and currently lives in Rome.

This is the final installment to feature the (original) chick and duck onscreen together. In "The One with Rachel's Book" (7.02), the duck is mentioned but unseen. At the time, there was no plan to eliminate the pets from the show because they were only used as needed, but after such a prolonged absence, the producers felt that bringing the pets back would be a desperate attempt at humor.

After the BFF hugging montage, Joey queries, "Hey, do we do this too much?" to which Chandler replies, "I think so. Yeah, get off me." The costars used this exchange to create a blooper moment. LeBlanc started the gag by saying that he was "uncomfortable" with the close contact, so Perry continued the bit by including some extra touching, and as they embraced, LeBlanc impulsively quipped, "What's that in your pocket?" (insinuating a hard-on). Everyone cracked up.

Jennifer Aniston's first acting role was an uncredited part in the 1988 movie *Mac and Me*, in which she played a dancer at a McDonald's fast food restaurant.

6.21 "The One Where Ross Meets Elizabeth's Dad" (04.27.00)
Bruce Willis and Matthew Perry costarred in *The Whole Nine Yards* (2000). One night while partying, prior to its theatrical release, the stars made a bet: if the movie topped the box office on its opening weekend, Willis would appear on *Friends* and donate his salary to charities of Perry's choice. And that's precisely what happened. Willis guest starred in three installments so he donated all the paychecks to five different nonprofit charities: UCLA Elizabeth Glaser Pediatric AIDS Foundation, AIDS Project Los Angeles, American Foundation for AIDS Research, Unicamp for underprivileged children, and Rape Treatment Center.

Although Bruce Willis informed *People* magazine Star Spotlight 2000 that he "agreed to a guest stint on *Friends* simply because he and Perry thought it would be fun," he also informed *Wired* in a videotaped interview that "I was on *Friends* because I lost a bet to Matthew Perry." In reality, Willis and Perry talked about a role on *Friends*, and Willis thought it would be fun, so that's why he made the bet.

As Rachel is perusing horoscopes in Central Perk, behind her on the shelf is Millstone Coffee. The company was founded in Everett, Washington, in 1981, by Phil Johnson. He started the business by selling 100-pound sacks of Arabica beans to high-end cafes in the greater Seattle area, and pioneered the notion of hawking whole-beaned coffees to supermarkets. In 2016 the brand was discontinued.

The horoscopes were meant to presage events in upcoming episodes: (1) the special gift is the wedding ring Chandler purchases in "The One with the Ring" (6.23), (2) the lovers quarrel is Monica and Chandler's relationship fallout after he refuses to get married in "The One with the Proposal, Part 1" (6.24), and (3) the secret crush is Richard's surprise proclamation of love to Monica in "The One with the Proposal, Part 2" (6.25).

Joey's television drama series is filmed at Pier59 Studios, at Chelsea Piers in New York City. The 110,000-square-foot structure is deemed the largest commercial photography and multimedia studio in the world.

In a blooper, Monica claims they were supposed to meet at six, and Chandler counters, "We said seven." Perry then improvises some colorful language to which Courteney Cox quickly responds, "If I had said seven, maybe I would've said something like this: 'Wow! My boyfriend's such a wiseass. Seven!'" Her ad-lib made it into the final edit.

6.22 "The One Where Paul's the Man" (05.04.00)
In the cold open in Central Perk, after Ross sits on the sofa arm, behind him is a blonde woman in a gray shirt who sips coffee and then starts chewing (even though there is no food on her table).

When Joey and Phoebe are in the dry cleaner store the first time, the same scene extras often walk past the window, most notably a woman wearing a brown shirt with mocha jacket and a blonde woman sporting a brown sweater with white stripe. In fact, all five dry cleaner scenes use the same extras, as well as a man in a lime green shirt, and they are visible multiple times walking past the storefront window.

While Joey is pointing out that his picture is next to Jim Belushi, the other headshots are Matt Lauer and fictional actress Zelda MacMurray, a portmanteau of writer Zelda Fitzgerald and actor Fred MacMurray. Other notable headshots include Harrison Ford, Steve Martin and Jay Leno.

At the dry cleaner store, Phoebe says that she and Matt Lauer (*Today*) would be great together. In real life, the two locked horns during an interview. "I almost got into a fight with Matt Lauer," Lisa Kudrow ardently declared, because he kept calling Phoebe dumb. "She's a nitwit, but she's not dumb. Phoebe knows about a lot of things, and she thinks of herself as an artist."

The dry cleaner owner (Ilia Volok) claims Joey's television show is offensive to Russians because it portrays them all as villains and terrorists, and that he never saw *Air Force One* (1997). This is a very subtle joke because, in the movie *Air Force One*, Volok plays Vladimir Krasin, one of the main Russian terrorists.

When Ross and Elizabeth (Alexandra Holden) are kissing on the couch, he pulls away so she asks what's wrong, and he states, "I'm just thinking about your father." During taping, the writers stopped production because they wanted another comeback to add to the joke. After a writers' huddle, they instructed Holden to respond, "Well, whatever works for you."

6.23 "The One with the Ring" (05.11.00)
Monica only appears in one scene for 50 seconds. Her storyline was removed because Courteney Cox was absent during production week to deal with personal issues related to a miscarriage. In total, she had seven miscarriages that were the result of antibodies attacking as her pregnancies tried to progress.

While Phoebe is trying on the tiara, she is using a fake mirror. The reflective side facing the camera has frosted glass paint to eliminate reflection, and a picture affixed to the surface. Mirrors are rarely used when filming because they often reflect images or set lighting, and can be distracting to the viewer.

The magna doodle reads "Rachel call D'ward St. George." This is a shoutout to Edward St. George, a hairstylist who worked on the set of *Friends*.

Joey and Ross talk about "freezing out" Chandler because they are infuriated with him. This idea becomes a future storyline in "The One with Ross's Tan" (10.03) where Monica and Phoebe try to freeze out a former neighbor (Amanda) who returns for a visit.

In the uncut DVD tag scene, Ross claims the engagement ring is beautiful. Phoebe then remarks, "And you should know, you've bought like a billion of them!" Rachel next asks why she never received a ring and asserts it would be nice to have a memento of their marriage, "something other than the divorce papers and the hangover." Ross counters that he never received sex when they were married, so she immediately and caustically retorts, "Well, yeah. No ring, no sex. Big surprise." Since this segment never aired, the writers added similar dialogue in the next episode.

This is Bruce Willis' final appearance. An interesting sidenote: he was elected homecoming king during his senior year at Penns Grove High School in New Jersey in 1973.

6.24 "The One with the Proposal, Part 1" (05.18.00)
Before writing the script, the producers contacted Tom Selleck to verify he was available and then pitched the story idea for his approval. "Tom has very strong opinions about the material so we wanted to make sure that he was happy with what we were doing before we went into it," David Crane explained.

The original plan was to have a season-ending cliffhanger where Elizabeth is pregnant with Ross' child, and after a yearlong story arc, the Season 7 finale would reveal he isn't the father. But the level of investment in their romance did not merit such treatment. The creators liked the irony, but it didn't warrant buildup for a whole year only to end feebly. Also, it wouldn't work with the cliffhanger involving Rachel's pregnancy at the end of Season 7.

Once it was decided that Elizabeth was not going to be pregnant, the producers were positive they didn't want her carrying over into the next season so they had to initiate a breakup. David Crane believed the writers sufficiently exhausted the stories of an older relationship—the student-teacher arrangement—so it was time to move on.

The engagement ring that Chandler gives Monica is modeled after the one Marta Kauffman received from her husband, Michael Skloff, which he personally designed for her.

After Richard recites a poem verse, Chandler has a quizzical look as he says, "What?!" This is one of Kevin Bright's favorite lines. It became a popular Chandler catchphrase to perplexing situations throughout the remainder of the series.

Following their breakup, Elizabeth bombards Ross with a water balloon from her dorm window. The short segment was filmed on Embassy Courtyard on the Warner Bros. lot, just around the corner from the *Friends* stage. Since it was filmed on location, the scene was preshot without an audience.

The restaurant kitchen scene was chosen because the writers wanted Richard to search for Monica to express his love. Although the scene staging is unrealistic because it lacks coworkers, it was purposely staged to focus attention on the drama without extraneous distractions from background extras.

During filming, as Richard confesses his love to Monica, Matthew Perry pranked Tom Selleck by unexpectedly entering the scene and yelling, "What the f*ck are you doing?" The audience went crazy. Selleck totally broke up. In the next couple takes, every time Selleck started the line, he had eyes looking over his shoulder just to make sure Perry wasn't going to crash the scene.

Several articles and viewer polls rank this installment as a top-10 *Friends* episode.

6.25 "The One with the Proposal, Part 2" (05.18.00)
Rachel and Phoebe discussing their happiness for Monica and Chandler—but actually feeling bitter and resentful—was inspired by Marta Kauffman's personal experience. "I think it's very relatable. I remember going through a period where all my friends were getting married and I was the only single one."

The backup husband storyline was inspired by Marta Kauffman's in-laws. "It just feels real. Feels like something I know that people do," she confided. "My sister-in-law talked about [it]. She has a backup and her backup is gay but at least she'd have someone and they both want children."

David Schwimmer's scenes (in Part 2) were filmed a week prior because he had to travel to London to shoot the HBO series *Band of Brothers*. This is the reason he's not in the last scene to partake in the group hug after Chandler proposes to Monica. (His absence is addressed in the dialogue.)

When Monica visits Richard at his residence, he is perusing *A Heartbreaking Work of Staggering Genius* by David Eggers. It's a memoir that chronicles the author's stewardship of his younger brother after the cancer-related deaths of his parents. The *Friends* prop department selected it for the title which represents the heartbreak Chandler is enduring due to his "ingenious" plan.

Originally, the final scene had Chandler down on one knee and Richard down on the other knee with Monica in the middle having to choose. This was changed because the audience knew who she would pick so the rest of the buildup would be pure silliness. It wasn't until production week that the showrunners crafted an ending where Chandler sufficiently muddles the relationship to the extent where it is believable that Monica rejects both men and goes home to her parents.

During filming, Monica's apartment was covered with a curtain to keep the audience at bay until the final reveal. All they saw was the hallway. The audience went crazy when Monica was unveiled in her apartment with a hundred burning candles. The creators needed "extra special permission" for all those candles, which required permits and fire department personnel backstage.

The proposal scene was performed twice. One was a bit more tearful. "It's probably one of the quietest moments ever in a *Friends* audience when he started proposing," Kevin Bright reminisced. "You could literally start to hear people starting to choke up and well in the audience."

The season ends without a cliffhanger. Rather than leaving Monica's decision unknown until the start of Season 7, the show's producers made the ending definitive because they thought the episode may serve as the series finale. At the time of filming, the cast had not signed contracts for another year. An agreement was finally reached four days before this episode aired.

This is one of Courteney Cox's favorite episodes. She loved her character's story arc.

Season 7: 2000-01

7.01 "The One with Monica's Thunder" (10.12.00)
This is one of the annual bottle episodes where no additional actors or sets are used.

Production was halted due to the lengthy honeymoon of Jennifer Aniston and Brad Pitt.

The episodic events occur on the same day as the prior episode (though filmed over five months later), which caused several continuity errors: (1) Matthew Perry is noticeably thinner after losing 20 pounds due to pancreatitis, and his hairstyle part changed, (2) Courteney Cox has much darker hair with a short side fringe, and (3) Jennifer Aniston shortened her long tresses.

Monica wants to celebrate her engagement at the Plaza Hotel which is one of New York's fanciest establishments. It appears in most Big Apple movies, such as *The Great Gatsby* (2013), *Eloise at the Plaza* (2003), *Serendipity* (2001), *Sleepless in Seattle* (1993) and *Moonstruck* (1987).

The Plaza Hotel was built in 1907 using the popular French Chateau style of the time. Originally, it was a residential building for the wealthiest New Yorkers, which explains its perfect downtown location (near Central Park, museums, and more). The interior was made to suit the most luxurious residents of the 20th century with gold, marble and crystal details.

This is the final episode where Lisa Kudrow wears a wig. She first started wearing it in "The One Where Ross Hugs Rachel" (6.02). The transition spans over two episodes. In the next episode she wears her hair in a bun, and in "The One with Phoebe's Cookies" (7.03) it is finally let down.

When Joey exits his bedroom dressed as a 19-year-old punk, Chandler is playing Play-Station *Crash Team Racing* (1999). The game is a preloaded sequence so Matthew Perry is just pushing buttons.

The magna doodle image has a giant cartoon girl—with two mini-buns atop her head and a flame tattoo above her right eye—sauntering about as she prepares to step on a small cartoon dog standing erect and holding a package. It represents Rachel crushing Monica's dream by stealing her thunder.

7.02 "The One with Rachel's Book" (10.12.00)
Ross' wedding advice to Chandler: "Take it from me, as the groom, all you have to do is show up and try to say the right name." This guidance is a callback to "The One with

Ross's Wedding, Part 2" (4.24) where Ross vowed to take Rachel as his bride during his nuptials to Emily.

This is the last time the duck is mentioned, though unseen. In "The Last One, Part 1" (10.17) it is revealed the duck and chick (rooster) were taken to a special farm for old pets (i.e., they died).

Rachel's novel involves a vicar, which Joey thinks is something like a hockey goalie. In reality, it's a religious post, e.g., representative or deputy of a bishop (Roman Catholic Church), member of the clergy in charge of a chapel (Episcopal Church), or incumbent receiving a stipend but not the tithes of a parish (Church of England).

During rehearsal, David Schwimmer suggested using the physical comedy bit where the massage table crushes Ross' foot. He loved doing physical comedy and often suggested ideas for scenes.

After Chandler puts his foot down and says "No" to Monica's dream wedding, he turns and raises a hand to his nose as if to adjust eyeglasses. This was a subconscious act by Matthew Perry. It was unscripted. He was first prescribed glasses during the summer hiatus which he wore during rehearsal, but not while filming. Consequently, adjusting his spectacles was a rote habit to correct his blurry vision.

Chandler claims he and Monica will have twin girls and two boys, live outside the city, and have a place for Joey to grow old. In Season 10, Monica and Chandler adopt twins, move to Westchester, and have a room set aside for Joey.

In an alternate epilogue, Phoebe gives Ross a massage which includes beating him with a phone book. She then asks if he wants a traditional massage with the hands. When Ross responds in the affirmative, Phoebe grabs a smilodon (saber-toothed tiger) skull to use for his rubdown.

7.03 "The One with Phoebe's Cookies" (10.19.00)

Chandler is sporting new eyeglasses but everyone thinks he already wore spectacles. In real life, Matthew Perry started wearing glasses in 2000 so it was written into the script.

Writer Ted Cohen once wore glasses into a steam room and accidentally sat on a gym member's knee. This became the inspiration for Chandler sitting on his future father-in-law's lap in the sauna.

When Rachel and Joey are on the sailboat, the background images shift between shots. The twin towers of the World Trade Center appear and disappear. Since the actors are actually performing on a soundstage in front of a green screen, the images are added in postproduction. Errors occur because editing is done after the images are set.

This is the last episode to feature Joey's boat. The producers were exasperated at how difficult it was to get the watercraft on the set to film scenes. Hereafter, the boat is only mentioned once, in "The One Where Ross is Fine" (10.02), where Joey reveals he sold it.

The idea of Monica discovering the cookie recipe on a bag of chocolate chips was a last-minute flash of inspiration from the episode writers. They thought it would be amusing to play off Phoebe's cultural naivete, and using the accent in the product name seemed perfect to them. They knew it was gold at the first table read when Lisa Kudrow's awry enunciation drew huge laughs.

According to staff writer Ted Cohen, this is not a Nestlé-sponsored product placement episode but it did result in an unexpected benefit for the creative team. "Literally 200 boxes of Nestlé Toll House cookie mix were delivered to the office," recalled Greg Malins.

Episode cowriter Sherry Bilsing-Graham claims she cannot make chocolate chip cookies without thinking about this installment. "Every time I see the name I think of the first time Ted pitched it and my realization of what he was saying," she recalls. "It was just as funny as watching Phoebe say it on TV and realizing what she's saying. You can't help but remember it."

Some of the Central Perk artwork created by pop artist Burton Morris

7.04 "The One with Rachel's Assistant" (10.26.00)

When *Mac and C.H.E.E.S.E.* is broadcast, the executive producers are Colleen Mahan, Eric Goldberg and Missy Krehbiel, the assistants to Marta Kauffman, Kevin Bright and David Crane, respectively.

The two pizza boxes on Monica's coffee table is a subtle in-joke for *Friends* fans because it represents the Joey Special.

In the first scene at Central Perk, Phoebe is reading *LOOT*, promoted as the UK's largest classified ads newspaper. It debuted in March 1985 on pale pink or salmon paper, and published every Thursday (LOOT stands for "Look Out On Thursdays"), but later started publishing a Monday edition on yellow paper.

When Phoebe is shown a photo of Tag, it is not the original snapshot taken by Rachel. The pic has stage lighting in the background (it was actually taken backstage during a rehearsal break).

On the wall outside Rachel's office is a print for Folies-Bergère's La Loïe Fuller by Jules Chéret. It's a poster promoting the Paris debut of American dancer Loïe Fuller (1862–1928) at Folies-Bergère cabaret music hall in 1893. Fuller caused a sensation with her "serpentine" dance, whirling across the stage in diaphanous costume, transformed by colored lighting. She is considered an innovator of both modern dance and theatrical lighting techniques.

In the show, Rachel is five years older than Tag, but in real life, Jennifer Aniston is nine years older than Eddie Cahill. At the time, Aniston was 31 and Cahill was 22.

Eddie Cahill claims Jennifer Aniston encouraged him to "have a voice on set" and that the rest of the cast was very accommodating of his nerves. He even established a lasting friendship with David Schwimmer. *Friends* fans still recognize him to this day.

7.05 "The One with the Engagement Picture" (11.02.00)

Joey ruins a shirt while eating a jelly-filled donut. It is actually a stage prop that has a hole filled with purple goo. When it is squeezed, the liquid oozes out. Notice that Matt LeBlanc never takes a bite.

Phoebe goes on a date with Hums While He Pees (Kyle), played by David Sutcliffe. This episode aired one month after he began his signature role as Christopher Hayden on *Gilmore Girls*.

Whitney is portrayed by Julia Campbell, best known as "mean girl" Christie Masters in *Romy and Michele's High School Reunion* (1997) costarring Lisa Kudrow.

The magna doodle has a drawing of a giant curling wave that causes a surfer riding a shortboard to crash while a dog is walking along the beach. The crew members had a recent surfing outing.

Rachel tells Joey, "I had a crush on you when I first met you." In reality Matt LeBlanc had a crush on Jennifer Aniston when they first met. As he reluctantly confessed: "I had a little crush on Jen in the very beginning, but I think the whole world did too, so what are you going to do?"

In Central Perk, Phoebe and Ross commence bickering like an old married couple as they defend their significant others. During filming, the actors could not stop laughing to finish their scene. At one point, David Schwimmer suggested shooting the scene line by line. Lisa Kudrow expeditiously quipped, "I did that once. Got an Emmy."

Joey is paired with Monica for the newspaper wedding engagement announcement. The accompanying write-up appears normal but midway thru the following text repeats: "We wouldn't want anything to ruin the big day now would we. Announcements will soon be arriving to the specially chosen guest list. This will be the wedding of the century." In addition, there are two other engagement announcements that repeat the following text: "They were married May 10th in Pasadena, CA. The happy occasion was witnessed by a homeless guy, Elvis and some Japanese tourists."

7.06 "The One with the Nap Partners" (11.09.00)
The scene where Joey and Ross take their first nap together required numerous takes because Matt LeBlanc and David Schwimmer could not stop laughing.

In the uncut DVD version, Chandler is watching *The Bikini Car Wash Company* (1992), a sex comedy about a group of young women who sport bikinis while washing vehicles to help a local business owner. The movie clip includes a topless woman—her bikini top lacks adequate coverage as she scrubs a car window with her soapy breasts.

The magna doodle image has a Ducati 916 motorcycle aka crotch rocket. The bike was produced from 1994 to 1998 and is often cited as one of the most beautiful motorcycles ever built. Matt LeBlanc had just bought the bike so he brought it to the studio to show it off. Paul Swain decided to sketch it.

While Chandler uses the toilet, Monica wants to have a conversation, so Matthew Perry added a couple bloopers. In one take he stated, "You girls got a measuring tape?" and then the next time he stated: "Honey, you gotta see this. This is like the size of my arm." Rather than breaking character to enjoy the easy laugh, Cox rolled her eyes, shrugged, and went in to check it out for herself.

The maid of honor competition in Joey's apartment is modeled after the improvisation series *Whose Line Is It Anyway?* (1998-2007) where members of the studio audience suggest ideas for the games and skits that four actors, usually improvisational comics, perform. The series features Ryan Stiles, Colin Mochrie and Wayne Brady as its regular performers, and a fourth seat for a guest panelist. FYI: Stiles costarred with Matthew Perry in FOX's ill-conceived pilot *LAX 2194*, the show that nearly cost Perry his defining role in *Friends*.

Rachel and Phoebe compete to be Monica's maid of honor. In real life, Courteney Cox was matron of honor for Jennifer Aniston's wedding to Justin Theroux in 2015.

During the tag scene where Ross and Joey are taking a nap, the coffee table contains a copy of *Cycle News* with the headline "The Return of Miguel" (August 9, 2000). This was added for Matt LeBlanc's benefit since he is an avid motorcyclist.

7.07 "The One with Ross's Library Book" (11.16.00)
This episode is directed by David Schwimmer.

In the opening scene at the university library, a woman passes in front of the camera reading the fictitious book *Co-Operative Dictums*. It is a subtle acknowledgment that the show's success is based on a collaborative effort.

This is the first episode where Rachel has a short blunt-bob hairstyle. Jennifer Aniston kept her hair long for over four years since abandoning The Rachel hairstyle. This is the most daring cut she adopted on the show. The bob lasts until "The One Where Rachel Tells Ross" (8.03).

Jennifer Aniston chose the hairstyle out of necessity. "The real reason I cut my hair? My real hair was getting thinned out again from all the extensions," she confessed. "It was starting to look fake." She ultimately regretted the cut, stating she feels sexier and more feminine with longer hair.

Australian Olympic swimmer Ian Thorpe appears as a scene extra in Central Perk. He is wearing blue jeans with a brown leather jacket and sipping coffee with a woman clothed in a green long-sleeve shirt. He first appears when Joey and Erin enter the coffee shop discussing the Mets. Thorpe was the youngest person to join the Australian men's swim team and set 22 world records. At age 15, he was the youngest gold medalist in World Championships history, winning the 400 m freestyle. On the morning of September 11, 2001 (9/11 terrorist attack), he was on his way to see the observation deck at the World Trade Center before realizing he had forgotten his camera. Thorpe returned to his hotel room to collect it and when he turned on the TV, he saw the North Tower on fire.

Phoebe asks Erin, "So, how's the second-greatest love affair of the century?" This is an inside joke referring to the marriage between Jennifer Aniston and Brad Pitt on July 29, 2000. The media circus surrounding their relationship was unparalleled. After Phoebe sidesteps Rachel's query as to whom is the first, Aniston breaks character by laughing because she knows the joke is about her.

Janice wore a lot of outrageous clothing, but one of Maggie Wheeler's favorites was the head-to-toe golden outfit—Betsy Johnson coat, lace pants and matching shoes. Unlike the main cast of *Friends*, Wheeler treasured wardrobe fittings. "You should see the stuff that didn't make it on the show," she said. "Just going down for those wardrobe fittings was comedy in itself because we would just try on this crazy clothing and just laugh our tails off, and then finally pick the things that we really loved the most."

7.08 "The One Where Chandler Doesn't Like Dogs" (11.23.00)
This is a bottle episode with only one guest actor, Eddie Cahill (Tag). Although it is a Thanksgiving episode, there is no dinner scene (only Monica eating dessert), and the holiday is barely mentioned.

In Monica's apartment, to the left of the hallway door, there is a print often overlooked, though present in nearly every installment of the series. Maïna La Voyante (Maina the Clairvoyant) is a vintage theater exhibition wall poster from 1920 by artist Louis Galice promoting a magic stage act. In 1924 it was made into a French silent film drama.

Joey asks Rachel if Tag likes her because if he doesn't "this is all a moo point. It's like a cow's opinion. It just doesn't matter. It's moo." Joey isn't alone in his mispronunciation. Many people believe it's a "mute point," which is a nonexistent phrase. The proper term is "moot point," which has opposing meanings. It can mean an issue that is open for debate (British English), or an issue no longer practically applicable and irrelevant for the present issue (American English).

One of Marta Kauffman's favorite moments on the show comes from this episode. "'Moo point' is the one that comes back to me all the time and just makes me laugh," she said.

Tag's description of a yearlong on-off relationship with his girlfriend parallels Ross and Rachel's past romantic turmoil. It was specifically written for comedic juxtaposition.

During the balcony scene, after Joey inadvertently reveals that Rachel likes Tag, there is a clear shot of a wooden sculpture of an old man. Of all the items set decorator Greg Grande curated for the show, this sculpture stands out in particular. "That was a really classic find," he proudly revealed.

Throughout Ross' tale that Monica is upset with Chandler for sending the dog away, the view outside the bay window features an apartment wing with exterior guard rails and entrance doors attached to the building (seemingly affixed to the secret hallway closet). In nearly every episode, Monica's balcony overlooks a street with an apartment building on the other side.

When asked about his favorite *Friends* moment, David Crane said, "Every Thanksgiving episode. I just love the Thanksgiving episodes."

7.09 "The One with All the Candy" (12.07.00)
During the neighborhood park scene where Ross is telling Ben that he has "one daddy, two mommies," Cole Sprouse (Ben) can be seen mouthing Ross' line.

At the start of Act 1, there is a winter park scene with people ice skating on Wollman Rink, a public ice rink in the southern part of Central Park. It opened in 1950 and is open for ice skating from late October to early April and then it is remade into Victorian Gardens, an amusement park for children, from late May to September.

After Rachel declares, "Oh, Monica, come on. You know I don't sleep with guys on the first date," Monica recites a list of boys' names to refute the claim. In a playful blooper, instead of saying the scripted names, Courteney Cox uttered David Crane, Kevin Bright and Marta Kauffman (the executive producers).

The magna doodle has a dreidel with the Hebrew letters that represent "Hey" and "Nun." A dreidel is a small four-sided spinning top used to play a game during Hanukkah. The Hebrew letters inscribed on a dreidel (transliterated as Nun, Gimel, Hey and Shin), form an acronym for the Hebrew saying "Nes Gadol Hayah Sham" ("a great miracle happened there"), referring to the miracle upon which Hanukkah is centered. The magna doodle image foreshadows the Hanukkah theme in the next episode.

In the scene outside Central Perk, a bike stand miraculously appears on the sidewalk; it was never there before and will never appear there again. It's where the fire hydrant is located in other episodes.

The motorcycle outside Central Perk is the same one that was the subject of a magna doodle drawing in "The One with the Nap Partners" (7.06). It is a red Ducati 916 (aka crotch rocket) that is owned by Matt LeBlanc. He wanted to show it off so he asked to include it as set dressing.

There are three pronounced errors in Phoebe's bicycling scenes: (1) she is smiling just before crashing the bike outside Central Perk, (2) the sound of her hitting the ground occurs before she actually would have hit the ground, and (3) when she falls off the bike in the park, she is actually standing beside it and then unhands it, instead of dropping from a sitting position.

7.10 "The One with the Holiday Armadillo" (12.14.00)
David Schwimmer directed this episode. It is one of his most memorable efforts.

Marta Kauffman used this installment for show-and-tell at her son's class. He attended Hebrew School and they had something called "Schmooze with Jews." She went to the school as one of the moms and talked to the children about her job. This episode was a great union of occupation and Jewish faith.

In the scene where Phoebe is freaking out about the word "probably," one bit was edited where she declares, "Your stepfather probably won't try to molest you." The producers thought the quip was too salacious for the younger viewing audience.

Joey's drum set was very popular during production week. Everyone tried it out, but the best beats came from Courteney Cox. She is an adept drummer and actually played the instrument for the 1995 music video "I'll Be There for You" (the *Friends* theme song).

The inability to slip someone cash was based on David Crane's personal limitations. "I have a phenomenal inability to do the graceful pass of money to the guy thing," he said.

The multifaith household and joint holiday celebration was inspired by Kevin Bright's home life. He is Jewish and his wife is not. As a trade-off, their family celebrates both holidays, Christmas and Hanukkah.

The magna doodle has five ducks ascending from a marsh as two hunters are standing in tall grass with rifles pointing at their prey. The *Friends* crew were avid duck hunters.

The holiday armadillo costume had to be specially designed and handcrafted to attain the desired effect. Costume designer Debra McGuire employed Doug White Productions because he is a "genius at doing these extra special things for us." McGuire praised the finished product as a "work of art" because it takes a ton of effort to make a costume like that in less than a week.

In 2019, Warner Bros. auctioned official *Friends* production materials, costumes, and props from the series with proceeds benefiting The Trevor Project, the world's largest suicide prevention and crisis intervention organization for LGBTQ young people. FYI: A studio-edition reproduction of the holiday armadillo costume fetched $4,100, much less than the expected $10,000 to $15,000.

7.11 "The One with All the Cheesecakes" (01.04.01)

This episode was inspired by an incident that occurred on set. "Somebody on staff had got sent a box of fruit that was not for him, and he ate it with the justification that by the time he tracked down the person it was supposed to go to, it would have gone bad. So he was really doing the world a favor," writer Shana Goldberg-Meehan declared. "We thought fruit was not tempting enough. We needed something better than fruit." They settled for irresistible cheesecake.

Joey uses the nickname "Big Daddy" when speaking with Phoebe. The writers added this plug for Cole Sprouse's benefit since he appeared in the movie *Big Daddy* (1999).

The magna doodle contains a house, van, police car with flashing cherry, and helicopter circling above. A cop has a gun drawn and the suspect is spread eagle on the ground with hands above his head. This is a crafty allusion to Chandler and Rachel as dessert-stealing scofflaws.

British journalist Sarfraz Manzoor has an uncredited role as a coffee shop patron. He was on set interviewing the show's creators for an article when he was given the part. Manzoor is sitting at the round table behind the couch wearing a black shirt and burnt-orange jacket (visible as Ross enters, after the Sam Goody bit).

Ross mentions being invited to a cousin's wedding, and plans on taking Joan Tudeski as his date. In *The Whole Nine Yards* (2000), the character Jimmy Tudeski is played by Bruce Willis. This naming credit was a nod to Willis for a recent Emmy Award win for his *Friends* performance in Season 6.

Writer Shana Goldberg-Meehan thought the storyline was pretty simple. "They have to keep upping the stakes, and eating it off the floor seemed like the logical ending," she stated. "[The] writers are super into food. There were definitely people who have eaten stuff off the floor in that room."

Initially, David Crane was very resistant to the idea of having Joey eat cheesecake off the floor. "I remember David being like 'He's not a cartoon. He doesn't see giant hams in people's eyes. He's a human being. He doesn't walk around with a fork in his pocket,'" Goldberg-Meehan said. "But on the second take, he let us try it, and it got a really good reaction. He was like, 'You know what? I guess Joey's a human who does walk around with a fork in his pocket.' He let us keep the moment, even though it was probably a little bit larger than stuff we normally did."

Most reviewers cite "The One with All the Cheesecakes" as a top-15 *Friends* episode.

7.12 "The One Where They're Up All Night" (01.11.01)

Aside from the rooftop scenes, none of the storylines intersect with each other. This is uncommon since *Friends* narratives often dovetailed, much like *Seinfeld*.

Ross wants the gang to watch the Bapstein-King comet. This is a fictional comet.

To illustrate how tiresome it is to read one of Monica's books, Chandler pretends to fall asleep. This is a callback to "The One with the Butt" (1.06) where the gang performed the same behavior. In real life, the cast would use the fake-sleeping gag whenever some-one began discussing a boring topic.

The magna doodle has a massive cup of coffee with steam rising above. This represents the gang being up all night and needing caffeine to stay awake.

After Phoebe shatters the smoke detector with a shoe heel and it continues to beep, she shrieks: "What do you want from me?!" This is a quote from *Jerry Maguire* (1996).

In the uncut DVD version, Phoebe wears earplugs, a hat and earmuffs to suppress the beeping sound of the smoke detector. Her thoughts focus on the song "Mickey" by Toni Basil (#1, 1982) and soon the vexing earworm is worse than the smoke detector beep. The song is Basil's only hit and the music video has the 37-year-old singer performing routines in a cheerleader outfit. Contrary to reports, her lyrics—"So come on and give it to me / Any way you can / Any way you want to do it / I'll take it like a man"—do not infer anal sex.

Phoebe's smoke detector didn't actually beep. The sound was added in postproduction. However, during filming, a noise was used so the audience could understand the scene.

While hanging from the fire escape, Matt LeBlanc is wearing a harness vest attached to the ladder. Thus, he is not actually carrying David Schwimmer's weight. The vest did all the work.

Ross' fall to the ground was only a couple feet with a thick padded mat below.

Most reviews of "The One Where They're Up All Night" have it listed as one of the worst *Friends* episodes of the entire series, consistently ranking it in the bottom 25.

7.13 "The One Where Rosita Dies" (02.01.01)
The magna doodle has the words "USDA PRIME" inside a 3-D shield. This is homage to Stephen Prime, director of this episode. It was his directorial debut. He was an editor for the series and credited with slicing 160 episodes.

When Rachel breaks the recliner, it is designed to split into two pieces. Jennifer Aniston simply pulls a lever attached to the side of the headrest cushion.

Phoebe is a telemarketer selling toner to businesses. When Jennifer Aniston moved to Los Angeles in the summer of 1989, her first job was a telemarketer selling timeshares in the Poconos (NY). In her words, she "sold her soul" by taking the job and never made one sale in three months. "I didn't like timeshare selling. I hated that job," she stated.

Marta Kauffman invited Jason Alexander to guest star on the show. She is good friends with him and his wife, Daena Title. Kauffman and Alexander first met in 1985 when he costarred in *Personals*, an off-Broadway play written by her and David Crane.

Joey's new recliner, the La-Z-Boy E-cliner 3000, is a modified version of the La-Z-Boy Oasis (Cool Chair). The writers thought it would be funny to have matching chairs with an arm that lifted up to store their cold beer. "I looked for the most obnoxious ones I could find," Greg Grande admitted. After ordering matching chairs, he bought leather and reupholstered both to match. The E-cliner 3000 brand name is fictitious (though La-Z-Boy does have a model called the Explorer e-cliner).

This is the first supersized episode, though not written as such. It was made longer by using extra footage that would have been otherwise cut. A typical sitcom is 30 minutes (with commercials) and has two act breaks while a supersized show is up to 40 minutes with three act breaks. Thus, the editor had to create act breaks in places that normally wouldn't be there. The syndicated version excises at least five minutes of footage, which is a significant number of scenes and dialogue.

Supersized episodes were created as a promotional stunt to compete against *Survivor*. On February 1, 2001, CBS switched its immensely popular reality series (No. 2 overall) to Thursday night, opposite *Friends*. NBC Entertainment President Jeff Zucker (who started in December 2000) bucked convention by extending *Friends* up to 10 minutes. Executives thought he was crazy but soon all the networks were doing it to their shows.

Despite Jeff Zucker's efforts, *Survivor* still crushed *Friends* in the ratings with 29 million viewers to *Friends'* 22.2 million, and dominated the rest of the season. Although *Friends* ended the season ranked No. 5, it had its lowest average audience (20.2 million) during its decade run.

7.14 "The One Where They All Turn Thirty" (02.08.01)

This is not a clip show. Despite the fact that there are numerous flashbacks, no archive scenes are shown. All flashback scenes are specially created for this episode.

Lisa Kudrow had a head cold so her voice is noticeably affected in most of her scenes.

Since Rachel was wearing a crown during her birthday celebration, the head costumer purposely dressed her in a designer Crown 12-4 tee for wardrobe juxtaposition.

During Monica's drunken speech, she falls next to the couch. A thick mat is positioned behind the sofa to break her fall.

While taping Rachel's birthday scene, Jennifer Aniston received an unexpected phone call which delayed production. She forgot to turn off the ringer before filming started. Although she was extremely embarrassed, the producers were not too pleased with her.

In the tag scene, as Joey and Ross walk down the thoroughfare, there is a Ducati 916 motorcycle parked in front of the newsstand. It is owned by Matt LeBlanc and appears in other episodes.

Throughout the series, Jennifer Aniston demonstrated a unique vocal tic. She clears her throat (often designated phonetically as "Ahem") before reciting lines that often involve an awkward situation. It has been documented in over 200 instances.

According to this episode, the oldest member of the group is Phoebe (after discovering she is a year older than expected) and the youngest is Rachel. Thus, the ranking from oldest to youngest: Phoebe, Joey, Chandler, Ross, Monica and Rachel. Of course, this is not absolutely certain since the writers lacked continuity in the birth month and year of various characters.

Although this is the second supersized *Friends* installment, it only has two minutes of additional run time. It was not written as a supersized episode. The episode was made longer using extra footage that was shot; however, the act breaks stayed the same.

7.15 "The One with Joey's New Brain" (02.15.01)

In the cold opening, Joey refers to *Days of Our Lives* as "*DOOL*." After *Friends* coined the term *DOOL* as a popular expression, NBC began using the acronym as a social media hashtag for viewers to use to discuss *Days of Our Lives* storylines and characters.

When casting the character Cecilia Monroe, the creators wanted an experienced actress with credibility, comedy and drama. Someone who could give a great performance like Susan Lucci in *All My Children*, and their first thought was Susan Sarandon.

Susan Sarandon agreed to the role because she, her husband (Tim Robbins), and all three children were huge fans of the show. The entire family was on set to watch her performance live.

Eva Amurri aka Eva Amurri Martino (Dina) is Susan Sarandon's daughter. FYI: When Sarandon agreed to appear on *Friends*, she stipulated that her daughter be cast on the show as well.

In "The One with Frank Jr." (3.05), Susan Sarandon was on Ross' celebrity freebie list but she was subsequently replaced after Chandler declared that she was too political and "probably wouldn't let you do it, unless you donated four cans of food first."

In the scene where Cecilia Monroe slaps Joey, Susan Sarandon was hesitant to hit Matt LeBlanc and kept trying to be careful. Finally, he insisted, saying, "Ah, just go ahead. Just smack me." And that's exactly what she did, so if the slap looks authentic, that's because it is.

David Schwimmer had professional bagpipe lessons during production week. In fact, he is playing the bagpipe in all the scenes. It is a very difficult instrument to learn so all week he practiced relentlessly, much to the chagrin of the entire cast and crew.

The producers told Schwimmer that he could pretend to play the instrument on-camera and they would hire a professional musician to play off-camera. He adamantly refused. He was determined to learn and perform the bagpipe live.

In Phoebe's abode, when Rachel uses her cell phone to call the mystery man's phone, Jennifer Aniston is using her real phone because she needed it nearby since she was expecting an important call. During filming, however, she forgot to turn it off. Naturally, as Rachel and Phoebe were arguing whether the phone still works, Aniston's phone began to ring.

While Joey is standing backstage by the food table, the entire sequence is filmed on the *Friends* soundstage, though it is redressed to resemble a soap opera set. The staircase behind him leads directly to the audience bleachers. During his discussion with Cecilia (Sarandon), all the exposed lumber behind her is the backside of actual sets being used in this episode. The backstage workers are real *Friends* stagehands, not scene extras.

Actor Matt LeBlanc was "very, very nervous to be working with Susan Sarandon," said Marta Kauffman. "He was terrified about it. He kept feeling like he would never live up to things, and then he ended up having to calm her down." She, too, was very nervous to do the show. Sarandon later reported, "Matt LeBlanc was so sweet and patient that we actually did work past the panic to a place where we enjoyed ourselves."

When Cecilia claims she is going to do a film in Guadalajara, Joey bewilderingly replies, "The airport?" In the writers room, this was their favorite dumb joke delivered by Joey. The actual New York airport is LaGuardia.

This is the third supersized installment but the first one written in that specific format with appropriately placed act breaks. Supersized shows extended filming sessions one to two hours because the script was 10 pages longer. This installment is 28 minutes in length; syndicated episodes are only 21 to 22 minutes.

Susan Sarandon is credited as playing Jessica Lockhart, but her *Friends* role is Cecilia Monroe (the actress who plays Jessica Lockhart in the fictional *Days of Our Lives*).

7.16 "The One with the Truth About London" (02.22.01)
David Schwimmer directed this episode.

In the uncut DVD version, there is an extra narrative where Phoebe takes painkillers (Hexadrin) for a headache. At first she loves the medication, however, after reading the medical information leaflet, she becomes paranoid and believes she is experiencing all the side effects.

There are two occurrences of product placement. First, while sitting at Monica's dining table, Matthew Perry adjusts a bottle of Yoo-hoo chocolate drink after a crew member offscreen instructs him that the bottle label is askew for the camera angle. Second, a bag of Rold Gold pretzels is openly displayed in front of the Cookie Time cookie jar.

While sitting on the recliner before opening the entry door for Ross, Rachel is diligently reading *To Kill a Mockingbird* by Harper Lee. This prop is used to portend Monica being wrongfully accused of a crime she did not commit, namely, having romantic feelings for Joey when everybody knows that Chandler is her true soul mate.

Carol is dressed in baggy clothing because actress Jane Sibbett had given birth shortly before filming this episode and was carrying some extra weight. She gave birth to her third child (daughter Violet) on November 28, 2000.

When Rachel confronts Ben about pulling pranks, he mimics her speech. This bit was written as a celebration of the movie *Big Daddy*, where Julian (Cole and Dylan Sprouse) imitates Sonny (Adam Sandler) as he watches hockey. The writers liked Sprouse's performance in that scene so they copied it.

David Schwimmer decided to end the installment by pranking Jennifer Aniston. After yelling at Ben and chasing him into the hallway, they ascend the staircase while Rachel stands nearby. In the script, Ross wasn't supposed to fall down the staircase, so as a prank, Schwimmer screamed and then tossed a life-size dummy onto the staircase and it landed directly in front of her. Aniston shrieked. She was completely mortified. After rushing to lend assistance and discovering it was a dummy, she was livid. Her reaction is completely genuine.

The tag scene is an alternate reality fantasy that hearkens to the original pilot concept where Monica and Joey were supposed to become lovers. In this episode, however, the added twist projects their romance into the future as a married couple.

Joey's fat suit is a specially designed one-piece outfit modeled after Monica's fat suit.

This is the fourth and final supersized episode of the season. In Season 8, NBC paused its promo stratagem after realizing that no program could compete against *Survivor* in the weekly ratings. Still, NBC resumed the advertising gimmick in Seasons 9 and 10.

7.17 "The One with the Cheap Wedding Dress" (03.15.01)

Gabrielle Union portrays Kristen Leigh, a romantic interest for both Ross and Joey. She has the honor of being the first black actor to have a guest starring role on *Friends*. Of course, she believes the part was given to her solely on merit, but in reality it was partly awarded to appease critics who complained that *Friends* lacked diversity.

Ross flirting with Kristen by using his knowledge of sewage is a callback to "The One Where Ross Can't Flirt" (5.19) where he discussed gas odors with the pizza delivery girl.

The bridal boutique owner is played by Kim Harris, the stand-in for Jennifer Aniston.

Monica's nemesis, Megan, is portrayed by Andrea Bendewald, one of Jennifer Aniston's best friends and a bridesmaid at her 2000 wedding to Brad Pitt. FYI: The following year, Aniston reciprocated as Bendewald's matron of honor for her wedding to Mitch Rouse.

Monica's discount wedding dress is not the same style or design as the original dress at the bridal boutique. The substitution was on purpose. The costumer didn't want to risk damage to the gown when the prospective brides wrestle for the garment at the store.

Dane Anthony Jungle Swing is a pseudonym for the real-life Dane Anthony Band. Kevin Bright wanted legitimate live entertainment at the wedding reception, and the band is renowned in the New York area. The quintet has been performing since 1988, primarily in Atlantic City, New Jersey.

This episode was supposed to air two months earlier but was pushed back. Thus, some scenes are inconsistent with events that occur in later episodes. The best illustration is the fully functional Barcalounger in Monica and Chandler's apartment. But in "The One Where Rosita Dies" (7.13), four episodes prior, the recliner was broken and discarded.

7.18 "The One with Joey's Award" (03.29.01)

Joey is a presenter at the Soapie Awards, where he is also nominated (but doesn't win). In real life, the six *Friends* costars were presenters at the 54th Annual Primetime Emmy Awards in 2002. In the sitcom's decade-long run, each costar (except Courteney Cox) received at least one Emmy nomination. *Friends*, as a show, was nominated six times for Outstanding Comedy Series, winning in 2002. Overall, the series was nominated for 62 Primetime Emmy Awards, and only brought home six trophies.

The writers created the fictitious Soapie Awards as an attempt to preserve the positive personal and professional reputations of the cast and to dissuade viewers from thinking that actors are arrogant and conceited when they win real-life television awards. This opened the door to having Jessica Ashley disparage the Soapie Awards and venerate legitimate acting honors.

The magna doodle drawing has an enormous fish with its mouth wide open and sharp teeth exposed as it prepares to swallow an approaching smaller fish. This is a metaphor for Joey being a small fish in the big pond of soap opera television and being swallowed by the more talented competition.

Monica's restaurant kitchen has a chalkboard with coworkers' names. In reality, they are names of *Friends* crew members, e.g., Jeff and Lisa (Jeff Astrof and Lisa Calderon).

Two pieces of art and a TV show cartoon poster that hung in Ross' apartment over the years

Matthew Perry has limited screen time. Other than a 15-second bit in Central Perk, he has only one scene (with Monica in their apartment). He appears for only 128 seconds due to a drug relapse on February 27, 2001, while filming *Serving Sara* in Texas. Perry entered rehab for addiction to Vicodin, methadone, amphetamines and alcohol.

During Matthew Perry's 28-day inpatient treatment, he was only given a couple short furloughs to visit the studio, which made rehearsal difficult. Thus, his plotline was cut. His drug problem was so bad the producers seriously contemplated writing him out of the series.

At the end of the episode, Phoebe yells the iconic catchphrase from *Saturday Night Live*: "Live from New York, it's Saturday night!" Incidentally, Lisa Kudrow auditioned to be a cast member in 1990 but the part was given to comedian Julia Sweeney. Coincidentally, after Sweeney quit four years later, Jennifer Aniston was offered the role but turned it down to costar on a TV pilot (later known as *Friends*). Of the six *Friends* costars, only Matt LeBlanc has been snubbed as host of *SNL*.

7.19 "The One with Ross and Monica's Cousin" (04.19.01)

Monica claims she and Chandler made a "no-sex pact" (to abstain from sex until their wedding night). This was written in response to media rumors that the *Friends* cast had a similar pact with each other once the series became a hit. The cast always denied this gossip, though Lisa Kudrow and David Schwimmer both admitted if there was a pact, it was definitely broken a few times. Twenty years later, at the *Friends* reunion, Matthew Perry claimed there was a pact but the female costars denied its existence.

At the time of her guest role, Denise Richards (Cassie) was dating Charlie Sheen, who appeared in "The One with the Chicken Pox" (2.23). The couple married in 2002 and divorced four years later after a tumultuous relationship, and then partook in a media-circus custody battle.

Chandler only appears in two scenes for a total of 105 seconds, making it his shortest appearance in the series. Matthew Perry was in rehab which had extremely limited and regimented furlough hours.

When Chandler meets Cassie, he awkwardly gawks at her. Matthew Perry and Denise Richards never actually shared a scene together because he was in rehab, leaving her to work with his stand-in.

The magna doodle image has a large head on a stick body. This pertains to Ross' ego for believing that his cousin Cassie is sexually attracted to him.

While watching TV with Cassie, Ross' inner thoughts believe *Logan's Run* (1976) is the sexiest movie ever made. In reality, it is not sexy at all. It depicts a dystopian society in 2274 where the population and consumption of resources are kept in equilibrium by killing everyone who reaches the age of 30. The story follows the actions of Logan 5, a man facing termination.

7.20 "The One with Rachel's Big Kiss" (04.26.01)

Winona Ryder portrays a former college sorority sister who once kissed Rachel after a fraternity luau party. In "The One with Frank Jr." (3.05), Ross included Ryder on his final celebrity freebie list.

As mentioned in "The One Where Joey Loses His Insurance" (6.04), Rachel is a Kappa Kappa Delta sorority sister. The fictitious organization is a twist on Kappa Delta Kappa, a sorority at Ursinus College in Collegeville, Pennsylvania. Marta Kauffman included the obscure reference because the educational institution is 25 miles from her hometown of Broomall, Pennsylvania.

The magna doodle sketch has a guy barely hanging onto the handlebars of a banana seat bicycle that is airborne after jumping a mound of dirt. The *Friends* crew members loved motorbiking in their spare time.

Rachel made out with Melissa after the Sigma Chi luau. Jennifer Aniston's then husband Brad Pitt was a member of the Sigma Chi fraternity at the University of Missouri.

When Monica calls Mrs. Tribbiani, some sources claim Matt LeBlanc accidentally dialed a real telephone number. This is false. Courteney Cox is using a prop phone.

This is the only *Friends* episode with an onscreen kiss on the lips between two women (other than a quick peck as a thank you or farewell). Carol and Susan never smooched, even at their wedding. When the series first aired in 1994, all networks forbade lesbian kissing so it was never shown, but their draconian rules slowly withered over the years.

Ryder was disappointed that viewers were never able to really see the Rachel-Melissa kiss, explaining, "When I saw the episode, all you see is hair and you don't see lips. I was kind of bummed out because we got a couple of chances to do some pretty nice kisses. She's a very good kisser."

Just over seven months after this episode aired, Ryder was arrested for shoplifting in Beverly Hills, California, and accused of taking $5,500 worth of designer clothes and accessories from a Saks Fifth Avenue department store. On November 7, 2002, she was found guilty of felony grand theft and vandalism but acquitted of burglary. The actress was sentenced to three years supervised probation, 480 hours of community service, $2,700 fine, and drug and psychological counseling.

7.21 "The One with the Vows" (05.03.01)

This episode is a clip show so it has no genuine substance or content. It was the last episode produced in Season 7. A vast majority of the scenes involve archive clips from past episodes. It was hurriedly assembled and hastily written to give the writers a break after working on the season finale script.

The French poster above the TV in Monica's apartment concealed a large hole that was cut in the wall so a camera could shoot a different angle into the residence. The special effects team designed a device to mechanically elevate the poster to expose the opening whenever the camera was needed.

The Aux Buttes Chaumont (French poster) wasn't the original artwork selected for that space. In the pilot, set decorator Greg Grande had hung an old 1900s tapestry that he found in the Warner Bros. drapery department. After studio and network executives did their final walk-through, they objected to the rug because it was overly religious. "I had to scramble a little bit and that's how I ended up starting to flip through my research books of circus and French posters from the early 1900s. I found that image, took it, and reproduced it for a poster," Grande stated. "It fit the apartment's feminine, eclectic style, and it was believable for Monica because it was good design on a budget."

Monica's cupboards were updated weekly by the art department but food types (pasta, canned goods, etc.) were always kept in the same place because she was so organized.

On the bathroom door of Joey's apartment is the advertising poster My Goodness My Guinness (c. 1939). It has been a staple in the apartment for most of the series' run. The print was illustrated by John Gilroy (1898–1985) who began working for Guinness in 1928. His work was so popular that he continued producing whimsical posters well into the 1960s, when the brewery moved away from their fun and playful campaigns and transitioned towards something more mature and serious. Nevertheless, Gilroy's work is still very popular to this day and Guinness continues to profit from it—selling merchandise, vintage posters, and even a range of collectible cans.

This installment holds the distinction of being the least-watched first-run episode in the *Friends* catalog with only 15.6 million viewers. It ranks as one of the worst installments, along with "The One with the Invitation" (4.21). Not surprising, both episodes are clip shows with little or no substance.

7.22 "The One with Chandler's Dad" (05.10.01)

This is the only episode utilizing two directors: Kevin Bright and Gary Halvorson.

In Central Perk, the beautiful woman sitting near the front door—who witnesses Rachel taking the car key (and money) from Ross' jacket—is the same extra who receives tennis lessons at Monica and Chandler's wedding reception in "The One After 'I Do'" (8.01).

Courteney Cox's sister-in-law Alexis Arquette portrays a waitress at the drag show. She also played a Central Perk customer in "The One with Rachel's Sister" (6.13). In 2016, Arquette died at the age of 47 of cardiac arrest after living with HIV for years.

Since the original series concept had Chandler as gay, the showrunners opted to make his father transgender. "I think it had to do with how Chandler had some interesting character traits. He had a disconnect from his family," Marta Kauffman said. "For us, especially considering there was an episode where everyone thought Chandler was gay, we thought we would stay in the LGBTQ area with him in his life."

The idea of casting Kathleen Turner just popped into their heads, and she was perfect. Turner was personally cast due to her deep, gritty voice and large frame which validates her portrayal of a transvestite. Turner was often likened to a young Lauren Bacall, and when they met, Turner reportedly introduced herself by saying, "Hi, I'm the young you."

The audience member from Bakersfield is actor Joe Everett Michaels, Matthew Perry's stand-in.

According to Marta Kauffman, if she were to make the show today, the scenes involving Chandler's dad would be done quite differently. She doubts the gay jokes would work. "I wish I knew then what I know now," she confesses. "The transgender stuff played very often as a joke. I'm not sure we had back then the sensitivity that I would have now."

After Kathleen Turner portrayed Chandler's father, Matthew Perry began referring to her as Dad. In fact, to this day he still affectionately refers to her as "Dad" even though it has been more than two decades since she last played his father on the show.

While younger actors quickly bonded with the cast, Turner slammed the sextet for being unfriendly: "I remember I was wearing this difficult sequined gown, and my high heels were absolutely killing me. I found it odd that none of the actors thought to offer me a seat. Finally, it was one of the older crew members that said, 'Get Miss Turner a chair.'"

7.23 "The One with Monica and Chandler's Wedding, Part 1" (05.17.01)

Even though Gary Oldman appears in Parts 1 and 2, all his scenes were filmed during the first week of production because he had other filming commitments the following week. Oldman's absenteeism was actually beneficial for filming because the soundstage could not hold all the sets. Once all his scenes were shot, the movie set was torn down to make room for the wedding sets. On the downside, the director had to make sure he had every shot he needed because there would be no pickups after filming wrapped.

Gary Oldman had never appeared in a sitcom so he was offended when the staff writers talked to him and offered notes to improve his performance. "He was very confused by that and wondered why we were being so disrespectful of the director," Marta Kauffman noted. This highlights the difference between television and feature films. It is commonplace to give notes in small-screen productions but anathema on the silver screen.

Matt LeBlanc helped secure Gary Oldman to appear. They had worked together on *Lost in Space* (1998) and discussed having him guest star on *Friends*. Once he agreed, the producers wasted no time crafting a memorable role, but waited until the finale to cast him because they wanted a big-name star as an advertising gimmick to boost ratings.

Movie set dialogue regarding Richard Crosby not winning an Oscar Award is an inside joke about Oldman who, at the time, had never been nominated for any major acting award, despite being known as one of the finest actors in the industry. He was finally nominated for a Screen Actors Guild Award in 2001, and then an Academy Award in 2011, and eventually won an Academy Award and Golden Globe Award for his role in the 2017 film *Darkest Hour*.

The inspiration for a spitting actor came from cast members who complained about an unnamed guest actor that intermittently overenunciated his words. The creative team discussed using it for the longest time but never found the right opportunity. "We were looking for something that would delay Joey getting to the wedding—maybe he's got work or a movie—okay, but what's funny about that? And then we went back to the spitting actor," David Crane fondly recalled.

The show's producers debated whether they needed to incorporate actual spitting into the sequence (which would be done in postproduction), but decided that Joey's reaction was sufficient, and adding any liquid to the scene would seem gross.

The formal wedding attire of Jack and Judy Geller are the same outfits they wear in the life-size photograph showcased at their 35th wedding anniversary party in "The One in Massapequa" (8.18). The only difference is a discarded waist-cinching accessory.

After casting Kathleen Turner, the producers debated hiring a different famous actress each time Chandler's father appears onscreen. The first time would be Kathleen Turner, then Tina Turner, then Cher. Basically, all the people he might portray in a Las Vegas burlesque show.

When Monica exits her bedroom and says, "I'm getting married today!!!" before falling to the ground, Courtney Cox performed the stunt without pads and there was no mat to break her fall.

7.24 "The One with Monica and Chandler's Wedding, Part 2" (05.17.01)

Joey claims he is having a hair transplant, so when the assistant director replies, "But you're not bald," Joey quickly retorts, "It's not on my head," (implying pubic hair). The comeback was not in the original script; Matt LeBlanc and Kevin Bright came up with the line during rehearsal.

Richard Crosby (Gary Oldman) is intoxicated on the movie set and admits he is wearing two belts. This bit was inspired by Kevin Bright who once came to work that way.

Chandler's office door has the nameplate "Mike Smith" (the construction coordinator).

In Mike Smith's office, the featured wall has an enlarged still of St. Patrick's Cathedral with a statue of Atlas. The neo-Gothic cathedral was erected between 1858 and 1878, across the street from Rockefeller Center. It is one of the most conspicuous symbols of the Catholic Church in the United States.

Series costumer Debra McGuire was given two weeks' notice to find Monica's wedding gown so she opted to design and put together the dress herself. "Right before the fitting, I decided I better have some backups because, what if my dress doesn't fit? So I had pulled some really simple, lovely backups, and of course, [Courteney Cox] put it on and I couldn't get the zipper up," McGuire recalls. "There was no time to do anything about it. Try the next one, we put it on, it zipped up, and fit perfectly. She was like, 'This is perfect!' And I was like, 'Shit!'"

When Joey is talking to Rachel on the phone and explaining that he is running late, his scene takes place on the actual *Friends* backstage. The crew members behind him are regular crew members. The soundstage was so crowded with sets that director Kevin Bright had to use the hole in the wall above Monica's TV set (normally covered with a French poster) to film this shot.

As Rachel is searching for a new officiate for Chandler and Monica's wedding, she meets a Greek Orthodox priest exiting the Anastassakis-Papasifakis wedding. Anastassakis is Jennifer Aniston's family name in Greece. It was her paternal grandfather (Antonio) who immigrated to the US in 1935.

Rachel informs the Greek Orthodox priest that the wedding couple is Monica Stephanopoulos and Chandler Acidophilus. Monica's surname is a fun callback to "The One with George Stephanopoulos" (1.04) where she was infatuated with their neighbor George Stephanopoulos. Chandler's surname is chosen because it sounds Greek and it's funny. Acidophilus is a species of bacteria in the stomach and intestinal tract which is used as a probiotic (good bacteria). It is found in some dairy products, such as yogurt.

After the couple is pronounced husband and wife, the instrumental is "Everlong" by Foo Fighters. Kevin Bright chose the song because it was Courteney Cox's favorite band at the time.

The wedding officiant is Father Karabetsos. The fictional character is named after Marta Kauffman's childhood friend, Kathy Karabetsos. They both attended Marple Newtown High School in Pennsylvania. Kauffman graduated in 1974, and Karabetsos in 1978.

After Joey interrupts the wedding ceremony, the Greek Orthodox priest is supposed to be clutching a Bible but it is actually a photo album. The images inside the "book" are photographs. The props department crew thought the photo album looked ecclesiastical enough to pass as a Bible.

The wedding scene is actually filmed inside Central Perk—the coffee shop interior was gutted and redecorated. The set had to be repurposed because there was not enough room on the soundstage to build another set, and it was cost effective.

Season 8: 2001-02

8.01 "The One After 'I Do'" (09.27.01)

Although this installment is a continuation in time from the last installment, several hairstyle changes are obvious: Monica (curled), Chandler (shorter), and Ross (cut and styled differently).

Friends fans love the bridesmaid dresses. "Those bridesmaid dresses got the most calls and inquiries of anything on the whole show," recalls Debra McGuire. "We bought them at Neiman Marcus, and they were so beautiful. They weren't by a big name, just some random formalwear brand." But its popularity didn't end with the show. "It went on for years and years, and I still get questions about them to this day," she declared. "I get emails every week about *Friends*, because people are always rediscovering it or else just seeing it for the first time."

Originally the producers envisioned Monica becoming pregnant, not Rachel, but decided otherwise because it was too conventional. They wanted a more dramatic cliffhanger.

Chandler's father is nowhere to be seen at his son's wedding reception. Kathleen Turner refused to reprise the role because of her unpleasant on-set experience with the cast. "The *Friends* actors were such a clique—but I don't think my experience with them was unique," she stated. "I think it was simply that they were such a tight little group that nobody from the outside mattered."

The wedding reception waiter who offers champagne to Rachel—who accepts and then spits it out—is played by Matthew Mullany. He and Kevin Bright have been best friends since high school.

In the original and syndicated broadcasts, Ben does not have any lines and functions more like a background scene extra. In the extended DVD version, he only has one line;

he is embarrassed by his father and asks, "Can't you go back to your table?"

In the DVD version, while Chandler is dancing, his legs slowly begin to drift apart so he latches onto Judy's dress, ripping it off her and exposing her lace garter belt and thigh-high stockings. Her skirt was fastened with Velcro strips for easy disrobing. The tearing sound was added in postproduction.

This is the first episode to air after the September 11 attack on New York. In the original airing, as the episode fades to black, a title card reads "To the people of New York City." The title card was later excluded from DVD and syndicated releases.

At the time of this episode, Rachel is four weeks pregnant. The wedding date was set for May 15th (and aired on May 17th), which would make her due date in mid-January. She actually gives birth in May, four months after her due date. The creators needed a grand event for the season finale so they purposely postponed her delivery.

8.02 "The One with the Red Sweater" (10.04.01)
David Schwimmer directed this installment of *Friends*.

In the teaser, Joey offers a meshuganut to Monica. This is clever wordplay for the term meshugana, which is Yiddish slang for someone acting in a crazy or nonsensical way.

As Ross is packing to leave the hotel, he pilfers all the guest amenities (soap, thread, ashtray, shampoo and complimentary items) because "it is built into the price of the room." His obsession would become a plotline in "The One with Rachel's Dream" (9.19).

Throughout Season 7, Monica had a yellow KitchenAid mixer on the counter, which is even visible in this installment when she tells Joey not to let her open any more gifts. Nevertheless, once she begins opening the wedding presents, one of the gifts is the very same yellow KitchenAid mixer, which is now absent from the counter. It then returns to its original place in the kitchen 30 seconds later.

Joey mentions that some dude with a red sweater spent the night with Rachel a month ago. In "The One with the Videotape" (8.04), Ross is wearing a red sweater and spends part of the day with Joey. Thus, Joey should have known that Ross was the father of Rachel's child.

During an establishing shot of Central Perk, the sign out front announces: "appearing today noon, Neighbor Tim." The message venerates a crew member whose unspecified altruism on the set went above and beyond the call of duty. Since then, "Neighbor Tim" has remained on the Central Perk message board.

As Phoebe and Rachel start walking down the street near Central Perk, they stop for a moment to talk. Behind them is a man wearing a red sweater. Costumer Debra McGuire dressed the extra to confuse viewers into believing that any man could be the father.

After Joey proposes marriage to Rachel and she turns him down, the uncut DVD has an extended scene where they hug and he unhooks her bra. In the syndicated version, she is trying to latch her bra while leaving the apartment which makes no sense to viewers unless they saw the entire scene.

8.03 "The One Where Rachel Tells Ross" (10.11.01)
One scene had to be rewritten after the 9/11 attack because it involved Chandler and Monica being detained as suspected terrorists. After observing the airport sign: "Jokes regarding aircraft hijacking or bombing are prohibited," Chandler banters, "You don't have to worry about me, I take my bombs very seriously." He and Monica are promptly whisked away for questioning. The rewrite had Monica becoming jealous of newlyweds who keep receiving perks and upgrades. Thus, the ticket counter segment is the only original airport segment kept intact; everything else was rewritten. (The original scene is included as a DVD extra.)

Since the series is set in New York, many fans wondered if the show would address the terrorist attack. The producers decided to not mention it directly; instead, they added subtle references in episodes.

Phoebe is wearing a red sweater similar to the style worn by Ross and Tag in the prior episode. It is not the same top but the costumer chose this clothing similarity to give the audience a visual cue regarding Ross being the father of Rachel's child.

Rachel sports a black sleeveless sheer top with ruffle details and matching decorative tie over a black halter. It is the same top that Buffy wore in *Buffy the Vampire Slayer* (ep Bargaining) which aired nine days earlier on October 2, 2001. The head costumer for *Buffy*, Cynthia Bergstrom, admits to borrowing the garment from the *Friends* wardrobe team. So, not only are Buffy and Rachel wearing the same designer and style, they are in fact wearing the exact same top.

In the cold open, Chandler departs the kitchen to pack his Speedo but when he returns, his hair is significantly shorter. This occurred because some of the airport scenes had to be reshot due to the 9/11 attack. Since the scene timing didn't sync, the writers filled the void with more dialogue in the apartment, specifically, Chandler discovering that Ross and Rachel are having a child.

The magna doodle image has King Kong grasping a person in one hand while holding onto the top of the Empire State Building with the other. The Manhattan Bridge is in view with an Albatros D.III fighter plane (The Red Baron) nearby. This is a 9/11 tribute.

The honeymoon establishing shot utilizes footage of Atlantis Hotel in Nassau, Bahamas. The actors didn't film their scenes on location. All scenes were filmed on Stage 24.

When Joey and Monica talk on the phone, their conversation does not use functional telephones; there is a walkie-talkie link between the phones so the actors can hear each other. In the segment, Matt LeBlanc is in Monica's apartment, and Courteney Cox is on another set listening to his voice, so that's how she knows when to say her lines.

Joey easily breaks the mismatched dining table chair in Monica's apartment. The prop department specially designed the chair so it would fall apart with minimal force.

Ross claims that Rachel can't be a single mother because she is unable to eat alone at a restaurant. In "The One Where Chandler Crosses the Line" (4.07), the subplot focused on Rachel eating alone at a restaurant. (This narrative is only available on DVD.)

In the original script, Ross was the one who freaked out about not seeing the baby on the ultrasound. The staff writers decided that it would make more sense for Rachel, an inexperienced mother, to be disconcerted.

8.04 "The One with the Videotape" (10.18.01)
This is one of the sitcom's annual bottle episodes. There is only one day player (actor) with a small part, and one additional set, Ross' apartment.

In the teaser, Monica and Chandler mention the couple they met on their honeymoon, Greg and Jenny. They are named after, and kind of based on, *Friends* staff writer Greg Malins and his wife, actress Jennifer Milmore.

Phoebe's fitted t-shirt has an image of Judy Garland (*The Wizard of Oz*). The costumer purposely chose this visage as a geographic link to Joey's Western Europe backpacking story. Garland spent most of the final six years of her life in London after burning all bridges in the US. She died from a barbiturate overdose in 1969 (age 47).

The magna doodle displays a walrus on the beach with a starfish in front and bird flying overhead. Later in the episode, it reads "I ♥ NY" with a swirling S-shaped horizontal line and a heart in the center. This is a tribute to New York after the 9/11 attack.

Rachel nearly stomping the videotape required numerous takes and 45 minutes to film because the cast kept cracking up. David Crane claimed it took "a million takes." Every time she went to step on it, the gang's reaction caused everyone to laugh, repeatedly, take after take.

Ross' private videotaping segment was preshot without a studio audience. The director wanted to air the segment for the audience so they would realize it was a videotape, not a live performance.

Office artwork: Folies-Bergère poster and St. Patrick's Cathedral with *Atlas* statue

Marta Kauffman came up with the idea of Ross and Rachel making a sex tape. She had a theory that people think they look better while they're having sex than they actually do. This is proven true in the tag scene when Ross and Rachel watch their performance.

The audience went insane when it was revealed that Rachel used the Western Europe backpacking story to seduce Ross. The screaming had to be edited in length. Then it was pandemonium after she claimed her friend heard the story from a guy named Ken Adams (Joey's alias).

While Ross and Rachel watch their sex tape, the audio is muted. As Kevin Bright stated, the series' producers "made a conscious decision not to put any sex sounds or anything that would make the audience feel uncomfortable. It was really about the comedy in the moment. The sex was silent."

This is one of Marta Kauffman's top-10 favorite episodes.

8.05 "The One with Rachel's Date" (10.25.01)

During the restaurant scene, when Phoebe sees Tim and seductively says, "I didn't see *this* on the menu," on a shelf behind her is a glass jar labeled "Monica's Jar" filled with paper currency. Later in the scene, Monica references the "Yell Jar" by refusing to put a dollar in it claiming she was not yelling in the kitchen. This is the only time the Yell Jar is present or mentioned.

According to Chandler, Ross enjoys frequenting the Hard Rock Cafe because he likes the Purple Rain display. This is a reference to the 1984 album and rock musical drama *Purple Rain.* Prince's semi-autobiographical feature grossed over 10 times its original $7.2M budget, and won an Oscar for Best Original Song Score. It is often regarded as one of the greatest musical films, and the soundtrack sold over 25 million copies, with two No. 1 hits and a No. 2.

Chris Parnell, who plays Bob, Chandler's coworker, is best known as a series regular in *Saturday Night Live* from 1998 to 2006, and playing Dr. Leo Spaceman in *30 Rock* from 2006 to 2013. Parnell is an accomplished voice artist for TV, film and videogames.

As Rachel leaves for her date, Joey is reading *Car and Driver* magazine New-Car Issue (October 2001). Two years prior, Phoebe was perusing the 1999 *Car and Driver* annual New-Car issue.

When Ross discovers that Rachel is taking a ferry to Staten Island, he panics, claiming the ferry is very dangerous for his baby. FYI: Nearly two years after this episode aired, on October 15, 2003, a Staten Island ferry crashed into a pier injuring 70 people with 11 fatalities.

The magna doodle image has wildflowers on the left, a bunny in the grass on the right, and a large mushroom with polka dots in the center with a hookah-smoking caterpillar on top. The sketch depicts a scene from Lewis Carrol's *Alice in Wonderland*.

In Central Perk, Phoebe is reading *Parabola* with the headline "Threshold" (vol. 25, no. 1). Founded in 1976, *Parabola*, aka *Parabola: The Search for Meaning*, is a Manhattan-based quarterly magazine on the subjects of mythology and the world's religious and cultural traditions. This prop lends credence to Phoebe's spiritual persona.

The newsstand offers shameless promotion for *New York Post* newspaper. The owner is wearing a vest with the latest edition featuring the headline "Return of the Lizziemobile" (August 16, 2001).

This episode is "Dedicated to the Memory of Richard L. Cox, Sr." He is Courteney Cox's father; he passed away from cancer on September 3, 2001.

8.06 "The One with the Halloween Party" (11.01.01)
This is the only Halloween episode of the series, which aired one day after the holiday.

This is the first episode filmed after the 9/11 attack. Production was postponed three weeks. The original table read was scheduled for Tuesday morning on September 11th.

At the beginning of the episode, Joey is wearing a t-shirt featuring the logo FDNY (Fire Department of New York) to commemorate their undertaking in the wake of the terrorist attack. This is one of several tributes to be featured on the show in upcoming episodes.

Director Kevin Bright wasn't a fan of Sean Penn's cameo. Of all the guest stars, Bright said that Penn was the least successful because "there was a little deer in the headlight effect." Matthew Perry disagreed. He thought the dramatic actor was "really funny," but felt intimidated working with such as star.

Sean Penn was offered the role after one of his many visits to the *Friends* set. He often observed the rehearsals with his two children, Dylan and Hopper, because they were fans of the show.

The two-time Oscar winner was referenced in "The One Where Dr. Ramoray Dies" (2.18) when Chandler mentions breaking up with a woman because she thought the capital of Cambodia was Sean Penn (it's actually Phnom Penh).

The third trick-or-treater to knock on Monica's door is Lelani Mayolanofavich dressed in a pink-and-white short-sleeve sweater and matching skirt. She is portrayed by Emily Osment, who later starred in *Hannah Montana* as Miley Cyrus' BFF, and the Freeform series *Young & Hungry*. Osment's entry into the entertainment industry began in 1997 (age 5) when she was cast in a commercial for the flower delivery company FTD.

This is the last time Lisa Kudrow portrays her twin sister, Ursula, in the series. Kudrow didn't like playing both characters in the same scene because she felt uncomfortable speaking the lines to her sister, Helene, who plays the body double for both characters.

The cast often cites this episode as one of their all-time favorites to film because they had a gigantic Halloween party afterwards even though it wasn't Halloween. The episode was shot four weeks prior so the costars thought it was fun to dress up and pretend.

This is one of Lisa Kudrow's favorite episodes because it's the first one shot after 9/11. "That whole week, while driving in LA, people would pull up and give me a very sad look and a quiet 'thank you' for making them laugh," she somberly recalled.

8.07 "The One with the Stain" (11.08.01)
In the opening scene in Central Perk, Phoebe's cell phone ringtone is "La Raspa." The song dates back to Veracruz, Mexico, as a dance often performed during celebrations and at dance schools. The "Mexican Hat Dance" is a combination of two tunes: "Jarabe Tapatío" and "La Raspa."

In an effort to procure an apartment from a Dutch-speaking neighbor, Ross is reading

Dutch for Beginners, a fictional book. It is used to explain his ability to communicate with the dying tenant.

Here is a translation of the Dutch conversation between Ross and Gunther: Ross states, "Thanks for the coffee," and Gunther says, "You speak Dutch? That's cool. Do you have relatives there?" Gunther's other lines are "Donkey," and "You have sex with donkeys." Surprisingly, NBC did not object to the last remark. "That's a little racy for primetime," James Michael Tyler (Gunther) opined. "But it was in another language."

Tyler admits that he doesn't speak Dutch. "There was a tutor who worked at the Dutch consulate in LA and he gave all the characters lessons on how to pronounce things. I speak German so it wasn't too far away," he stated. Tyler always assumed his fictional character was Dutch. "It's kind of established that the character is of Dutch heritage. That was my assumption that was never specifically said by the writers," he stated.

The magna doodle has a sketch of Rock 'Em Sock 'Em Robots. Joey and Phoebe played the game in "The One Where Rachel Tells Ross" (8.03) and it was frequently used as set dressing in his abode, typically stationed on the coffee table.

When Joey asks Rachel to remain living with him after the baby is born, she is reading *The Girlfriends' Guide to Pregnancy* by Vicki Iovine. The book provides the lowdown on all those little things that are too strange or embarrassing to ask, as well as practical tips and hilarious takes on everything pregnant. The prop department added this book to remind viewers that Rachel was pregnant, and not unexpectedly gaining weight.

While lying in bed, Eric is perusing *The Alchemist* by Brazilian author Paulo Coelho, an allegorical (hidden moral meaning) novel that follows a young Andalusian shepherd on his trip to the pyramids of Egypt, after having a recurring dream of finding a treasure there. The book is intended to foreshadow Eric's pursuit of his treasure, Phoebe, but he faces a moral crossroad after sleeping with her twin sister, Ursula.

This episode is "Dedicated to the memory of Pearl Harmon."

8.08 "The One with the Stripper" (11.15.01)
David Schwimmer directed this episode.

The pop-art piece in Central Perk is a headshot of the Statue of Liberty in front of the American flag. This is a tribute to New York City after the 9/11 attack.

In one scene, Chandler states: "You know that the two pillars of marriage are openness and honesty." Monica frustratingly comments, "I knew giving you that book was gonna come back and bite me in the ass." This dialogue was in the original script of "The One Where Rachel Tells Ross" (8.03) before the couple went on their honeymoon. After their honeymoon scenes were rewritten (due to the 9/11 attack), this exchange was put on the writers' ideas board for future use.

When Phoebe states she doesn't eat chicken, Rachel's father says, "I'll never understand you lesbians." The word "lesbians" is deleted in syndication to avoid offending fans.

In India, the word "hooker" is muted throughout the episode. Also, one scene is excised for being culturally insensitive—where Ross and Mona are making out on the sofa and she unintentionally breaks the Lord Ganesha statue (which Ross refers to as an 18th-century Indian artifact). Ganesha (or Ganesh) is one of the most worshiped and best-known deities in the Hindu pantheon.

The magna doodle drawing shows the moon with an American flag planted in the lunar surface, the galaxy filled with stars, a crescent moon (which makes no sense since the lunar surface is already pictured), cross symbol, and Earth (with an outline of North, Central and South America). This is a tribute to NYC after the 9/11 attack.

In the tag scene, Rachel is reading *The Complete Idiot's Guide: Pregnancy and Childbirth* by Michele Isaacs Gliksman MD. The prop is featured to foreshadow Rachel's idiocy as it pertains to her lack of knowledge about pregnancy, childbirth, and infant care.

Bonnie Somerville (Mona) shared a majority of her scenes with David Schwimmer, and spoke highly of their time together. "It was great working with him as a director because here's a guy who was so experienced and knows so much of what he's doing but he was so into my ideas and what I thought," she said with genuine sincerity.

8.09 "The One with the Rumor" (11.22.01)

This episode was filmed on November 2, 2001, less than three weeks before airing. This is quite unusual. Typically, an episode is taped four to six weeks prior to its release. The 9/11 attack caused the entire production to fall behind schedule.

The magna doodle image has the US flag overlaid on a basketball above the words "One New York" and to the right is written "1 People." This is a tribute to the people of New York and the country's solidarity after the 9/11 attack.

Brad Pitt portrays high school classmate Will Colbert. At the time, Pitt was married to Jennifer Aniston. He often visited her at the studio during production week rehearsals and Friday night tapings, but stayed out of sight during the live performances to avoid being a distraction.

During one of Brad Pitt's on-set visits, the producers asked him to appear for a special episode. He happily agreed because the cameo offered a platform to promote his latest feature, *Spy Game*. The movie was released November 19, 2001, three days before this episode aired. It's an American action thriller costarring Robert Redford.

At the time of his appearance, Brad Pitt was a longtime fan of the show. "It's a happy show," the actor said. "It comes on and it makes me happy. It's always been that way since its first incarnation, before I met my wife [Aniston]."

While promoting the episode, NBC made no mention of Brad Pitt and blurred his face in television spots, teasing about a high-profile guest star. Nonetheless, trade publications reported that Pitt would appear in Season 8, and most media outlets correctly predicted he was the mystery guest star.

Despite being a Hollywood A-list star, even Brad Pitt is fallible. While filming in front of a studio audience, he actually mishandled the opening line on his first cued entrance: "I flubbed my first line. We had to stop and start again," he confessed.

Rachel is wearing the fashionable Laundry by Shelli Segal (ivory lace with bell sleeve). In *Buffy the Vampire Slayer* (ep Smashed), Buffy wears the same top in an installment that aired two days earlier, on November 20, 2001. *Buffy*'s head costume designer, Cynthia Bergstrom, confessed that the blouse was on loan from the *Friends* wardrobe team.

The LGBTQ community was upset by the way the show's creators handled the topic of hermaphrodites as a hurtful rumor. The Intersex Society of North America delivered a sternly worded letter of complaint to NBC, characterizing the installment as "ignorant, insulting, degrading, and absolutely unprofessional." ISNA urged the network to learn about intersex individuals via the Society's website and read an on-air apology before future reruns. Nearly two decades later, in a direct reply to the subject at hand, Marta Kauffman stated, "I might have not done the hermaphrodite stuff today if I had that to do over. It really is a period piece."

8.10 "The One with Monica's Boots" (12.06.01)

A menorah is visible in front of Monica's microwave at the beginning of the installment. This alludes to her and Ross being part Jewish. In Central Perk there is a menorah by the entrance door, hanging menorah artwork, and Star of David on the coffee machine. Kevin Bright added Jewish symbols to Christmas-themed episodes because he comes from a multifaith household.

This episode has several New York City–related 9/11 tributes: (1) Central Perk artwork has the Statue of Liberty overlaying the American flag, (2) Rachel's corporate office has an American flag pillow on the windowsill, (3) the school hallway has a framed picture of the US flag waving in the wind with the inscription "This is Our Flag, Be Proud of It!" (4) Joey's apartment has an American flag hanging on the wall, (5) a background extra is wearing an FDNY baseball cap, and (6) the magna doodle has the Statue of Liberty on the right with fireworks bursting in the sky to the left and FDNY at the bottom left.

Joey's sister Dina is reading *Pregnancy for Dummies* by Joanne Stone, et al. Although Dina and her boyfriend are clueless, Joey is the "dummy" in his handling of her pregnancy. Rachel is the voice of reason as she educates him on the hypocrisy of thinking Dina's not ready to have a baby.

Rachel is reading *The Girlfriends' Guide to Pregnancy: Or Everything Your Doctor Won't Tell You* by Vicki Iovine. This is a reminder to the viewers that Rachel is pregnant.

The establishing shot for the residence of Sting and his wife Trudie Styler begins with a photograph of the happy couple. She provided the snapshot for the producers to use in this episode. Styler also included framed family photos for the background tables.

The ottoman contains a copy of *Sting: The Illustrated Lyrics* by Roberto Gligorov. It is a collection of artwork collages that blend Gligorov's art with fully written lyrics of various Sting songs. Gligorov also happens to be a Sting doppelganger, to the point where he has been chased in public by rabid groupies. Interestingly, Sting and Gligorov seem to be fans of each other's work.

Sting was scheduled to have a cameo but canceled at the last minute so his wife Trudie Styler filled in on his behalf. He claims he never agreed to appear, just his wife, since he was on tour at the time of filming. In truth, Sting agreed to appear otherwise the show's producers wouldn't have hastily replaced him with a plot involving his wife.

Due to Sting canceling, the writers added a jab at the rocker by having his wife claim he is unavailable for a meeting with Phoebe and Ben because he has a concert, to which Phoebe sarcastically replies: "Concert. Yeah. That does put us in … quite a pickle."

8.11 "The One with Ross's Step Forward" (12.13.01)
An alternate title for this installment is "The One with the Creepy Holiday Card" which is actually the title used in the UK, Netflix and original DVD release.

Phoebe mentions it being the fourth month of Rachel's pregnancy but in reality it's the ninth. The writers purposely skewed the pregnancy timeline to feature her childbirth as the season finale.

The Central Perk coffee table has a copy of *Time* magazine with the headline "Lifting the Veil" (December 3, 2001). This is a thematic signal for Ross as he lifts the veil to expose all the flaws in his and Mona's relationship. It is also blatant product placement.

After Mona leaves Central Perk, Ross can be seen reading *Will the Circle Be Unbroken? Reflections on Death, Rebirth, and Hunger for a Faith* by Studs Terkel. The book explores the possibility of life after death. It is meant to presage Ross' relationship problems with Mona. The joint holiday card illuminates their relationship flaws and Ross immediately realizes he made a mistake. The metaphor is whether he will have a future love life after the death of his current commitment.

Throughout the course of the series' run, all the holiday-episode sets were decorated by a private company. The Warner Bros. Studio warehouse lacked sufficient storage for holiday-themed decorations so a private business had to be hired to perform the task.

Phoebe's friend Roger, the virgin who volunteers to have sex with Rachel, is played by Ashley L. Clark, who also appeared in "The One with All the Candy" (7.09), as one of the tenants standing outside Monica's apartment demanding candy from the Candy Lady.

In the tag scene, Rachel is wearing an FDNY t-shirt as a tribute to the Fire Department of New York and their efforts after the September 11 attack.

The studio audience was mostly comprised exclusively of family members of firefighters or police officers who lost their lives in the 9/11 attack. The executive producers asked Warner Bros. to finance an all-expense-paid trip for 400 family members to honor the first responders.

8.12 "The One Where Joey Dates Rachel" (01.10.02)

David Schwimmer directed this episode.

Phoebe's wedding gift to Monica and Chandler is a *Ms. Pac-Man* arcade game. Released in 1982, multiple names were considered for the game, including Super Pac-Man, Miss Pac-Man and Mrs. Pac-Man, before settling on the name that was easier to pronounce.

While playing *Ms. Pac-Man*, Chandler is wearing a red long-sleeve shirt with the phrase "United We Stand" as a tribute to New York after the 9/11 attack.

Joey's date, Mabel, is portrayed by Krista Allen. In 1994, she starred as the eponymous character in the erotic cable series *Emmanuelle in Space*. She later played Billie Reed on *Days of Our Lives* from 1996 to 1999, and Jenna Avid in *Baywatch* from 2000 to 2001.

During her date with Joey, Mabel mentions actor Stephen Baldwin to foreshadow the appearance of his older brother Alec who plays Phoebe's fervent boyfriend Parker in a two-episode story arc.

This is the first installment where Joey develops romantic feelings for Rachel. When the cast saw the script for the first time, they all "freaked out." Matt LeBlanc kept repeating, "It's wrong. It's like I want to be with my sister." The creators said, "Yes, it's absolutely wrong. That's why we have to do it. You can't just keep spinning the same plates. You have to go places where you're not expected to go." David Crane said, "Once it actually started, it was heartbreaking because it couldn't go anywhere. It was always going to be Ross and Rachel."

Phoebe is actually swearing while playing *Ms. Pac-Man*. The scene was preshot without an audience. After Lisa Kudrow's vulgar tirade, Kevin Bright started laughing and told her not to worry because "no one should even be able to read it on your lips."

This is the last appearance of Ben Geller in the series. Actor Cole Sprouse is credited for an appearance but doesn't have any lines. He is basically an overpaid scene extra.

8.13 "The One Where Chandler Takes a Bath" (01.17.02)

In the opening scene, Joey is wearing an FDNY t-shirt with the name Capt. Billy Burke. He was a New York City firefighter who lost his life on September 11, 2001, at the World Trade Center. Other Big Apple tributes in this episode include the US flag in the back of the coffeehouse, and the song "Only Time" by Enya (while Chandler soaks in the tub).

During the summer and fall of 2001, NBC used the song "Only Time" by Enya in ads to promote *Friends*. It subsequently became the unofficial national grieving hymn after the 9/11 attack, spending 32 weeks on the US Billboard charts, peaking at No. 10, her only top-10 single as a solo artist. Enya donated profits from the sale of that single to the Widows' and Children's Fund founded by the Uniform Firefighters Association to help families of firefighters in the aftermath of 9/11.

As Ross and Rachel are discussing baby names, he suggests Thatcher, and she proffers Sawyer. Both are surnames of characters from Mark Twain novels: Becky Thatcher and Tom Sawyer.

During Chandler's first bath, as Monica enters the bathroom, on the back of the door is a small pink needlework art. Marta Kauffman stitched the artwork using a design that was created by an acquaintance.

When Monica suggests giving Chandler a facial after his bath, he proclaims, "I'm going to need a bigger boat." This is an allusion to the horror movie *Jaws* (1975) where Roy Scheider uttered the phrase, "You're gonna need a bigger boat," which is now a popular response to any situation that seems more difficult than originally thought. Chandler needs a bigger boat because his masculinity is being called into question if he agrees to a facial after the bubble bath.

The doctor's office has a corkboard with dozens of baby photographs. The *Friends* crew members contributed the pics.

The magna doodle image features an old-time coal-burning train barreling down a track with the engine blowing smoke into the air, coupling rods connecting the wheels, and an attached coal car.

The writers penned Joey's dialogue to mimic cereal commercial slogans hoping to get permission from Kellogg's and General Mills to use their products in the scenes. Both corporations declined, so mock cereal boxes were used as an allusion to these brands. The dialogue was also changed to avoid trademark infringements associated with the signature phrases uttered by the cereal mascots (Tony the Tiger's "They'rrre Greaaat!" became simply "Greaaat!" and Sonny the Cuckoo Bird's "Cuckoo for Cocoa Puffs" was simply "Cuckoo").

8.14 "The One with the Secret Closet" (01.31.02)

According to production designer John Shaffner, "This episode was written to finally explain why there was a random door between the bathroom and balcony in Monica's home." When he designed her abode, the hallway closet had a typical purpose though it was never utilized in an episode. For the longest time, many people wondered what was behind the door. The staff writers finally found a way to incorporate it into the series by characterizing Monica as a closet hoarder.

In Season 1, the hallway door was often ajar to alert the audience to its presence and utility as a walk-in closet. The following year, the set designer believed the hall storage was a waste of space since it was never used so it was dismantled. In reality, the closet door was a backstage passage used by the crew. The hall closet was reconstructed for "The One with the Routine" (6.10) but only because it was integral to the storyline as a possible hiding place for Monica's Christmas presents.

Set decorator Greg Grande used this episode to prank Matt LeBlanc and Matthew Perry. During rehearsal the closet was empty so the guys were expecting an empty closet while filming. Between filming breaks, when the cast returned to their dressing rooms, the crew kept filling it a little at a time. When the big reveal finally occurred, and the guys opened the closet door, LeBlanc and Perry were truly shocked by its bulging contents.

When Rachel enters the bedroom so Joey can feel her pregnant belly, he is supposed to be naked but his boxer shorts are visible at the end of the scene. In a blooper, Jennifer Aniston actually saw his penis when his boxers failed to keep his "mouse in the house."

Ross enters Central Perk wearing winter attire. After he discovers Rachel's baby kicked, he tries to remove the mittens with his teeth and then shakes them off. Costar David Schwimmer suggested the physical comedy bit and worked with the director to stage it.

The magna doodle sketch is a closeup of a hockey goalie in front of the net with a puck approaching. It commemorates the crew members attending a hockey game.

In the scene where Joey takes Rachel to the hospital, Ross rushes into the waiting area. In a blooper, David Schwimmer ran past the waiting room causing Jennifer Aniston to burst out laughing. In the next take, Aniston and LeBlanc intentionally hid to confuse their costar. Schwimmer calmly walked into the waiting room, looked around, and did not see his castmates, so he continued down the corridor. He truly believed he missed his mark again. Later, when he forgot his line, Aniston shouted in jest, "You just suck! What happened to you? You used to be able to act!"

The comedy bit involving sex noises during a massage was copied in *Modern Family* (ep Regrets Only) where Claire moans orgasmically during a mall rubdown. FYI: In 2009, Lisa Kudrow auditioned to play Claire, and Matt LeBlanc turned down the role of Phil.

8.15 "The One with the Birthing Video" (02.07.02)

In the uncut DVD version, after Rachel rattles off random facts on how rats started the plague, she is perturbed at Ross for making her watch the Discovery channel 24/7, and declares: "Oh, dear God, Ross. Nick at Nite, once in a while." Nick at Nite is the evening programming on Nickelodeon for adult audiences with a lineup of classic TV shows, like *Friends*, which started airing on the network in 2011.

The magna doodle drawing has a guy with his left leg fully extended as he takes a tight curve with the motorcycle angled low to the ground. The stagehands were avid riders.

After watching a birthing video (and just before Monica entices him with sex), Chandler is antithetical so the song "Fallin'" by Alicia Keys (#1, 2001) overlays the scene. Kevin Bright selected the number because it totally captured the moment. Chandler is in love with Monica but the birthing video makes the thought of sex repulsive. He is falling in and out of love with her.

Marta Kauffman used personal experience to inspire the birthing video plotline. She had the unenviable task of watching her cousin's videotape of the event. It was horrifying.

While filming a scene in the coffee shop, Ross realizes the foolishness of asking Rachel to move in with him while he still has a girlfriend. During one take, David Schwimmer forgot his line so after sighing, he interjected a personal commentary on his character: "Poor Ross." The remark left Lisa Kudrow in stitches before she quipped, "Have you ever seen this show?" (citing Ross' history of bad luck and terrible timing). It was a delightful moment of jocularity amongst castmates.

In the tag scene, the DVD version has Rachel watching what she thinks is the birthing video but it's actually a porn movie. In her thoughts, she ponders if the film commences with how they get pregnant, but once they start having sex, she comments, "No, nope. You can't get pregnant that way." She is insinuating anal sex.

8.16 "The One Where Joey Tells Rachel" (02.28.02)
This is one of the few episodes with only two storylines, not the typical three. Ross and Joey lock horns due to their mutual love for Rachel, and Joey confesses his love to her but she does not reciprocate. Phoebe realizes her date (Don) is Monica's soul mate, and Chandler is jealous of Don's undeniable connection with Monica.

There's a hint that Ross still has feelings for Rachel when he tells Monica: "It's Rachel, you know?" The producers often added dialogue to lay the groundwork for a possible romantic reunion.

Phoebe's date (Don) is portrayed by Harry Van Gorkum, who had a memorable role in *Seinfeld* (ep The Wig Master) as Elaine's boyfriend whose luscious mane is cut and sold to a wigmaster.

The magna doodle drawing has a very worried face. It represents Joey's concern over his friendship with Ross, and whether Rachel will reciprocate romantic feelings toward him.

In Central Perk, Phoebe is perusing *InStyle* magazine featuring Michelle Pfeiffer on the cover with the headline "Celebrity Weddings." The back cover has an advertisement for Arianna Skincare products, which are natural Dead Sea products containing minerals, salt and raw black mud.

In Ross' building corridor, after Joey schedules a dinner date with Rachel, a man exits the apartment across the hall. The tenant is staff writer Andrew Reich.

While dining with Rachel in a fancy restaurant, Joey claims he is wearing a t-shirt with a picture of Calvin doing Hobbes. The famed comic strip, *Calvin and Hobbes*, covers the fanciful world of a boy (Calvin) and his imaginary tiger (Hobbes). Syndicated in 1985, it quickly became one of the most popular comic strips of all time, appearing in more than 2,400 newspapers when creator Bill Watterson retired on December 31, 1995. Calvin is named for a 16th-century theologian, and Hobbes for a 17th-century philosopher with a dim view of human nature.

After Rachel takes a peek at Joey's t-shirt, she remarks, "Wow, I wouldn't think Hobbes would like that so much." This is an allusion to bestiality.

8.17 "The One with the Tea Leaves" (03.07.02)
At the start of Act 1, when Ross is inquiring about his faded salmon (pink) shirt, he is wearing a gray t-shirt containing a motif of two hands with interlocking index fingers. This is the American Sign Language symbol for the word "friend."

In Monica's apartment, she asks Chandler, "Honey, why is the Bruce Springsteen CD in the Cat Stevens case?" This is a subtle allusion to the 1984 music video "Dancing in the Dark" where Courteney Cox was pulled onstage to dance with The Boss for 23 seconds. She was selected from a swarm of over 300 contenders for the $350, two-day job. This seemingly innocuous gig changed her life forever. FYI: Carlton's dance from *The Fresh Prince of Bel-Air* was inspired by Cox's rhythmic motions in the music video.

NBC casting chief Joel Thurm saw Cox's music video and was impressed. He pressured producer Stephen Cannell into casting her for a nonspeaking role in *Code Name: Foxfire* as Flight Attendant (ep Slay It Again, Sam) (01.27.85), and then a speaking role as Amy (ep Pick a Hero, Any Hero) (03.08.85). After one of her auditions, Cox discovered that producers were across the hall casting for *Misfits of Science* so she brazenly auditioned and earned a costarring role. The rest is history.

Despite visiting different restaurants, Phoebe and Jim are holding the same menu that Rachel, her father, and Phoebe were using in "The One with the Stripper" (8.08).

The name of the dry cleaner store is Bleeker Street Dry Cleaners. The art department misspelled the name of the actual New York Street, which is Bleecker (with a "c").

When Phoebe and Monica visit the dry cleaner store, they enter from the street. Once inside, the thoroughfare inexplicably becomes a hallway with a light fixture and framed painting on the wall.

Alec Baldwin plays Phoebe's overly enthusiastic boyfriend, Parker. The character was inspired by a real-life boyfriend of Marta Kauffman. Alec Baldwin was cast for the role because he is extremely passionate in real life. When asked about his brief time on the show, Baldwin commended Lisa Kudrow: "I was very grateful I had my scenes with Lisa because she is so unique, beautiful and funny, but slightly odd in a wonderful way."

Technically, all of Phoebe's tea leaf predictions come true: (1) Rachel is going to have a baby (she does), (2) Monica will be promoted (she gets an even better job at Javu), and (3) Phoebe will meet the man of her dreams (which occurs in Season 9).

8.18 "The One in Massapequa" (03.28.02)
This episode is also known as "The One with the Zesty Guy."

Before leaving for the apartment, Parker asks about the location of the party. Monica tells him Massapequa, and he replies that he's never been there. Alec Baldwin (Parker) was raised near Massapequa.

In the first party scene, Jack and Judy Geller walk past a life-size portrait on an easel. Several sources falsely claim there is a clothing blooper, asserting that Jack and Judy Geller are wearing the same outfits in the photograph. This is false. Judy is wearing a plain gray dress, not a light-blue jacket with tan pattern and silver skirt, and Jack has a brighter red tie. The photo is actually an enlarged promotional print used by NBC to hype the Season 7 finale.

After Ross and Rachel speak with his parents, a guest says, "Congratulations on your wedding." At that moment, the stand-in for Elliott Gould (Jack Geller) is visible behind Rachel. Since Gould is a recurring guest star, no effort is made to find a doppelganger. In this instance, the stand-in is significantly shorter than Gould, wearing glasses, and sporting a different suit and tie. This error is only visible in the wide-screen format.

When Ross chronicles how he proposed to Rachel, he claims their first date was at the planetarium. This was actually their second date. Their first date was the movies to see an unnamed foreign film with subtitles; Rachel had trouble following the plot because she didn't want to wear her glasses.

Nearly everyone at the party believes Rachel and Ross are married, yet no one notices the lack of wedding bands on their fingers. However, at the end of the episode (in Ross' apartment), after they say goodnight to each other, Rachel places her hand on her belly, revealing a wedding ring on her left hand. (It is actually Jennifer Aniston's engagement ring from Brad Pitt.)

David Schwimmer with Aisha Tyler and Greg Kinnear, and consulting with the show's creators

During her celebratory toast, Monica mentions the family's childhood dog Chi-Chi. This is a callback to "The One with the Thumb" (1.03) where Ross learned that their beloved pet was not taken to a farm, it actually died.

8.19 "The One with Joey's Interview" (04.04.02)

This is another clip show with no real substance or content. Most of the scenes involve archive clips from past episodes. This was the last episode produced in Season 8. The writing team was emotionally and physically spent after the finale so they hastily inked a script to fulfill their episode commitment to the network. The producers intentionally delayed producing the installment so the staff writers wouldn't waste time and effort on an irrelevant clip show.

When shooting this installment, the producers knew it would air prior to the finale but didn't know when. This created continuity problems regarding Rachel's pregnancy. They guessed the episode would air right before the birthing episode but then it was moved up a month. Thus, Rachel appears extremely pregnant compared to the prior episode.

Shelley, the interviewer, is portrayed by Sasha Alexander. She asks Joey how it feels to have a huge gay fan base. Coincidentally, Alexander, while costarring in *Rizzoli & Isles* (2010-16), amassed a large lesbian and bisexual female fan base, which even spawned a lesbian drinking game.

The Central Perk coffee table has a copy of *Blue Dog Love* by George Rodrigue. The book highlights the paintings of Rodrigue who, upon meeting his wife, often created artwork based on his life with her, though substituting a blue dog in place of himself.

As an artist, Rodrigue chronicled Cajun life and was best known for his signature Blue Dog images. He authored more than 12 books including *Are You Blue Dog's Friend?* and *A Blue Dog Christmas*. He died in 2013 (age 69) after a two-year battle with cancer.

James Michael Tyler (Gunther) earned a fortune as a secondary character on *Friends*. During the first season, he earned $500 per episode appearance. His salary doubled in Season 2. For the third and fourth seasons, he earned $20,000 per episode. The next two seasons had a bump to $30,000. For the remainder of the series' run, he took home $40,000 per installment. In all, Tyler earned $4.65 million playing Gunther in *Friends*. Moreover, since *Friends* is a SAG (Screen Actors Guild) show, he kept earning residual royalties from syndication, which added another $1 million in his lifetime.

In the tag scene, the *Soap Opera Digest* periodical is actually a prop designed by the art department. It has Joey's headshot on the cover with the headline "Joey Tribbiani: The Days of His Life." The issue release date is April 1, 2002 (an April fools' joke).

Throughout the first eight years, Joey's apartment featured the 1933 Кенгуру-Боксер (Boxing Kangaroo) wall poster, advertising a boxing match between the animal trainer Vladimir Durov Jr. and a kangaroo. The bottom text reads "Vladimir Durov Junior" and the logo by the kangaroo's shoulder is GOMET—the Soviet State Department's Ministry of Enlightenment established for the regulation of musicals, theaters and circuses. The Durovs were a family of performers who brought renown and prestige to the Russian circus, and their descendants still perform today.

8.20 "The One with the Baby Shower" (04.25.02)

The game show *Bamboozled* was included as a DVD extra in the white box set.

In the uncut DVD version, Heather Sims appears as a party guest saying "Hey there!" to Phoebe, who in turn blows her off. Sims is the stand-in for Lisa Kudrow.

Joey asks Chandler, "In what John Huston film would you hear this line, 'Badges? We don't need no stinkin' badges!'" Chandler answers *The Treasure of the Arachnid Madre* (1948). However, this line is actually from *Blazing Saddles* (1974). The original line in Huston's film is "Badges? We ain't got no badges. We don't need no badges. I don't have to show you any stinking badges!"

One of the game show audition questions is "Which monarch has ruled Great Britain the longest?" and Ross answers "Victoria" which, at the time of filming, was the longest-serving monarch (1837-1901). In 2015 Queen Elizabeth II surpassed Victoria with her recent reign (1952-2022).

The quiz question, "Which monarch has ruled Great Britain the longest?" is technically incorrect. It should be "Which monarch has ruled the *United Kingdom* the longest?" FYI: British monarchs rule the United Kingdom (which includes Great Britain). Great Britain is the island comprising the countries of England, Scotland and Wales. United Kingdom (UK) is a country that is a union of the countries on the island of Great Britain, as well as the country of Northern Ireland (which shares the island of Ireland with the Republic of Ireland.)

When Joey goes to the *Bamboozled* audition, the names on the eraser board are *Friends* producers, writers, assistants and crew members.

Lisa Calderon (aka Lisa Avery) portrays Erin at Joey's *Bamboozled* audition. She is best known as the stand-in for Courteney Cox.

When Monica falls down the hallway staircase, a green safety mat covers the steps. The sound of her tumbling down the stairway was added in postproduction.

This is the last appearance of Marlo Thomas as Sandra Green. It's her first appearance since "The One with Two Parties" (2.22), which was 144 episodes ago.

8.21 "The One with the Cooking Class" (05.02.02)

The Central Perk artwork features *Uncle Sam* by Burton Morris. This is his last original painting to appear in the series. During the series' run, more than a dozen of his pop art paintings and designs were featured in Central Perk which encompassed more than 70 episodes.

Monica receives a terrible review for her cooking at Allesandro's restaurant. Ironically, in "The One Where They're Going to Party!" (4.09) she composed a scathing review of Allesandro's which prompted the owner to hire her as head chef for the restaurant.

In the uncut DVD version, Joey looks at the Cookie Time cookie jar atop the refrigerator and states, "I gotta get going," and heads for the door. Coincidentally, Lisa Kudrow did the same thing in a prior installment (but it never aired) which caught Matthew Perry's attention. When the series ended, he immortalized that notable goof by stealing the jar from the set and giving it to her as a memento.

Katie initially mistakes Ross and Rachel as a married couple. So does Janice shortly after Emma's birth in "The One Where Rachel Has a Baby, Part 2" (8.24). Both innocent comments were meant to presage the future union of Ross and Rachel two years later.

Katie asks Ross if he read the latest Walter Alvarez book, which is the 1997 nonfiction *T. Rex and the Crater of Doom*. It is a saga exploring the exhilaration of discovery that forever altered our grasp of Earth's geological history. Ross states that he teaches the book in his class.

The baby store has a product placement poster for Mustela baby lotion. Mustela offers a complete range of specially formulated skin care to best address changes in the delicate skin of newborns, babies, children and mothers.

At the baby store, the cashier (Katie) flirts with Ross by stating, "A paleontologist who works out, you're like Indiana Jones." This is a reference to the classic film *Raiders of the Lost Ark* (1981). In truth, Indiana Jones was an archaeology professor.

When Rachel asks Ross, "How serious are you about keeping Ben in your life?" he says, "My son? Pretty serious." Ironically, Ben doesn't appear in any future episodes, though he is mentioned.

8.22 "The One Where Rachel is Late" (05.09.02)
In the opening scene in Monica's apartment, on the coffee table in front of Joey is a can of Sprito soda, which is designed to resemble Sprite. When the producers failed to get corporate permission, they frequently purchased (or made) props designed to resemble national brands.

One common product placement is Bertolli Classico olive oil. It is usually displayed in Monica's cupboard, though twice it was promoted through use of a printed apron, e.g., "The One Where Monica & Richard Are Friends" (3.13) (Monica preparing lasagna) and "The One with the Ultimate Fighting Champion" (3.24) (Ross grilling on the balcony).

The poster above the television in Monica's apartment is Aux Buttes Chaumont: Jouets et Objets Pour Étrennes (toys and gifts for New Year's) by French artist Jules Chéret (1836–1932). The 1885 poster is promoting toys at a department store near Paris' Parc des Buttes-Chaumont. It conveys the image: "We are très chic ... We have joie de vivre!" (We are very stylish. We have joy of living). Chéret started producing advertisements in the 1870s and his work helped to move art out of the gallery and into the streets. He is known as the father of the modern poster.

Chandler provided financial support to Joey for nearly a decade so the once-struggling actor shows his appreciation by taking his friend to a movie premiere. Considering rent for a New York apartment at that time, food for one adult, and other various expenses revealed in the show, it is estimated that Joey owed Chandler around $120,000.

The movie premiere for *Over There* is the same WWI epic that caused Joey to be late for Monica and Chandler's wedding. The exterior movie theater scene used for Joey's movie premiere was filmed on New York Street on the Warner Bros. lot in Burbank, California.

British TV host Ben Shephard has an uncredited role as the man with the microphone at the movie premiere as Joey and Chandler walk the red carpet. Shephard was on the set to shoot a behind-the-scenes feature for the UK's GMTV (Good Morning Television).

Rachel enters Monica's apartment wearing a short top to accentuate her pregnant belly. Jennifer Aniston was fitted with a latex prosthetic device that weighed less than two pounds and attached behind her, which explains why it looks so real at every angle.

The only problem with the pregnancy prosthetic was its "terrible smell." According to Debra McGuire, "There's a fume that came out ... it was a chemical that would emit so we couldn't keep it on her that long." The fetid fumes made Aniston nauseous.

While Ross is eating spicy foods, there is product placement for Tapatío hot sauce.

When Monica asks Phoebe to wager whether the baby is a boy or girl, this is a callback to "The One Hundredth" (5.03) where baby Chandler was born as a girl instead of a boy.

8.23 "The One Where Rachel Has a Baby, Part 1" (05.16.02)
The plotline of vexing hospital roommates was based on Marta Kauffman's experience giving birth to her first child (Hannah), though Rachel's roomies were worse. "Everybody had a baby but me that day," she stated. "I went in [at] six o'clock in the evening, and between six in the evening and eight o'clock the next evening in the labor room, I had five different roommates. Two women, actually, couldn't even get out of the room to give birth they came so fast. It was very depressing."

Monica and Chandler decide it is time to have a child. Originally, the *Friends* creators never fathomed the couple having children. Once the idea was broached as a subplot for this episode, it became the motor that drove the narratives for Season 9.

The second hospital roommate, Evil Bitch, is played by Debi Mazar, who was actually pregnant during the shooting of her scene.

After the scene featuring Evil Bitch and Sick Bastard, Chandler is seen staring into the nursery. The on-duty nurse is *Friends* staff writer Sherry Bilsing-Graham.

The elevator scene where Phoebe and Cliff first meet is a very small area, yet it took five cameras to film this seemingly simple segment. When Cliff enters the elevator, a female extra was placed on a mark to conceal a hole cut in the back of the elevator (which was used to film Phoebe).

The elevator door is manually operated by a stagehand pulling a rope.

Rachel endures contractions as her third roommate (Asian woman) enters the antenatal room. The husband pushing the wheelchair is Matt LeBlanc's stand-in, Douglas Looper.

The Asian woman, whose contractions are only mild annoyances, was based on Marta Kauffman's cousin. "For her, the worst part of it was as she was heading into pushing, which is the worst time of labor, she literally would go 'Oww, that hurts,' and I hated her so much. It was too easy for her." Kauffman channeled her anger into comedic gold, and thought to herself, "that might be really fun comedy to watch someone else not be affected by it."

While pretending to be Dr. Drake Ramoray, Joey requests the chart for a patient (Cliff) and then slaps Phoebe's butt cheek. The smack was suggested by Matt LeBlanc during rehearsal. This is a direct callback to "The One with Ross's Sandwich" (5.09) where he first introduced the move on Monica.

This is the first of three consecutive episodes set in the hospital. The producers had to dismantle Central Perk and both apartments to construct the hospital sets. To save on construction costs, they kept the hospital sets intact through the Season 9 premiere.

8.24 "The One Where Rachel Has a Baby, Part 2" (05.16.02)

When Cliff's foot itches, Phoebe grabs a spoon to scratch it. He then quips, "I usually get to know a girl a little better before I let her spoon me." She quickly retorts, "Relax, it's not like we're forking." This is clever wordplay using utensils to represent a vulgar term for a sexual act.

Rachel's birthing scene was preshot without a studio audience. The infant was 8 weeks old and premature so it was smaller in size which made it appear newborn. The woman in the background is a real nurse working as an extra. The director wanted her on set. "The baby was a very delicate situation," Kevin Bright explained. "I wanted to make sure that somebody was close by that knew what they were really doing."

From pregnancy to birth, Rachel's gestation period is 13 months.

To create the appearance of a newborn covered in birthing fluid, the baby is slathered with grape jelly. According to director Kevin Bright, "The baby's skin is sensitive so you can't use fake blood or anything like that because they tend to have allergic reactions and have rashes. Somehow in the history of television they discovered that grape jelly works best."

Rachel's first time holding the infant was shot twice—with a real baby on Thursday, and then a doll on Friday in front of a studio audience. The same filming arrangement was used when the gang first viewed the infant.

In the touching hospital scene after Rachel gives birth to Emma, Monica is aflutter and blissful. However, in real life, Courteney Cox was conflicted; she had to partake in such a joyous event on camera when only a couple days earlier she suffered a miscarriage. "That was hard," she confided. "Oh my God, it was terrible having to be funny."

The infant doll was a mechanical robot the producers borrowed from the set of *ER*. The robot baby is heavier and larger than a real-life newborn. Thus, it is wrapped differently in a blanket which explains the continuity errors between edits.

The creators like using dolls because the actors tend to speak softer when a live baby is in the room. A doll allows for better enunciation and dialogue clarity for editing.

Isabella was one of the names the writers seriously considered for the newborn. It was suggested by Kevin Bright to honor his niece, Isabelle Bright (b. 1988). After graduating from UC–Santa Cruz, she worked as a production assistant on *Mike & Molly* (2012-16) and is currently a coordinating producer on *Bob Hearts Abishola* (2019-present).

Originally, Janice was going to be introduced simply as a joke—a gag reveal—but then when the writers were trying to figure out an ending, they thought Janice could be used to make Rachel feel insecure about her relationship with Ross.

This is Jennifer Aniston's favorite episode. Maggie Wheeler cites this as one of her three favorite episodes in the series because she "loved being in the labor room with Rachel."

Season 9: 2002-03

9.01 "The One Where No One Proposes" (09.26.02)
Rachel spends the entire installment in a hospital bed. This was written into the script because Jennifer Aniston broke her toe during the summer filming hiatus. She had to stay off her feet throughout the entire week of production.

A mechanical baby with moving arms was used during the breastfeeding scenes.

When Joey observes Rachel's breast, he exclaims "Yowzah." Ross uttered the same word when he saw her breast in "The One with a Chick and a Duck" (3.21).

As Ross and Phoebe discuss whether or not he proposed marriage to Rachel, the studio stage lighting and backstage bleacher area are reflected in the metal garbage can.

Rachel's flowing hair is back in full swing by Season 9, along with her signature layers. Her coloring fluctuates from light to a bit darker, but the length remains intact.

When Joey tells Chandler about seeing Rachel's breast, Chandler wonders what it looks like. He already saw her breasts in "The One with the Boobies" (1.13).

Elliott Gould played Trapper John McIntyre in the original 1970 telepilot for *M*A*S*H*. Two years later the part was recast using Wayne Rogers for the TV series.

This episode is often considered one of the worst *Friends* episodes, and usually ranks in the bottom 20 by most reviewers.

9.02 "The One Where Emma Cries" (10.03.02)
When Joey enters Rachel's hospital room, there is a corridor wall directly behind him. In the prior episode, Rachel's door opened to a long hallway. The set designer purposely constructed a wall because the corridor and waiting area had to be dismantled to erect Central Perk for this episode.

Jennifer Aniston is wearing after-birth padding to maintain an accurate depiction of the female form shortly after giving birth. Also, she is still limping from a broken toe.

When Ross enters Central Perk, Gunther is behind the bar wearing a designer tie created by artist Burton Morris. The tie was produced by Pittsburgh clothier Charles Spiegel.

In the scene where Ross punches the interior post, he is actually hitting memory foam. The *Friends* construction crew cut a segment out of the pole, replaced it with memory foam, and then repainted it so he would hit the soft part.

Ross punching the interior post was a special filming moment for James Michael Tyler (Gunther). After the first take, everybody in the coffee shop reacted with shock so David Schwimmer turned to the director and said, "Oh my gosh. Gunther needs to love this." Tyler had the same idea, "Gunther would thoroughly enjoy seeing Ross get hurt." Thus, in the scene, Gunther is in the background grinning, treasuring the moment.

After Joey hits Ross, the camera pans to Gunther who is wearing a wedding ring. In the show, Gunther is single but actor James Michael Tyler was married. He simply forgot to remove the band.

In the episode, the baby is not actually crying. The sound was added in postproduction. However, a crying noise was relayed to the audience so they could follow the scene.

Emma is only subdued when snuggling in Monica's arms. This is the exact opposite of what occurred in "The One with the Baby on the Bus" (2.06) where Ben was calm until she held him, then he cried incessantly. The role reversal was intended. Monica reading parenting books and her soothing embrace were all meant to foreshadow her success at motherhood, which occurs in Season 10.

9.03 "The One with the Pediatrician" (10.10.02)

Roger Christiansen directed this episode. He normally worked on *Friends* as a technical coordinator.

Monica's apartment is featured for the first time since Season 8, and one memorable set dressing error occurred: the set dresser forgot to place Pat the dog on the balcony. Also, a bassinet by the bay window appears misplaced since Rachel had a child, not Monica. However, this mistake was intentional to foreshadow Monica and Chandler's effort to conceive a child.

This episode was filmed around the one-year anniversary of the 9/11 attack. There are many subtle visual tributes to NYC residents and first responders: Ross wears a New York City t-shirt, Joey sports an FDNY tee, and his abode has an NYC cap on a hook by the door and US flag on the wall.

The magna doodle image has a shark fin protruding above the water with a giant shark leaping skyward—its mouth wide open and teeth exposed—as two birds soar overhead. The sketch is meant to foreshadow the next episode, where Monica purportedly catches Chandler watching shark porn.

This is the first appearance of Paul Rudd as Mike Hannigan. He is best known as the title character (Scott Lang) in the *Ant-Man* movies. After earning a BA degree in theater from the University of Kansas, Rudd studied at the American Academy of Dramatic Arts with thespian Matthew Lillard, while also employed as a deejay at bar mitzvahs. After graduation, he had many odd jobs, such as glazing hams at the Holiday Ham Company in Overland Park, Kansas.

Already a longtime pal of Jennifer Aniston, Rudd credits their friendship for making his *Friends* experience more enjoyable. Many sources claim the pair were brief lovers after starring together in *The Object of My Affection* (1998). They have joked around about it but never definitively confirmed it.

Joey's blind date (Mary Ellen Jenkins) is portrayed by Dedee Pfeiffer, the younger sister of famous actress Michelle. Dedee's memorable roles include Sheri Winston in *For Your Love* (1998-2002) and Rachel Blanders in *Cybill* (1995-97). She also posed for *Playboy* in February 2002. Pfeiffer is a social worker but will occasionally accept acting gigs.

In Central Perk, Phoebe finds a random patron whom she claims is her best friend. The stranger is played by Kim Harris, Jennifer Aniston's stand-in.

9.04 "The One with the Sharks" (10.17.02)

Phoebe claims she has never been married but this is inaccurate. She had a green card marriage for six years with an ice dancer (Duncan) and in "The One After Vegas" (6.01), she intimated having a prior Las Vegas marriage to an unnamed man.

Chandler's move to Tulsa was the creators' unique way of hiding Matthew Perry's drug addiction. By removing his character from the daily activities of the gang, the writers could easily write Perry out of installments in case he happened to relapse again. At the time, there was serious concern that he was abusing drugs.

Central Perk artwork by artists George Rodrigue, Burton Morris and Susan Winget

Ross claims that Phoebe's former long-term boyfriend was named Vikram. The writers selected this obscure moniker because an India TV series, *Hello Friends* (modeled after *Friends*), which aired from September 6, 1999 to February 28, 2000, utilized the name Vikram for its Ross counterpart. Ross even employs an Indian accent when leaving a message on Phoebe's answering machine. The Indian series also had a character that fused Monica and Rachel—Sanjana, a clothing designer who detested untidiness.

The establishing shot for Chandler's temporary residence is supposed to be the Tulsa Ramada Hotel. However, the televised clip is not the actual hotel. It is stock footage of a random hotel that was used to represent the Tulsa Ramada.

As Phoebe speaks to Mike about Vikram, the coffee table has a copy of *InStyle* magazine with the headline "Celebrity Weddings" featuring Michelle Pfeiffer on the cover. This was an intentional addition by the prop department since her sister Dedee appeared in the prior episode. It is the same issue used in "The One Where Joey Tells Rachel" (8.16).

The set dresser forgot to place Pat the dog on Monica's balcony.

In the tag scene, Joey is wearing an Alpinestars shirt. Alpinestars is a manufacturer of clothing and protective gear for motorsports and action sports. It was founded in Asolo, Italy, in 1963, and has two fashion design centers in California. Joey's sports shirt was from Matt LeBlanc's personal collection.

9.05 "The One with Phoebe's Birthday Dinner" (10.31.02)

The establishing shot for Tulsa features The Golden Driller statue. It was built in 1952 by the Mid-Continent Supply Company of Fort Worth, Texas, as a temporary feature for the International Petroleum Exposition (IPE). The oil company donated the statue so it could be installed in front of the Tulsa Expo Center for the 1966 IPE. The statue's right hand rests on an oil derrick. His statistics include: Belt (48 feet in circumference), shoe (393DDD), and hat (112 hard hat). The original belt engraving was "Mid-Continent" but was changed in 1979 to "Tulsa."

Chandler admits to smoking three cartons of cigarettes in two days, i.e., 600 cigarettes in 48 hours (three cartons have 30 packs, each pack has 20 cigarettes), which is the equivalent of smoking one cigarette every five minutes without sleeping.

At the restaurant, after Joey and Phoebe are relocated to a smaller table, the back wall has the celebrated *The Four Seasons* portraits by 16th-century Italian painter Giuseppe Arcimboldo. Each portrait uses fruits, vegetables, and plants appropriate to the season: Spring is a woman facing left made from a wide variety of flowers; Summer is a woman facing right created out of fruits and vegetables; Autumn is an irascible man with rough features facing left, also composed of fruits and vegetables; and Winter is a scraggly old man facing right, whose skin is a gnarled trunk, representing the wrinkles of old age.

On the bedroom nightstand, Monica has a jar of Crème de la Mer moisturizer, a favorite brand of Courteney Cox. Infused with cell-renewing Miracle Broth, this ultrarich cream immerses skin for instant and all-day moisture, helping heal dryness.

According to Judy Geller, Ross was so distressed "he took off all his clothes, tucked his penis between his legs and cried out, 'Mommy, I'm a girl, take me with you.'" This is a callback to "The One Where Nana Dies Twice" (1.08) where the gang discovered an old photograph of a little girl but it was actually Ross (with his penis tucked) who timidly admitted, "I'm just trying something."

For Phoebe's birthday party, Monica is wearing a gaudy jade-and-opal Y necklace. It's the same accessory Phoebe wears in "The One with Phoebe's Rats" (9.12).

9.06 "The One with the Male Nanny" (11.07.02)

Monica's coworker, Jeffrey the maitre d' (the funniest guy she knows), is named after Jeffrey Klarik, David Crane's life partner. "I get a lot of points for getting his name into the script whenever I can," Crane playfully asserted.

Lisa Kudrow improvised the physical comedy bit where she places Mike's hand on her breast. Her husband was on set the day they filmed which made Paul Rudd (Mike) feel rather awkward and uncomfortable.

The male nanny plot was based on Marta Kauffman's personal life. "Finding a nanny is truly the hardest thing to do in the world," she stated. "I had just gone through a period where we were interviewing nannies, and I met my first, as my daughter said, 'manny.' And he was wonderful. He was so fun to work with and so game."

Tom Hanks was scheduled to appear but canceled at the last minute when a production delay occurred while filming a movie, so Freddie Prinze Jr. was offered the nanny role. He swiftly accepted but was shocked when his agent said, "Yeah, it shoots tomorrow." He had less than 24 hours to learn his lines and how to play a musical instrument. On set, Prinze was "totally nervous" until David Schwimmer offered comforting words and said, "You'll have a ton of fun, don't worry about a thing."

The creators had difficulty deciding between David and Mike as Phoebe's long-term love interest. They eventually selected Mike because Paul Rudd fit so well with the cast and just felt more real. Moreover, Hank Azaria's filming schedule would have made it nearly impossible to lock him down for a recurring character commitment.

The Mike-Phoebe-David love triangle was supposed to span over two episodes but the writers couldn't get the story to work, so the romance was culled to a one installment.

In the uncut DVD version, Ross says, "You're just a guy who's a nanny? You've got to be at least bi," (meaning bisexual). In syndication, this comment is edited. The producers made a concerted effort to remove nearly all dialogue that may be construed as offensive or insensitive.

David's reference to a "Vladnik" carnival is a random fictitious Russian word created by the writers. David does speak real Russian words when he bids farewell to Phoebe.

Freddie Prinze Jr. and Matt LeBlanc received professional lessons on the recorder. The actors didn't play the instrument during the live performance; they were simply doing the proper fingering technique. A professional musician was hired to record the music which was added in postproduction. The two songs were "Greensleeves" (solo) and "Hot Crossed Buns" (duet). Prinze only had four hours of lessons before the show filmed.

This is the 200th episode and a supersized installment so it is one-third lengthier with three acts. The DVD version has a run time of 34:08, while the syndicated version times out at 21 to 22 minutes.

9.07 "The One with Ross's Inappropriate Song" (11.14.02)

The inappropriate song is "Baby Got Back" by Sir Mix-a-Lot (#1, 1992). Every time Ross or Rachel sing the tune, they stop before uttering the inappropriate lyrics. The song was controversial for its blatant sexual objectification of women, which resulted in it being briefly banned by MTV. Nevertheless, it became the second-best-selling song in the US in 1992 (behind Boyz II Men's "End of the Road"). In 2008, it was positioned No. 17 on VH1's 100 Greatest Songs of Hip Hop.

At the start of the episode, Joey is wearing a sweatshirt with "Greenwich" stitched on it, which is, of course, the primary setting for *Friends*. The costumer frequently chose New York–themed shirts.

While touring Richard's apartment, Joey sits on the couch and puts one hand down his pants like Al Bundy in *Married... with Children*. FYI: The series launched Matt LeBlanc's 1991 sitcom *Top of the Heap*.

Richard's apartment features original artwork from Jeff Schaller. He is good friends with pop artist and customary *Friends* contributor Burton Morris. When Morris became too busy to create new pieces for the series, he formally introduced Schaller to Kevin Bright. The artist recalled the meeting: "I remember getting the call and the set designer saying they needed a piece for Richard's apartment. I was so excited because I thought Monica and Richard were going to get back together! I was in the know!" He promptly became a regular art contributor for the final two seasons.

Actress Cristine Rose (incorrectly credited as Christine Rose) portrays Mike's mother in this episode. She also portrayed Ted Mosby's mother in *How I Met Your Mother*.

Andre Lachaumette, who portrays Tom, a friend of the Hannigans, also appeared as an extra in two other *Friends* episodes: "The One with the Screamer" (3.22) (theater after-party attendee) and "The One After Ross Says Rachel" (5.01) (wedding reception guest).

While the guys are watching Richard and Monica's sex tape, Monica enters the abode so Joey pulls her to the floor. Courteney Cox is wearing injury-prevention knee pads, and a safety mat was also used but it was edited out of the frame.

9.08 "The One with Rachel's Other Sister" (11.21.02)
Marta Kauffman purchased Monica's good china after the series went off the air.

Chandler's joke involving his use of the word "y'all" was added by Matthew Perry as an inside joke aimed at Courteney Cox because she frequently used the contraction in real life. The joke is in the DVD version for "The One with the Male Nanny" (9.06).

Reese Witherspoon was asked to reprise the role of Jill but declined because she was terrified at the idea of performing in front of a live studio audience. The producers opted to develop the character Amy, Rachel's other sister, since she had been mentioned in prior episodes.

This is the first appearance of Christina Applegate as Amy Green. Marta Kauffman had nothing but adulation for the special guest star: "This was, as far as I'm concerned, the best bits of casting we ever did." Applegate reprises the role in "The One Where Rachel's Sister Babysits" (10.05).

The executive producers all worked with Applegate on the TV series *Jesse* (1998-2000), so when it came time to cast the part of Amy Green, they instantly thought of her.

Prior to this installment, Christina Applegate already knew most of the *Friends* costars. She met Matthew Perry in 1988 while making the telefilm *Dance 'Til Dawn* (they played teen lovers), knew Courteney Cox and Lisa Kudrow since the late 1980s, and worked with Matt LeBlanc in 1991 on *Married... with Children* and *Top of the Heap*. Although she didn't know Jennifer Aniston, she dated Brad Pitt in 1989, and he, of course, ended up marrying Aniston in 2000.

The bit where Amy repeatedly misspeaks Phoebe's name was not in the original script. It was added during filming in front of a live studio audience. This comedy bit was one of Applegate's favorite "funny moments on the show."

The original script didn't have china breaking. It evolved as the story unfolded and after multiple rewrites. When it was pitched, the writers liked the idea since it would cause Monica consternation.

After Chandler packs the good china, it is swapped out during filming with another box containing broken plates. Director Kevin Bright tried all sorts of ways to dump the box and have the plates break but nothing worked. He opted to go with pre-broken china.

HD versions reveal filming errors such as Elliott Gould's stand-in during a scene pickup

9.09 "The One with Rachel's Phone Number" (12.05.02)
The installment opens with an establishing shot of the Tulsa skyline. This is the actual Tulsa skyline.

In the cold open, Joey is wearing a gray Foursquare sweatshirt while talking on a cell phone in his apartment. The brand is promoted more than half a dozen times in various episodes, starting with "The One with All the Resolutions" (5.11).

When visiting Ross' apartment, Mike brings a fake six-pack of Australian Foster's Lager. The label was modified to "Father's" to prevent a trademark infringement.

Monica's bedroom features a fleur-de-lis (lily flower) wall hanging. The image has been used by French royalty and throughout history to represent Catholic saints of France, e.g., the Virgin Mary and St. Joseph. The symbol is profoundly ingrained in Louisiana's history. It is seen in architecture, the state flag, and the NFL helmet for the Saints, but originally it was once used to mark slaves.

Joey's countertop features a box of Flutie Flakes, a frosted corn flakes breakfast cereal named for NFL quarterback Doug Flutie. The brand was introduced in 1998, after Flutie saw his popularity soar because of his scrambling, last-quarter heroics, and impressive win-loss record. At first, PLB Sports intended to produce just 50,000 boxes, but wound up selling more than 3 million.

In the later years of the series, Puma received sizable product placement on the show. In this episode, when Chandler and Joey enter Monica's abode to check whether she is having an affair, Chandler is wearing Puma gray sneakers with white logo. FYI: Matthew Perry was the main actor used to promote the footwear brand.

Ross is carrying a Ray Bari pizza carton. This was a frequent image used to sell the idea that the sitcom was based in New York.

9.10 "The One with Christmas in Tulsa" (12.12.02)
This is the last Christmas episode of the series. Unfortunately, it is also a clip show so the writers wasted another opportunity to actually entertain their fans. Although it has more substance than other clip shows, it was still hastily prepared by the staff writers.

In the teaser, Phoebe entertains Joey with a magical tale of a jolly man delivering toys, and claims the story as her own. It is actually the 1823 poem *A Visit from St. Nicholas* (aka *The Night Before Christmas*) by Clement Clarke Moore. Arguably, the composition contains the best-known verses ever written by an American and is largely responsible for some of the conceptions of Santa Claus from the mid-19th century to today. It had a massive effect on the history of Christmas gift-giving. The poem was eventually set to music and has been recorded by many artists.

Ross is wrapping a T-Rex Dino Kit. This is a fake toy created by the art department.

This episode offers an instrumental of "We Three Kings" (aka "Three Kings of Orient"). The 1857 carol was inked for a Christmas pageant in New York by John Henry Hopkins Jr. when he was the rector of Christ Episcopal Church in Williamsport, Pennsylvania. Numerous versions of this song have been composed and it remains a popular carol.

When Rachel and Ross are urging Chandler to answer Monica's questions quicker and better, this is a callback to "The One the Morning After" (3.16) where Joey and Chandler prompted Ross to give better answers when being grilled by Rachel about his tryst with Chloe, the copy girl.

Monica proposes the rhetorical question, "Do you think it's snowing in Tulsa where my husband is having sex on a copy machine?" This remark is a callback to "The One with Phoebe's Husband" (2.04) where Joey's porn movie featured a couple having sex on a photocopier.

9.11 "The One Where Rachel Goes Back to Work" (01.09.03)
In the opening scene after credits, it is very obvious that Lisa Kudrow is wearing a wig.

The wooden beam archway in Monica's apartment is reinstalled for this episode. It had to be rebuilt because it got lost after five years of storage. Customarily, the set designer only installed the beam when James Burrows directed an installment. However, in this case, director Gary Halvorson deemed it essential for this episode.

Outside Rachel's office is a mammoth print for El Siglo Exposicion y Venta (The Century Exhibition and Sale) by Leonetto Cappiello, circa 1920s. It features two women studying a swatch of fabric for an exhibition and sale of cloth carpets and upholstery. Cappiello is one of the most influential artists in the history of poster art and known as the father of modern advertising posters.

In the start of Act 1, Ross positively asserts that Emma's "gonna be hotter than peasant blouses and A-line skirts." Due to this dialogue, the *Friends* costumer dressed Rachel and Monica in peasant blouses to illustrate the point.

Dermot Mulroney (who plays Gavin Mitchell) makes his first guest appearance. He was introduced to fuel romantic conflict between Ross and Rachel. FYI: The character is not named after the actor with the same name.

When Rachel first meets Gavin in her office, the door nameplate displays her surname as "Greene." In all other episodes, except "The One with the Invitation" (4.21) and "The One with Phoebe's Rats" (9.12), her last name is spelled "Green" (without the extra "e").

This is the first appearance of Alexandra and Athina Conley as Emma. Although Emma appeared in nearly two dozen episodes of *Friends*, the Conley twins only played her in four installments, from January 2003 to March 2003.

As a soap opera extra, Phoebe repeatedly botches her scene as a surgical assistant. In real life, Lisa Kudrow repeatedly botched this scene during filming because she couldn't keep a straight face.

During the *DOOL* restaurant scene, Joey is dining with a soap opera colleague played by Paul Logan, who actually starred as Glen Reiber in multiple installments of the real *Days of Our Lives*.

In the soap opera restaurant scene, two women claim Joey slept with them and never called the next day. The blonde is played by Lisa Kudrow's stand-in, Heather Sims.

9.12 "The One with Phoebe's Rats" (01.16.03)
Actress Melissa George portrays Molly the nanny. The Australian native was a national rollerskating champion and won bronze medals in the National Championships in 1989 and 1990, and a silver medal at the Junior World Championship in 1991. George began modeling in her early teens, and in 1992 was named Western Australia's Teenage Model of the Year. She began her acting career playing Angel Parrish on the Australian soap opera *Home and Away* from 1993 to 1996.

In the uncut DVD version, Chandler is watching television and asks, "Who shot J.R.?" which refers to *Dallas* (1978-91), a primetime soap opera revolving around an affluent and feuding Texas family, the Ewings. The show was famous for its cliffhangers, like the popular 1980 installment "Who Done It" (promoted as "Who shot J.R.?"). It remains the second-highest-rated primetime telecast ever, and ended up No. 69 on *TV Guide*'s 2009 list of TV's Top 100 Episodes of All Time.

During one scene, Ross says "Whassup!" to which Chandler remarks, "Seriously dude. Three years ago." This is an allusion to Budweiser's 1999 television ad that popularized the catchphrase "Whassup!" and made it part of popular culture and urban vernacular.

Ross' apartment contains a large giclée (ZHē′klā) print entitled *Questions and Answers* by artist Jeff Schaller from Downingtown, Pennsylvania. It has a giraffe from the neck up with an all-white man and boy sketching overlaid and For Sale at the bottom. Giclée is a special technology for fine art or photograph reproduction using high-quality inkjet printers to make individual copies.

While Monica and Rachel discuss cleaning the apartment after the party, a remarkable wood carving of an old man is visible in the hallway. This is a favorite piece curated by set decorator Greg Grande.

This episode alludes to the fact that Ross still loves Rachel based upon his forlorn facial expression after witnessing the kiss between her and Gavin. The writers wanted to keep the audience invested in the idea of a future romantic union for Ross and Rachel.

9.13 "The One Where Monica Sings" (01.30.03)

Phoebe declares that Joey is high maintenance because he needs his eyebrows plucked and knuckle hair removed, so he retaliates by stating that she dyes her hair. In real life, Matt LeBlanc started dyeing his hair in Season 2 when it began graying at the temples. At first he tried doing it himself to save time, but after dyeing the back of his ears black, he decided to have the on-set makeup artist handle the task.

When Joey visits the spa to have his eyebrows waxed, there is a shelving unit with OPI products, as well as several promotional posters. OPI is an American nail polish maker headquartered in Calabasas, California.

This is the last appearance of Dermot Mulroney as Gavin. The producers considered a lengthier arc but felt Mulroney lacked sufficient chemistry with Jennifer Aniston.

Mike is a lawyer turned pianist. Likewise, Courteney Cox is an actor turned pianist. She admits to being "obsessed with playing the piano" and frequently shares on Instagram practice sessions with her daughter singing. Cox stated, "I host music nights a lot at my house. It just makes me happy."

Monica sings karaoke quite poorly which came natural to Cox. She admits to having a "bad voice" despite taking singing lessons.

As two women enter Central Perk, the blonde (Michelle) is crying after breaking up with Eric. Her black-haired friend is played by Lisa Calderon, Courteney Cox's stand-in.

The fake eyebrows attached to Matt LeBlanc's face melted several times during filming due to the intense heat of the stage lighting. Multiple production breaks were needed to replace the eyebrows.

9.14 "The One with the Blind Dates" (02.06.03)

The magna doodle has three-dimensional ABC blocks with A stacked atop B and C. The C block has a cat, B a basketball, and A an apple. This alludes to Emma living in Joey's apartment.

At the start of Act 1, Joey is wearing gray Nike pants and a black Fox Racing tee. Matt LeBlanc is an avid racing enthusiast so he chose this shirt and asked costumer Debra McGuire to work it into an episode according to her color palette.

Joey's kitchen contains a shelf above the stove. It's the most recent addition to the set. Production designer John Shaffner wanted a focal point to better display and promote products for the corporate sponsors. The top of the refrigerator was the original product placement location but many labels were obscured or out of frame so a shelf was built to make brand names more visibly accessible to the audience.

Ross waits for his date at Delmonico's Steak House, a real restaurant at 56 Beaver St. in Manhattan. In 1837, the Delmonico brothers opened the first fine-dining restaurant in the country. It offered unheard of luxury—private dining rooms (located on the third floor) where discriminate entertaining was the order of the day—and the largest private wine cellar in the city, featuring an impressive collection of 1,000 bottles of the world's finest vino.

The waiter at Delmonico's is portrayed by Sam Pancake. He had the same occupation at another restaurant in "The One Where Joey Tells Rachel" (8.16), where Joey and Rachel occupied his table all night.

Rachel's blind date, Steve, is portrayed by Jon Lovitz, in a reprisal of the character. He previously appeared in "The One with the Stoned Guy" (1.15), which aired 193 episodes ago, the longest span between recurring character roles. Although it is a blind date, the characters previously met in an earlier episode where Rachel was working as a waitress during Monica's cooking audition for him.

9.15 "The One with the Mugging" (02.13.03)
This episode was filmed on Friday, December 13, 2002, but did not air until February 13, 2003.

Rachel only appears in two scenes. This was to accommodate Jennifer Aniston's broken toe that she injured at home a week prior. Her original storyline was cut and she was relegated to a secondary character. Fortunately, Aniston had a month to heal before the next episode was shot.

Jennifer Aniston's publicist originally claimed that her client banged her foot on a piece of furniture. She later expounded, stating that Aniston broke her toe on an ottoman at home while rushing for the phone.

Monica says that Ross was not the originator of the "Got Milk?" advertising campaign. It was created in 1993 and featured famous actors and athletes drinking and promoting milk with a "milk mustache." From 1995 to 1999, approximately 300 celebrity posters were produced. One of the first ads featured Lisa Kudrow and Jennifer Aniston.

At the audition, Joey demonstrates a Southern accent, but it sounds Jamaican. This is a callback to "The One Where Rachel is Late" (8.22) where he worked 20 hours with a dialect coach to learn the drawl (which Chandler paid for) but it was actually Jamaican.

Kyle Gass portrays the part of Lowell, the mugger. Gass is a guitarist in Tenacious D, a comedy rock duo. During filming breaks, he played guitar to entertain the audience.

Monica sports an ecru long-sleeve graphic tee with a giant question mark on it. This is an allusion to the Riddler, a nemesis of Batman. Costumer Debra McGuire selected the attire to evince superhero notions that correspond with Ross' childhood comic book. It was also an inside joke. In the first part of Season 1, "The Riddler" was a nickname the writers used to describe the Monica character.

Ross' comic book *Science Boy* is a fictional publication intended to reiterate his interest in science as a teenager, and to further explain his career as a paleontologist. It is also meant to illustrate that his quirky, geeky persona as an adult originated in childhood.

9.16 "The One with the Boob Job" (02.20.03)
In the cold open of the uncut DVD version, Rachel is hobbling as she runs around the apartment in stockings attempting to get the gang to witness Emma crawling. Jennifer Aniston is still recovering from a broken toe incident that happened in early December. She has remarkable mobility because the scene was filmed in early February, as part of another episode. In this installment, Rachel's storyline of babyproofing the apartment was written to limit Aniston's movement.

There is a transitional establishing shot featuring John's Pizzeria on Bleecker Street, a historic Manhattan pizzeria founded in 1929. It is publicly known for serving coal-fired brick oven pizzas prepared in the style of a tomato pie. In 2015, it was ranked the 10th best pizzeria in the United States by TripAdvisor. John's Pizzeria is memorialized for its graffiti-carved wooden booths where any patron can whittle their name.

As Phoebe and Mike discuss his vow to never get married, the background prints vary with each edit. Often it is a black-and-white photo in front of a poster labeled Liqueur.

Monica, Chandler, and Joey describing how difficult it is moving Mike's couch up the stairs is a callback to "The One with the Cop" (5.16), where Ross, Rachel and Chandler attempt to "pivot" a sofa up the stairs to Ross' apartment.

Phoebe's apartment number is 16 (on the door), which has stayed consistent since she started living there. However, in "The One with Joey's New Brain" (7.15), she tells the mystery cell phone guy that she lived in apartment 14, and in "The One with Phoebe's Dad" (2.09), the designation 12B was used when her grandmother lived there.

The establishing shot for Phoebe's apartment is 5 Morton St. in New York. However, the invitation for Ross' wedding was addressed to 143B Howton Ave., New York, NY 10001. In real life, the invitation address is located in Staten Island, New York.

9.17 "The One with the Memorial Service" (03.13.03)

This episode is also known as "The One with the Start of Social Media Networking" but it is more of a retrospective moniker used by some viewers.

To accommodate Jennifer Aniston's broken toe, Rachel's involvement was minimal and the camera blocking limited her movements. She is primarily in the apartment playing with Emma or discussing Hugsy with Joey. Aniston wore slippers because it was too painful to wear shoes.

When Ross uses the alumni social network webpage to "out" Chandler (as gay), Monica says it's a cruel joke because it could be true, and then provides an example: "I guess I should have known ... He just kept making me watch *Moulin Rouge!*" She knows that it could be true. Monica thought Chandler was gay the first time they met, as revealed in "The One Where Nana Dies Twice" (1.08).

Phoebe's coat rack features the emerald green jacket with black plaid that she pilfered while attending Rachel's birthday party in "The One with Phoebe's Rats" (9.12).

After Monica snatches the cell phone, Phoebe yells, "Damn you, Monica Geller hyphen Bing." In "The One with Princess Consuela" (10.14), however, it is revealed that Monica never changed her surname. Courteney Cox, on the other hand, changed her stage and legal name after her marriage to David Arquette. In contrast, Jennifer Aniston kept her surname professionally but legally changed it to Pitt following their marriage in 2000. After the couples divorced, Cox restored her maiden name in both realms and Aniston legally reclaimed her birth name.

After only four episodes, this is the final appearance of Alexandra and Athina Conley as Emma. It was their only acting gig. The twins never pursued an acting career.

In the spinoff series *Joey*, two personal possessions follow the titular character to his new Los Angeles residence. First, and foremost, his bedtime penguin pal, Hugsy. The other prized possession is the 1983 Al Pacino *Scarface* poster in his bedroom.

9.18 "The One with the Lottery" (04.03.03)

This is one of the annual bottle episodes where the entire episode consists of the main cast, two or less secondary characters, no special guest stars, and no elaborate sets.

When this episode originally aired, Powerball was not sold in the state of New York. On January 31, 2010, the New York Lottery started selling Powerball tickets so residents no longer had to travel to adjacent states to buy an entry. Powerball is an American lottery game currently offered by 45 states, the District of Columbia, Puerto Rico and the US Virgin Islands.

This is the first episode where Rachel is able to wear shoes since Jennifer Aniston broke her toe in early December 2002. Nevertheless, the director still limited her movements;

in most scenes she is simply standing around or barely moving.

Rachel is wearing an MC5 t-shirt, which stands for Motor City Five, a popular Detroit-based rock band from the 1960s and 1970s known for such singles as "Teenage Lust" and "Kick Out the Jams." *Friends* head costume designer Debra McGuire was a fan of the rockers since high school.

If Joey wins the lottery and buys the Knicks, he promises to select Rachel as starting forward for the team. Rachel replies, "You would do that? I never get picked!" This is a callback to "The One with the Football" (3.09) where she was sad after being picked last for a football game.

After Phoebe drops the bowl of lottery tickets from the balcony, everyone evacuates the apartment without jackets, but upon their return, they are all sporting outerwear.

The televised Powerball lottery is stock footage purchased by the production company and is from a prior broadcast. During filming, a loop of the drawing played on the TV for the audience. After filming, a clip of the lottery telecast was added in postproduction.

On the wooden shelf next to Monica's refrigerator, there is a glimpse at the novel *Ellis Island* by Fred Mustard Stewart. It was added as set dressing to reinforce the sitcom's New York roots. The same book appears in Carol and Susan's apartment.

9.19 "The One with Rachel's Dream" (04.17.03)
As Joey is talking dirty to a pineapple, Rachel exits her bedroom to eavesdrop. This is a recycled bit from "The One with the Stoned Guy" (1.15) where Ross practiced dirty talk with Joey as Chandler exited his bedroom to eavesdrop.

The *Days of Our Lives* scenes are taped on Stage 24 using video cameras, instead of the usual 35 mm film. Rachel is backstage watching a live feed of the soap opera scene.

This episode has the only scene inside Javu restaurant, where Monica is the head chef. Javu is a fictional eatery. It's a chic spot that's especially appealing to Monica because of its squeaky clean kitchen: "It's not just Health Department clean, it's Monica clean!"

Outside Javu, Phoebe strums a Gibson classical guitar and then later a Gibson acoustic (with black pickguard). The guitar case offers product placement for the manufacturer.

While running lines with Joey, Rachel is supposedly holding a *Days of Our Lives* script, but actually, it is the official *Friends* script for this episode.

This is the second time Rachel has erotic dreams featuring Joey. In "The One with the Ick Factor" (1.22), her dreams involved multiple romantic encounters: (1) Chandler, (2) Joey and Chandler, and (3) Ross.

In the Vermont hotel, Chandler pridefully displays a recent edition of *USA Today*. The newspaper was first promoted in "The One with Five Steaks and an Eggplant" (2.05).

The magna doodle has a donkey tied to an old-time covered wagon and is stubbornly sitting on the ground. This is a metaphor for the characters' obstinacy: Ross mulishly pilfering hotel amenities to offset the exorbitant cost of a room, and Monica and Phoebe steadfastly refusing to capitulate in their turf war at Javu.

9.20 "The One with the Soap Opera Party" (04.24.03)
In the cold opening, Joey invites the gang to a one-woman play called *Why Don't You Like Me? A Bitter Woman's Journey Through Life*. Ross remarks: "Yeah, it does sound interesting, I mean, to listen to a woman complain for two hours, I don't think it gets bett ..." (Ross starts snoring, faking sleep). This act of falling asleep to the thought of something boring was an off-camera behavior used by the cast as a joke. The writers liked the quirky conduct so they added the bit to a couple episodes.

In the opening scene of Act 1, Monica is perusing *Mental Floss'* The 10 Issue with the headline "This One's a Knock Out." Courteney Cox's husband David Arquette thought it was an interesting periodical so he suggested that she include it in the show.

***The Four Seasons* portraits by Giuseppe Arcimboldo**

The character Charlie was created to quell criticism that *Friends* lacked racial diversity. Aisha Tyler was the first black actor to earn a recurring role on the series. She appeared in nine episodes.

After arriving on set, the first thing Aisha Tyler did was walk into Monica's apartment and look out the window to see if she could see Ugly Naked Guy. Of course, it's just a backstage area but that's how well the show sold the imagery.

Jane Rogers, the voice on Joey's answering machine tape, is actually spoken by Heather Sims, Lisa Kudrow's stand-in.

The magna doodle has a closeup drawing of Hello Kitty. Costumer Debra McGuire was a huge fan of the fictional cartoon character. She always kept a doll on a podium in her office. A crew member stole the doll so the sketch was an inside joke related to the theft.

In the scene where Joey enters Monica's apartment and opens his robe, the audience reaction is uproarious laughter because of a prior blooper. In the outtake, Matt LeBlanc opened his robe to expose his boxer shorts, and covering the genitalia area was a headshot of David Schwimmer.

During Joey's rooftop soap opera party, time stands still on all the clocks in the distant buildings. The background image is a still photo overlaid on a blue screen so there is no clock movement.

Four *Days of Our Lives* stars have cameos as rooftop party guests. The featured actors are Kyle Lowder (as Brady Black, 2000-05) and Matthew Ashford (as Jack Deveraux, 1987-2012). In the background is Farah Fath (as Mimi Lockhart) and Alexis Thorpe (as Cassie Brady).

Charlie reveals she previously dated Professor Benjamin Hobart, a double Nobel Prize winner. The writers added the name-drop to foreshadow his appearance in Season 10.

9.21 "The One with the Fertility Test" (05.01.03)

In the teaser, Monica is reading *Mental Floss* magazine. Since 2017, it became an online publication focusing on millennials. The website offers facts, puzzles and trivia written in a humorous tone, and draws 20.5 million unique users a month.

The magna doodle has a lion's face and the words "Happy Birthday Gizzy 5-1-91." This is a tribute to a stagehand's daughter (Gisella) who was celebrating her 12th birthday.

When Joey seeks advice on dating Charlie, he is wearing two belts. This is a recycled joke from "The One with Monica and Chandler's Wedding, Part 2" (7.24). The writers admit they simply forgot the bit had already been used.

After achieving fame on *Friends*, Maggie Wheeler (Janice) auditioned for the female lead as Debra Barone in the sitcom *Everybody Loves Raymond* (1998-2005). Despite being the producers' first choice, CBS insisted on Patricia Heaton. As a consolation, Wheeler was cast in a recurring role as Linda, Debra's friend.

Monica and Chandler discover they can't naturally conceive a child. In Season 10, this becomes the continuity roadblock that derails any effort to write Courteney Cox's pregnancy into the script.

Courteney Cox had problems naturally conceiving a child. Sadly, she experienced seven miscarriages and numerous failed IVF treatments. Thankfully, IVF and blood thinners eventually worked for her and she gave birth to a daughter, Coco Arquette, in 2004.

Monica and Chandler's inability to conceive a child was not meant to mirror Courteney Cox's real-life trauma. It was purely accidental. The writers were looking for something unconventional and the idea of adoption fascinated them. Plus, they did not want the blame to be borne by one person, which would cause resentment, so both characters were equally incapable of conception.

9.22 "The One with the Donor" (05.08.03)
The Bloomingdale's department store employee who spritzes Phoebe with men's cologne is played by Kim Harris, Jennifer Aniston's stand-in.

Charlie mentions wanting a jacket with shoulder pads and asks where she can find one, to which Rachel replies, "On Melanie Griffith in *Working Girl*." The 1988 rom-com movie encapsulates the entire decade of women's fashion where shoulder pads were meant to give women the kind of sharp, defined silhouette that men had with their luxury suits and power ties. Fittingly, the apparel is dubbed linebacker shoulders or Working Girl shoulder pads. As of 2019, the fashion was making a revival.

John Stamos (Zack) is best known for his work on *Full House*. His parents supported his career so he skipped college to focus on acting, and after just three weeks, landed a role as Blackie Parrish on *General Hospital*, which earned him immediate recognition. Stamos is also a competent musician. In 1985 he began touring with The Beach Boys, playing drums and other percussion instruments. He would later appear in the band's music videos, play drums on albums, and record lead vocals on songs.

While sitting in Monica's living room, Zack is reading *Saveur* magazine with the caption "The Saveur 100" (Jan/Feb 2003). It is a gourmet food, wine, and travel periodical that specializes in essays about various world cuisines. *Saveur* became an online publication in February 2021.

During a transition clip, the World Trade Center is visible despite it being almost two years since the 9/11 attack that destroyed the twin towers. The editor used old stock footage and no one in the production company noticed the continuity error.

When Phoebe enters Central Perk wearing a stunning black dress, Joey glances at her and remarks, "Wow! You look ... (drops the cookie) ... stop-eating hot! Which is like the highest level of hotness!" This line was added for Lisa Kudrow's benefit because she felt "like this mountain of a woman" standing next to her younger, hotter costars. Kudrow still struggles with her body image and it's an ongoing battle, but she's coming to terms with aging and accepting her large-frame physique.

This episode is the lowest-rated non-flashback episode of the entire series.

9.23 "The One in Barbados, Part 1" (05.15.03)
This is the episode debut of identical twins Cali and Noelle Sheldon as Emma.

All the tropical images are either stock footage or well-dressed purpose-built studio sets used to create the illusion of a Caribbean paradise. No scenes were filmed in Barbados.

Barbados was randomly chosen during a brainstorming session. The creators wanted a big event, like a birth or wedding, but both had been done to death, so they opted for a vacation destination to give the season finale a little promotional punch for ratings.

Most fans don't know that Matthew Perry and Hank Azaria are best friends. From the moment Azaria was cast for this episode, Perry began lobbying the producers for screen time together. The writers finally inked a scene in Central Perk, which is quite fortunate since Azaria never reprised the role. After filming wrapped, the duo went to London for three months to costar in *Sexual Perversity in Chicago* at the West End Theatre.

While in Ross' hotel room, Rachel has her arm bandaged. In real life, Jennifer Aniston cut her arm during nonworking hours and it was serious enough that it could not be concealed with makeup. By the time Part 2 was filmed, the cut had sufficiently healed so the bandage was discarded.

After Joey opens the hotel room door, Ross says, "You're never going to guess who I just saw downstairs." The answer is Dr. Kenneth Schwartz, which is a name-drop. Kenny Schwartz is a writer-friend of Shana Goldberg-Meehan and Scott Silveri, the writing duo who penned this episode.

Phoebe inadvertently saying "I love Mike" instead of "I love David," is a callback to Ross' wedding with his misspoken vows: "I take thee Rachel" instead of "I take thee Emily."

In the hotel lobby, as Joey and Rachel are deciding how to spend their day together, a waiter is carrying a tray of hors d'oeuvres. The extra is Joe Everett Michaels, the stand-in for Matthew Perry.

Joey and Rachel attend a pharmaceutical convention using fake IDs, and she grabs the name tag for Kate Miller. The moniker is a throwback to "The One with the Tiny T-Shirt" (3.19) where Joey fell in love with an actress named Kate Miller.

While filming this installment, Hank Azaria was also filming the movie *Shattered Glass*. He awoke at 6am to shoot the movie scenes and then went directly to the *Friends* stage to film his sitcom scenes. The marriage proposal scene wrapped around 1am so Azaria endured a 20-hour workday.

9.24 "The One in Barbados, Part 2" (05.15.03)

The bandage on Jennifer Aniston's arm is finally removed after wearing it for a month. She was left with a long, prominent scar on her left forearm as a remembrance.

The conference room for Ross' speech is the same swing set used for David's marriage proposal at the restaurant. The producers opted to save money on construction costs by repurposing the set.

With an episode having two romance plots (Ross-Charlie and Rachel-Joey), the writers needed a third narrative to encompass Monica, Chandler and Phoebe. They opted for a silly story to balance the seriousness of the other two, and selected one of their favorite fallback themes—Monica's competitiveness.

For the ping pong competition, the producers hired table tennis professionals to assist the actors with form and teach them the basics. The creators thoroughly researched the topic of table tennis to understand the rules and other aspects of the game.

The television in Rachel's hotel room is the same TV set used in Monica and Chandler's apartment.

Although the cast adamantly objected to a Rachel-Joey relationship, an audience straw poll was taken and half the people wanted them together while the other half wanted her with Ross.

In the scene where Monica hurts her hand playing ping pong, the first take caused the audience to gasp because they thought the injury was real. It was just good acting on Cox's part. She sold it.

When a group of paleontologists gather to accost Ross to throw him into the pool, one of whom is Professor Klarik. He was named after David Crane's life partner, Jeffrey Klarik.

David Schwimmer was worried about the audience judging him for kissing Charlie, so he asked the creators to write dialogue that would cast him in a less judgmental light. Thus, a playful segment was included where they are running around the hotel, hiding, and having drinks which ultimately culminates with their closeness in proximity and inevitable kiss.

Joey and Rachel's passionate kiss was not filmed in front of a live studio audience. The showrunners wanted this revelation to remain a secret to shock viewers when it aired.

Pop art prints by Jeff Schaller that were featured in Seasons 9 and 10

Season 10: 2003-04

10.01 "The One After Joey and Rachel Kiss" (09.25.03)

The three hotel rooms are not adjacent sets. The visual effect was created by repeated through-wall pans during postproduction editing. It was necessary to accommodate the eavesdropping, but other scenes show at least one room is separated by a hallway.

Monica and Chandler's hotel room has a bathroom door near the window. In the prior episode, there was no door in that location.

Rachel wears a white t-shirt with a stitched pair of lips and scrolled inside is the phrase "Save the drama for your mama." The series costumer chose this shirt to highlight the complicated relationship status of the characters vis-à-vis Ross and Rachel swapping partners with Joey and Charlie. In 2020, singer Harry Styles paid homage to Rachel by sporting a replica tee stitched by his sister Gemma.

While on the plane, Ross speaks to Joey about kissing Charlie, and then Joey excitedly shouts "You kissed?" As Ross awkwardly snickers, in the background Jennifer Aniston breaks character by laughing at the scene while watching from afar.

Anne Dudek portrays Mike's current-girlfriend Precious. In this episode, she suffers a relationship breakup on her birthday. In *How I Met Your Mother*, Dudek plays Natalie, one of Ted's girlfriends, who endures a relationship breakup on her birthday (twice).

Phoebe refers to Precious as "Susie" because the name Precious reminds her of a pet's name. This is a callback to "The One with Phoebe's Rats" (9.12) where her pet mouse was called Susie.

Monica gets her hair caught in the shower curtain hooks while dancing to the tune "No Woman, No Cry" by Bob Marley and the Wailers. The live version is ranked No. 37 on *Rolling Stone*'s 500 Greatest Songs of All Time.

The magna doodle has an adult kangaroo with a baby in its pouch with the word "Joey" and an arrow pointing to the baby. Obviously, a "joey" is an infant marsupial.

10.02 "The One Where Ross is Fine" (10.02.03)

The Joey-Rachel romance was not initially accepted by the cast. "In the beginning, Matt LeBlanc did not want to do that story," Kevin Bright stated. "He was very firmly against it, saying that he's Ross' friend, and that the type of friend that Joey is, would never go and take someone else's girlfriend." Bright added that it took "a lot" to convince LeBlanc to agree to the narrative.

At the start of Act 1, there is an M&M collectible in Joey's oven. As a game, the *Friends* crew had a regular Easter egg hunt where someone would hide a prop around the set for others to find. The oven proved to be a good hiding place. The toy remained hidden in the oven for the rest of the series.

Elle Fanning (*Super 8*, *Maleficent*) auditioned to play one of Frank Jr.'s daughters, but didn't get the part. After being rejected for the role, she vowed never to watch the show, and remained headstrong even after her older sister Dakota was cast to appear in "The One with Princess Consuela" (10.14).

Frank Jr. wants to give Phoebe one of his kids, which is a role reversal from "The One Hundredth" (5.03) where she wanted to keep one of the triplets after giving birth.

This is the final appearance of Giovanni Ribisi as Frank Jr. He previously appeared in "The One Hundredth" (5.03), a span of 120 episodes. Debra Jo Rupp (Alice) does not appear. Both actors were too busy with other projects to regularly appear on *Friends*.

The prominent Spanish wall poster hanging in Bill and Colleen's home is Bailes Rusos Teatro Liceo (Russian Dances Lyceum Theater) by Russian artist Leon Bakst (c. 1911), which is promoting a Russian dance performance at a Barcelona theater.

According to numerous sources, this is a top-20 *Friends* episode.

10.03 "The One with Ross's Tan" (10.09.03)
Ross visits Mystic Tan, a real business with franchises across the US. In exchange for the use of its equipment, the company received free advertising with a wall poster and tanning booth sign: Mystic Tan UV-Free Tanning. Applied with Magnetan Technology.

Joey and Rachel realize neither of them paid for dinner. This is a recycled bit from "The One with All the Cheesecakes" (7.11) where she and Chandler forgot to pay for lunch.

When Rachel and Joey are kissing on the davenport and she keeps slapping his hand, Jennifer Aniston actually smacks Matt LeBlanc in the head. They talked about this bit beforehand and he agreed to take a hit for the betterment of the scene.

Phoebe and Monica's vexing former neighbor (Amanda) is played by Jennifer Coolidge. Her only improvisation in this episode was her dance routine. Coolidge would later play Joey's agent, Bobby Morganstern, in the spinoff series *Joey*, though she is best known as Stifler's mom in the *American Pie* franchise and Sophie Kachinsky in *2 Broke Girls* (2012-17). Coolidge attended Emerson College, Kevin Bright's alma mater, and in 1985 she graduated with a BA in theater.

Jennifer Coolidge felt disconcerted the moment she strolled onto Stage 24. "I was kind of intimidated, even though I knew Lisa [Kudrow] because she was in a comedy group," she stated. "But I didn't know the rest of them, and I was very intimidated because they were all so attractive and had it going on."

The scene where Rachel successfully removes her bra through her sleeve is a callback to "The One with the Fake Party" (4.16) where the same maneuver failed in her effort to seduce Joshua. In most syndicated versions, the bra removal scene is removed because Jennifer Aniston's nipples prominently protrude through her shirt.

This installment is often ranked as a top-20 *Friends* episode by numerous sources.

10.04 "The One with the Cake" (10.23.03)
This installment is supposed to be Emma's one-year birthday celebration. Based on its airdate, Emma is actually 17 months old because she was born May 16, 2002.

Judy mentions that her parents died young, but in "The One Where Nana Dies Twice" (1.08) her mother passed away at a very old age.

The magna doodle image is a three-dimensional candle in the shape of a large "1" with a wick and flame on top and the words "Happy Happy" next to it, which honors Emma's first birthday.

During a panning shot of a Porsche on the highway, Ross is wearing a white shirt with the seatbelt latched. The interior view has him sporting a black jacket and gray shirt without a seatbelt.

Emma is played by Noelle and Cali Sheldon. The twins have performed in local theater, college films and a 2007 pilot. With nearly a dozen acting credits, their prime role was the 2019 thriller *Us*.

The cake box has Rachel's last name spelled Green (without an extra "e") which is the most frequent spelling, though a couple episodes have it spelled Greene.

10.05 "The One Where Rachel's Sister Babysits" (10.30.03)

This episode is directed by Roger Christiansen. He worked as an associate director on the series for 25 episodes from 2002 to 2003 where his duties included supporting and executing the show's objective, managing the day-to-day activities, and looking after the important project and assignment deadlines.

The magna doodle drawing has an apple pierced on both sides with a bullet exiting the fruit. This is a metaphor for the 9/11 attack on New York: Terrorists can attack the Big Apple but the strike will pass quickly while the city as a whole remains intact.

Phoebe and Mike's hockey scenes are supposed to be taking place in Madison Square Garden but were actually preshot using the audience bleachers on the *Friends* set.

The baby playing Emma did not get her ears pierced. She wore clip-on earrings.

Amy claims the earrings will help people realize that Emma is a girl. This is a callback to "The One Where Rachel Goes Back to Work" (9.11) where Rachel was incensed that everyone thought Emma was a boy.

Amy mentions that her sister Jill gained about 15 pounds, and is getting fat in the ass and face. This is an inside joke for Reese Witherspoon (Jill), because she was pregnant at the time this episode was filmed. She gave birth to her son Deacon one week before this episode aired.

This is Christina Applegate's final appearance as Amy. In 2021 she was diagnosed with multiple sclerosis. She previously had breast cancer in 2008 which resulted in a double mastectomy and the removal of her ovaries and fallopian tubes.

10.06 "The One with Ross's Grant" (11.06.03)

Greg Kinnear appears as Benjamin Hobart. At the time of his appearance, Kinnear was a first-rate Hollywood star, which is obvious from the audience ovation upon his first cued entrance.

At the restaurant, as Benjamin Hobart prepares to sit down, he takes the chair that was vacated by Ross. This is a callback to "The One with the Race Car Bed" (3.07) where Dr. Green occupies Ross' chair after joining him for dinner, as well as "The One Where No One's Ready" (3.02) where Chandler discovers the club chair he previously occupied has been usurped by Joey.

The magna doodle drawing has a one-legged man balancing on his left leg because the right one was ripped off by a dog that is chewing on the other extremity. This represents the battle for Charlie's affection where Benjamin Hobart is the mongrel tearing apart Ross' romance with Charlie.

A transition clip features Jefferson Market Library fka Jefferson Market Courthouse, a National Historic Landmark at 425 Avenue of the Americas in Greenwich Village.

The outfits worn by the girls in the Ichiban commercial are nearly identical to Rachel's attire. The costumer wanted to show a parallel between the females to presage Rachel and Joey's breakup, i.e., the ad was a mistake, much like his romance with Rachel.

Joey's lipstick commercial was a jab at famous actors who made embarrassing foreign commercials on the assumption no one in the Western world would ever see them. At the time, it was true. With the emergence of YouTube and the internet, some of these TV commercials have resurfaced. The list of actors include Leonardo DiCaprio, Charles Bronson, John Travolta, Dennis Hopper, Sean Connery, Roger Moore and Brad Pitt.

One potentially humiliating gig that Matt LeBlanc refused to accept was an advertisement for cold sore cream. He was worried it would negatively impact his marketability as a model.

Phoebe's 3-D artwork (Gladys) was created by a private artist. It was not commissioned for the show. Set decorator Greg Grande bought it at a flea market because he thought it "would be really funny as artwork for Phoebe's apartment wall." The art department enjoyed creating Glynnis, a comparably creepy 3-D piece.

10.07 "The One with the Home Study" (11.13.03)
Ross says he'll have his next wedding in Hawaii at sunset. He then alludes to his future divorce by declaring that he plans to have a City Hall wedding *after* the Hawaiian union. According to the spinoff series *Joey*, his next marriage is to Rachel soon after "The Last One, Part 2" (10.18).

The magna doodle drawing has a massive snail and a tiny man yelling at it through a megaphone. This is a metaphor for Ross' incessant procrastination in his romance with Rachel. He is the snail that needs a relationship coach to motivate him to act.

Monica gives her veil to Phoebe but it is not the one she wore at her wedding. Monica's veil is full length with a comb attachment; the one she gives Phoebe is shorter with an Alice band headpiece.

The park playground is actually a set built on Stage 24.

Ross is kicked in the head and knocked to the ground by a boy on a swing. This is Ross' third head trauma in the series. In "The One with the East German Laundry Detergent" (1.05), he walked into a dryer door, and in "The One Where Rachel Has a Baby, Part 2" (8.24), Rachel head-butted him.

Actress Maria Pitillo plays the home study interviewer (Laura). While Pitillo was working as a department store clerk, her friend invited her to audition for a TV commercial. Her first job was an ad for Pepto-Bismol. In 2002 she married David R. Fortney and then six years later retired from acting to raise her family and preside over Ice Box Foods, Inc., a small business in San Anselmo (outside San Francisco) with her husband.

Rachel doesn't hand a spider to Ross, nor does he have one trapped in his hands.

10.08 "The One with the Late Thanksgiving" (11.20.03)
Monica's angst-driven storyline was inspired by Marta Kauffman's exasperating holiday experiences. She, too, endured many thankless holidays and vowed never to do it again. "This is where I really connect with Monica," she confessed. "Every year I say, 'I'm not gonna do it again.' And there I am with 40 people in my house for Thanksgiving."

Rachel states it's Emma's first Thanksgiving but Monica corrects her and says it's not. This is a jab at critics for unabatedly publicizing the flawed timeline involving Rachel's 13-month gestation. It also serves as an in-joke for *Friends* fans who are well aware of the inconsistencies over the years regarding the birthdays of the characters, particularly Ross, Rachel and Phoebe.

A baby beauty pageant plotline was strongly debated in the writers room but ultimately chosen because the staff needed a legitimate reason for Rachel and Phoebe to be late for Thanksgiving. Then, they had to pitch the narrative to the cast. "Jennifer had a really strong response," Crane confessed. "She was horrified that she's entering her baby in a beauty pageant." Since it was only one scene, Aniston agreed. "If it was a whole story," he opined, "she may not have gone along with it."

Joey's cabbage patch doll storyline was inspired by a writer who owned the collectible. The name Alicia Mae Emory was a composite of names from the writer's doll collection.

During the beauty pageant scene, the public address announcer calls for "Rebecca Holt, contestant #16 from Younkers." This was a shoutout to Marta Kauffman's nanny.

At the beauty pageant, Rachel is holding Emma but the infant is fidgeting. While taping, the baby didn't feel well and had a runny nose so the only thing that kept her content was food. In the background, there is a woman in a pink blouse who is responsible for feeding her Goldfish crackers. Thus, throughout the entire scene, the infant is looking for food, reaching for a cracker or chewing snacks.

The hallway scenes were shot in one continuous take. In other words, the actors had to learn 20 pages of dialogue and perform it straight through, rather than the usual four pages and then take a break while another scene was shot.

During the hallway scene, the gang mentions the vein in Monica's forehead. The writers considered having the makeup artists configure and attach a vein but opted to keep the segment dialogue driven.

Having four heads peeking through the door was complicated to coordinate. The most laborious positioning was David Schwimmer's. He had to stand on apple boxes, which explains his inability to fully extend his head through the door opening. All the actors were quite uncomfortable holding their position during the scene. The whole sequence was shot live in front of an audience.

10.09 "The One with the Birth Mother" (01.08.04)
This is the last episode directed by David Schwimmer.

In the uncut DVD version, Joey advises Emma, "You better appreciate this while it lasts because when you get older you're not going to be able to just sit around all day." After Rachel agrees, the camera cuts to her, Ross and Phoebe sitting on the couch sipping coffee (implying that is what they do all day). This joke was written to poke fun at critics who blasted the show for having its characters in the coffee shop at all hours of the day.

Monica and Chandler visit an adoption agency in Cincinnati, Ohio. In the establishing shot, a placard painted on a building is advertising 700 WLW, a commercial news/talk radio station serving Greater Cincinnati and surrounding Southern Ohio.

This is the debut performance of Anna Faris as Erica, the birth mother for Monica and Chandler's adopted twins. Despite a successful film career, Faris is best recognized as Christy Plunkett (from 2013 to 2020) on the sitcom *Mom*.

During the adoption interview in Ohio, the periodicals on the table are the same issues present in most Central Perk scenes.

This is the first utterance of Joey's catchphrase: "Joey doesn't share food!" This line was parodied in the animated series *The Penguins of Madagascar* (ep Roger Dodger/Skorca!) where Joey the kangaroo declares, "Joey doesn't share."

When Sarah starts making orgasmic sounds while eating chocolate cake, Joey says, "I'll have what she's having." This famed line from the film *When Harry Met Sally* (1989) was uttered by a patron after Meg Ryan demonstrates her ability to fake an orgasm.

10.10 "The One Where Chandler Gets Caught" (01.15.04)
This was the last episode produced. It was filmed after the finale. The cold opening uses an unaired segment from a prior episode.

This is the last clip show of the series. Once again, the staff writers were indolent. Clip shows became an annual event to provide the writers a break after exhausting sessions formulating the yearly finale.

Courteney Cox is looking particularly thick during the apartment scenes because this installment is aired out of order. It was filmed over two months after the previous and subsequent episodes. Thus, to conceal her pregnancy, she is mostly filmed above the waist, seated at a table, or wearing baggy layered clothing.

In the teaser, in order to keep the baby happy, the cast had to feed her throughout the scene. The cake prop was added to the scene so Courteney Cox could feed the toddler.

In the cold open, after Monica says, "I think I could show this cake a good time," Emma smiles and waves (she was acknowledging her mother who was watching off-camera).

In Central Perk, Phoebe and Rachel are seated on a love seat by the front window. This is only the third episode where the friends are unable to secure the orange sofa because it's already occupied.

Although not present in this episode, during the series' run, the magna doodle appeared in 108 episodes with 117 original messages or images (five times it was left blank, twice there were duplicate messages, and once the board was absent from the abode).

10.11 "The One Where the Stripper Cries" (02.05.04)

When the cast agreed to one final season, Courteney Cox insisted on doing one episode with Fat Monica. The writers accommodated her request with this installment.

Unlike other Fat Monica appearances, the crew had to take special precautions to make sure the fat suit was safe. "Courteney was pregnant at this point and we had to be very, very careful," explained Marta Kauffman. "The fat suit is really, really hot, and she was not supposed to get overheated. We had this thing rigged up, it was a big tube hooked up to an air conditioner that we stuck under the costume and down her shirt so that she could cool down between takes."

Joey participating in a game show was inspired by the creators who earned extra cash in their 20s writing math and history quiz questions for a local Philadelphia game show called *The Knowledge Bowl.* David Crane's father arranged the gig.

The creators use the class reunion as a shoutout to friends and family, such as John Rosove (Marta Kauffman's rabbi), Andrea Tamburino (Kauffman's sister), Michael Skloff (Kauffman's husband), Jeffrey Klarik (David Crane's life partner) and Missy Goldberg (portmanteau of assistants to the producers, Missy Krehbiel and Eric Goldberg). Later in the installment Chandler shouts "Adrienne Turner!" who was David Crane's former assistant, and currently an executive at Warner Bros.

Director Kevin Bright tried to create two realities when filming the *Pyramid* segments. Joey talking to his game show partner was shot on 35 mm film, and the actual game show scenes were shot on videotape. Bright wanted to make the inside conversations look different from the game show.

The game show scenes were filmed on the actual *Pyramid* set using its usual audience. The crowd came that day expecting to see *Pyramid* and instead received an unexpected pleasant surprise.

The *Pyramid* production crew consists of members of the *Friends* team, such as second assistant director Carlos Piñero, but the cameramen belong to the *Pyramid* crew. Kevin Bright also gave his friend from high school, Matthew "Matty" Mullany, a bit part as the stage manager.

Actor Danny DeVito was the first person approached for the role of an old, washed-up stripper. The 4'9 actor had no problem with all the jokes being made at his expense.

When DeVito first entered the apartment, the audience went crazy. They loved it. His wife (Rhea Perlman) was in attendance for the filming and she was howling, and their son Jacob, who was friends with Marta Kauffman's daughter Hannah, was cackling.

Danny DeVito invented the dance routine, which was polished by choreographer Robin Antin, of The Pussycat Dolls. She worked with him for four days during rehearsal.

The flashback scene where Chandler has a tear rolling down his cheek is a recycled bit from "The One Without the Ski Trip" (3.17). The tear was created by blowing air through a small tube with a menthol stick inside, and when it hits the eye it forces a tear out.

According to Kevin Bright, the editing room made DeVito a better dancer. The actor had issues tearing off his clothes and getting the sleeve between his legs. The audience loved the bloopers, but the mishaps delayed filming.

The bombshell ending—Ross being Monica's midnight mystery kisser—was not decided until two days before filming started. "This was our last rewrite before camera blocking," Marta Kauffman stated. "The actors were a little horrified when they first read it but the audience went crazy."

10.12 "The One with Phoebe's Wedding" (02.12.04)

The magna doodle has a champagne bottle, two glasses, and a popped cork in honor of Phoebe and Mike's wedding.

The Central Perk artwork has a giant Statue of Liberty on the right and a drawing of the United States on the left with a woman's face above it. It is called *American Lady* (36 x 36 encaustic) by Jeff Schaller. The piece also appears in the next two episodes.

At one time the writers contemplated an alternative ending where Phoebe reunites with David (Hank Azaria), rather than Mike (Paul Rudd). The creators really wanted to have Azaria back on the show but ultimately decided on Rudd.

Series costumer Debra McGuire wanted to design Phoebe's wedding gown but was not given enough notice to accomplish the task so she had to raid Warner Bros.' costume warehouse. When that failed, she bought it from a bridal store in Westwood, California.

McGuire designed the embroidered coat that Phoebe wore over her dress. It was from McGuire's personal collection. "I had the fabric made in India—it was gorgeous—and it's lined in faux fur ... It's just so Phoebe!" she stated. McGuire could not resist upgrading the bridesmaid outfits. "The bridesmaid dresses were Michael Kors, and I loved them," she declared. "But here's the thing: When you're in a bridesmaid dress, you're not really showing your character. They're kind of homogeneous. So I thought, why not also do coats on the girls that show their individuality?"

Courtney Cox and Lisa Kudrow respected Debra McGuire's fashion sense so they both commissioned her to design their awards-show gowns. McGuire's couture line has also outfitted stars such as Dolly Parton and Tracy Ullman.

Lisa Kudrow's 1995 wedding gown was designed by *Friends* costumer Debra McGuire. The designer's biggest regret, which she dubbed "a crushing blow," was not being able to use the bridal dress she designed for Monica's TV wedding in 2001.

After Joey asks for the rings, there is a wide-angle shot of the wedding party showing a mysterious third bridesmaid in a pink jacket standing next to Monica. The scene extra is Lisa Calderon (aka Lisa Avery), Courteney Cox's stand-in.

As Phoebe begins reciting her vows, Rachel is visibly weeping. These are genuine tears of Jennifer Aniston. Filming the scene brought back memories of her faltering marriage to Brad Pitt. Later in the year, he would have an affair with Angelina Jolie.

This is a supersized episode which runs 32:05 on the DVD version. A typical sitcom is 21 to 22 minutes so many scenes, segments and dialogue were removed for syndication.

10.13 "The One Where Joey Speaks French" (02.19.04)

When Rachel and Ross visit her father in the hospital, there is an establishing shot of the supposed Long Island medical facility. The actual building is the John P. Robarts Library at the University of Toronto, in Toronto, Canada.

The establishing shot for Rachel's childhood home uses stock footage from the hit movie *Planes, Trains and Automobiles* (1987). The real-life abode is located at 230 Oxford Rd. in Kenilworth, Illinois. Built in 1916, it has six bedrooms, four baths, over 3,500 square feet, and sold in 2009 for $1.4M.

In addition to a French dictionary, Joey is reading *Essential French*, a fake book used to sell the belief that he is actually learning a foreign language. Although Joey is trying to learn French for an audition, the book actually foretells Rachel's relocation to Paris.

When Phoebe speaks to the casting director, she mentions the French town of Estée Lauder. This is a crafty reference to the New York–based multinational manufacturer and marketer of prestigious skin care, makeup, fragrance, and hair care products.

The syndicated release excludes one of Phoebe's comments to the director: "Listen, I will tell you the truth. He's my little brother. He's a bit retarded." The producers deemed the dialogue insensitive and politically incorrect.

***Friends* finale: the cast sharing their last supper and giving an ovation to the audience**

Contrary to many reports, Lisa Kudrow is not fluent in French. She can speak a little French which she learned from her French husband. Similarly, castmates Matt LeBlanc (French-Canadian father) and Matthew Perry (Canadian citizenship) can speak French but not fluently.

Joey consuming a gallon of milk in 10 seconds is a parody of the movie *Jackass* (2000), which involves drinking a gallon of milk within one hour without vomiting. Joey's gulp time was 30.69 seconds.

10.14 "The One with Princess Consuela" (02.26.04)

The Gucci executive, Mr. Campbell, is portrayed by Brent Spiner who previously worked with Courteney Cox in the unsold sitcom pilot "Sylvan in Paradise." The concept follows the adventures of Sylvan Sprayberry (Jim Nabors), a blundering bell captain working at the Hawaiian Hotel Lindalani, manager Clinton C. Waddle (Spiner), owner Polly (Ann Wedgeworth) of Polly's Puka Gift Shop, bellboy Sparky McMann (Glenn Withrow), and Sparky's romance with Sylvan's niece, Lucy Apple (Cox). It aired on August 9, 1986.

Brent Spiner had an uncredited role in *Joey* (ep Joey and the Premiere). In the episode, Joey cannot decide who to take to the premiere of *Deep Powder*, so he tries to get extra tickets for Gina, Alex and Michael. After Michael meets a girl and Brent Spiner, he must choose who will attend the premiere.

As Phoebe enters Central Perk to discuss her new name, Chandler is reading *Ideas for Great Kids' Rooms* by the editors of Sunset Books. The prop was meant to foreshadow Monica and Chandler's final decision to purchase a home in the next episode.

When Phoebe reveals her new name to Monica and Chandler, and they object to it, she states that her friends can call her Valerie. This is Lisa Kudrow's middle name. It was also the name of her character in the webseries *The Comeback*.

Although *Friends* never used an establishing shot to represent Monica and Chandler's suburban home, the neighborhood includes the McCallisters' abode from *Home Alone* (1990). A view out the living room window shows the same blue-and-white garage for the house across the street. The *Friends* production company simply bought the stock footage. It is common for studios to reuse footage that already exists rather than paying to create their own, especially for inconsequential background images. The real *Home Alone* residential address is 671 Lincoln Ave., Winnetka, Illinois.

The Mackenzie character is named after director Will Mackenzie who oversaw the pilot episode of *Family Album*, a short-lived series created by Kauffman and Crane.

This is the last of six guest appearances by Steven Eckholdt as Mark. He was last seen in "The One with the Tiny T-Shirt" (3.19), a span of 165 episodes.

After Joey returns to the living room after speaking with Mackenzie, the coffee table has a copy of *The Orchid* by k. tolnoe. It's a poetry collection highlighting the eternal truth that all humans, like orchids, are uniquely singular and divine in their own way. This is meant to signify the oneness that each friend exhibits as they enter a new and unique phase of their life.

10.15 "The One Where Estelle Dies" (04.22.04)

Rachel's boss, Mr. Zelner, has a son named Ross who likes dinosaurs. This is the staff writers' attempt at humor using juxtaposition since Rachel's on-off boyfriend is named Ross and also likes dinosaurs, and yet, ironically, Zelner can never remember Ross' name (calling him Ron).

The magna doodle drawing has a pickle with stick arms and legs, one hand waving and the other holding a striped umbrella. This is a metaphor for the predicament Ross faces with Rachel's relocation to Paris. He is in a pickle.

Monica and Chandler tour the house next door to the residence they already agreed to purchase. Contrary to numerous reports, the establishing shot utilized to represent the neighbor's home (i.e., the one Janice considers purchasing) is not the same home used to signify the Gellers' residence in "The One Where Rosita Dies" (7.13).

Jane Lynch plays the real estate agent. Despite numerous reports, she never auditioned to play Phoebe on *Friends*. "At that time in my life I wasn't getting that level of audition, that's for sure," she admitted.

Chandler discloses Janice's full name: Janice Litman Goralnick (née Hosenstein). The surname Goralnick honors a good friend of the creators, Deborah A. Franzblau, whose mother's maiden name was Goralnick.

Maggie Wheeler loved playing Janice so much that she thinks the character has become part of her and had hoped to continue portraying the role in her own spinoff. She even pitched the idea of having her character appear in the *Friends* spinoff *Joey* but neither proposal was embraced.

In the original script, Rachel resigns from Ralph Lauren after Ross agrees to help her move to Paris. "They go to Paris and have this big romantic time and that's when we see he's starting to fall in love with her again. And it actually went too far, and so we pulled back and were just counting on the finale to do a lot of the work. And it did," said David Crane. The unproduced script, "The One Where Jetlag Wins," was aptly titled because the pair ended up falling asleep in their hotel room.

Actor EJ Callahan, who plays Al Zebooker, Estelle's paper-eating client, also appeared in "The One with the Ballroom Dancing" (4.04) as a massage client.

10.16 "The One with Rachel's Going Away Party" (04.29.04)

The magna doodle image has a simple message: "Joey ... Call Reid." This refers to Reid Haessig, a gaffer on the set. His job is to position the lights and quickly change lighting setups between shots.

In response to Rachel leaving for Paris, Chandler reminiscently adds, "It feels like when *Melrose Place* got canceled." *Melrose Place* was a popular primetime soap opera that ran from 1992 to 1999. Matthew Perry auditioned for the role of Billy Campbell but lost to Stephen Fanning. Days before shooting the pilot, Fanning had gained significant weight so he was fired and replaced by Andrew Shue, brother of actress Elizabeth (*Cocktail*). Coincidentally, Paul Rudd was a finalist for the role.

Ross complains about not getting a hug from Rachel so Joey hugs him. This is a callback to "The One with the Monkey" (1.10) where Chandler complained about not being kissed on New Year's Eve so Joey kissed him.

When Erica is going into labor, Monica has to sit down to calm herself and behaves as if she is the one in labor. Although a comical bit because of the role reversal, the writers actually wrote it as an in-joke for Courteney Cox to acknowledge her real-life pregnancy at the time of filming.

In the tag scene, Joey is stuffing packing peanuts down his pants to see if Phoebe can hurt him with a knee to the groin. In reality, Matt LeBlanc is fitted with a protective cup and padding to prevent damage to the family jewels. Lisa Kudrow did initiate contact but the force was minimal.

According to Marta Kauffman, the Ross-Rachel relationship dynamic was fascinating to even the most unlikely viewers. "My rabbi, when I dropped my daughter off for Hebrew school, would stop me and say, 'When are you going to get them together?'"

10.17 "The Last One, Part 1" (05.06.04)

In preparation for writing this episode, the show's producers watched finales from other sitcoms, paying attention to what worked and what did not, and *The Mary Tyler Moore Show* was the gold standard. They spent several days thinking about the final scene without being able to write a word. The ultimate goal was to be true to the series and not do something "high concept, or take the show out of the show."

The coffeehouse scenes (Part 1) were shot on January 16, 2004 because Central Perk needed to be dismantled to build the airport set for Part 2. One week later they taped the airport scenes.

The hand-selected audience included Hank Azaria, David Arquette and Maggie Wheeler, among others. Missing from the set was Brad Pitt. He told the producers that he wanted to be surprised when it aired on TV. In reality, he and Aniston were having relationship difficulties so he was not feeling supportive.

Director Kevin Bright reflected upon the first night of filming: "We did the first take and everything went well. And then David [Schwimmer] mentioned to the rest of the actors the realization that this was the last coffee shop scene that they were ever going to do together. Tears started to flow." Marta Kauffman dutifully added, "It was impossible to get through. We stopped several times because of tears."

The magna doodle has a mountain range with clouds in the sky, and a person planting a flag at the peak of the larger mountain in the center. This is a metaphor for the show leaving its mark on the world and going out on top.

The Central Perk scene is filled with background extras that include family, friends and colleagues of the executive producers. When Ross stands, at the round table (from left) is the creators' agent Nancy Josephson, their unidentified lawyer, Lisa Kudrow's husband (Michel Stern), and David Crane's life partner, Jeffrey Klarik.

The Central Perk artwork *Cup o Joe* by Jeff Schaller was specifically commissioned by the producers for the finale. It was purchased by the Warner Bros. Museum for their permanent collection and displayed in Central Perk as part of the studio tour. Schaller's work is collected nationally and internationally and displayed in the Coca-Cola Museum and Lancaster Museum of Art.

In the scene where Monica and Chandler hold the twins for the first time, the producers hired three sets of twins just to make sure there would not be a problem with crying. During this scene, a nurse can be heard paging Dr. Matthew Perry and Dr. Green on the intercom (a nod to the actor and recurring character).

After Part 1 finally wrapped, everyone celebrated. "We tore down the coffeehouse at the end of the night and we ended up with an impromptu party, about 80 people—crew, cast, producers stayed, office staff—and we just watched it go down," Kauffman fondly recalls. "It was like losing a little piece of yourself. A number of us took souvenirs." Her memento was the neon sign with "Service" inside an arrow, Kevin Bright snatched the big milk can sign (which he still has at his estate in Saratoga, New York), and Jennifer Aniston snatched a neon coffee cup sign. "We all signed walls," Kauffman added. Matt LeBlanc's immortalized message was "I shit here—Matt LeBlanc." Courteney Cox didn't take anything from the set but wishes she had. "I'm not a person that collects things," she revealed. "And then I regret it."

Other mementos were pilfered by the cast. Kudrow took Phoebe Buffay's rings. LeBlanc swiped an "I Love *Friends*" license plate and put it on Schwimmer's car. "It took him a week to realize," LeBlanc remarked. And Schwimmer swiped a Professor Geller placard from Ross' office at NYU.

The cast and crew passed around yearbooks, custom-made by the staff, and signed them for each other. The cast gave the producers inscribed Cartier SA watches, while the producers reciprocated with Neil Lane jewelry. As the Central Perk set was struck, the cast and crew received a keepsake—a chunk of the street encased in a glass box.

This two-part episode ran 66 minutes in its original airing. Thus, the syndicated version has 11 to 12 minutes of valuable footage trimmed from Part 1 to time out at 30 minutes (with commercials).

10.18 "The Last One, Part 2" (05.06.04)

This episode was filmed on January 23, 2004. The studio audience was 75% legitimate fans and 25% friends and family.

As Ross and Phoebe get into the cab, Marta Kauffman's cousins are scene extras.

When devising a third plot, the creators wanted to address the Joey-Chandler dynamic because the pair developed a type of bromance that needed closure. The trio thought, "What better way than the foosball table?" This promptly evolved into the story of the chick and duck and the foosball table. "We loved it because it brings back all these sort of icons of the show," David Crane stated.

As Ross and Phoebe first arrive at the airport, the visitors standing by the pay phones are Missy Krehbiel, Eric Goldberg and Colleen Mahan, the assistants to David Crane, Kevin Bright and Marta Kauffman, respectively.

In the next airport scene, where Rachel is standing in the ticket line, the background extras include Kevin Bright's kids, casting director Leslie Litt, and Marta Kauffman's Pilates instructor. As Rachel arrives at the ticket counter, the blonde woman seated behind her is NBC publicist Barbara Brogliatti.

As Rachel is boarding the plane, she hands the flight attendant her passport. Some sources falsely report it has a photo of Monica instead of Rachel. It is a random picture of a brunette hired to pose for the photo which was issued by a prop company.

During another airport scene, Ross is running through the stanchion maze as Phoebe bypasses it. This was not in the script. David Schwimmer added the physical comedy bit during rehearsal.

When Phoebe and Ross are buying tickets, behind them is a woman (wearing a scarf) and a young man in a black shirt. In the very next scene, where Rachel is looking for her boarding pass, the same extras are standing behind her. However, the two scenes take place in different airports.

After Rachel locates her boarding pass and returns to the ticket counter, behind her in line is Jeffrey Klarik (David Crane's life partner) and Nancy Josephson (agent for the executive producers). As Crane noted, "We really went to great lengths to get the people we love in this show."

When Ross learns he went to the wrong airport and Rachel prepares to board the plane, the production song is "Yellow Ledbetter" by Pearl Jam, which is often the band's final encore song. As of 2019, it was used 337 times in the final encore position. The series creators chose this song for that reason. This is also the first time the band licensed a song for a television show.

After rescuing the fowl, Joey's kitchen counter has two Chinese takeout boxes with the symbol 友 for "Friend" (Yǒu) written in red. It is a tribute to the show's own title and its main characters.

The airplane is packed with *Friends* writers. Behind Rachel is Shana Goldberg-Meehan, Andrew Reich is across the aisle from Shana, and Scott Silveri is positioned two rows behind Rachel in the right seat.

The writers worried about mentioning mechanical problems with the airplane. In the aftermath of the 9/11 attack, this topic was no joking matter. However, once they came up with the phalange defect, a callback to Phoebe's alias, it made the scene funny.

As the passengers are standing in line to board the plane (after the phalange mishap), the queue includes Marta Kauffman's children (Sam and Hannah), her then husband (Michael Skloff), and Kevin Bright's niece Isabelle Bright.

Set decorator Greg Grande has a cameo as one of the movers. He is escorting the dog statue out of the apartment—the last piece of furniture. The creators told Grande that he deserved to be in the scene so he asked a couple crew members (Kai Blomberg and Quent Schierenberg) to join him onscreen. "The best part for me, was in the last episode of the show," Grande said. "I got a little sentimental."

NBC heavily promoted the series finale weeks in advance. The advertising rate reached historic levels, averaging $2M for 30 seconds of commercial time, breaking the previous record of $1.7M set by *Seinfeld* six years earlier for its finale.

The *Friends* finale was watched by 52.46 million viewers, making it the most watched entertainment telecast in six years. It was the fourth-most-watched series finale in TV history, behind *M*A*S*H*, *Cheers* and *Seinfeld*, which were viewed by 105M, 80.4M and 76.2M, respectively.

In the UK, 8.6 million fans watched the series finale. It set three records for Channel 4, the UK's distributing channel: (1) highest-rated program of 2004, (2) highest-rated non-British program, and (3) second-highest-rated program (excluding films, special events and sports), trailing the third season finale of UK's *Big Brother* (2000), which roped in 10 million viewers.

The *Friends* finale was not the show's most watched episode. That distinction goes to "The One After the Superbowl" (2.12, 2.13) in 1996, which had 52.9 million viewers.

There were three finale wrap parties: (1) dinner at the Aniston-Pitt residence on January 19, 2004, (2) sit-down event at the cast's favorite hangout, Il Sole in West Hollywood, on January 22, and (3) blowout for 1,000 guests on January 24 at LA's Park Plaza Hotel where The Rembrandts performed and the cast reenacted a scene from the pilot.

When the spinoff *Joey* began production, Matt LeBlanc experienced a strong sense of nostalgia because his fledgling series was filmed on Stage 24 (The *Friends* Stage).

Matt LeBlanc was not the first choice for a spinoff series—he was the third. NBC desired Jennifer Aniston but she wanted to pursue a film career so they approached Courteney Cox and Matthew Perry, but they didn't want to play those parts anymore.

Episode Index

Note: Bold page number denotes main listing for episode

After "I Do" (8.01) 135, **137**

After Joey and Rachel Kiss (10.01) **167**

After Ross Says Rachel (5.01) 89, **93**, 157

After the Superbowl, Part 1 (2.12) 23, **56**, 59, 61, 179

After the Superbowl, Part 2 (2.13) 32, **57**, 178

After Vegas (6.01) 103, **106**, 154

Apothecary Table (6.11) 109, **113**

Baby on the Bus (2.06) 32, **52**, 62, 154

Baby Shower (8.20) **150**

Ball (5.21) 98, **104**

Ballroom Dancing (4.04) **80**, 82, 175

Barbados, Part 1 (9.23) 13, **165**

Barbados, Part 2 (9.24) **166**

Barry & Mindy's Wedding (2.24) 47, 63, **64**, 95

Beach (3.25) **78**

Birth (1.23) **48**

Birth Mother (10.09) **171**

Birthing Video (8.15) **146**

Blackout (1.07) **39**, 64

Blind Dates (9.14) **160**

Boob Job (9.16) **161**

Boobies (1.13) **42**, 71, 95, 153

Breast Milk (2.02) **50**, 73

Bullies (2.21) 54, **62**

Butt (1.06) **38**, 48, 49, 100, 128

Cake (10.04) 13, **168**

Candy (7.09) **127**, 144

Candy Hearts (1.14) **43**

Cat (4.02) **79**

Chandler Can't Cry (6.14) **114**

Chandler Can't Remember Which Sister (3.11) **70**, 76

Chandler Crosses the Line (4.07) **82**, 139

Chandler Doesn't Like Dogs (7.08) **126**

Chandler Gets Caught (10.10) 117, **171**

Chandler in a Box (4.08) **83**

Chandler Takes a Bath (8.13) 29, **145**

Chandler's Dad (7.22) **135**

Chandler's Work Laugh (5.12) **99**

Cheap Wedding Dress (7.17) **132**

Cheesecakes (7.11) 23, **128**, 168

Chick and a Duck (3.21) **76**, 153

Chicken Pox (2.23) **63**, 133

Christmas in Tulsa (9.10) **158**

Cooking Class (8.21) **150**

Cop (5.16) **101**, 103, 162

Could Have Been, Part 1 (6.15) **115**

Could Have Been, Part 2 (6.16) **116**

'Cuffs (4.03) **80**

Dirty Girl (4.06) **81**

Dollhouse (3.20) 71, **76**

Donor (9.22) **165**

Dozen Lasagnas (1.12) **42**

Dr. Ramoray Dies (2.18) 23, **60**, 79, 141

East German Laundry Detergent (1.05) 12, **38**, 170

Eddie Moves In (2.17) **59**

Eddie Won't Go (2.19) **61**

Embryos (4.12) **85**

Emma Cries (9.02) **153**

Engagement Picture (7.05) **124**

Estelle Dies (10.15) 81, **175**

Everybody Finds Out (5.14) 69, **100**

Evil Orthodontist (1.20) **47**, 64

Fake Monica (1.21) **47**

Fake Party (4.16) **87**, 168

Fertility Test (9.21) 22, **164**

Five Steaks and an Eggplant (2.05) **52**, 163

Flashback (3.06) 61, **67**, 76, 117

Football (3.09) 47, **69**, 163

Frank Jr. (3.05) **67**, 130, 134

Free Porn (4.17) **88**, 115

George Stephanopoulos (1.04) **37**, 137

Giant Poking Device (3.08) **69**

Girl From Poughkeepsie (4.10) **84**

Girl Who Hits Joey (5.15) **101**

Halloween Party (8.06) 82, **141**

Haste (4.19) **89**

Heckles Dies (2.03) **51**

Holiday Armadillo (7.10) 13, **127**

Home Study (10.07) **170**

Hypnosis Tape (3.18) **74**, 86

Ick Factor (1.22) **48**, 163

Inappropriate Sister (5.10) **98**

Invitation (4.21) **90**, 135, 159

Jam (3.03) **66**, 77

Jealousy (3.12) **71**, 110

Jellyfish (4.01) **79**

Joey Dates Rachel (8.12) **145**

Joey Loses His Insurance (6.04) **108**, 134

Joey Moves Out (2.16) **59**

Joey Speaks French (10.13) 40, **173**

Joey Tells Rachel (8.16) **147**, 155, 161

Joey's Award (7.18) **132**

Joey's Bag (5.13) **99**

Joey's Big Break (5.22) **104**

Joey's Dirty Day (4.14) **86**

Joey's Fridge (6.19) **117**

Joey's Interview (8.19) **149**

Joey's New Brain (7.15) 23, **130**, 162

Joey's New Girlfriend (4.05) **81**, 84

Joey's Porsche (6.05) 108, **109**

Joke (6.12) **113**

Kips (5.05) **95**, 107

Kissing (5.02) **93**, 95

Last Night (6.06) **109**

Last One, Part 1 (10.17) 123, **176**

Last One, Part 2 (10.18) 15, 170, **177**

Late Thanksgiving (10.08) **170**

Lesbian Wedding (2.11) **55**

List (2.08) **53**

Lottery (9.18) **162**

Mac and C.H.E.E.S.E. (6.20) **118**

Male Nanny (9.06) 110, **156**, 157

Massapequa (8.18) 136, **148**

Memorial Service (9.17) **162**
Metaphorical Tunnel (3.04) 59, 61, **66**
Monica & Richard Are Friends (3.13) **72**, 151
Monica and Chandler's Wedding, Part 1 (7.23) **135**
Monica and Chandler's Wedding, Part 2 (7.24) 22, **136**, 164
Monica Sings (9.13) **160**
Monica's Boots (8.10) **143**
Monica's Thunder (7.01) **122**
Monkey (1.10) **41**, 47, 175
Monkey Gets Away (1.19) 31, **46**, 47
Morning After (3.16) **73**, 95, 159
Mrs. Bing (1.11) **41**
Mugging (9.15) **161**
Nana Dies Twice (1.08) **40**, 83, 156, 162, 168
Nap Partners (7.06) **125**, 127
No One Proposes (9.01) **153**
No One's Ready (3.02) 22, 30, 46, **65**, 73, 169
Old Yeller Dies (2.20) **61**
One Hundredth (5.03) **94**, 151, 168
Paul's the Man (6.22) 39, **119**
Pediatrician (9.03) **154**
Phoebe Hates PBS (5.04) **95**, 102
Phoebe Runs (6.07) **110**
Phoebe's Birthday Dinner (9.05) **155**
Phoebe's Cookies (7.03) 122, **123**
Phoebe's Dad (2.09) **54**, 162
Phoebe's Ex-Partner (3.14) 60, **72**
Phoebe's Husband (2.04) **51**, 159
Phoebe's Rats (9.12) 156, 159, **162**, 167
Phoebe's Uterus (4.11) 29, **84**
Phoebe's Wedding (10.12) **173**
Pilot (1.01) **35**, 42, 61, 68, 89
Poker (1.18) **46**, 89
Princess Consuela (10.14) 75, 76, 162, 168, **174**
Princess Leia Fantasy (3.01) **64**, 77, 110, 117
Prom Video (2.14) 32, **58**
Proposal, Part 1 (6.24) 119, **120**
Proposal, Part 2 (6.25) 119, **121**
Race Car Bed (3.07) 22, **68**, 71, 169
Rachel Finds Out (1.24) **49**, 66
Rachel Goes Back to Work (9.11) 13, **159**, 169
Rachel Has a Baby, Part 1 (8.23) 98, **151**
Rachel Has a Baby, Part 2 (8.24) 150, **152**, 170
Rachel is Late (8.22) **151**, 161
Rachel Quits (3.10) **70**

Rachel Smokes (5.18) **102**
Rachel Tells Ross (8.03) 125, **138**, 142
Rachel's Assistant (7.04) **124**
Rachel's Big Kiss (7.20) **134**
Rachel's Book (7.02) 119, **122**
Rachel's Crush (4.13) **85**
Rachel's Date (8.05) **140**
Rachel's Dream (9.19) 22, 138, **163**
Rachel's Going Away Party (10.16) **175**
Rachel's Inadvertent Kiss (5.17) **102**
Rachel's New Dress (4.18) **88**
Rachel's Other Sister (9.08) **157**
Rachel's Phone Number (9.09) 76, **158**
Rachel's Sister (6.13) **114**, 135
Rachel's Sister Babysits (10.05) 157, **169**
Red Sweater (8.02) **138**
Resolutions (5.11) **98**, 101, 158
Ride-Along (5.20) 96, **103**
Ring (6.23) **119**, 120
Rosita Dies (7.13) **129**, 132, 175
Ross and Monica's Cousin (7.19) 64, **133**
Ross & Rachel Take a Break (3.15) 64, **73**
Ross and Rachel...You Know (2.15) **58**, 79
Ross Can't Flirt (5.19) **103**, 132
Ross Dates a Student (6.18) **117**
Ross Finds Out (2.07) 27, **53**
Ross Got High (6.09) **111**, 112
Ross Hugs Rachel (6.02) **107**, 122
Ross is Fine (10.02) 123, **167**
Ross Meets Elizabeth's Dad (6.21) **119**
Ross Moves In (5.07) **96**, 98
Ross's Denial (6.03) **108**
Ross's Grant (10.06) 22, 68, **169**
Ross's Inappropriate Song (9.07) 93, **156**
Ross's Library Book (7.07) 64, **125**
Ross's New Girlfriend (2.01) **50**
Ross's Sandwich (5.09) **97**, 152
Ross's Step Forward (8.11) **144**
Ross's Tan (10.03) 23, 120, **168**
Ross's Teeth (6.08) **110**
Ross's Thing (3.23) **77**
Ross's Wedding, Part 1 (4.23) **91**
Ross's Wedding, Part 2 (4.24) 14, **92**, 104, 123
Routine (6.10) **112**, 146
Rugby (4.15) **86**
Rumor (8.09) **143**
Russ (2.10) 15, **55**

Screamer (3.22) **77**, 157
Secret Closet (8.14) **146**
Sharks (9.04) **154**
Soap Opera Party (9.20) 39, **163**
Sonogram at the End (1.02) **36**, 68, 98
Stain (8.07) **141**
Stoned Guy (1.15) 22, **44**, 161, 163
Stripper (8.08) **142**, 148
Stripper Cries (10.11) 23, **172**
Tea Leaves (8.17) 117, **147**
Thanksgivings (5.08) **97**, 109
They All Turn Thirty (7.14) **130**
They're Going to Party! (4.09) **83**, 150
They're Up All Night (7.12) 39, **128**, 129
Thumb (1.03) **36**, 52, 149
Tiny T-Shirt (3.19) **75**, 166, 174
Truth About London (7.16) **131**
Two Parties (2.22) **42**, 62, 150
Two Parts, Part 1 (1.16) 43, **44**, 52
Two Parts, Part 2 (1.17) **45**
Ultimate Fighting Champion (3.24) **78**, 151
Unagi (6.17) **116**, 117
Underdog Gets Away (1.09) 36, 38, **40**, 41, 42, 48
Vegas, Part 1 (5.23) **105**
Vegas, Part 2 (5.24) **105**
Videotape (8.04) 138, **139**
Vows (7.21) **134**
Wedding Dresses (4.20) 30, **89**
Without the Ski Trip (3.17) 23, **74**, 172
Worst Best Man Ever (4.22) 23, **90**
Yeti (5.06) **96**, 98

General Index

A

According to Jim 114
Act II Light Butter 102
adoption 165, 171
Agassi, Andre 57
Air Force One 120
Alamo (art) 73
Alchemist, The 104, 142
Alcott, Louisa May 72
Alexander Hamilton United States Custom House 36, 87, 98
Alexander, Jason 14, 36, 92, 129
Alexander, Sasha 149
All My Children 17, 130
Allen, Krista 145
Allen, Rick 94
Allen, Thomas and John Christopher 13
Allesandro's 84, 87, 150
Alvarez, Walter 150
Amazing Discoveries 59, 66
America's Greatest GAME 1931 poster 88
Amurri, Eva 130
Amy *see* Green, Amy
Anastassakis 137
Anderson, Pamela 102
"Angel of the Morning" 52
animal filming 31
Aniston, Jennifer 1-2, 4-9, 11-15, 25-28, 35, 37-38, 42-43, 45-47, 51-53, 55, 58-59, 61-62, 66-67, 73-74, 80-82, 85, 87-91, 94, 96-97, 99-101, 103, 105, 109, 114-19, 122, 124-26, 129-34, 137, 143, 146, 148, 151, 153-54, 157, 160-62, 165-68, 170, 173, 176, 178
Aniston, John 55
ankh 56
Anthem: An American Road Story 81, 84
Anthropology Weekly 48
Antin, Robin 112, 172
Applegate, Christina 14, 157, 169
Archie Show 116
archway 159

Arianna Skincare 147
Arquette, Alexis 114, 135
Arquette, David 66, 85, 106-07, 162-63, 176
Arshack, Daniel 23, 61
Art of Happiness 114
Ashford, Matthew 164
Ashley, Jessica 132
Astrof, Jeff 37, 46, 53, 56-57, 132
Atlantic City 96, 132
Atlantis Hotel 139
Atlas (art) 136, 140
Austen, Jane 49, 54
Austin Powers: International Man of Mystery 105
Aux Buttes Chaumont poster 104, 134, 151
Avery, Lisa *see* Calderon, Lisa
Aykroyd, Dan 97
Azaria, Hank 3, 12, 41, 156, 165-66, 173, 176

B

baby beauty pageant 170
"Baby Elephant Walk" 68
baby filming 31
"Baby Got Back" 156
baby names 145
background extras, *see* extras
Bailes Rusos Teatro Liceo poster 168
Balaban, Bob 100
Baldwin, Alec 148
Baldwin, Stephen 140
Bamboozled 150
Banbury, Jen 87-88, 93, 107
Band of Brothers 51, 121
Bapstein-King comet 128
Barbie 67
Bari, Ray 158
barista 10, 30, 54
Barone, Anita 6, 36, 41, 164
Barry *see* Farber, Barry
Basil, Toni 129
Batman 161
Battaglia, Matt 78
Baxendale, Helen 28, 86-87, 89-91, 93, 95-96, 103
Bayer, Vanessa 51

Baywatch 44, 60, 67, 77, 82, 145
Be Your Own Windkeeper 61
Beach Boys, The 165
Bear Went Over the Mountain 77
Beatles, The 55
Beavis and Butt-Head 59
Beck, Heidi 94
Becker, Pete 7, 75, 77-78
Beeson, Joel 50
Belushi, Jim 120
Ben *see* Geller, Ben
Benay's Bird and Animal Rentals 31
Bendewald, Andrea 132
Benson, Robby 2, 72
Bentley, Jim 30
Bergstrom, Cynthia 111, 139, 143
Berkley, Elizabeth 6
Berle, Milton 80
Bernhard, Sandra 4
Bertolli Classico 151
"Best Friends" 8
bestiality 147
Bethesda fountain 21, 24
Beverly Hills, 90210 6, 77
BFF 78, 119, 141
Bieres de Chartres poster 62, 86
Bierko, Craig 8, 59
Big Brother 178
Big Daddy 115, 128, 131
Big Gulp 78, 100
Bijan for Men 50
Bikini Car Wash Company 125
Bilsing-Graham, Sherry 123, 152
Bing, Nora 41
Blazing Saddles 150
"Bleecker Street" 19
Bleeth, Yasmine 60, 67, 77, 82, 102
Blender magazine 26
Blomberg, Kai 178
Bloomingdale's 71, 76, 85, 165
bloopers 52, 60, 74, 102, 119, 125, 127, 146, 148, 164, 172
Blue Dog 108, 149
Blue Dog Love 149

Blue Dog Man 108
Bob Newhart Show 77
Boddingtons 93-94
body doubles 15, 39, 59, 66, 141
Bon Jovi 75-76
Bon Jovi, Jon 75
Bonerz, Peter 53, 77
Borkow, Michael 64, 89, 91
Borns, Betsy 23, 52
bottle episode 46, 65, 103, 109, 122, 126, 139, 162
Bourgeois Pig 54
Bowie, David 103
Boxing Kangaroo poster 49, 149
Boyle, Brian 65
brand integration 93, 109, 111
Brandeis University 23, 36, 45, 61
Branson, Richard 91, 100
Brewster, Paget 28, 81, 86
bridesmaid dress 58, 64, 137, 173
Bright, Isabelle 153, 178
Bright, Jackie 14, 49, 64
Bright, Kevin 1, 9, 14, 20, 22-25, 28, 32-33, 37, 39, 42, 45, 48-49, 54, 57-58, 60, 64, 69, 74, 78, 81, 83, 85, 91, 93-94, 97-98, 100, 105, 107, 109, 111-13, 116, 121-22, 124, 127, 132, 135-37, 140-41, 143, 145, 147, 152-53, 157, 167-68, 172, 176-78
Brogliatti, Barbara 177
Brontë, Charlotte 97
Brontë, Emily 97
Brown Brothers Harriman 75
Bruza, Scott 15, 77, 99
BTS 33
Buckman, Zoe 118
Buffay Jr., Frank 28, 53, 62, 67-68, 75, 85, 167-68
Buffay Sr., Frank 100
Buffay Sr., Phoebe 78-79
Buffay the Vampire Layer 114-15
Buffy the Vampire Slayer 107, 111, 115, 139, 143
Bugs Bunny 113
Burgin, Joshua 85, 87, 89-90, 168
Burke, Billy 145
Burke, Karey 59
Burke, Richard 12, 59, 61, 63-64, 72, 83, 88, 105-06, 119, 121, 157
Burr, Fritzi 64
Burrows, James 2, 9, 13, 20, 24, 30, 36, 39, 46, 48, 73, 86, 105, 159

C

Caesar's Palace 105, 108
Cahill, Eddie 124, 126
Calderon, Lisa 15, 114, 116, 132, 150, 160, 173

Calhoun, Wil 67
Callahan, EJ 81, 175
Calvin and Hobbes 147
Campbell, Julia 124
Campbell, Larry Joe 114
Canova restaurant 75
Capricorn One 103
capuchin 11, 31, 41, 46, 56
Car and Driver 140
Carno, Jennifer 11
Carol 5-6, 23, 36, 41-42, 48, 56, 68, 74, 88, 95, 102, 116, 131, 134, 163
cast camaraderie 26
cast clique 26, 137
casting lead actors 1
Cat in the Hat 62-63, 70
Cavazos, Lumi 35
Cecilia *see* Monroe, Cecilia
censors (NBC) 22-23, 32, 64, 74, 81
Central Perk logo 53
Central Perk pop-ups 11
Chadsey, Barbara 11, 54, 63
Channel 4 (UK) 76, 91, 178
character development 8
characters, naming 17
Charlie *see* Wheeler, Charlie
Charlie Brown Christmas 112
Chase, Adam 11, 37, 53, 57, 60, 64, 69, 91, 98, 105-06, 116
Cheers (series) 21, 178
cheesecake 128
Chelsea Reporter 83
Chéret, Jules 124, 151
Cherry Hill fountain 24
childbirth, unconventional 28
Chinese posters 92, 102, 110
Chloe (Xerox copy girl) 64, 66, 73, 91, 159
Christiansen, Roger 24, 154, 169
Cimoch quadruplets 13
City Hall fountain 21, 24, 170
Clark, Ashley L. 144
cliffhanger 64, 78-79, 90, 121-22, 137, 159
clip show 90, 118, 130, 134-35, 149, 158, 171
Clooney, George 1, 33, 45-46
Clueless 46
Co-Operative Dictums 125
Coca-Cola 176
Cocker, Joe 63
Coffee Book, The 108
Coffee Joe 18
Cohen, Ted 84, 98, 123
Cold Feet 87
Coleman, Dabney 21
Collins, Joan 48, 106
Comeback, The 174
Comedy Central UK 34
comet 128
Complete Idiot's Guide: Pregnancy and Childbirth 142
concept, series 17
condom 23, 52, 60-61, 90
Condom Boy (character) 62

Conley, Alexandra and Athina 13, 159, 162
Connolly, Patrick 113
continuity 10, 40, 53, 67-68, 70, 79, 122, 130, 149, 153, 165
Cookie Time jar 54, 131, 150
Coolidge, Jennifer 14, 168
Cooper Union 18, 72
copy girl *see* Chloe
Coster-Praytor, Marjorie 58, 70
Cougar Town 15, 48
Couples (series) 1
Cox, Courteney 1, 4-5, 8-9, 11-12, 14-15, 18-20, 26-27, 29, 33, 37, 39-40, 44, 46, 48, 52, 58-59, 66, 73, 78-80, 84-85, 96, 101, 106-07, 112, 114-16, 119-20, 122, 125, 127, 132, 134-37, 139, 141, 148, 150, 152, 155, 157, 160, 162-63, 165-66, 171-76, 178
Crane, David 1-3, 9-10, 14, 16-19, 22-23, 26-28, 30, 32-33, 35, 38, 45, 48, 53-54, 57, 60, 65-66, 70, 73-74, 76, 83, 85-86, 92-94, 102, 112, 114, 120-21, 124, 126-29, 136, 139, 145, 156, 166, 170, 172, 174-77
Crane, Gene 70
Crème de la Mer 155
Critchlow, Roark 61
Crosby, Richard 136
Cryer, Jon 7
Crystal, Billy 14, 78
Curtis, Michael 51, 65
Cycle News 125

D

D'Agostino Supermarkets 67
dadao 46
Daily, Elizabeth "E.G." 60, 72
Dalai Lama 114
Dallas (series) 159
"Dancing in the Dark" 148
Dane Anthony Band 132
Dane Anthony Jungle Swing 132
Danny (the yeti) 96, 98
Danza, Tony 9
Dateline 101
Davidson, Elizabeth and Genevieve 13
Davis, Kristin 14, 46
Days of Our Lives 39, 55, 60-61, 115-16, 130-31, 145, 159, 163-64
De Niro, Robert 33
Decourcelle, Pierre 90
DeGeneres, Ellen 2, 19
Delmonico's Steak House 161
DeLuise, Peter 62
Demarco, Tony 23
Desperate Housewives 6
deVally, Dana 24, 85, 95
DeVito, Danny 14, 172
Diet Coke 78, 100

directors 24
Dirt 15
Dirty Dancing 47
Disney 22
diversity 22, 72, 84, 132, 164
dollhouse 76
Donovan, Tate 85, 88-90
Dostoyevsky, Fyodor 72
Dot's Spot 23, 117
Dottie & Herman's bodega 23
Dr. Seuss 70
Dream On 1-2, 17, 33, 63
dreidel 127
Drescher, Fran 43
Dreskin, Billy 23, 45
dressing room 8, 26, 46, 50,
    82, 86, 111, 146
dressing *see* set dressing
dry cleaner 39, 120, 148
Ducati 125, 127, 130
Dudek, Anne 167
Duffy, Karen 4
Duncan (character) 51, 83, 154
Dutch for Beginners 142

E

Easter egg hunt 83, 167
Eckholdt, Steven 71, 174
Ed (movie) 47
Eisner, Michael 22
El Siglo Exposicion y Venta
    poster 159
Elizabeth *see* Stevens,
    Elizabeth
Elizabeth II, Queen 106, 150
Ellen (series) 3, 5, 19, 36
Ellen's Stardust Diner 62
Emeril Live 95
Emerson College 39, 168
Emily *see* Waltham, Emily
Emma 12-13, 29, 150, 152,
    154, 159-62, 165, 168-71
Emmy Award 72, 125, 128,
    132
English trifle 111-12
Entertainment Weekly 107, 113
Enya 145
Episodes (series) 11
ER (series) 45-46, 49, 152
erection 35
Erica 171, 175
erogenous zones 84
Essential French 173
Estevez, Emilio 14
Ethan 48
"Everlong" 137
Everybody Loves Raymond
    100, 164
Excelsior poster 71
Exploits of Elaine 90
extras 10, 15-16, 36-37, 39,
    51, 54, 57, 69, 79, 120-21,
    126, 131, 135, 137-38, 143,
    145, 152, 157, 159, 166, 173,
    176-77

F

Facts of Life (series) 5-6

Fairchild, Morgan 41
"Fallin'" 147
Family Album 174
Family Jewels 63
Fancy, Richard 83
Fanning, Dakota 117, 168
Fanning, Elle 13, 167
Fantasy Island 52
Farber, Barry 1, 36, 47, 64, 68,
    116
Faris, Anna 171
Fat Monica 58, 115, 172
fat suit 39, 58, 101, 115, 132,
    172
Fath, Farah 164
Favreau, Jon 7, 75, 78
Featherstone, Angela 73
"Feel So Good" 89
Fenn, Sherilyn 72
Ferguson, Sarah (Fergie) 14,
    91-92
Ferris Bueller (series) 7, 47
Field & Stream 118
film noir 79
flashback 28, 58, 68, 97, 130,
    165, 172
fleur-de-lis 158
Flock of Seagulls 97
Flowers of Evil 71
Flutie Flakes 158
Flutie, Doug 69, 158
Folies-Bergère poster 124, 140
Fontaine, Jillian 39
Fonz aka Fonzie 68, 94-95
Foo Fighters 137
Fools Rush In 71
foosball 75, 86, 177
Fortunata 70
Foster, AJ 105
fountain (*Friends*) 21, 24-25,
    88, 92, 115
fountain scene *see* title
    sequence
Four Seasons (art) 155, 164
Foursquare 158
Fox Racing 160
Fox, Michael J. 63
Frank Jr. *see* Buffay Jr., Frank
Frankie Goes to Hollywood 75
Frankie Say Relax 75
Franzblau, Deborah A. 23, 42,
    48, 94, 175
Frasier (series) 3, 62
Free Being 23
French posters 62-63, 71, 86,
    90, 104, 124, 126, 134, 137,
    140, 151
friend pairings 26
friend zone 39
"Friends Like Us" 1, 3-4, 8, 19,
    21
Friends
    porn 88, 115
    reunion 71, 106, 109, 112,
        124, 133
    soundtrack 23, 52
    theme 25, 41, 45, 127
Friends: A XXX Parody 88
FriendsFest 11, 34

Frye, Soleil Moon 101
Full House 30, 165
Fuller, Loïe 124
Fun Bobby 41, 55
Fusco, Cosimo 42, 118-19

G

Gable, June 39, 49, 57
Gall, Franz 103
Gant, Robert 78
Garland, Judy 98, 139
Garofalo, Janeane 2, 4
Garr, Teri 79
Gass, Kyle 161
Gavin, *see* Mitchell, Gavin
gay *see* homosexuality
Geddes, Anne 111
Geller Cup 70
Geller, Ben 13, 52, 61-62, 67,
    95, 103, 115, 127, 131, 137,
    144-45, 151, 154
Geller, Jack 13-14, 103, 148
Geller, Judy 13-14, 136, 138,
    148, 156, 168
George, Melissa 159
Gertz, Jami 5-6
"Get Ready For This" 70
"Get Ready" 70
Gibson guitar 163
Gilpin, Peri 3
Gilroy, John 134-35
Gingrich, Candace 56
Ginsu knife 88
Girenel, AK 86
Girlfriends' Guide to Pregnancy
    142, 144
GLAAD 56
Gladys (art) 54, 117, 170
Glantz, Yehuda 53
Glynnis (art) 170
going commando 65
Goldberg-Meehan, Shana 64,
    128, 166, 177
Goldberg, Adam 60
Goldberg, Eric 124, 172, 177
Golden Driller 155
Golden Globe Award 72, 136
Gómez, Carlos 71
Good Will Humping 115
Gordon, Michael 106
Got Milk? 161
Gould, Elliott 13-14, 103, 112,
    148, 153, 158
Gould, Sandra 70
Grammy Award 76, 112
Grand Jury Secrets 55
Grand Prix poster 98
Grande, Greg 29-30, 35-36,
    50, 59, 64, 68, 101, 106,
    113-14, 126, 129, 134, 146,
    160, 170, 178
Grateful Dead 72
Great Eastern Dispensary 110
Greek Orthodox 137
Green, Amy 157, 169
Green, Jill 114-15, 157, 169
Green, Leonard, Dr. 14, 62-63,
    68, 169, 176

Green, Sandra 150
"Greensleeves" 156
Greenstein, Jeff 18, 40, 44, 49, 54
Greenwich Village 19, 24, 67, 73, 81, 157, 169
Grey, Jennifer 14, 47, 64
Griffin, Kathy 2
Grinch 62
guest stars 14
Guggenheim Museum 61
Guinness poster 68, 134-35
Gunderson, Michael 13
Gunther 10-11, 13, 22, 30, 36, 54, 61-63, 71-74, 82-83, 113-14, 142, 149, 153-54

H
Haessig, Reid 175
Hagerty, Michael 69, 80
Hahn, Kristin 81
Halvorson, Gary 135, 159
Hanging Up 107
Hankin, Larry 51
Hanks, Tom 15, 156
Hannah Montana 141
Hannigan, Mike 11-12, 93, 154-58, 160, 162, 166-67, 169, 173
Hanukkah 112, 127
Happy Days 68, 94-95
Hardin, Melora 44
Haredevil Hare 113
Harington, Kit 55
Harmon, Pearl 142
Harris, Kim 15, 73, 91, 99, 109, 117, 132, 154, 165
Haugen, Jon 69
Heartbreaking Work of Staggering Genius 121
Hecht, Jessica 5, 42, 116
Heckles, Mr. 51
Heston, Charlton 33
Hexadrin 131
High Fidelity 105
Hines, Cheryl 114
Hitchcock, Alfred 97
Hobart, Benjamin 164, 169
Hocus Pocus 25
Holden, Alexandra 117, 120
Holt, Rebecca 170
Hombre Man 50
Home Alone 174
Home Improvement 19
homosexuality 10, 22, 40, 48, 56, 85, 121, 135, 149, 162
Hootie & the Blowfish 52
"Hot Crossed Buns" 156
How I Met Your Mother 157, 167
How Stella Got Her Groove Back 77
"How you doin'?" 86
Howard Stern Show 7, 66
Hugsy 38, 98, 100, 113, 162
Hunt, Helen 33
Hunt, Lamar 56
Hupp, Jana Marie 47, 64

Huston, John 150
Hynde, Chrissie 23, 52-53

I
I Dream of Jeannie 87, 112
"I Go Blind" 52
"I Ran (So Far Away)" 97
"I'll Be There for You" 25-26, 127
Ichiban 169
Ideas for Great Kids' Rooms 174
Idiot, The 72
Il Sole 31, 178
IMDB 10
In & Out... and In Again 88, 115
infomercial 59, 66, 73, 88
Insomnia Cafe (business) 17
"Insomnia Cafe" 19
Inspect Her Gadget 115
InStyle 147, 155
International Harvester 80
Isaak, Chris 14, 56, 59

J
Jack Russell terrier 62
Jackson, Shoeless Joe 108
Jacobson, Danny 3, 45
Jane Eyre 97
Janice 5, 12, 38, 41, 43, 51, 64, 67-68, 86-87, 117, 126, 150, 153, 164, 175
Javu restaurant 148, 163
Jaws 145
Jay-Z 25
Jefferson Market 18, 169
Jefferson Market Library 18, 169
Jeremy, Ron 88
Jerry Maguire 108, 129
Jesse (series) 14, 77, 95, 157
Jill *see* Green, Jill
Jillette, Penn 80
Joanie Loves Chachi 35
Joanna (boss) 71, 76, 80, 83
Joey (series) 15, 60, 71, 105, 162, 168, 170, 174-75, 178
John's Pizzeria 161-62
Jones soda 87
Jones, Sebastian 65
Joseph, Gail 111
Josephson, Nancy 16, 176-77
Joshua *see* Burgin, Joshua
Judy *see* Geller, Judy
Junge, Alexa 57-58, 64, 100

K
Kanner, Ellie 1-4, 7
Kaplan International 33
Kaplan, Gabe 57-58
Kapp Horner, Alex 107
Kappa Kappa Delta 134
Karabetsos, Kathy 137
Kate *see* Miller, Kate
Katie (animal actor) 11, 31, 46
Katt, Nicky 62
Kauffman, Dorothy 23, 80, 117

Kauffman, Herman 23
Kauffman, Marta 1-2, 8-10, 14, 17-19, 21-23, 25-26, 32-33, 35-36, 38, 41, 45, 48, 51, 54-58, 60-61, 63-66, 69, 73, 75-76, 79-80, 91-92, 94, 100-01, 107, 117, 121, 124, 126-27, 129, 131, 134-35, 137, 140, 143, 145, 147-48, 151-52, 156-57, 170, 172, 174, 176-78
Keaton, Diane 49
Kensit, Patsy 87
Keys, Alicia 147
King of Queens 5
King of the Hill 59
King, Stephen 72
Kinnear, Greg 149, 169
Kirsch, Stan 48
Klarik, Jeffrey 3, 16, 19, 23, 38, 156, 166, 172, 176-77
Klopp, Jürgen 33
Knight, Wayne 7
Knowledge Bowl 172
Krakowski, Jane 6
Krehbiel, Missy 124, 172, 177
Krog 109
Kubrick, Stanley 104
Kudrow, Lisa 1, 3, 5, 9-11, 14-16, 19, 23, 26-30, 32-33, 36, 41, 44-45, 53-55, 57, 61, 63, 66, 69-70, 75, 84, 86, 89-91, 93-94, 99-101, 106-07, 115, 117, 120, 122-25, 130, 133, 141, 145-48, 150, 156-57, 159, 161, 164-65, 168, 173-76
Kurland, Seth 85

L
L.A. Law 61
Lady Gaga 33
LaPlaca, Alison 76
Las Vegas 57, 58, 80, 85, 105-06, 108, 136, 154
Last Thing He Wanted 78
Lauer, Matt 120
Laurel and Hardy 36, 38
Lauren, Ralph 88, 111, 175
Laurie, Hugh 92
Law & Order 103
LAX 2194 (series) 8, 125
Le Matin 55, 90
leather pants 98-99
Leave 'em Laughing 36
LeBlanc, Matt 1, 4-5, 9, 11-12, 14-15, 20, 26-28, 30, 33, 35, 37, 39, 47, 50-52, 58, 60, 63, 65-67, 69, 71, 74, 77-78, 85-86, 91, 94, 97, 99, 101, 107, 109, 112-14, 117, 119, 124-25, 127, 129-31, 133-34, 136, 139, 145-46, 152, 155-57, 160, 164, 167-69, 174-76, 178
Lecroix, Janine 28, 110-11, 113
Ledbetter, Mr. 98

Lee, Harper 102, 131
Leibman, Ron 14, 62
Lembeck, Michael 57-58, 63
Lennon, Thomas 105
Leno, Jay 120
Leo Carrillo State Park 32, 79
Leonard, Estelle 39, 49
Leoni, Téa 5
Les Mystères de New-York 55, 90
Levy, Mike 66
Lewis, Jerry 63
LGBTQ 56, 128, 135, 143
Like a Hole in the Head 87-88, 93, 107
Lillard, Matthew 154
Linus 112-13
"Lion Sleeps Tonight" 46
Lipson, Dean 56
Litt, Leslie 11, 89, 177
Little Engine That Could 57
Little White Chapel 106
Little Women 72
Littlefield, Warren 5, 7, 18-19, 61
lobster 58
location shooting 32
Lockhart, Jessica 131
Logan, Paul 159
Logan's Run 133
London episodes 91-92
London Marriott 91
Looper, Douglas 15, 50, 77, 97, 114, 152
LOOT 99, 124
Lost in Space 14, 136
Lovato, Demi 13
love interests 28
LoveBug 110
Lover's Revenge 55
Lovitz, Jon 14, 44, 161
Lowder, Kyle 164
Lucas, George 65
Lucci, Susan 130
Lynch, Jane 2, 175

M

*M*A*S*H* 153, 178
M&M collectible 83, 167
Mac and C.H.E.E.S.E. 118, 124
Mackenzie, Will 174
Macpherson, Elle 28, 110-11, 113
Mad About You 3, 21, 36, 44-45, 55, 114
Madagascar 171
Madman of the People 21
Madonna 49
magna doodle 75, 77, 80-84, 86-87, 89-90, 95-99, 108, 110-11, 113, 117-18, 120, 122, 124-25, 127-29, 132-34, 139, 141-44, 146-47, 154, 160, 163-64, 167-70, 172-73, 175-76
Mahan, Colleen 124, 177
Maïna La Voyante poster 104, 126

Malcolm (stalker) 77
Malcolm in the Middle 25
Malins, Greg 59, 61, 65, 70, 76, 78, 89, 91, 93-94, 100, 106, 112, 123, 139
man purse 99-100
Man with a Plan 15
Mancini, Henry 68
Mancuso, Gail 50
Mandell, Brown 63
Mandylor, Louis 4, 116
Mangione, Chuck 89
Mann, Cynthia 42
Mann, Thea 89
Manzoor, Sarfraz 16, 128
Marcel (pet) 11, 31-33, 35, 41, 45-48, 56
Marcoux, Sierra 13
marijuana 111
Married... with Children 157
Martin, Steve 120
Martino, Eva Amurri 130
Marvin the Martian 113
Mary Tyler Moore Show 176
Master and Margarita 10
Masters of the Universe 109
masturbation 61, 112
Matthews, Chip 117
Mazar, Debi 152
MC5 163
McCartney, Paul 15
McCormack, Eric 1
McDaid, John 48
McDonald, Kevin 77
McGuire, Debra 11, 38, 46, 56, 58, 61, 64, 70, 89-90, 99, 111, 116, 127-28, 136-38, 151, 160-61, 163-64, 173
McKeon, Nancy 5
McMillan, Chris 38, 77
menorah 143
Mental Floss 163-64
Mercedes-Benz poster 98
Merchant, Natalie 25
Meyer, Angela 35
Meyer, Dina 77
Michaels, Joe Everett 15, 109, 135, 166
Michelangelo 109
"Mickey" 129
midget wrestling 52
Mike *see* Hannigan, Mike
Mike & Molly 24, 153
Miller, Barbara 4
Miller, Kate 77, 166
Millstone Coffee 119
Milmore, Jennifer 61, 76-77, 139
Minetta Lane Theater 45
Minnesota 22
Minsk 41
Misfits of Science 40, 148
Mitchell, Gavin 28, 159-60
mockolate 53-54
Modern Family 146
Moistmaker, The 98
Mona (girlfriend) 55, 142-44
Mona Lisa 55

Monkey (animal actor) 11, 31, 46
Monkeyshine 56
Monroe, Cecilia 130-31
Montalbán, Ricardo 52
moo point 126
Moondance Diner 62, 71, 76
"Moonlight" 28
Moonves, Les 8
Moore, Clement Clarke 158
Morley (cigarettes) 103
Morning Show 115
"Morning's Here" 89
Morris, Burton 37, 44, 71, 87, 99, 101, 114, 124, 150, 153, 155, 157
Moulin Rouge! 162
movie posters 39, 55, 90, 162
Mr. Destiny 44
Ms. Pac-Man 145
MTV 4, 118, 156
Muddling Through 4, 7
Mullally, Megan 2, 92
Mullany, Matthew 94, 113, 137, 172
Mulroney, Dermot 28, 159-60
multifaith 127, 143
Murphy Brown 98, 110
Museum of Prehistoric History 36, 98
music video (*Friends*) 26
Mustela 150
My Big Book of Grievances 51
My Goodness My Guinness 134
MyHeritage 33
Mystic Tan 168

N

Naked City 103
Naked Truth 6
Nanny, The 43, 156, 159
National Education Association 62-63
Naysee, Deborah 24
Neiers, Mikel 80
Neighbor Tim 138
Nestlé Toll House 123
Netflix 72, 144
network run-through 20, 43
New York Park 110
New York Post 141
New York University 108, 117, 176
Newbern, George 96
Newsweek 104
Nick at Nite 146
Nicky St. Hubbins 81
Night Before Christmas 158
Nike 37, 99, 160
9/11 tribute 81, 126, 138-39, 141-45, 154, 165, 169, 177
nipple 23, 51, 73, 90, 110, 168
no-sex pact 133
Noguchi, Isamu 75
Nora *see* Bing, Nora
Nutrisystem 6, 66
NYPD Blue 104

O

O'Donnell, Rosie 4, 14

Oberman, Rona 23, 36, 42, 48, 88, 94

Object of My Affection 154

Odd Couple, The 105

Office, The 44

Officer and a Gentleman, An 63

Ohlmeyer, Don 20, 22, 25

Oldman, Gary 14, 135-36

Olympics posters 66, 68

On Dante Alighieri 109

One Life to Live 55

"Only Time" 145

OPI 160

orange couch 30, 35-36, 171

Orchid, The 174

orgasms 146, 171

Oscar Award 136

Osment, Emily 141

Outbreak 33

Over There 151

P

Pacino, Al 39, 162

Pakzad, Bijan 50

Pallbearer, The 104

Pancake, Sam 161

Paolo (boyfriend) 39, 41-42, 118

Parabola (magazine) 141

Paramount Studios 32, 52

Paris 22, 86, 112, 119, 124, 151, 173, 175

Park Lincoln, Lar 2

Parker, Ricky 29

Parton, Dolly 173

Paste (magazine) 26

Pastula, Dante 13

Pat the Cop 18

Pat the dog 59, 154-55

Paul the wine guy 23, 35, 61

Pauley, Jane 101

Pearl Jam 98, 177

penis 7, 23, 37, 80, 88, 146, 156

Penn, Sean 14, 33, 141

People (magazine) 75, 119

Pepto-Bismol 95, 170

Perlman, Rhea 172

Perry, John Bennett 33, 88

Perry, Matthew 1, 7-10, 14-15, 22, 26, 30, 33, 38-39, 41, 46-48, 50-54, 57-61, 67-68, 70-72, 74, 76-77, 80-83, 88, 91, 93-95, 97, 99-102, 105-06, 109-10, 115, 119, 121-23, 125, 131, 133, 135, 141, 146, 150, 154, 157-58, 165-66, 174-76, 178

Personals 45, 129

Pete *see* Becker, Pete

Pfeiffer, Dedee 154

phalange 177-78

Phalange, Regina 93, 106

PhilloSophie 52

Phoebe's songs 23

phrenology 103

Physicists, The 38, 49

Pickles, Christina 13-14

Pier59 Studios 119

Pieters, Thomas 33

pilot 17

    changes 18

    debut 26

    filming 19

Piñero, Carlos 172

ping pong 166

Pitillo, Maria 170

Pitt, Brad 6, 14, 33, 105, 122, 126, 132, 134, 143, 148, 157, 162, 169, 173, 176, 178

pivot 102, 162

Planes, Trains and Automobiles 173

Planet dish detergent 59

Playboy (magazine) 113, 154

PlayStation 103, 111, 122

Plaza Hotel 37, 45, 122, 178

Popeye 91

Porsche 26, 108-09, 168

Portos Ramos-Pinto poster 63, 66

Posey, Parker 6

Pottery Barn 113

Powers That Be 8

Practical Intuition in Love 96

pranks 65, 88, 97, 109, 121, 131, 146

Pregnancy for Dummies 144

pregnancy issues 28

pregnancy, unplanned 29

premature ejaculation 59, 79

Premium saltines 86

Presley, Elvis 85, 125

Pretenders, The 23

Pride and Prejudice 54

Prime, Stephen 24, 129

Prinze Jr., Freddie 14, 156

product placement 37, 59, 80, 86-88, 95, 100, 102, 108-09, 111, 113, 123, 131, 144, 150-51, 158, 160, 163

prom dress 58

props 12, 29, 31, 39-40, 51, 59, 67-68, 70, 76, 78, 83, 86, 88, 95-97, 100, 102-03, 108, 116, 121, 124, 128, 131, 134, 137, 139, 141-42, 149, 151, 155, 167, 171, 174, 177

Prosek, James 64

Psycho 97, 103

Pulitzer fountain 21, 24

Puma 158

Purple Rain 140

Pyramid 172

Q

Quinn, Charlie 25

R

R.E.M. (band) 20, 25, 41, 45

Race: How Blacks and Whites Think About the American Obsession 72

Rachel, The 38, 64, 125

Ralph Lauren (company) 88, 111, 175

Ramone, Joey 23

Ramoray, Dr. Drake 23, 55, 60-61, 79, 141, 152

Rapaport, Michael 104

Rash, Jim 33

Ravelo, Caridad 35

real-life inspirations 23

Rebuilding the Indian 114

recliners 76, 80, 99, 129, 131-32

recurring regulars 10

recycled jokes 22

Red Cube (art) 75

Red Shoe Diaries 51

red sweater 138-39

Reformatory poster 55

Reich, Andrew 84, 98, 101, 147, 177

Reilly, James E. 60

Reiser, Paul 101

Rembrandts, The 25-26, 178

Remini, Leah 5, 49

Resorts International Hotel Casino 96

Ribisi, Giovanni 53, 62, 68, 85, 168

Ribisi, Marissa 68

Richard *see* Burke, Richard

Richards, Denise 6, 133

Riff's bar 44-45

ringtone 141

Ritter, Adam 23, 44

Rivers, Melissa 6

RM (singer) 33

Robbins, Tim 130

Roberts Gillan, Lisa 57

Roberts, Julia 14, 33, 57, 60, 67

Robinson, Chase 33

Rock 'Em Sock 'Em Robots 142

Rockstar 118

Rodin, Auguste 49

Rodrigue, George 108, 149, 155

Rold Gold 131

Rolling Stone (magazine) 167

Romijn, Rebecca 81

Romy and Michele's High School Reunion 41, 106, 124

Rose, Cristine 157

Rosove, John 172

Rossellini, Isabella 67

Roth, Peter 113

Rudd, Paul 11-12, 154, 156, 173, 175

Rupp, Debra Jo 75, 85, 168

Russian posters 38, 43, 49, 66, 68, 72, 90, 149

Russian Thinker poster 49, 90

Ryder, Winona 14, 67, 134

S

safe sex 61

"Sailor's Hornpipe" 91

Saks & Company 50-51, 134

Sandler, Adam 115, 131

Santa Claus 158
Sarandon, Susan 14, 33, 67, 130-31
satchel *see* man purse
Saturday Night Live 2, 4, 26, 44, 51, 97, 133, 140
Saunders, Jennifer 92
Saved by the Bell 6
Scarface 39, 162
Schaller, Jeff 133, 157, 160, 167, 173, 176
Schierenberg, Quent 178
Schlamme, Thomas 55
Schulz, Charles M. 113
Schwimmer, David 1-2, 10-11, 19, 24, 26-27, 30, 36-37, 39, 44, 48-49, 51-52, 55, 58, 65, 72, 74, 84, 89-90, 93, 95, 97, 99-100, 102, 104, 109, 112, 115-18, 121, 123-25, 127, 129-31, 133, 138, 142-43, 145-47, 149, 153, 156, 164, 166, 171, 176-77
Science Boy 161
Score, Mike 97
Scream 66, 79, 85
Scream 2 79
Screen Actors Guild Award 136
script ideas 21-22
script ideas, unused 22
Search for Tomorrow 6
secret closet 86, 146
Secret Santa 83
Seinfeld 2-3, 17-18, 21-22, 36, 45, 60-61, 73, 83, 99-100, 128, 147, 178
Selleck, Tom 12-13, 28, 59, 62, 72, 88, 106, 120-21
Selz Shoes 108
series facts 32
Serving Sara 133
Sesame Street 37, 95
set dressing 29, 50, 76, 83, 88, 102, 127, 142, 154, 163
sets 29
17 Again 105
Sex and the City 37, 44, 62
Sex Toy Story 2 115
Shaffner, John 29-30, 42, 69, 78, 146, 160
Shakespeare 74
Shanghai posters *see* Chinese posters
Shearer, Harry 48
Sheen, Charlie 14, 63, 133
Sheeran, Ed 112
Sheldon, Noelle and Cali 12-13, 165, 168
Shephard, Ben 16, 151
Shepherd, Sherri 84
shepherd's pie 111
Sheridan, Nicollette 6
Sherman, Helene Marla 15-16, 66, 141
Shields, Brooke 14, 57
Shining, The 72
"Shiny Happy People" 20, 25, 41
Shout (magazine) 102

show titles 18
Shutter Speed 32, 105
Sibbett, Jane 6, 36, 41, 74, 131
Siegel, Robin 91
Sigma Chi 134
Sikowitz, Mike 37, 54, 56
Silveri, Scott 28, 37, 54, 59, 84, 92-93, 166, 177
Silverman, Jonathan 14, 48, 94
Silverstone, Alicia 46
Simmons, Sue 76
Simpsons, The 48
Sims, Heather 15, 117, 150, 159, 164
Sir Mix-a-Lot 156
"Six of One" 19, 21
Skloff, Hannah 69, 151, 172, 178
Skloff, Michael 25, 66, 121, 172, 178
smell the fart acting 55
"Smelly Cat" 23, 53, 60
Smith, Mike 136
Snaro 55
SNL see Saturday Night Live
Snyder, Allisyn 13
Soap Opera Digest 60, 149
Soapie Awards 132
SoHo (magazine) 62
Solow Building 37
Somerville, Bonnie 143
Soviet aviation poster 43, 49
"Space Oddity" 103
Spanish posters 62, 86, 118, 159, 168
Speed Racer 116, 133
Spiegel, Charles 99, 153
Spin City 63, 100
Spiner, Brent 174
Springsteen, Bruce 8, 148
Sprouse, Cole 13, 103, 115, 117, 127-28, 131, 145
Spy Game 143
Square Pegs 5
St. George, Edward 120
St. John's Church 91
St. Patrick's Cathedral 136, 140
St. Paul's Chapel 18, 81
Stage 5 30, 50
Stage 24 29-30, 42, 50, 52, 57, 74, 78-79, 91, 116, 139, 163, 168, 170, 178
Stamos, John 14, 165
stand-ins 15, 50, 73, 77, 91, 97, 99, 109, 114, 116-17, 132-33, 135, 148, 150, 152, 154, 158-60, 164-66, 173
Star of David 76, 143
Star Trek 10, 95, 105
Star Trek V: The Final Frontier 105
Star Wars 65
Stephanopoulos, George 37, 137
Stern, Michel 16, 84, 176
Stevens, Cat 148

Stevens, Elizabeth 32, 117, 121
Stevens, Fisher 33, 43
Stevens, Todd 77, 80
Still Standing 5
Stiller, Ben 77
Sting 15, 144
Sting: The Illustrated Lyrics 144
Stipe, Michael 25
Strauss, Jeff 11, 18, 38, 40-41
studio tour 115, 176
Styler, Trudie 15, 144
Suddenly Susan 57, 84
Suite Life of Zack & Cody 45
sunflower (t-shirt) 77
Super Bowl 57-58
supersized episode 129-32, 156, 173
surrogacy 27, 29, 75, 84, 94
Survivor (series) 129, 132
Susan 5, 23, 42, 48-49, 56, 74, 88, 95, 102, 116, 134, 163
Sutcliffe, David 124
Swain, Paul 77, 110, 125
Swift, Taylor 23, 72

T
T. Rex and the Crater of Doom 150
Tag (character) 83, 124, 126, 139
"Take a Bow" 49
Tale of Two Cities 71
Tamburino, Andrea 172
Tapatío 141, 151
tattoo 59, 114, 122
Tattoo (TV character) 52
Taxi (series) 21, 59
Taylor, Christine 14, 78-79
10 (movie) 25
Terkel, Studs 72, 144
That Girl 69
theme song (*Friends*) 25
Theroux, Justin 15, 125
These Friends of Mine 3, 5, 19, 36
They Might Be Giants 25
Thiessen, Tiffani-Amber 6
Thinker, The 49
30 Rock 11, 140
Thomas, Marlo 69, 150
Thorpe, Alexis 164
Thorpe, Ian 16, 126
Three Headed Monster 24-25
"Three Kings of Orient" 158
Thurm, Joel 148
Thyne, TJ 94
Tickon, Charles 90
Tiffany firefly lamp 35, 89
Timberlake, Justin 15
Time (magazine) 105, 144
title sequence 20, 24-26, 35, 88-89, 92-93, 115
Title, Daena 14, 36, 129
To Kill a Mockingbird 102, 131
Toblerone 88
Tokens, The 46
Tom, Lauren 50-51, 53

Top Gear 109
Top of the Heap (series) 157
transgender 56, 135
transvestite 14, 135
Treasure of the Arachnid Madre 150
Treeger, Mr. 69, 80, 82
Tres Destinos (series) 35
Trevor Project 128
trifle *see* English trifle
Trout: An Illustrated History 64
Tulsa 154-55, 158-59
Turner, Adrienne 172
Turner, Kathleen 14, 56, 135-37, 172
Tuttle, Sarah 70
TV Guide 58, 61, 85-86, 106, 159
Twin Peaks 72
twin towers *see* World Trade Center
Two and a Half Men 63, 72
Tyler, Aisha 15, 149, 164
Tyler, James Michael 10, 13, 30, 54, 61, 63, 72-74, 82, 113, 115, 142, 149, 153-54

U
U2 (band) 53-54
Ugly Naked Guy 69, 88, 100, 164
unagi 116-17
Ungerleider, Ira 11, 65, 70
Union, Gabrielle 132
Unitel Video Studio 55 95
Universal Studios 33
"Up Where We Belong" 63
Ursula 15-16, 44-45, 66, 101, 114, 141-42
US Custom *see* Alexander Hamilton United States Custom House
USA Today 76, 163

V
vagina 84, 108
Vale, Nancy 43
Van Damme, Jean-Claude 57-58
Van Gorkum, Harry 147
Vasquez Rocks State Park 32, 105
Vassar College 3, 9, 61, 84
Vaughn, Michael 83
Vaughn, Vince 4

Velveteen Rabbit 82
Ventresca, Vincent 41, 55
Veronica's Closet 95
VH1 156
vicar 123
Village Cigars 73
Village Voice (newspaper) 67
Villechaize, Hervé 52
Vincent, René 63
Vinnie & Bobby 4
Virgin Atlantic 91
Virgin Cola 100
Virgin Group 100
Visit from St. Nicholas 158
Volok, Ilia 120
Voltaire, Susanna 69

W
Waltham, Andrea 92
Waltham, Emily 15, 23, 28, 85-87, 89-91, 93, 95-96, 103-04, 123, 166
Wang, Joel 10
Warner Bros. 4, 7-8, 17, 19-21, 24, 30, 32-33, 35, 37, 39-41, 46-47, 50, 54, 57-58, 68-70, 78, 88-89, 105, 108, 110, 113, 115, 121, 128, 134, 144, 151, 172-73, 176
Warner Bros. Studio locations 32
  Blondie Street 32, 40
  Brownstone Street 32, 47
  Embassy Courtyard 32, 121
  French Street 32
  Hennessy Street 32, 37, 41, 57
  Midwest Residential Street 32, 54
  New York Street 32, 148, 151
Warnes, Jennifer 63
Washington Square Arch 18, 81, 96, 110
Washington Square Park 81, 108
Waterlily 111
Waxine 73
"We Three Kings" 158
wedding dress 56, 89, 132, 136, 173
Welcome Back, Kotter 58
Wembley 91
Wentworth Institute of Technology 67
Westinghouse 80
Westminster Abbey 91, 94

What to Expect When You're Expecting 87
"What's the Frequency, Kenneth?" 45
Wheel of Fortune 65
Wheeler, Charlie 164-67, 169
Wheeler, Maggie 5, 12, 38, 43, 51, 87, 99, 117, 126, 153, 164, 175-76
Whelchel, Lisa 6
When Harry Met Sally 171
White, Stanford 81
Whitfield, June 92
Whitfield, Mitchell 1, 7, 47, 92
Whole Nine Yards 14, 119, 128
Whose Line Is It Anyway? 125
"Wicked Game" 14, 59
Will (Colbert) 143
Will & Grace 1, 24, 92
Williams, Olivia 92
Williams, Robin 14, 33, 78
Willis, Allie 25
Willis, Bruce 14, 119-20, 128
Wilson, Dorien 63
Wilson, Owen 15
Winget, Susan 155
Winston, Ben 154
Wired (magazine) 1219
"With or Without You" 53-54
Witherspoon, Reese 14, 33, 96, 114-15, 157, 169
Wizard of Oz 139
Wollman Rink 127
Working Girl 165
world record 126
World Trade Center 81, 123, 126, 145, 165
Wright, Max 40
Wuthering Heights 97
Wyle, Noah 1, 45

Y
Y necklace 156
"Y.M.C.A." 62
"Yellow Ledbetter" 98, 177
Yoo-hoo beverage 131
You Are Welcome! Poster 66, 68
YouPorn 52

Z
Zahn, Steve 51
Zebooker, Al 81, 175
Zelner, Mr. 102, 175
Zucker, Jeff 129